LEARNING TO TEACH

Language Arts

IN A FIELD-BASED SETTING

Donna L. Wiseman
UNIVERSITY OF MARYLAND–COLLEGE PARK

Laurie Elish-Piper
NORTHERN ILLINOIS UNIVERSITY

Angela M. Wiseman
FAIRFAX COUNTY PUBLIC SCHOOLS

Holcomb Hathaway, Publishers

Scottsdale, Arizona

Library of Congress Cataloging-in-Publication Data

Wiseman, Donna L. (Donna Louise)
    Learning to teach language arts in a field-based setting / Donna L. Wiseman, Laurie Elish-
Piper, Angela M. Wiseman.
        p. cm.
    Includes bibliographical references and index.
    ISBN 978-1-890871-60-4
    1. Language arts (Elementary)—United States.   2. Teachers—Training of—United States.   3.
Student teaching—United States.   I. Elish-Piper, Laurie.   II. Wiseman, Angela M.   III. Title.

LB1576.W53 2005
372.6'044'0973—dc22

                                                            2004024275

Holcomb Hathaway, Publishers, Inc.
6207 North Cattletrack Road
Scottsdale, Arizona 85250
480-991-7881
www.hh-pub.com

10 9 8 7 6 5 4 3 2 1

ISBN 978-1-890871-60-4

Printed in the United States of America.

Contents

CHAPTER 3

Speaking and Listening   82

CHAPTER 4

Writing   138

CHAPTER 5

Reading   196

CHAPTER 6

Literacy and Visual Representation, Interpretation, and Evaluation *278*

CHAPTER 7

Using Assessment to Make Instructional Decisions   328

The author and publisher have made every effort to provide accurate and current Internet information in this book. However, because the Internet and URLs change constantly, some of the Internet addresses listed in this textbook will change. We regret any inconvenience this may cause readers.

Preface

We believe that future teachers benefit enormously from the opportunity to work in schools with students, and that teacher preparation programs should facilitate these opportunities. Courses that are field-based allow students to learn about teaching and learning language arts from professors, mentor teachers, and students. *Learning to Teach Language Arts in a Field-Based Setting* is designed for university methods classes that are closely linked to K–6 classrooms. This text, used in conjunction with such school–university collaborations, enables future teachers to learn in an environment where theory and practice are connected in relevant and meaningful ways.

Our experiences with school–university partnerships have guided the development of our textbook. We know that texts used in field-based courses need to be flexible so that educators can adapt the content to their unique settings, time frames, and field experience situations. For this reason, we have organized our book into chapters around eight broad topics related to language arts instruction and then divided each chapter into two to five "articles" that focus on a specific aspect of the chapter topic. You will have the option of assigning articles to be read individually, since each stands on its own, or together across an entire chapter.

We believe that this article format better facilitates in-depth understanding and discussions as compared to traditional textbook chapters, which tend to introduce multiple topics with less internal structure than we have provided. The articles found in this book are also appropriate to share with preservice teachers, and on occasion with partner teachers, in a seminar format, often characteristic of classes in field-based settings. At the end of each article, a list of readings related to the central topics will allow you to expand and extend reading assignments when necessary.

Language arts methodologies are fraught with differing philosophical approaches in both research and practice. This text recognizes the importance of dealing with challenging topics such as phonics, approaches to spelling, and teaching children whose native language is not English. Our goal has been to include research-based discussions of such topics while recognizing that teachers and schools are accountable for developing certain reading and writing skills, seeking a balance between research-driven theory and practical application.

This text reflects the belief that all learners construct meaning and understanding through active engagement and meaningful involvement in their own learning. To this end, the book provides a wide variety of activities, reflective writing ideas, and field-based projects that will stimulate and involve preservice teachers in their learning just as they will later use such active engagement to teach their own students. This book also integrates topic-specific coverage for English language learners throughout the articles.

IMPORTANT FEATURES OF THIS BOOK

Several features of this text are designed to make learning to teach language arts in a field-based setting a comfortable and productive learning process that moves effortlessly between elementary schools and university classrooms. These features include:

- **Window to the Classroom:** Future teachers in field-based assignments find themselves immersed in teaching, and during their first classroom work much of their attention is focused on classroom contexts. The vignettes at the beginning of chapters, which describe real-life language arts teaching and language processes, help future teachers recognize how the theory discussed in a chapter supports and relates to practice.

- **Teacher Viewpoints:** Exposure to the views of experienced teachers helps future teachers understand how teachers think, solve problems, and learn from their classrooms. These viewpoints, found throughout the text and featuring future, beginning, and experienced teachers, illustrate a great variety of challenges and successes and remind readers that teaching is a lifelong learning process.

- **Field Notes:** These numbered activities help readers connect the surrounding text discussion to classroom practices by asking them to choose and apply specific strategies and lessons to their field-based classrooms.

- **Personal Reflections:** Independent and collaborative explorations allow future teachers to formulate their beliefs and describe their experiences, and they encourage interaction with peers. Many require the reader's participation in hands-on activities in the university classroom that support their growth as language arts teachers.

- **Professional Readings:** A list of recommended professional readings related to the topics discussed is provided at the end of each chapter. Annotations help future teachers select additional reading that will be of most interest and use to them.

- **Literature Links:** Students are asked to read one or more of the suggested children's literature books and complete the related activity, designed to help future teachers gain insight into the experiences, perceptions, and realities of language arts learning from the perspective of the characters in the books.

Finally, *Learning to Teach Language Arts in a Field-Based Setting* helps readers create a professional portfolio as a capstone to related field experience and course work. The field notes, personal reflections, and professional readings provide multiple opportunities for developing portfolio exhibits. As future teachers work through the content in each chapter, they are encouraged to expand or illustrate one or more of the personal reflection activities or field notes, design their own exhibit, or develop one of the suggestions at the end of each chapter. By developing portfolio exhibits for each chapter in this text, future teachers can document, reflect upon, and track their growth as professionals. When they finish this course, the series of exhibits or a representative subset of the exhibits can become part of their on-going teaching portfolio.

In summary, this text is designed specifically for use in field-based courses. It offers you and your students the theoretical and practical content, the flexibility, and the pedagogy to make the most of classroom learning experiences.

ACKNOWLEDGMENTS

We have learned a great deal from the many experienced teachers who work with us in field-based settings and the future teachers who are participating in our university teacher preparation programs. The ability of experienced teachers to manage the changes and challenges associated with teaching elementary students about language arts has taught us many valuable lessons about flexibility, teaching, and learning. Our university students who want to be teachers exude a refreshing optimism and joy about teaching and constantly impress us with the energy they bring to the profession. We are always amazed at what new and experienced teachers accomplish through inspired and caring teaching.

We would like to thank the following reviewers for their constructive suggestions: Sheila C. Baldwin, Monmouth University; Clara Carroll, Harding University; Elizabeth Day, Santa Clara University; Linda Ellis, University of Houston; Judith Greig, College of Notre Dame; Rachael Hungerford, Lycoming College; Tina Jacobowitz, Montclair State University; Ina Katz, California State University–San Bernardino; Lucia Lu, Clark Atlanta University; Lynn K. Rhodes, University of Colorado at Denver; Sherron Killingsworth Roberts, University of Central Florida; and Mary Shake, University of Kentucky. Their assistance helped to make this a better book.

The production of this textbook has been a long process and we appreciate the Holcomb Hathaway professionals who worked with us. Our editor, Colette Kelly, never gave up or became frustrated with the starts and stops we experienced. Her quiet encouragement and belief that we had an important product kept us motivated when we were ready to stop. During the last phase of the process, Gay Pauley and others worked with us to make sure that the text was as good as it could be and gently maintained the pace of production in spite of our work schedules and other interferences.

We also want to express gratitude to our spouses and children. They have been patient and amazingly supportive during long hours when we seemed permanently attached to our computers working on our book and related professional tasks.

Many thanks to all these people.

—DONNA L. WISEMAN
—LAURIE ELISH-PIPER
—ANGELA M. WISEMAN

To the Reader

Learning to Teach Language Arts in a Field-Based Setting is designed for field-based courses such as yours. One of the main purposes of a field-based course is to develop a scaffold that connects what you learn in the professional literature you read, your university classrooms, and the classrooms where you are completing your field experiences. In order to develop a stronger link between theory and practice, your university program and the public schools may have formed a collaborative relationship. If this is the case, at least a portion of your course work will be taught on the campus of a local school by a combination of school and university faculty. The courses you take that are taught in school settings or with close connections to schools will provide concrete connections between what you hear in your university methods courses, what you read in this book, and what you see in the classroom. The purpose of this book, therefore, is to introduce current instructional theory and practices and provide immediate opportunities to link theory and practice.

You may already have noticed that this book looks different from many textbooks you have used in university courses. It is organized by chapter around eight broad topics related to language arts instruction. Each chapter consists of two to five "articles" that focus on specific aspects of the chapter topic. The articles are concise and practical, while still incorporating the most important research and theory. They can be read individually, since each stands on its own, or together across an entire chapter. We believe this format allows for in-depth understanding and discussions, in contrast to the typical textbook structure, which often introduces all related ideas rather than developing the most important concepts fully.

Another unique aspect of this book is the use of the following features to help you understand the content, strategies, and theories more deeply:

- *Window to the Classroom:* Each chapter begins with a vignette that paints a picture of a classroom or other learning context involved in a process related to the chapter. In these vignettes, you will see examples of best practices in language arts in action.

- *Teacher Viewpoints:* In this feature, preservice teachers, beginning teachers, veteran teachers, and teacher educators talk about the challenges and successes they have experienced related to teaching language arts.

- *Field Notes:* These activities are designed to be completed in your school-based classroom. They are directly tied to specific content and strategies discussed in the articles and will allow you to make connections between the theory in the text and your practice in the elementary classroom.

- *Personal Reflections:* These activities provide opportunities for you to reflect on your beliefs and experiences, interact with your class peers to enhance your understanding, and participate in hands-on activities in the university classroom to support your growth as a teacher of language arts.

- *Professional Readings:* At the end of each chapter, we provide a list of recommended professional readings. These professional readings will allow you to deepen your understanding of specific language arts topics and strategies. Annotations are provided to help you select those that are of most interest to you.

- *Literature Links:* At the end of most chapters, we list several children's books or young adult books that relate to the ideas in the chapter. By reading one or more of these books and completing the suggested activity, you will gain insight into the experiences, perceptions, and realities of language arts teaching using the perspective of the characters in the books.

Finally, *Learning to Teach Language Arts in a Field-Based Setting* focuses on creating a portfolio as a capstone to your field experience and course work. A teaching portfolio is a collection of work and documents that illustrates your experiences in becoming a teacher. It is an excellent tool for reflecting on what you are learning; for illustrating to others what you have learned; for helping you formulate and communicate your teaching philosophy; and for sharing specific experiences you have had in the teacher education program. Developing a portfolio exhibit for each chapter in this text allows you to reflect upon and track your growth as a professional. As you work through the content in each chapter, you may expand or illustrate one or more of the Personal Reflection activities or Field Notes, design your own exhibit, or develop one of the Literature Link suggestions. When you finish this course, the results of these activities can become part of your teaching portfolio.

We hope you find this text to be a useful tool as you learn and grow as a teacher this semester. Best wishes as you embark on the most exciting, meaningful profession—teaching!

LEARNING TO TEACH

Language Arts

IN A FIELD-BASED SETTING

The streets of the Pilsen area of Chicago are bustling with activities. In this predominately Mexican section of the city, conversations and communication are mainly in Spanish. The culture and businesses reflect Mexican life. It is possible to live in this area of the city and never interact with written or spoken English.

A young boy, Juan, stands on the street corner accompanied by his mother and big brother. He is aware of the traffic and store signs. Some of them are written in English and others in Spanish. The voices around him mostly speak Spanish. His mother almost always speaks Spanish, except for a few words and phrases she knows in English. Some of his new friends from kindergarten speak English, but mostly they speak Spanish when they are not

Chapter 1

PERSPECTIVES ON TEACHING LANGUAGE ARTS

at school. Within walking distance of his home live large enclaves of Chinese, Vietnamese, Middle Eastern, and Italian families. He has greeted others and listened to conversations in several languages. Since he has watched a great deal of American television and has interacted with his older brother's friends, he does understand and speak some English. Occasionally, he or his brother must help older family members interpret English conversations.

As he follows his mother and brother into their home, he goes directly to their new computer. There, he sees from the flashing icon that there is an e-mail message for the family. It is probably from his aunt, who lives in Mexico. The families communicate regularly through e-mail, and although he has never spoken to his young cousin the same age who lives in Mexico, he knows they share many of the same games and toys. His father is seated on the couch in the living room reading a Spanish-language newspaper, and he tells the family about the upcoming festival in the neighborhood. The family talks about the

festival activities—the music, art, and craft exhibits—and anticipates the good food that they will be able to eat.

Juan will start first grade in the fall. He doesn't know it yet, but his teacher has agreed to work with a university student, Diane, who is studying to be a teacher. Diane has never visited Pilsen, and she attended elementary and secondary school in a suburban location in which everyone spoke English.

When Diane was growing up her mother and father read to her regularly, and the family valued times when they were able to discuss current events and happenings. Her bedroom and living room had several shelves of her favorite books, and she visited the local library often to pick out books to read. Each weekend she looked forward to reading the Sunday comics, she regularly checked on the television programming schedule in the television listings, and she often sat at the table while her mother and father paid the monthly bills. On trips to the grocery store and shopping center Diane often studied labels and signs. Older members of her family would talk to her about her favorite brand names, such as Oreos, Cheerios, and Kool-Aid, pointing them out as they shopped for clothes or food.

Diane enjoyed reading and writing throughout her elementary and secondary education. She was a good student, known for her ability to speak before groups and explain things to others. She traveled extensively throughout the United States but had very little exposure to languages other than English.

Diane is learning to be a teacher at a university located outside the city. Most of her classmates come from backgrounds that are similar to hers. While in college, she has read many books, including children's literature. One or two of her professors have backgrounds that are different from her own, but almost everyone at her university shares her values and experiences with the English language. She is keeping a journal about her college years. She is active in her community, volunteering to tutor elementary children who are having difficulty learning to read and write.

Diane's methods classes have introduced her to the idea of multiculturalism. Her courses and student teaching assignment in Pilsen have caused her to think about the impact of her life experiences on her views about language and literacy. She knows that some children in her future classrooms will have very different backgrounds from her own. She knows she has lots to learn, but preparing herself to work with children whose backgrounds are different from her own is one of the reasons she looks forward to her field experiences.

INTRODUCTION

As an elementary teacher, you will be responsible for teaching your students all areas of the curriculum, including language arts. You will face a diverse group of students including those of different abilities, language groups, cultural backgrounds, and economic levels. As the opening of this chapter illustrates, the literacy experiences of teachers and students may be very different. What you believe about language arts is based on your personal literacy experiences, professional knowledge gained from your course work and professional reading, and practical knowledge you gain from working in classrooms with children, teachers, and parents. This chapter will help you understand the concepts of literacy and language arts. In addition, you will have the opportunity to consider your own literacy experiences and how these influence your teaching and expectations for your students.

GUIDING QUESTIONS

Consider these questions as you read this chapter. Jot down your initial responses to each question. After reading the articles, revisit your responses. Would you make any changes to them? If so, what would those changes be? Discuss your responses with one or more of your classmates, your professor, or your mentor teacher.

1. What is literacy?
2. What are the language arts?
3. What are some of the literacy experiences that you remember from your childhood?
4. How do your personal literacy experiences affect your beliefs about language arts?
5. What dispositions do teachers need to teach language arts effectively?

Understanding Literacy and the Language Arts

This course will introduce you to teaching language arts in the elementary classroom. Although you probably accept the necessity of attending classes, you may be impatient to spend an extended period of time in field classrooms, work with teachers, and teach your first lessons. If you are like most future teachers, you often sit in your university class thinking, "Let's get to the classroom, the important part of what will make me a teacher."

Spending time in classrooms actively involved in language arts teaching and learning processes is a meaningful aspect of your preparation to be a teacher. But in order to be a thoughtful teacher who is ready to make decisions about teaching language arts, you must also understand what you are teaching and know how to make instructional decisions. You need to develop a *philosophy* of teaching language arts, which will be applied to issues, strategies, standards, and assessments. The university and elementary classroom experiences you have this semester will help prepare you to become a thoughtful, effective teacher.

This is an important semester—one that will prepare you for your student teaching or internship. It will require a balancing act as you are exposed to different ideas and approaches. Because teaching philosophies vary from teacher to teacher, you will encounter a variety of perspectives. It is normal for your beginning teaching experience to raise questions and contradictions. Navigating through the wealth of knowledge and ideas available in schools and universities is a little tricky and sometimes stressful. It may be intimidating to work for the first time with a small group of children on your own or to be in front of the classroom with the teacher or your professor sitting in the back of the room watching you. Other times you may question things your university professor or your mentor teacher tells you, yet you might hesitate to ask why they are saying different things or offering differing perspectives. All of these insecurities and frustrations are normal as you progress toward becoming a teacher. This process will include integrating the professional knowledge you gain from your methods courses and professional reading, personal knowledge about literacy from your own experiences, and practical knowledge from working in the classroom with children and teachers.

JESSICA, BEGINNING TEACHER ▶ I was so confused when I first started teaching. For each idea I learned, I saw teachers use it in the classroom in many different ways. For example, in many classrooms, I watched teachers teach "writers workshop." But it looked different in each class, and no one interpreted the strategy exactly as it was presented in my college classes! I wasn't really sure how I would make it work when I began teaching. Sometimes I felt like I wanted someone to just tell me exactly how to teach something so that it would work out.

Now that I am in my second year of teaching, I can honestly say that I benefited from seeing the different ways of teaching and learning in the classroom. It wasn't until later that I realized it was okay to teach things in various ways and even to disagree with teachers who wrote books that seemed full of good ideas. In fact, I now know I have to consider a teaching method and adapt it to the way I run my classroom and how my students learn. I always think, "Now that's a good idea, but how can I make it effective with my students?"

Sometimes things don't work out the way they are supposed to. That's when I have to consider how I might change the plan or if it is worth trying again. Sometimes it is, and sometimes it isn't.

Questions and Concerns About Learning to Teach Language Arts

field note

1.1

Consider the viewpoint that Jessica expresses. What questions does this viewpoint raise for you? What questions or concerns do you have about teaching language arts? Jot these down and share them with a classmate. Discuss your ideas with a small group or your whole class. Compile a class list of major issues and questions that have arisen. When you visit your field experience classroom, ask your mentor teacher for his or her opinion on these questions and issues. When you return to the university classroom, share the viewpoints of your mentor teachers. Revisit this task and these questions near the middle and end of the semester to see how your understanding of teaching language arts has changed.

WHAT IS LITERACY?

The concept of literacy is a good place to begin thinking about the language arts. Literacy is a complex, ever-evolving concept that is defined by society. Each society and culture has a different perception or view of what it is to be literate. In most western cultures, literacy is an important socialization process in which children learn to use oral and written language. Conversely, language is also used to socialize children, a means of teaching them how to behave, express themselves, and communicate with others. "A literate person not only learns language, they learn about language and they learn through language" (Gutierrez, Baquedano-Lopez, & Turner, 1997, p. 369). Your future students' success in school, in the workplace, and in society depends a great deal on their development of personal literacy skills.

Literacy comprises social interactions, communication skills, and empowering opportunities. As you read about these components of literacy, consider how they relate to your own life and literacy history.

Social Interaction

From birth, language becomes the basis of social interaction. Our relationships with family, friends, colleagues, and acquaintances are built on our ability to talk, interact, and share in appropriate and diverse ways. Without a shared knowledge of language, we are cut off from social interaction and communication.

The converse is true too: Social interactions are essential to developing literacy skills. Literate people both learn from other people and are able to navigate social, educational, and workplace environments effectively. At school, students interact with and learn from the teacher, and they are strongly influenced by peer responses and relationships. Peer interactions have significant implications in the classroom: Students learn from each other, and classroom teachers who recognize the importance of peer influences will provide opportunities for students to interact and learn together.

Communication

Literate people are able to communicate ideas with others by sharing thoughts, feelings, and opinions. From an early age it is necessary for children to express their needs. Young children who are just beginning to develop oral language will be able to tell parents that they are hungry, happy, or upset. As children mature they learn to use language to communicate about many different things. They may communicate what they are learning at school, share their ideas and feelings with family and friends, and begin to develop communication skills that will eventually assist them in the workplace. Effective communication occurs on a daily basis and develops throughout an individual's lifetime.

Empowerment

Literacy gives us the power to understand our world, create new thoughts and ideas, and accomplish tasks necessary for living. Those who are not literate do not have the same opportunities to change their world, to participate with the mainstream of life, to help make decisions, or to be in control of their own learning. In a literate society, success is directly related to language skills. Providing children and young people with literacy skills can give them the opportunity to succeed in our society.

Literacy is needed to exercise the rights and responsibilities of citizenship. Early in our country's history, individuals like Thomas Jefferson realized that literacy was an important element in maintaining a democracy. He knew that making decisions in a democracy required thoughtful interactions among citizens. Jefferson established an American public educational system so young people could become literate and participate in the democratic process. It is still true that individuals need to understand formal language and other forms of communication to take part in the democratic process.

Characteristics of Literacy

Think about a person whom you consider to be literate. Why did you select this person? What behaviors does that person display? Explain to a small group of your classmates how this person demonstrates literacy. Describe the characteristics that identify literacy for you. After everyone in the group has shared an example of a literate person, list the literacy characteristics that you and your classmates value. Do you see differences? Similarities? Be prepared to talk about the literacy characteristics with your entire class.

personal reflection

WHAT ARE THE LANGUAGE ARTS?

The traditional definition of language arts is pretty simple. For years language arts education has referred to *activities that utilize reading, writing, speaking, and listening skills.* In addition, "thinking" and "problem solving" were often included in the definition. These basic components of language arts—reading, writing, speaking, and listening—provide a basic definition; however, language arts education is evolving into a more complex aspect of the curriculum (Gutierrez, Baquedano-Lopez, & Turner, 1997). In today's modern world, where information is exploding as fast as the new technologies deliver it, language arts education is expanding to incorporate important processes such as viewing and creating visual representations (NCTE/IRA, 1996). In addition, the use of technology has become a key component in the definition of language arts.

Language arts is often referred to as the hub of the elementary curriculum because reading, writing, listening, speaking, viewing, and understanding visual representations are essential in all areas of the curriculum. For example, in math, students encounter and must interpret charts, graphs, and tables; they listen as teachers provide explanations; they speak about problem-solving strategies with partners; and they read word problems. Students must also use their language arts skills to comprehend and apply social studies and science concepts.

The building blocks of language arts begin early.

While closely associated with literacy education, the term *language arts* is most often used in discussions of teaching and learning in the schools. Effective language arts education helps students become people who read, write, listen, discuss, and think about ideas in a variety of contexts. They are effective language users—they are literate.

personal reflection

Linking the Components of the Language Arts

Work with your classmates and design a way that reading, writing, listening, and speaking can be graphically described. To do this, try to think of as many characteristics as you can related to reading, writing, listening, and speaking. Based on your lists, do the four processes have anything in common? Would you pair them together in any way? For example, how are reading and writing different from speaking and listening? How are they alike? What characteristics might link reading and listening? Writing and speaking? Now that you have worked through this exercise with some of your classmates, continue reading this article to find out how they are often linked and described.

By their very nature, the language arts are integrated and connected to each other. Learners do not develop one aspect of language arts independently of the others. The basic components of language arts are closely linked, but at the same time they have important differences. Compare the processes of writing and speaking, which are at the same time similar and different. A writer and a speaker create meaning by using similar thinking processes, words, and language structures. One produces speech and the other generates text. Talk that occurs in everyday usage is informal—it is often repetitive, hesitant, and sprinkled with "uhs and ahs," and much of the meaning comes from body language and nonverbal cues. Those who are listening to a speaker can ask questions, watch body language, and read the context to clarify what the speaker is trying to convey. Writing is more permanent, so the writer is usually more careful and precise about how language is phrased. Writing is governed by rules and is much more structured than everyday speaking. The writer must be more specific and explanatory because the reader does not usually have the opportunity to reduce confusion or clarify the intended meaning through interaction with the author.

Listening and reading are alike in that oral and printed symbols are taken in and used to construct meaning. Insights that the listener constructs are based on cues from the speaker's voice, actions, and facial expressions and from the context in which the encounter occurs. Interpretations from listening are based on immediate reactions or memories. Unless a spoken event is recorded in some way, it cannot be exactly reconstructed. On the other hand, reading is an interaction with an author who is usually not present. The author produces printed symbols that represent ideas, then the readers rely on texts, illustrations, and their own interpretations. Reading is an interaction

Reading is an interaction between reader and author that the reader can revisit often.

between the reader and the author that the reader can revisit as many times as desired and that is not always the same.

Oral and written language also have similarities and differences. Talking and listening both involve oral communication processes: A speaker produces oral language, and a listener receives oral language. Likewise, reading and writing are written communication processes: Readers use their knowledge and experiences to receive cues and construct meaning from texts. Writers construct meaning by producing written texts based on knowledge and experience. Oral and written communication have common elements—they both are "purposeful, express meaning, share the same functions, and use the same print conventions" (Ministry of Education, 1996).

Language Arts Across the Curriculum

Although language arts is often taught as a separate part of the curriculum, it is also a foundation for all areas of the elementary curriculum (Luke, 1998). Choose an area of the elementary curriculum (e.g., science, social studies, math, art, physical education, music, health) and brainstorm how students must use reading, writing, listening, speaking, and viewing and creating visual representations in that area of the curriculum. When you are in your field classroom, ask your mentor teacher to share his or her ideas about how the language arts are integrated into the various areas of the curriculum. Share these ideas with your classmates when you return to the university classroom.

EXPANDING THE DEFINITION OF LANGUAGE ARTS

Recently, a broader view of language arts has developed—one that includes technological, communicative, and visual communication (NCTE/IRA, 1996). The *Handbook of Research on Teaching Literacy Through the Communicative and Visual Arts* (Flood, Heath, & Lapp, 1997) explains language arts as a process that:

> explores the possibilities of broadening current conceptualizations of literacy to include the full array of communicative arts (reading, writing, speaking, listening, viewing) and to focus on the visual arts of drama, dance, film, art, video, and computer technology. The communicative and visual arts encompass everything from novels and theatrical performances to movies and video games. In today's world new methods for transmitting information have been developed that include music, graphics, sound effects, smells, and animations. While these methods have been used by television shows and multimedia products, they often represent an unexplored resource in the field of education. By broadening our uses of these media, formats, and genres, a greater number of students will be motivated to see themselves as learners. (front flap)

We are preparing children to live and work in a world that is experiencing a transformation (Leu, 2000), and the dramatic changes suggest the need to think about literacy and language arts education in new and different ways. Many changes are related to the rapid growth of technology and the increasing impact of media. It is no longer enough for students to be effective readers, writers, listeners, and speakers; there is now a need to develop a number of "specialized vocabularies and concepts in order to be considered functionally literate" (Mikulecky, 2000, p. 379). Media and technology are constantly changing—almost before we learn how to use one computer, another new model with additional communication processes is available. Consider the understanding of print, symbols, and social structures needed to navigate the World Wide Web. Already we take the literacy associated with the Web almost for granted. In addition to being capable of accessing and using the tools that are currently available, literate individuals will need to learn new skills and strategies as our world changes (Mikulecky, 2000). The wide range of technology and visual tools used to communicate requires students to be literate in multiple venues, contexts, and situations. Understanding a wide range of messages delivered in a wide range of materials and media is sometimes referred to as *multiliteracy*.

The concept of multiliteracy expands the concept of "text." Traditional literacy is generally associated with printed materials—literature and writing are the core (Leland & Harste, 1994; Hobbs, 1997). Multiliteracy implies that literacy skills must be applied to a variety of message forms (Hobbs, 1997). E-mail messages, Web graphics, and Internet research processes are current technologically enhanced texts that help us learn and communicate with others. Some classrooms, now referred to as "smart classrooms," demonstrate the concept of multiliteracy. During a single class a teacher may use videos, a PowerPoint presentation, Internet resources shown on a large screen, and a document camera to support the ideas and concepts discussed during the class period. The use of multimedia tools opens up a wide range of options for teaching and communicating to children in educational settings.

TEACHER Viewpoint

HILDA, VETERAN TEACHER ▶ I was so amazed at how technology helps me teach concepts that were so difficult to explain or understand by reading a textbook. It also helps me link language arts instruction with other subject areas. My classroom has Internet access, and the computer is hooked up to a large television monitor that the students can see from their desks. When we began talking about molecules in science, I found a website that showed a 3-D interactive model of what a molecule looks like. I went to the website during the lesson. Not only were the kids talking and reading about it, they could see it! I think it really helped them to understand these concepts.

After viewing it in class, we went to the computer lab and students teamed up in partners to explore two websites I found. The first one was through the Smithsonian Institution (**americanhistory.si.edu**); it explained how atoms form molecules and gave visual examples such as a water (H_2O) molecule and a DNA molecule. The students could compare the differences between the two. Some of the students were ready to learn about protons and neutrons in the nucleus of the atom and how to calculate atomic mass, so we went to **www.nyu.edu/pages/mathmol,** which had a hypermedia textbook for elementary students. Not only did they learn about parts of the atom, they were able to learn how these ideas applied to cooking and everyday compounds. They discussed the shape and function of the molecule and researched questions they had about it.

We concluded the lesson by constructing molecules out of playdough and toothpicks. They recorded their observations and drew the diagrams they created in their learning logs. Technology really added to our classroom resources!

Experiences with Technology and Literacy

Think of a type of technology you have recently learned to use (e.g., e-mail, the Internet, PowerPoint, CD-ROM, a personal digital assistant (PDA), TIVO or other television recording device, voice mail, text messaging, instant messaging, a video camera, a digital camera). What were your reasons for wanting to learn to use the new technology? How did you learn to use the technology? What challenges did you have in learning to use it? Did this new technology change or enhance your use of the language arts (reading, writing, listening, speaking, and viewing and creating visual representations)? If so, how? If not, why not? Share your experience with your peers.

personal reflection

Learning with Technology

Can you think of a time a teacher or professor used technology in instruction in such a way that you understood a concept, idea, or skill more fully than you would have from more traditional methods of instruction? What was it about the technology that helped you learn so effectively? If you cannot think of an example, choose a time when it was very difficult for you to learn a concept, an idea, or a skill. Would technology have helped to enhance your learning? Why do you think so? Share your ideas with your peers.

personal reflection

FINAL REFLECTIONS

Becoming an effective teacher of the language arts is a multifaceted task. Teachers must prepare students to communicate in a world that is becoming more and more diverse and technologically connected. The long-range goal of language arts instruction is to help students become effective language users who operate within the expectations of today's society. While this is a challenging goal, many effective approaches and strategies can help students develop and enhance their use of the language arts. These approaches and strategies are the focus of the remainder of this book.

Teaching Language Arts

Teaching language arts can take many different forms and require a wide range of teaching and learning skills. By now you are probably realizing that teaching language arts is a bit like being a juggler. When teaching language arts you must consider many aspects of language and communication. Language arts instruction can be just as complex as a field trip to the museum where background information must be provided and students are exposed to multiple visual displays, technology-assisted explanations, and verbal explanations. Language arts instruction can also be as straightforward as teaching the beginning consonant sounds, explaining syllable markings, or reading aloud to students. No matter what the teaching activity, the focus of language arts instruction is to increase your students' ability to understand and communicate through a variety of signs and meanings, including those that are related to linguistic, gestural, pictorial, musical, and mathematical ways of expression (Suhor, 1992).

You may be wondering how you could possibly prepare yourself to teach such a multidimensional subject to the widely diverse group of children who will occupy your future classroom. You may also be curious to see how teachers approach language arts instruction. This article will explain language arts instruction and the roles teachers play when teaching language arts. In addition, the article will introduce you to several language arts teachers who differ in expertise, background, and teaching style.

TEACHER *Viewpoint*

NADIA, FUTURE TEACHER ▶ When I was growing up, I loved spending time with my family on Saturday afternoons. One of the most common pastimes was reading books and going to the library. With one of my parents, my sister and brother and I would walk a few blocks down the road to the red brick public library on the corner of the street. I remember walking among the shelves of books and wishing I had read each one of them. Mom usually had to give me a limit of books I could check out, because I was almost greedy about wanting to take as many as I could. When we got back home, we had milk and cookies in the living room and sat around browsing through our books. Sometimes we talked about what we read, but there were a lot of quiet pauses as my siblings and I enjoyed our selections and read through the stories.

CONNECTING PERSONAL LITERACY EXPERIENCES

The first step to understanding how to go about teaching language arts is to think about your own language learning experiences. The process of becoming a language arts teacher starts long before you enter a formal university program. Many beliefs, attitudes about language, and learning and educational values are established in early life experiences. Your own language learning, early role models, learning experiences, and the contributions of significant people in your life have helped form your definition of and attitude toward language arts and your use of communication skills. Your personality development, socialization patterns, and ways of interacting with others become integral parts of your attitude toward communication and beliefs about children's language learning (Wiseman, Knight, & Cooner, 2004).

Literacy Stories

Think about your own literacy experiences. Consider the following questions:

1. What are your earliest memories of reading and writing at home and in school?
2. Are these positive or negative memories? Why?
3. What are some of your strongest memories related to literacy?
4. Why are these memories important to you?
5. Who are some of the people who have influenced your literacy development throughout your life, and how did they influence you?

Record your thoughts and feelings in your journal and share some of your ideas with a small group of your classmates. Discuss how your literacy stories are different and similar. Finally, consider these reflection questions:

6. How have your literacy experiences influenced how you view the language arts?
7. What implications for your future teaching can you draw from reflecting on your literacy stories?

personal reflection

You probably developed your first notions of good communication in response to the way your parents and early teachers felt about language. If your parents were avid readers and felt it was important to discuss what they were reading, then you likely grew up feeling that reading was important. In homes where storytelling is valued as a way to entertain and communicate, the children learn that verbal explanations are important. Your attitude toward writing may have been partially built by how your elementary, middle, or high school teachers approached writing instruction. If teachers encouraged experimentation in writing, your experiences would be different than if you only had teachers who focused on form and structure.

JON, FUTURE TEACHER ▶ In my home, we had a strong sense of community. Families were often outdoors, and we looked at the neighborhood as one big front yard. We often sat on our front porch and talked to neighbors, or we would go and visit other families outside. When a group gathered together, it was the prime time for storytelling. We had one neighbor—Mr. Jones—who could weave the most outrageous tales but made them just as believable as if you had lived through them yourself! I always liked it when he began telling his stories.

My dad and my mom had different ways of telling stories. My dad was very animated, using his hands, changing voices for different characters, and pausing to build

Teacher Viewpoint

suspense or for effect. My mom, on the other hand, had a quiet way of talking with a drawn-out Southern accent. I loved the way her voice just seemed to slide out of her mouth and right into my head.

All of us are language users and are influenced by our particular social and cultural contexts. You come to teaching with your own expectations about language learning. You may believe that it's important for a teacher to stress certain aspects of communication, such as reading classic literature or public speaking. Each of the children in your classroom also comes to school embedded in her or his own language and cultural experiences, needs, and resources. Often, your students' language and cultural experiences will be different from your own. Students' cultural, socioeconomic, and community contexts are some of the most important considerations when planning for instruction (Hull & Schultz, 2002). In the past, many teachers felt that there was one standard way in which all children must learn, think, talk, or communicate. Instead, the goal of language arts instruction is to help all of the children in your classroom learn to communicate effectively in many different situations and settings, recognizing that they may start from different points and bring diverse but valid ways of using language and communicating.

You may never be an expert on all cultures, nor could you possibly speak all the languages that could be present in your classroom. You may never know what it is like to live in poverty, but this may be a reality for some students in your classroom (Payne, 1998). You can, however, recognize, accept, and appreciate the differences among your students. Expanding your experiences and developing an understanding of diversity will help you create meaningful lessons and activities. Get to know your students, their communities, and their families. Depend on colleagues from different cultural backgrounds to help you understand how the differences might influence language and communication processes. Visit the neighborhoods where your students live to gain a greater understanding of their lives and communities. Then accept and expect the wonderful diversity of language and language styles that will be represented in your classroom.

TEACHER Viewpoint

CARLA, BEGINNING TEACHER ▶ During my first year of teaching math to students who were learning English as a second language (ESL), I decided that we needed to focus on learning math words so that we could talk more about concepts. In order to do this, we started writing books about how we use math in our everyday lives. I started off by introducing phrases that they might use in their book, such as, "In math, I like to learn about . . ." or "I want to find out more about . . . ." We brainstormed some sentences we might use in our stories, and then students began writing independently.

As I was circulating around different groups of students, one child asked, "Ms. Diaz, I like my book. I want to read it to my family. Can I write it in Spanish?" What a wonderful idea! I gathered the class together so that we could talk about how to use both English and our native language in our books. Most students liked the idea and published their books in two languages. Some students worked together and used friends' native languages, too. They loved sharing these stories! They will be perfect to share for parents' night!

Researching Languages, Cultures, and Ethnicities in a Classroom

Talk to your cooperating teacher and ask him or her how many different languages are represented in the classroom and what they are. Ask about specific dialects that are used by children in the classroom. Ask about the cultural and ethnic groups represented in the classroom. Select one language, dialect, culture, or ethnicity and gather information about it by observing and interacting with the child(ren), talking to the teacher and others in the school, visiting the community, and conducting research in the library or on the Internet. Share your information with your classmates.

DISPOSITION OF TEACHERS OF THE LANGUAGE ARTS

Effective language arts teachers must be comfortable with a range of communication processes. A broad definition of literacy that includes multiple forms of representation allows us to expand ways of knowing and the extent to which diverse learners internalize new knowledge (Sweet, 1997, p. 273). An effective language arts teacher realizes there are many pathways to communicating meaning. By expanding the ways of developing meaning in the classroom, we can help all students communicate in multiple ways (Eisner, 1994).

A strong comfort level with written and oral communication, including multiple forms of visual and communicative arts, is invaluable. It is important for teachers to model effective communication skills. They need to read, write, listen, speak, and visually communicate in ways that their students can observe. An effective teacher is willing to share her language processes with her students. One of the easiest ways to do this is to talk about the books she is reading. Teachers should bring a book to read during time designated for silent reading. They can also participate in the classroom or schoolwide reading challenges by reading each night and recording the titles of the books on the same reading log the students may be using. Teachers can involve students in their own writing process as well (Angeletti, 1993). They can begin a story, then ask students to question them about the details. They can share their plans for what they will write and then ask the children to read the story when they have finished writing. When a teacher takes the time to talk through the language and communicative processes, the descriptions provide children with a window into ways they can communicate with others.

By now you may understand that many aspects of your personality are essential to teaching. Your students will learn from *you*—you are a strong role model for social and intellectual behaviors. As a teacher, you bear an amazing responsibility. Some essential components of your own attitude and actions are cultural respect, knowing your students, fostering home–school connections, and collaborating.

Language and Cultural Respect

As you will hear over and over, the first place where children learn language is their home and community. Including home and community communication processes extends the boundaries of the classroom and allows families to contribute a great deal to children's language learning (Hull & Schultz, 2002). Effective teachers recognize and accept that every home is an educational setting, and they recognize and respond to this contribution (Moll & Greenberg, 1990). The concept "funds of knowledge" (Moll, Amanti, Neff, & Gonzalez, 1992) asserts that all families possess important knowledge about a variety of topics. By acknowledging and appreciating these funds of knowledge, teachers can encourage families to share their knowledge about the practical (e.g., auto repair), the aesthetic (e.g., needlework), the sciences (e.g., natural remedies), and other meaningful areas. Some teachers hold family learning days, events where families can set up stations for children to learn about various topics (McIntyre, Kyle, Moore, Sweazy, & Greer, 2001). Beyond the obvious benefits of sharing new knowledge with children, this approach also builds strong home–school ties and demonstrates your respect and appreciation for your students' families and cultures.

There are many ways to demonstrate that you respect your students' language and cultural background, but a great part of the acceptance is your own attitude. At the very least, you must recognize that much learning occurs in the social structure. The classroom, teacher, and textbooks are not the only way that your students will learn. Their lives outside the classroom will teach them a great deal, too. The more you know about your students' family and community contexts, the better you can connect the experiences in the classroom to what your students already know and have experienced, and the more effective your teaching will be.

Knowledge of Students

As mentioned above, language arts teachers must have access to a wide range of knowledge and materials. However, the resources are useless unless the teacher understands his students. Teachers must take into account developmental needs, learning styles, academic and personal interests, and background experiences of their students. This involves piecing together observations and information about students from a variety of sources and backgrounds. Some methods that teachers can use to learn about their students include:

- student interviews or questionnaires
- parent interviews or questionnaires
- student-of-the-week activities
- frequent and open communication with parents

- classroom observations noted as anecdotal records
- classroom activities and discussions such as "Day in the life of . . ." activities (see Exhibit 1.1).

High expectations are an important aspect of understanding and monitoring students in your classroom. Effective teachers have appropriate high expectations for all their students and see their job as facilitating students' learning. The relationship between teacher and student is crucial to sharing and achieving high expectations.

Literacy and Home–School Connections

Since language arts instruction should build on how children have learned to use language at home, it is important to understand as much as possible about your students' experiences with literacy in their homes, including the many different interpretations and uses of language. This is an important aspect of your knowledge of your students. Your role as a teacher includes gathering information about each student by involving family members. To get to know your students well, you will need to take the time to learn about students' lives outside of school and use that information to inform the way you teach. Involving families in the educational process is an important step toward accomplishing this. This textbook will provide many ideas and strategies to help you learn about your students, their families, and their communities. In addition, you will read about a variety of effective instructional strategies that support students' literacy and language arts development.

"Day in the life of. . ." activities to learn more about students.	**1.1**

- Have a group discussion about "a day in the life of" your students. Ask them to explain what they do most mornings, after school, in the evening, and on the weekend.

- Brainstorm with students to think of questions to ask other people about their daily lives.

- Have students write their own questions, then work in pairs interviewing each other (taking notes as they do).

- Have students keep a journal (in writing for older students or in pictures for younger ones) for one week about their daily activities (what they do, where they go, what they read and write, what television shows they watch, and so forth).

- Have students give oral reports about a day in their life.

- Create a bulletin board with a collage of images featuring one student at a time.

Adapted from Wikelund, K. R. (1990). *Schools and communities together: A guide to parent involvement.* Portland, OR: Northwest Regional Educational Laboratory.

SAMANTHA, BEGINNING TEACHER ▶ For one of my first assignments, I had my students draw maps to and write detailed descriptions of their homes. Students were highly motivated to complete the task, for if I could follow their maps and directions, I delivered a small package of cookies to them. On a weekend during the first month of school, I was able to visit almost all of my students' homes!

As I pulled up the gravel, stone, and paved driveways, I could see my students' faces in the windows awaiting my arrival. When I stepped foot into their homes I entered their worlds away from school. Prized 4-H rabbits, newly weaned puppies, and chained pit bulls greeted me. Crawfish étouffée, fried chicken, and biscuits invited me to sit down and stay awhile. I was welcomed into both crowded houses and empty houses. Grandpas dressed in their Sunday best and younger siblings barely dressed at all were eager to meet their loved one's new teacher.

During our poetry unit, students started by writing "Where I'm From" poems. I was able to build upon details I already knew about their home lives as I helped them revise their poems. For example, I was able to say, "Fred, now I know your mother's corn-bread is more than just 'all right'—tell me what the air tastes like when she is making it." My initial home visits gave me abundant information about students' lives that I was able to use in my lessons throughout the year.

In the end, home visits not only allowed me to see the environments my students lived and learned in, but they also made that first important personal connection to the student's family. Later, one parent told me that I was the first teacher she ever felt comfortable talking to about her son's progress in school. The mother said she and her son felt connected to me since I had visited their home. Spending some time reaching out to families in the beginning of the year really pays off.

Note. Some school districts may have policies about home visits. Be sure to check with the building administrator before planning a home visit.

It is important to understand as much as possible about your students' experiences with literacy in their homes.

Reflective Decision Making

Teaching language arts means making many decisions and taking various actions in a classroom setting. Teachers must consider their instructional goals and what they will do to provide instruction to help all children reach these goals. Decision-making skill comes partly from teachers' knowledge about communication and partly from teaching experiences. As you gain more knowledge about teaching and more experience in the classroom, you will be able to base your decisions on what you know about language arts instruction, teaching, learning, and your students. "Thinking like a teacher" means considering the options for and potential of various situations in order to revise your lessons, differentiate or modify instruction for varied student levels, group students, and respond to linguistic and cultural diversity.

All teachers are researchers, testing new ideas and hypotheses about learning, and creating theories based on observations and assessments of students' performance. Learning from your classroom as well as from other educators is an important aspect of your teaching experience (see Chapter 8, Article I, for more about reflective teaching). Teaching is a learning process. Even experienced teachers are constantly learning better ways to approach language arts instruction and new strategies that meet the needs of their students.

Collaborating

Even though much of their work is done in isolation with groups of children, teachers are rarely truly solo performers. Teachers improve their effectiveness by collaborating with their colleagues. Often elementary teachers are part of a grade-level team that establishes goals for learners, develops curriculum, coordinates instruction, interprets state and local goals and objectives, and implements student services. Teachers also work with a variety of special service teachers to meet the many different needs of their students. In any given classroom, teachers could have students who work with the reading specialist, speech teacher, LD resource teacher, occupational therapist, English-as-a-second-language teacher, and social worker. These students may receive this extra support in the classroom or in a pull-out setting. Either way, it's imperative that the classroom teacher collaborate with the special service teachers so that the student receives the most effective support. Effective teachers work with their administrators, share their knowledge and skills with others, and participate in developing strong school programs. In addition, teachers must work collaboratively with parents and take advantage of community resources.

Membership in a professional organization facilitates professional collaboration and exchange of ideas. Two professional organizations related to language arts are the International Reading Association (IRA) and the National Council of Teachers of English (NCTE). These organizations sponsor conferences that you may want to attend and even present at; they also publish books, journals, and other materials about language arts instruction. You can find out more about membership benefits by visiting their websites, **www.reading.org** and **www.ncte.org.**

To summarize, teaching language arts has many facets. A teacher is influenced by formal and informal experiences in and out of the classroom. Various individuals and experiences contribute to teachers' dynamic socialization and education. However, learning to be a good teacher requires conscious reflection on biographical events, professional training, personal experiences, readings, classroom experiences, collaboration, and other meaningful events. The following section will help you begin to do this.

DEVELOPING A PERSONAL PHILOSOPHY

There is more to teaching than loving children, knowing content, and implementing instructional procedures. The decisions you make as a language arts teacher may have a long-lasting impact on your students. Your actions are based on how you know and understand the world (Clark, 1995). Your philosophy of language arts and communication accounts for your unique teaching style, contributes to your decision-making process, and influences your interactions with learners. Your experiences in this methods course should help you begin to understand your teaching philosophy and how your beliefs influence your language arts teaching.

Developing a personal philosophy of language arts education involves clarifying educational issues, justifying your instructional decisions, and integrating your understandings into the teaching/learning process. Developing a personal philosophy requires self-examination and honest thought about communication, language learning, meaning making, teaching, and learning. It is a continual process of seeking answers to hard questions over a long period of time. Before developing a philosophy of language arts education, you may find it helpful to identify some of your major beliefs about language arts, teaching, and learning. You can use these "I Believe" statements to formulate your personal philosophy statement after you have gained more knowledge about language arts and more experience in classrooms.

personal reflection

Preparing "I Believe" Statements About Language Arts Education

Complete the following statements about language arts education, teaching, and learning. Be honest; there are no right or wrong answers. The purpose of this activity is to get you thinking about your beliefs related to language arts education.

1. I believe language arts is . . .
2. I believe an effective teacher should . . .
3. I believe students should . . .

Record your ideas and discuss them with a partner. Save your responses and review them near the middle and end of the course to see if you want to make changes. At the end of this course, you may want to finalize and print your statements for your portfolio.

TEACHERS AS LANGUAGE USERS

Have you ever thought about how your ideas about literacy might be changed by teaching and working with children's literacy? The following real-life stories describe some of the natural connections between literacy and the personal and professional lives of teachers. These teachers are at different points in their careers, and the contexts in which they are teaching and learning require different skills. They are involved in language and communication in a multitude of ways, and their specific interactions teach them about language and communication. Hence because of the requirements of their work, they view literacy in very different ways.

Preservice Teacher

Jane is enjoying her studies in teacher education. This is the first college semester where she has been totally immersed in courses about teaching and learning in the elementary school. She has always felt that she wanted to be a science and math teacher for upper grades, but she is surprised how much she enjoys the courses related to literacy. One of her courses focuses on the language arts and another on reading instruction. The previous semester she completed a course about children's literature in which she read many children's books. She particularly enjoyed some of the young adult science fiction literature. She reread *A Wrinkle in Time* (L'Engle, 1990) and was introduced to the rest of the books in that trilogy. Although she hadn't been a recreational reader in the past, she began to take time to become familiar with books that she observed students reading during her practicum experiences. The most popular current book, *Harry Potter and the Order of the Phoenix* (Rowling, 2003), became a topic in many of her methods classes. She meant to keep reading children's literature as she prepared to student teach, but she is finding that the reading demands of her methods courses are very high and it is hard to find the time to read new children's literature.

Even though Jane is a natural in front of a group of children, she struggles to feel comfortable talking in front of her university classmates. She doesn't have a problem talking in the small groups that are formed in many of the methods classes, but she dreads getting up in front of a classroom to talk about teaching. Jane feels so different in front of her fifth-grade classroom, where she enjoys learning and talking with students. The students in the classroom where she is working this semester also make her feel more comfortable about her writing abilities. Her cooperating teacher has asked her to respond to some of the fifth graders' journal entries, another comfortable way for her to interact with fifth graders.

Jane is rather surprised that methods courses are helping her reflect on her own literacy. She is beginning to see why an elementary teacher must understand strengths and weaknesses related to literacy and communication. She sees herself growing as a language learner and teacher.

Beginning Teacher

This is Delray's first year of teaching. In addition to planning for daily instruction, he is constantly looking in reading materials for suggestions about his bilingual classroom, where many of the five-year-olds speak English as their second language. He is also trying to learn some Spanish so he can greet the parents of his students when they bring their children to school. One day each week, Delray holds a Spanish "lunch bunch" where students eat their lunch with him and teach him Spanish. They enjoy introducing Delray to new vocabulary words and phrases, and Delray keeps notes of what he learns in a notebook that he reviews now and then.

He is constantly on the lookout for books that have pictures of concepts familiar to the students in his classroom, but he has found that often he must make his own posters and ABC books with magazine pictures that represent his students' cultures. His students' favorite book is *Hairs/Pelitos* by Sandra Cisneros (1994). This story, which uses characteristics of a narrator's family's hair to describe their personalities, is in both English and Spanish. Rocio, who is able to read in Spanish, helps Delray read the story to the classroom. They both sit at the front of the classroom, holding the book. Delray reads the phrases in English and then Rocio reads the story in Spanish.

Delray thinks the most effective language activity in his classroom is his morning meeting. After students enter the classroom, get settled, and read and look at books for 15 minutes, they gather at the front of the room to discuss the schedule for the day, share concerns or stories, and read poems or stories together. The meeting begins when the student who has the job of changing the calendar and the weather report calls the class together. In unison, students read the date and report on the weather. Another student records the information on their weather graph. Delray discusses their daily schedule as he reads it from the board. Then students have sharing time, when they tell stories from their lives or pose questions they have. Delray ends the morning meeting by teaching the students a poem or rhyme that involves actions, hand gestures, or special sounds. Together, they recite the rhyme several times.

Veteran Teacher/University Instructor

Betty has been teaching for 25 years. She has always loved teaching, but she has particularly enjoyed teaching reading and language arts. She has seen many changes in the teaching of language arts. She continually reads research and other articles about how to teach language arts, and she tries to share what she reads with the new teachers in her building.

For the past several years she has been enrolled in a graduate program that helps her keep up with cutting-edge instruction in reading and language arts. Her involvement in a graduate education program has required her to do extensive reading and writing in many areas of education. In addition, Betty reads as many children's books and novels as she can possibly read each year. She feels this is an important activity related to her teaching.

Betty became involved with a group of teachers who write and share their writing. This resulted in her publishing an article about teaching in her district's newsletter for teachers. The group is trying to organize a teacher research group in their school district to study various issues related to language arts instruction. They are currently reading about how other groups of teachers have organized and implemented such groups within their own schools.

Last year, the local university asked Betty to teach an undergraduate course in language arts methods. She began to think about how future teachers understand and apply the language arts during their methods courses and later in their initial teaching experiences. She had thought about this before, when she worked with student teachers. This kind of work gave her an opportunity to learn about current methods as well as talk to enthusiastic future teachers about her own knowledge. It reminded her how important it is for teachers to be aware of their own language and communication processes.

Teachers as Language Users

Think about the stories of Jane, Delray, and Betty, and write down the ideas and insights that are most important to you about each of these teachers as a language user. Consider how they use reading and writing in their lives. Consider how you use language in a typical day. To make connections between their stories and your own experiences, try using prompts such as

"That reminds me of . . ."

"That is like something that happened to me when . . ."

"That makes me think of . . ."

"That makes me wonder about . . ."

Share your ideas with your classmates. Then make a list of the three to five most important ideas about teachers as language users that you gained through this reflection.

FINAL REFLECTIONS

To become a teacher of language arts, you must learn to adjust to new groups of students and situations. Effective teachers understand and respect their students' language processes, collaborate with others, and constantly reflect upon their own practice. Throughout their careers they focus on different aspects of language arts instruction, always searching for new and effective ways to teach the diversity of students in their classrooms.

Reflecting on Guiding Questions

Look back at the guiding questions at the beginning of this chapter. Read your initial responses to these questions. Note any changes you would make now. Discuss your responses with your classmates.

PROFESSIONAL REFLECTIONS

To continue to reflect on your Field Note responses from this chapter, consider these suggestions:

- Compare your definition of language arts with that of your classmates and experienced teachers. Use a graphic such as a Venn diagram or a concept map to show similarities and differences.

- Choose a way to present your literacy story. It could be a timeline, collage, poem, life-map (graphic display of literacy events plotted as a concept map), photography, drama, painting, or sculpture. Consider using technology such as hypertext, Web pages, or digital video to tell your literacy story.

Professional Readings

Some books that expand your understanding of the content of this chapter include:

Ballenger, C. (1999). *Teaching other people's children.* New York: Teachers College Press.

Ballenger writes about what happens when a teacher does not share a cultural background with her students. Her initial teaching plans for reading to children do not produce the results she expects. She has a difficult time with communication, which adversely affects the children's classroom behavior. She examines her own attitudes about books and reading, learns from the community, and restructures the way she teaches. This book will help you understand how your views of literacy can be different from those of your students.

Graves, D. (1991). *Build a literate classroom.* Portsmouth, NH: Heinemann.

This book provides step-by-step suggestions that will help you understand your own literacy behaviors and how what you believe affects your teaching. It includes actions and reflections that would be valuable support for professional reflections, portfolios, and inquiry.

Heath, S. B. (1984). *Ways with words.* Cambridge, England: Cambridge University Press.

This classic text describes the connections between culture, language learning, and school experiences. Even though it was written two decades ago, this text remains an important source of information about the impact of home experience on our view of language. Heath writes about the literacy development in two contrasting communities that are seven miles apart. She illustrates how the community and family ways of communicating and learning affect children's classroom experiences. She chronicles how the teachers in this community respond to the differences in attitudes toward literacy by creating student-centered curricula.

Meier, D. (2000). *Scribble scrabble: Learning to read and write, success with diverse teachers, children and families.* New York: Teachers College Press.

Meier questions his own ways of teaching in a kindergarten classroom. He emphasizes the multitude of different factors that influence a child's belief system regarding literacy. By using the voices of parents and teachers, Meier provides a deeper understanding of the factors that influence a child's literacy development.

Select one of the following books listed below and read it. Reflect on the insights you gained about diversity, community, family, or culture from reading the book. Consider how your insights can help you work more effectively with the diversity of students you will find in your classroom.

Children's Books

The following examples of children's literature provide insights into the content of this chapter:

Clymer, E. (1995). *Santiago's silvermine.* New York: Dell.

This story describes how two Mexican boys looking for treasure to help their families find something unexpected and valuable.

Myers, W. D. (1993). *Brown angels: An album of pictures and verse.* New York: HarperCollins.

The author and illustrator collected pictures of African American children and wrote about their experiences, family interactions, and memories.

Rosen, M. J. (1992). *Home*. New York: HarperCollins.

This is a collection by several authors that illustrates varied perceptions of home to illuminate cultural differences.

Say, A. (1993). *Grandfather's journey*. Illustrated by A. Say. New York: Scholastic.

This story describes the cross-cultural experiences of a Japanese American family that feels loyalty to both countries. The book addresses the strong and constant pull that bicultural families feel for two countries.

Other children's books mentioned in this chapter are:

Cisneros, S. (1994). *Hairs/pelitos*. Illustrated by T. Ybanez. New York: Alfred Knopf.

L'Engle, M. (1990). *A wrinkle in time*. New York: Farrar, Straus, and Giroux.

Rowling, J. K. (2003). *Harry Potter and the Order of the Phoenix* (Book 5). New York: Scholastic.

REFERENCES

Angeletti, S. R. (1993). Group writing and publishing: Building community in a second-grade classroom. *Language Arts, 70,* 494–499.

Clark, C. M. (1995). *Thoughtful teaching*. New York: Teachers College Press.

Eisner, E. W. (1994). *Cognition and curriculum reconsidered* (2nd ed.). New York: Teachers College Press.

Flood, J., Heath, S. B., & Lapp, D. (Eds.). (1997). *Handbook of research on teaching literacy through the communicative and visual arts*. A Project of the International Reading Association. New York: Macmillan.

Gutierrez, K., Baquedano-Lopez, P., & Turner, M. G. (1997). Putting language back into language arts: When the radical middle meets the third space. *Language Arts, 74,* 368–378.

Hobbs, R. (1997). Literacy for the information age. In J. Flood, S. B. Heath, & D. Lapp (Eds.), *Handbook of research on teaching literacy through the communicative and visual arts* (pp. 7–14). New York: Macmillan.

Hull, G., & Schultz, K. (Eds.). (2002). *School's out: Bridging out-of-school literacies with classroom practice*. New York: Teachers College Press.

Leland, C. H., & Harste, J. C. (1994). Multiple ways of knowing: Curriculum in a new key. *Language Arts, 71,* 337–345.

Leu, D. J. (2000). Our children's future: Changing the focus of literacy and literacy instruction. *The Reading Teacher, 53,* 424–429.

Luke, A. (1998). Getting over method: Literacy teaching as work in "new times." *Language Arts, 75,* 305–313.

McIntyre, E., Kyle, D., Moore, G., Sweazy, R. A., & Greer, S. (2001). Linking home and school through family visits. *Language Arts, 78,* 264–272.

Mikulecky, L. (2000). What will be the demands of literacy in the workplace? *Reading Research Quarterly, 35,* 379–380.

Ministry of Education. (1996). *Dancing with the pen: The learner as a writer*. Wellington, New Zealand: Learning Media.

Moll, L. C., Amanti, C., Neff, D., & Gonzalez, N. (1992). Funds of knowledge for teaching: Using a qualitative approach to connect homes and classrooms. *Theory into Practice, 31,* 132–141.

Moll, L., & Greenberg, J. (1990). Creating zones of possibilities: Combining social contexts for instruction. In L. Moll (Ed.), *Vygotsky and education: Instructional implications and applications of sociohistorical psychology* (pp. 319–348). New York: Cambridge University Press.

National Council of Teachers of English & International Reading Association. (1996). *Standards for the English language arts*. Urbana, IL: NCTE and Newark, DE: IRA.

Payne, R. K. (1998). *A framework for understanding poverty* (Revised ed.). Highlands, TX: RFT Publishing.

Suhor, C. (1992). Semiotics and the English language arts. *Language Arts, 69,* 8–230.

Sweet, A. P. (1997). A National Policy Perspective on Research Intersections Between Literacy and the Visual/Communicative Arts. In J. Flood, S. B. Heath, & D. Lapp (Eds.). *Research on teaching literacy through the communicative and visual arts* (pp. 264–285). International Reading Association. New York: Macmillan.

Wikelund, K. R. (1990). *Schools and communities together: A guide to parent involvement*. Portland, OR: Northwest Regional Educational Laboratory.

Wiseman, D. L., Knight, S. L., & Cooner, D. (2004). *Becoming a teacher in a field based setting* (3rd ed.). Belmont, CA: Wadsworth.

Debra, a first-year teacher, has waited all summer to get into her classroom. After she was hired at her new job, she was told that she would not be able to work in her room until planned repairs and painting were complete. Finally, soon after the first of August, her principal calls to tell her she can pick up the key to her classroom and begin setting up for the beginning of the year. When she finally opens the door, the freshly painted classroom is large and bright, but looks abandoned. The bookcases are empty except for several sets of textbooks, and the bulletin boards are bare except for a few tacks. Chairs perch upside down on the tops of 25 desks. She knows she has two weeks to prepare for her first class of fourth graders, who are represented only as names on the roster she finds in her mailbox.

Debra sets about preparing to teach all the subjects in her elementary curriculum, but the development of language arts is the focus of her efforts since she feels it is basic to all other subjects. Right away, she realizes that she will need support from experienced teachers. She quickly develops a list of questions to ask the teacher who was assigned as her mentor. Her student teaching experience exposed her to many ideas that she wants to implement in her classroom, but her mentor suggests that she select one framework or strategy that will guide her instructional planning. It will be possible to include

Chapter 2

PLANNING AND ORGANIZING FOR LANGUAGE ARTS INSTRUCTION

some of her other ideas as she gains experience. Since her school has scheduled a block of time specifically for teaching language arts, Debra decides to use the workshop approach as a framework for planning and implementing language arts instruction. She talks to other teachers who are using this approach, reviews the state and local language arts standards,

rereads some of the materials from her methods courses, and takes into account her own goals as she plans for her first weeks of class. Eventually she decides she would like to integrate language arts instruction throughout all the subjects that she teaches, but she decides to wait to make a formal plan for that during the second part of the year.

After making preliminary plans for her approach to language arts instruction, Debra arranges her classroom so she can have space for her students to work independently and in small and large groups. She places the desks in groups of four and five, and she designates small round tables as math, reading, art, science, and social studies work stations. She clusters her three classroom computers in a central area so that students have easy access to them. She also creates a small classroom book collection in the corner that includes the books she collected during her university training. She is a bit disappointed at how small her collection looks once the books are in the cases, but she feels sure that she will be able to add to it during the next few years. After a trip to the local secondhand furniture store, she adds a rug and big pillows to her book center to make it look and feel more comfortable.

Debra balances her own goals and philosophy and her school's standards and curriculum requirements with the challenges of selecting an instructional approach. As she organizes her classroom, her efforts seem more involved than what she observed in her student teaching environment, where her cooperating teacher seemed to get ready for the beginning of school so effortlessly.

By the time her students arrive on the first day of school, Debra has started to collect the instructional resources she will need, arranged the classroom in ways that support her instructional approach, and planned activities that introduce workshop routines for the classroom and provide opportunities for her and her students to read, write, talk, and listen together. Her overall goal is to connect all the components of instruction and create a literate environment that will encourage her students to engage in language learning opportunities. Debra has put in a lot of thought into the best ways to do this, and she is now ready to start her first year of teaching. After a busy couple of weeks, she is now looking forward to meeting her students on the first day of school.

INTRODUCTION

Establishing environments that support language arts teaching and learning requires careful planning and organization. Your ideas, thoughts, and theories about literacy and language arts affect classroom organization, curriculum planning, and material selection, but you must consider other factors, such as state and local standards, as well. This chapter will help you consider various aspects of establishing a classroom environment.

GUIDING QUESTIONS

Consider these questions as you read this chapter. Jot down your initial responses to each question. After reading the articles, revisit your responses. Would you make any changes to them? If so, what would those changes be? Discuss your responses with one or more of your classmates, your professor, or your mentor teacher.

1. How do teachers plan and organize for language arts instruction?
2. What must teachers know about their students when planning for instruction?
3. What standards and curricular plans guide language arts instruction?
4. What student groupings support language arts instruction?
5. What room arrangements are effective for teaching language arts?
6. What books, materials, and supplies, including technology, are needed to teach language arts?

Structures for Language Arts Instructional Planning

How does a new teacher choose what to teach and how to present language arts instruction to her students? This is a question that most any new teacher like Debra will have. Planning for instruction is a balancing act that requires teachers to match what they know and understand about their students with curriculum standards and instructional requirements. Effective teachers are very aware of students' backgrounds, families, and communities, and they use what they know about their students to plan relevant instruction. By becoming familiar with the neighborhood where the school is located and providing opportunities for students to talk about themselves through reading, writing, listening, speaking, and visual representation, you will gain a great deal of information that you can use in instructional planning. (Refer back to Exhibit 1.1 for a list of specific activities for getting to know your students.) Developing knowledge of students, their diversity, and their lives is a crucial step in developing a structure for language arts instruction.

Standards, specific instructional approaches, and general guidelines for developing lessons are all important building blocks of language arts instruction. Teachers take the basic ideas about instructional planning, include their understanding of their students' backgrounds, and add their own inventions and routines to meet the needs of their students. Even if you are familiar with your students, language arts strategies, and curricular goals, it will still seem as if you have to make many decisions about where to begin. This article explains the role of standards, gives three examples of instructional approaches, and provides guidelines for planning language arts lessons.

USING STANDARDS TO PLAN FOR INSTRUCTION

Standards provide guidance for planning, implementing, and evaluating language arts instruction by describing behaviors students should exhibit. Standards are "clearly stated expectations of what students should know, both in knowledge and process . . . if they are to be functional members of society" (Hammer, 1998, p. 7). Standards are developed and established to create a sense of direction for what is taught and how it is taught in order to foster higher achievement for students. They form the basis of instructional objectives that guide lesson planning and establish learning intentions for students.

Professional groups such as the International Reading Association (IRA) and the National Council for Teachers of English (NCTE) have developed national standards for literacy education. These standards were established by specialists in language arts, English, and reading to provide guidance and ideas for instruction. An example from the NCTE and IRA standards reads as follows:

Students apply knowledge of language structure, language conventions (e.g., spelling and punctuation), media techniques, figurative language, and genre to create, critique, and discuss print and non-print texts. (National Council of Teachers of English, 1996)

For a complete reference to NCTE/IRA standards, see Exhibit 2.1 or log on to **www.ncte.org/about/over/standards/110846.htm.**

Understanding the NCTE/IRA Standards for the English Language Arts

Read the NCTE/IRA Standards for the English Language Arts (see Exhibit 2.1 or consult the website **www.ncte.org/about/over/standards/110846.htm).**

With a partner, discuss each standard, and write it in your own words. Share your ideas about each standard with your classmates. As a group, brainstorm examples of how each standard might look in action in the classroom.

Note: You may also find the NCTE book series *The Standards in Practice* useful for understanding how the standards look when implemented in classrooms at the K–2, 3–5, and 6–8 grade levels. These books are available for purchase on the NCTE website, **www.ncte.org.**

All except one state in the United States have developed standards for all subject areas, and these standards take priority over the NCTE/IRA standards. The detail presented in state standards helps teachers and administrators identify the most important things for students to learn in the various subjects and grade levels. The example in Exhibit 2.2, taken directly from the state standards, illustrates the specificity of standards for language arts instruction for the state of Illinois. The Illinois English language arts standards are presented in five broad strands: reading, literature, writing, listening and speaking, and research. Each of the strands is introduced by the statement of an overall goal and a list of many sub-goals. For example, the broad goal stated for listening and speaking is, "Students will listen and speak in a variety of situations." The learning standards are broken down into more detailed statements that delineate many ways in which the learning standard is met and specify the grade level at which the standard should be achieved. Be sure to review a copy of your state's language arts standards. They can be easily accessed on the Internet at your state department of education's website.

Teachers and administrators collaboratively work together to develop local standards for the school district. School districts connect their standards with state standards by cross listing or using a numbering system that will help teachers make connections. It is most important to review the standards for language arts learning that are used in the district where you are observ-

exhibit **2.1** *Standards for the English language arts.*

STANDARDS FOR THE ENGLISH LANGUAGE ARTS
Sponsored by NCTE and IRA

The vision guiding these standards is that all students must have the opportunities and resources to develop the language skills they need to pursue life's goals and to participate fully as informed productive members of society. These standards assume that literacy growth begins before children enter school as they experience and experiment with literacy activities—reading and writing, and associating spoken words with their graphic representations. Recognizing this fact, these standards encourage the development of curriculum and instruction that make productive use of the emerging literacy abilities that children bring to school. Furthermore, the standards provide ample room for the innovation and creativity essential to teaching and learning. They are not prescriptions for particular curriculum or instruction. Although we present these standards as a list, we want to emphasize that they are not distinct and separable; they are, in fact, interrelated and should be considered as a whole.

1. Students read a wide range of print and non-print texts to build an understanding of texts, of themselves, and of the cultures of the United States and the world; to acquire new information; to respond to the needs and demands of society and the workplace; and for personal fulfillment. Among these texts are fiction and nonfiction, classic and contemporary works.

2. Students read a wide range of literature from many periods in many genres to build an understanding of the many dimensions (e.g., philosophical, ethical, aesthetic) of human experience.

3. Students apply a wide range of strategies to comprehend, interpret, evaluate, and appreciate texts. They draw on their prior experience, their interactions with other readers and writers, their knowledge of word meaning and of other texts, their word identification strategies, and their understanding of textual features (e.g., sound-letter correspondence, sentence structure, context, graphics).

4. Students adjust their use of spoken, written, and visual language (e.g., conventions, style, vocabulary) to communicate effectively with a variety of audiences and for different purposes.

5. Students employ a wide range of strategies as they write and use different writing process elements appropriately to communicate with different audiences for a variety of purposes.

6. Students apply knowledge of language structure, language conventions (e.g., spelling and punctuation), media techniques, figurative language, and genre to create, critique, and discuss print and non-print texts.

7. Students conduct research on issues and interests by generating ideas and questions, and by posing problems. They gather, evaluate, and synthesize data from a variety of sources (e.g., print and non-print texts, artifacts, people) to communicate their discoveries in ways that suit their purpose and audience.

8. Students use a variety of technological and information resources (e.g., libraries, databases, computer networks, video) to gather and synthesize information and to create and communicate knowledge.

9. Students develop an understanding of and respect for diversity in language use, patterns, and dialects across cultures, ethnic groups, geographic regions, and social roles.

10. Students whose first language is not English make use of their first language to develop competency in the English language arts and to develop understanding of content across the curriculum.

11. Students participate as knowledgeable, reflective, creative, and critical members of a variety of literacy communities.

12. Students use spoken, written, and visual language to accomplish their own purposes (e.g., for learning, enjoyment, persuasion, and the exchange of information).

Example of an Illinois state learning standard.   *exhibit*   **2.2**

4.A. LISTEN EFFECTIVELY IN FORMAL AND INFORMAL SITUATIONS.

4.A.1a Listen attentively by facing the speaker, making eye contact and paraphrasing what is said.

4.A.1b Ask questions and respond to questions from the teacher and from group members to improve comprehension.

4.A.1c Follow oral instructions accurately.

4.A.1d Use visually oriented and auditorily based media.

4.A.2a Demonstrate understanding of the listening process (e.g., sender, receiver, message) by summarizing and paraphrasing spoken messages orally and in writing in formal and informal situations.

4.A.2b Ask and respond to questions related to oral presentations and messages in small and large group settings.

4.A.2c Restate and carry out a variety of oral instructions.

4.A.3a Demonstrate ways (e.g., ask probing questions, provide feedback to a speaker, summarize and paraphrase complex spoken messages) that listening attentively can improve comprehension.

4.A.3b Compare a speaker's verbal and nonverbal messages.

4.A.3c Restate and carry out multi-step oral instructions.

4.A.3d Demonstrate the ability to identify and manage barriers to listening (e.g., noise, speaker credibility, environmental distractions).

Illinois State Board of Education, 1997.

ing and teaching. They can usually be found on the Internet website for the district, or your mentor teacher should have a copy for you to review.

Current policies require teachers to pay a great deal of attention to standards during instructional planning. This emphasis sometimes makes it easy to forget that what teachers know about their students should be the first consideration when they develop teaching and learning activities. Although standards provide guidelines and suggest goals, instructional goals should be driven by students' needs and strengths. Knowledge of curricular standards in combination with an understanding of students' needs and strengths is the foundation for high-quality instructional planning.

2.1

Language Arts Standards

Locate and review the language arts standards for your state and/or the school district where you are doing your internship. Observe a language arts classroom over several days and determine how many of the standards are met in routine instructional practices. Match specific activities with the standards. Share with your classmates and determine which standards are not routinely met in most classrooms. Talk to your mentor teacher about how the standards affect teaching.

Standards influence teachers' instructional planning in many ways. After teachers assess students' knowledge related to a standard, the standard may suggest an appropriate activity. For example, Illinois state standard 4.A.2b states that students should be able to "Ask and respond to questions related to oral presentations and messages in small and large group settings." Nadia, a fourth-grade teacher in that state, observes that many of her students are hesitant to speak and to ask questions during whole-class discussions. She decides to develop a lesson to help them meet standard 4.A.2b. Knowing that her students are interested in current events, Nadia invites a speaker to the classroom to discuss life in a Middle Eastern country. In preparation for the speaker's visit, she provides background about Middle Eastern geography and cultures. The class also brainstorms questions about this part of the world. After the class has agreed on several questions, Nadia models an appropriate way to ask them. She plans the speaker's visit and her preparatory activities to help her students overcome their hesitancy in speaking and asking questions in front of groups.

Teachers may also review standards during lesson planning to make sure that a lesson is appropriate and comprehensive, to ensure that it addresses standards in a meaningful way, and to determine if planned activities can be expanded. For example, a teacher who brings in a speaker may also meet reading and writing standards while preparing students to ask questions and respond to the speaker. A teacher's input into instruction is very important even when state standards suggest a framework for literacy instruction. Although the standards provide a general goal to work toward, "in the end, it is the teacher [and how the teacher considers the skills and abilities of students], not the standards, that make a difference in the classroom" (Klein, 1999, p. 27).

Standards provide a guideline for assessment and evaluation (Elmore & Furhman, 1995), and they correlate with standardized tests. Standards and their connections with standardized tests have a major impact on the teaching of language arts. A discussion of connections between standards and student assessment is found in Chapter 7, Article I. After you review the NCTE/IRA standards, your state's learning standards, and your district's curriculum standards, you will know the broad goals and important areas that should be taught in language arts at your grade level. Standards, however, do not provide the routines or activities that are implemented in the classroom. Instructional approaches are also helpful in suggesting potential planning structures for your classroom.

APPROACHES TO PLANNING LANGUAGE ARTS INSTRUCTION

Two basic approaches form the foundation of most language arts instruction. One approach is the *literacy block*, where lessons and schedules focus entirely on the development of language arts skills. The literacy block primarily concentrates on the natural connections among the language arts processes that result in a great deal of overlap among reading, writing, speaking, and listening activities. Units and lesson plans use literature as the foundation, and a variety of themes—such as literature genres (e.g., the study of poetry, mysteries, short stories, and so forth), authors, or topics selected for special events or interests (e.g., study of popular culture, comparing celebrations across cultures or special issues)—support instructional planning.

The second approach to planning for language arts instruction is an *integrated curriculum approach*, in which language arts instruction is embedded in the teaching of content areas such as science, social studies, mathematics, art, drama, and even physical education. An integrated curriculum approach presents language arts skills with thematic content instruction throughout the school day. Language arts instruction is organized by themes, such as Space, Communities, Courage, or Cultures, and it occurs during science, mathematics, social studies, and arts instruction as well as language arts. The descriptions given below of the literacy block and integrated approaches will help you understand how language arts instruction is presented in most classrooms.

Literacy Block

Many elementary and middle schools schedule a language arts period that focuses entirely on reading, writing, speaking, and listening activities. Teachers plan for the literacy block in multiple ways. Reading/writing workshops (Atwell, 1998; Calkins, 1994), Four Blocks (Cunningham, Hall, & Sigmon, 1999), and guided reading instruction (Fountas & Pinnell, 1994), are three popular examples of how teachers plan for literacy block instruction.

Reading/Writing Workshop

Nancie Atwell (1998) is a New England teacher who wanted to replicate the discussions that she and her own children had around the dinner table about children's literature. What emerged as she attempted to embed the reading, writing, and sharing into her own classroom instruction was the reading/writing workshop, a framework that has been implemented in many classrooms. The purpose of the workshop format is to provide daily time for students to read and write, to encourage students to be involved in self-selection of reading materials and writing topics, and to share student-authored texts. (See Chapter 4, Article II, for a complete discussion of writers' workshop and Chapter 5, Article IV, for literature circles.) Some teachers use a workshop format as a general guide for their entire language arts program; others use it in combination with other approaches and strategies. Atwell developed the workshop model for adolescent writers, but her plan provides a structure that is applicable with many different developmental stages. Lucy Calkins (1994) developed a similar framework for teaching early primary grades. Workshops provide predictable routines that include opportunities to engage in reading and writing. They take on many forms, depending on how teachers consider unique settings and student needs, but they almost always include the following routines:

Reading–writing mini-lesson. Short, planned, teacher-directed sessions begin the workshops each day. The mini-lessons are presented to the whole class, small groups, pairs, or even one student and focus on a multitude of topics including workshop routines; author studies; discussion of a poem, short story, or opening book chapter; or the introduction to a certain genre. The teacher may use mini-lessons to model comprehension strategies, develop vocabulary concepts, teach writing conventions, or complete a word study. The short lessons provide opportunities for the teacher to focus on the development of literacy behaviors. Although mini-lessons typically last no more than 15 minutes, the time needed for a specific mini-lesson will be determined by the needs, age, and attention span of students and by the focus of the lesson.

Effective language arts teachers are guided by standards and by their students' knowledge and backgrounds when planning instructional activities.

Independent reading/writing. The time allowed for independent reading and writing is called *work time* by Calkins (1994), while Atwell (1998) suggests planning for a period of independent reading and writing in which students self-select their reading texts or writing topics. Students use their time to work on various individual projects that may be at very different stages. The teacher begins the independent reading/writing time by modeling and engaging in personal reading and writing. At some point during this part of the workshop, the teacher will stop her own reading and writing and move around the classroom to provide advice, feedback, encouragement, and support to students.

Conferences. A portion of the workshop structure is designed to allow time for students to talk about their personal reading and writing. During conference times, students may meet with the teacher or a peer to talk about their writing, share what they have been reading and writing, react to what they are reading and writing, or talk about issues that emerge during their reading and writing processes.

Sharing. Sharing is an important part of workshop instruction and is usually done in a large-group setting. Three or four students talk about what they have written or read during the workshop. They ask their peers for advice, share something they feel is well written, or talk about the processes they use to read and write.

Scheduling for the workshop approach involves providing large blocks of time for students to read, write, think about and respond to ideas they have read, listen to others, share insights, and make discoveries (Au, Carroll, & Scheu, 2001). Ideally workshops are scheduled for $1\frac{1}{2}$ to 2 hours each day, providing time for students to read and write, listen and share, and participate in instruction. When teachers feel they cannot devote this amount of time each day to the workshop approach, they schedule in creative ways. Exhibits 2.3 and 2.4 illustrate two ways teachers may schedule workshop activities.

Typical schedule for workshop approach (two-hour block).	*exhibit* **2.3**

8:30–8:45	Reading–Writing Mini-lesson
8:45–9:30	Independent Reading and Writing
9:30–10:00	Conference Time
10:00–10:30	Sharing Time

Creative schedule for workshop approach ($1\frac{1}{2}$ hours, not in a block).	*exhibit* **2.4**

8:30–8:45	Reading–Writing Mini-lesson
8:45–9:15	Independent Reading and Writing
9:15–9:50	Break for Music Class
9:50–10:00	Status of the Class (to remind students what they are working on, what their goals are, and the focus of the mini-lesson from the morning)
10:00–10:20	Conference Time
10:20–10:35	Sharing Time

Four Blocks

The Four Blocks literacy framework is an instructional structure developed for primary grades (Cunningham, Hall, & Sigmon, 1999) and adapted for upper grades. The main focus of this structure is reading, but the Four Blocks concept supports a multilevel approach to language arts instruction that includes attention to all literacy skills. This structure emphasizes flexible groupings of children who are rearranged as they experience and learn more about language arts. Routines associated with the Four Blocks framework are as follows:

Self-selected reading block. Students are given time during the day to read self-selected reading material. They are encouraged to read a variety of books and other texts independently. Teachers provide baskets or shelves of books divided into various levels and help students select appropriate materials.

Guided reading block. Teachers plan explicit instruction focusing on specific reading skills. Students are divided into groups randomly or based on their specific reading strengths and needs, depending on the focus of the lesson. Guided reading groups typically consist of at least three but no more than eight students. The guided reading block includes pre-reading activities, during-reading activities, and after-reading activities. In the pre-reading activities, teachers help students establish prior knowledge, learn vocabulary, set a purpose for reading, and make predictions about the texts they are reading. Familiar books written at grade level and below grade level are used during the guided reading session, but teachers provide students time to read new materials and texts. The teacher closely monitors the reading to make sure students comprehend the material. The after-reading portion of the block supports practice and application of the reading process by allowing students to engage in additional reading, discussion, or questioning.

Working with words block. During this block the students focus on vocabulary development and explore words, letters, sounds, and patterns. Students work together in small groups, or the teacher may lead them through activities that focus their attention on words and word patterns. Teacher guidance helps them focus on spelling and decoding strategies in various ways, such as by making words, sorting words for patterns, doing word wall activities with basic sight words or other important words, or playing word games.

Writing block. Teachers begin the writing block by modeling something about writing that their students need to learn, then encouraging their students to practice the new skill or idea. During this time, students engage in independent writing and conference with the teacher about their writing. Sharing students' writing is an important aspect of the writing block.

The Four Blocks approach is typically implemented for a period of two hours, with time divided differently based on the grade level of the classroom. Sample schedules for a primary and an intermediate classroom using the Four Blocks approach are provided in Exhibit 2.5.

Guided Reading

A third model for literacy instruction is guided reading (Fountas & Pinnell, 1996), which provides explicit skill instruction for a small group of students at similar levels of development. Because guided reading depends on grouping children based on their reading level, it requires the teacher to assess students' reading by using ongoing assessment strategies such as running records and observations (see Chapter 7, Article II). Based on teacher assessment of instructional needs, students are grouped and regrouped as appropriate. As students become more proficient, they move into reading groups with higher skill levels, and the focus shifts more toward building meaning. The structure of guided reading groups places four to six children together and proceeds through the following sequence.

Introducing a new book. The introduction of a leveled book, sometimes called a "little book," is teacher directed. Leveled books are sets of books organized by levels from easy enough for a beginning reader to more complex for experienced readers (Fountas & Pinnell, 1999). One grade level may

Sample schedules for the Four Blocks approach.   *exhibit* **2.5**

PRIMARY CLASSROOM SCHEDULE

8:30–9:00	Self-Selected Reading Block
9:00–9:30	Working with Words Block
9:30–10:00	Guided Reading Block
10:00–10:30	Writing Block

INTERMEDIATE CLASSROOM SCHEDULE

8:30–9:10	Self-Selected Reading Block
9:10–9:25	Working with Words Block
9:25–9:50	Guided Reading Block
9:50–10:30	Writing Block

have several sets of leveled books to use for reading instruction. Usually more levels are available at the kindergarten and first-grade level (as many as 10) and fewer (perhaps three or four) for upper grades.

During the introduction of the new book, the teacher establishes the general idea of the book, introduces the language of the book, focuses on the print in the book, connects children's prior knowledge to the book, and makes a strategy statement to let the children know the focus of the lesson. With groups of young children or struggling readers, teachers may also use a "picture walk" to have children look at and discuss the pictures in the text and make predictions of what they think the book will be about, prior to reading the book.

Reading the book. Children read the book independently, either silently or orally. Very young readers receive assistance from the teacher, who reads the book aloud, points to the text as they read, and helps them use appropriate reading strategies. Students reread the book to establish fluency and comprehension. After repeated readings, when children are able to read the book fluently and on their own, the process is repeated with a new book.

After reading. During this time, students discuss the story, focus on specific skills or strategies, talk about their own reading processes, and talk about words in the story. In this phase students may engage in additional language arts activities such as writing, additional reading, drama, or choral reading. Teachers may conduct conferences with students to talk about their reading and writing.

Scheduling for guided reading. A consideration for scheduling the guided reading approach is what the other students will be doing while the teacher works with a guided reading group. Typically, primary teachers have other students participate in learning centers. Learning centers, such as a listening center, writing center, and library center, are locations within the classroom that present children with instructional materials, directions, objectives, and provisions for self-evaluation. At these centers, either working by themselves or with a few others, students can self-select an activity from a group of related activities and work independently (see Article II in this chapter). If a classroom aide or a parent volunteer is available, he may be responsible for monitoring the centers while the teacher works with a guided reading group. A teacher of older students often has the other students participate in independent reading, writing, response journal activities, or projects while the teacher works with a guided reading group. Teaching students to work without teacher support during guided reading is challenging but essential. This process typically takes several weeks at the beginning of the year and includes clarifying expectations, establishing routines, and modeling appropriate behavior.

When scheduling guided reading groups, most teachers plan to see struggling readers more often than stronger readers (in the sample schedule below, the teacher works with most of the groups four days per week, the struggling reader group daily, and the strongest readers three days per week). A sample schedule for guided reading groups is provided in Exhibit 2.6.

Sample schedule for guided reading groups (five groups).		*exhibit* **2.6**
Monday	8:40–9:00	Group A
	9:00–9:20	Group B
	9:20–9:40	Group C
	9:40–10:00	Group D
	10:00–10:40	Other Language Arts Instruction
Tuesday	8:40–9:00	Group E
	9:00–9:20	Group A
	9:20–9:40	Group B
	9:40–10:00	Group C
	10:00–10:40	Other Language Arts Instruction
Wednesday	8:40–9:00	Group D
	9:00–9:20	Group E
	9:20–9:40	Group A
	9:40–10:00	Group B
	10:00–10:40	Other Language Arts Instruction
Thursday	8:40–9:00	Group C
	9:00–9:20	Group D
	9:20–9:40	Group E
	9:40–10:00	Group A
	10:00–10:40	Other Language Arts Instruction
Friday	8:40–9:00	Group B
	9:00–9:20	Group C
	9:20–9:40	Group D
	9:40–10:00	Group A
	10:00–10:40	Other Language Arts Instruction

GROUP KEY

Group A = Struggling readers   Group D = Good readers
Group B = Low-average readers   Group E = Very skilled readers
Group C = Average readers

TEACHER *Viewpoint*

ARICELI, BEGINNING TEACHER ▶ During the first couple of months of school, I was so worried about finding the right or best way to teach language arts. I felt frustrated that no one told me the BEST way to teach during my teacher education program or during faculty meetings at the school where I'm a first-year teacher. When I asked my mentor about the best approach, she told me that the first step to planning instruction is to know my students' interests and needs, but she also emphasized that finding routines and strategies for teaching language arts was necessary. She suggested that I find a format that I am comfortable with and that fits my students; use the standards as guidelines; observe the children's learning closely; and teach with creativity and enthusiasm. She also suggested that I visit other teachers' classrooms during my preparation time to see how they teach language arts. I have learned so much from seeing experienced teachers in their classrooms. I have also realized that while some of them structure their teaching in different ways, they are still teaching to the standards and getting good results. I guess you could say I'm starting to realize that my mentor's advice is right after all!

MIRIAM, VETERAN TEACHER ▶ I've been teaching for 21 years, and I think I'm a good teacher who really helps all children learn. About a year and a half ago, my district adopted the Four Blocks format, which worried a lot of the teachers in my building. After I read about the format, attended professional development workshops, and talked with other teachers who were already using the approach, I realized that it was not all that different from the approach I had been using successfully in the past. In fact, I think the format helped me be more aware of including all of the important components of language arts in my classroom every day. I still find ways to incorporate my creative, fun ideas into the format, and it is exciting to see my students' progress and enthusiasm for the Four Blocks.

field note **2.2**

Observing Different Approaches

Observe a teacher who uses a workshop, Four Blocks, or guided reading framework for her instructional approach in the language arts. Identify what she does during each component and how the students respond to instruction. Do students read, write, speak, and listen as they are involved in lessons? Are they working as a whole class or in small groups? Also, note the teacher's role in each component of the approach. After you have observed the lesson, interview the teacher. Ask questions about why she selected her approach to language arts and the strengths and weaknesses of the approach. Consider the different philosophical frameworks associated with each approach. Ask the students which of the components they enjoy the most and what they think they are learning. Use the information you have gathered to examine the benefits and challenges of different instructional approaches. If possible, share your observations and findings with your classmates to gain greater insight into the various instructional approaches for language arts.

Comparing the Three Examples of Block Literacy Instruction

The three examples of language arts instruction given previously present frameworks to guide planning and reflect philosophies about teaching language arts. Each of the three approaches has a different perspective on teachers' roles, grouping children, and guiding instruction. For example, one of the obvious differences in philosophy is the amount of teacher-directed instruction that occurs. The workshop approach is almost totally student centered. Self-selected reading material and writing topics comprise the major instructional strategies. workshop mini-lessons are planned and presented by teachers, but they are based on the specific needs of the students. The manner in which children are grouped also illustrates differences in the three approaches. The workshop and Four Block approaches are based on flexible, heterogeneous small groups formed from student interests and needs, and the guided reading approach is presented to small, homogeneous groups of students.

The three approaches also have many aspects in common and suggest the basics of language arts instruction. The following routines occur each day in effective instruction, regardless of the framework.

- *Modeling and demonstrations* include the teacher explaining the task or process while demonstrating or describing the steps involved.
- *Guided practice* allows the teacher and students to practice together or the teacher to help the students engage in language arts activities.
- *Independent practice and application* provides opportunities for students to try the reading and writing on their own.
- *Sharing and reflecting* about reading and writing takes place after students have practiced the task. They apply it to different situations and the teacher continues to provide feedback.

An important aspect of instruction is helping students make connections to their own lives and experiences. Routines included in successful language arts instruction should provide a way for students to talk about events in their lives, connect class material to their own family and community contexts, and express their opinions and feelings about what they are experiencing in the classroom. Understanding how to put the students in the center of all instruction is crucial to good instruction, no matter what approach is used.

Integrated Curriculum Approach

In contrast to the literacy block, a second broad approach to planning and implementing language arts instruction

Language arts instructional activities provide opportunities for students to make connections to and communicate about their lives and experiences.

integrates reading, writing, speaking, and listening with other subject areas. Instead of treating language arts as a separate subject, integrated instructional planning involves presenting two or more subjects as overlapping and interacting (Seely, 1996). The most common technique for implementing an integrated curriculum approach is the use of integrated thematic units. Integrated thematic units are developed around important topics, books, or big ideas. They frequently emerge from popular culture (TV, movies, or books), current events (presidential elections, community celebrations, the Olympics), or common interests (favorite books, sports, or pets).

Planning an Integrated Curriculum

Planning for integrated instruction includes:

- selecting a theme with student input
- identifying goals
- planning activities
- locating resources

Some teachers find the use of a planning web helpful as they consider how to link the various content areas around a central theme. Exhibit 2.7 provides an example of a preliminary planning web for a primary level unit on the ocean.

exhibit 2.7   *An integrated thematic unit planning web.*

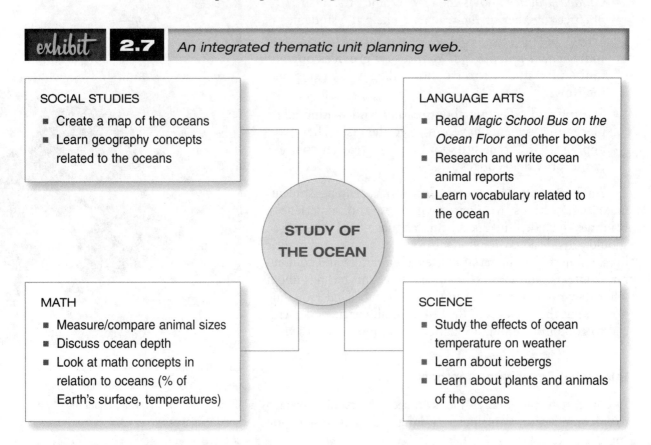

SOCIAL STUDIES
- Create a map of the oceans
- Learn geography concepts related to the oceans

LANGUAGE ARTS
- Read *Magic School Bus on the Ocean Floor* and other books
- Research and write ocean animal reports
- Learn vocabulary related to the ocean

STUDY OF THE OCEAN

MATH
- Measure/compare animal sizes
- Discuss ocean depth
- Look at math concepts in relation to oceans (% of Earth's surface, temperatures)

SCIENCE
- Study the effects of ocean temperature on weather
- Learn about icebergs
- Learn about plants and animals of the oceans

ELYSE, VETERAN TEACHER ▶ After I started linking subjects together by teaching thematically, I was amazed at how often connections are made across the curriculum. For example, we were reading the Tomie dePaola book *Watch Out for Chicken Feet in Your Soup,* and we made the recipe in the back of the book. I had the students measure the ingredients as a group after I demonstrated at the front of the room. Some of the students were confused about fractions and asked about them as we were mixing the flour. I gave a brief mini-lesson on fractions while they were cooking. I decided to begin a fraction unit the next week so they would understand. Next time, I will teach the book with the fractions unit. It will make more sense that way!

Identifying a theme. The theme selected for an integrated unit provides a framework for planning and instruction in language arts and other subjects. Students' needs, interests, and developmental levels are some of the first items a teacher should consider when identifying a theme (Smith & Johnson, 1994). Themes focus on important topics, issues, and concepts such as friendship, survival, or the ocean—ideas that are relevant to students and fit well with district curriculum. When planning integrated units, the teacher will not only consider language arts standards but content area standards as well. Some sample themes for the elementary and middle school grades are provided in Exhibit 2.8.

Identifying goals. District and statewide standards and local curriculum must be considered in the selection of a theme. Reading and writing standards may suggest genre or author studies, for example. When planning integrated units, the teacher will consider not only language arts standards but also content area standards. For example, the Virginia standards of learning pro-

---

Sample themes for integrated curriculum units. *exhibit* **2.8**

Grade 1: Healthy Lifestyles

Grade 2: Communities

Grade 3: The Ocean

Grade 4: Water Quality in Our Community and State

Grade 5: Examining the Revolutionary War from Multiple Perspectives

Grade 6: Ancient Egypt

Grade 7: Overcoming Adversity

Grade 8: Examining World War II from Multiple Perspectives

vide guidelines for fourth graders to study science topics such as force, motion, energy, life processes, and living systems. The Virginia standards also call for teaching about Greece and Rome in third-grade social studies.

Planning instructional activities. Thematic instruction should be more than a series of activities; it should provide support, encourage interaction, and make connections between language arts and other subject areas. Integrated units include plans for cross-curricular activities and incorporate science, mathematics, social studies, the arts, and, of course, language arts. Unless activities are developed around important ideas and connected by themes and standards, they are nothing more than a loosely connected series of ideas. Activities appropriate for individual, small group, and whole class learning suggested throughout the articles in this textbook can be a part of an integrated thematic unit.

Integrated thematic units typically contain three different types of activities:

- *Initiating activities.* These activities occur at the beginning of the unit and serve to build and activate the students' prior knowledge, pique interest in the theme, and set purposes and goals for the unit.
- *Developmental activities.* These activities make up the bulk of lessons in thematic units and provide the actual instruction and learning experiences related to the theme and various content areas.
- *Culminating activities.* These activities occur near the end of the unit and help students pull together their learning, celebrate their new knowledge, and put their learning into action. Often thematic units end with a project, such as a field trip, student presentations, a dramatization, or an action project that allows students to apply their new knowledge to real-life situations and share with others beyond the classroom. Examples of action projects include writing letters to the editor about water quality concerns in the community or holding a food or clothing drive to help community shelters, houses of worship, or food banks.

Locating resources. One challenging aspect of unit planning is gathering the resources needed for successful implementation. Teachers have the primary responsibility for locating resources such as children's literature, textbooks, reference materials, audiovisual aids, and computer software related to the theme. Materials at varying levels of reading difficulty and in various media should be available to encourage all students in your classroom to develop concepts.

Collaboration and Integrated Teaching

Integrated teaching occurs naturally in early elementary grades when one teacher teaches all subjects. But as more content is presented and different teachers are responsible for content instruction due to departmentalization, the situation becomes more complicated. Even so, developing integrated curriculum is worth the effort at all levels, and collaborative teachers can deliver very effective lessons across the curriculum. The development of an effective integrated approach does not just happen, but rather evolves as a result of a well-articulated theme and thoughtful planning. Usually when teachers develop a unit, they work collaboratively with colleagues to plan lessons. They share children's and adolescent literature, textbooks, and other instructional materials that relate to the theme. Teachers get ideas for integrated units in many places. Commercially prepared units are available, and the Internet provides examples and support for integrated teaching. Teachers typically adapt prepared units to match their students' needs and curriculum standards. Several examples of thematic units are reviewed at the websites listed in Exhibit 2.9.

Because of the planning and many resources required, building a thematic unit from the beginning is a difficult task even for experienced teachers (Lipson, Valencia, Wixson, & Peters, 1993). Beginning teachers may want to use prepared thematic units, modify existing units, or gradually integrate subjects, starting with two that are easily related, such as language arts and social studies. Thematic instruction is best planned in collaboration with teachers of other subjects or a grade-level team. When teachers work together they contribute from differing perspectives and share responsibilities.

DEVELOPING LESSONS

Regardless of the approach you use to plan and implement language arts instruction, lessons offer the day-to-day guidance so necessary for effective teaching. Lesson planning for language arts instruction follows common formats. Many of these formats exist, but generally they consist of the elements described in Exhibit 2.10.

Websites offering thematic unit ideas.   *exhibit* **2.9**

THE TEACHER'S GUIDE

www.theteachersguide.com/Thematicunits.html

UNIT PLANS

www.cccoe.k12.ca.us/bats/welcome.html

http://curry.edschool.virginia.edu/go/Whales/home.html

www.sbcss.k12.ca.us/sbcss/specialeducation/ecthematic/

www.okaloosa.k12.fl.us/technology/training/tools/elem/k-2.htm

2.10   *Sample lesson plan format.*

Content: _____

Grade Level: _____

Date: _____

Objective: What should students be able to do after completing the lesson? Include state and/or district curriculum standards that will be met.

Materials needed: List all the resources needed to teach the lesson. Be sure to include what is to be used by both the teacher and the learner and indicate how they will be used.

Why are you teaching this lesson? What led you to plan a lesson to meet this instructional objective? Include what role this lesson has in future classroom learning.

Instructional procedures: Describe what you will do in teaching the lesson to students. A brief outline of the lesson (for a 12–20 minute lesson) could include:

- Motivation/introduction: How will you introduce the lesson and capture students' attention? (Allow 2–3 minutes for this step.)

- Teaching procedures and student activity: What instructional techniques will you use? What things, specifically, will students do during the lesson? (Allow 5–10 minutes.)

- Closure/evaluation: How will you bring closure to the lesson and how will students demonstrate new learning? (Allow 5–8 minutes.)

Follow-up activities: Describe how you will reinforce and extend this lesson. You might describe homework, other assignments and projects, and/or links to other subject areas.

Classroom management concerns: Identify possible problems and plan for them.

Self assessment (to be completed after the lesson is presented): Answer questions such as the following:

- What was the most effective part of the lesson? The least effective?

- What were the students most enthusiastic about and why?

- If you had the opportunity to teach this lesson again, what would you do the same? What would you do differently?

- Were there any surprises, and how did you handle them?

- How did the actual results differ from the desired and planned for results? (Analyze the difference between the learning objective and what was actually learned.)

Lesson plan sites on the Internet.	*exhibit* **2.11**

www.askeric.org/Virtual/Lessons

http://lessonplanspage.com

http://lessonplanz.com

One of the most helpful tips in writing your first lesson plans is to look at lesson plans that are already fully developed to get a better idea of what needs to be in a lesson plan. You can do this by reviewing your teacher's lesson plans or lesson plans available in numerous books and journals or on the Internet. The sites listed in Exhibit 2.11 provide examples of lessons written by practicing teachers.

Lesson plans are to teaching as roadmaps are to traveling. A good lesson plan helps teachers know where the lesson is going, how they will help students get to the end goal or objective, and what materials and steps are needed. Some teachers' lesson plans may make planning look so easy that you will be surprised by the difference when you begin to think about your own instruction. After teaching for several years, they may go for several weeks with only notes or a short outline written in the small space in their lesson plan books. This does not mean that they have not planned for instruction. As a new teacher you will find that you need clearly written lesson plans that provide a framework veteran teachers may have internalized through years of experience.

PLANNING FOR UNIQUE STUDENT NEEDS

Today's classrooms comprise students from diverse cultures, speaking different languages, and possessing different learning abilities. Good planning involves taking the wide range of student needs into account and considering suggestions for modifications that will meet those needs. A teacher who is culturally aware recognizes that children have different interests, learning styles, and abilities as well as different experiences. Lessons will need to be differentiated or modified to accommodate children who learn in different ways. Some students will need tasks presented explicitly and with shorter explanations; others will need more time to finish their tasks, more opportunities to practice new skills and strategies, or more support from teachers until they learn routines or concepts.

No one instructional approach takes care of all the different linguistic needs of students in diverse classrooms. The activities planned for language arts instruction should also benefit those children who are learning English. Teachers who are planning instruction for English language learners (ELLs) should consider the suggestions listed in Exhibit 2.12.

exhibit **2.12** *Suggestions for planning instruction for English language learners.*

1. Provide many opportunities for hearing, speaking, reading, and writing English.

2. Use children's literature as a foundation for activities and to provide opportunities to play with the English language.

3. Provide opportunities for peer interaction between ELLs and English speakers.

4. Use flexible grouping to vary language interactions.

5. Use nonverbal clues, visuals, demonstrations, and concrete objects.

6. Use thematic approaches to teach the language arts.

Children who speak languages other than English should have many opportunities to hear English, speak English, and read and write English. They will need to see others read and write and take part in discussions. Children's literature, especially picture books, serves as the foundation for all activities designed to expose non-English speakers to English. Wordless picture books, alphabet books, and books with repetitive and predictable texts can provide ELLs an opportunity to play with the English language. Providing opportunities for ELLs and children who are fluent in English to talk and work together benefits all children in a classroom. Peers are often the best teachers of children who are learning to speak English. In addition, students who speak only English may learn phrases from their ELL classmates and develop an interest in other languages if their teacher provides the opportunities and encourages the language interactions.

Flexible grouping offers many opportunities for language interactions. Group work that involves ELLs should include nonverbal clues, visuals, and demonstrations so that a child who is learning English can understand what is happening. Children's learning is enhanced when language arts activities are accompanied by real objects. For example, if a lesson requires that a student understand friendly (or personal) letters, then a trip to the post office, actual letters, or pictures of letters provide concrete examples. Another way to increase understanding is to encourage physical activity and creative expression. Acting out stories in pantomime will include speakers of different languages in meaningful ways.

Thematic approaches to language arts are particularly valuable for English language learners. Themes may be based on stories or texts accompanied by illustrations that support meaning. Thematic units also usually incorporate many hands-on activities that provide concrete experiences ELLs can connect to their new language learning. Hands-on activities support the texts of books such as *Strega Nona* (DePaola, 1975, 1999) and *The Magic Porridge Pot* (Galdone, 1986) and lead to discussions in which each child builds understandings from a combination of pictures and words. In conjunction with *Strega Nona,* children could make spaghetti and invite guests to the classroom. The language and dialogue around such activities will promote understanding and encourage attempts to use newly acquired English skills.

Looking at Thematic Units

Obtain a thematic unit to review. Examples may be found at the school where you observe and teach, on a website, or in commercially prepared materials. Highlight language arts activities that are used across the curriculum. In small groups discuss the instructional goals, strategies, and methods used to teach language arts. If possible, sit in with a group of teachers either planning a thematic unit or discussing how one might be implemented. What topics do they cover as they talk about implementing the unit plan? What materials and resources are needed to implement the plan? Reflect on your insights about thematic units.

FINAL REFLECTIONS

Planning and organizing for language arts instruction requires a great deal of thought and preparation, as Debra found out in the Window to the Classroom at the beginning of the chapter. Even before the students arrived in her classroom, she established her teaching philosophy through the materials she included in her classroom, its physical arrangement, and the decisions she made about approaching language arts instructional processes. In addition, she considered the needs of her students, how they learn best, and the goals, objectives, and requirements of the state and local curricula. Debra learned that good instructional planning is the basis for effective language arts instruction.

Organizing the Classroom and Students for Instruction

Instructing language arts effectively is rather like being an orchestra conductor. Many components must be managed and fine-tuned in order for harmony to exist in your classroom. In addition to making instructional plans, a teacher organizes 20 to 30 learners and establishes a comfortable environment that supports learning. Student grouping procedures and the physical layout of the classroom are important elements in a comfortable, productive learning environment.

GROUPING STUDENTS

Students may be grouped in a variety of ways and for many purposes, depending on the type of language arts activities that are occurring (Au, Carroll, & Scheu, 2001). Groupings of students provide time for supported practice, completion of shared tasks, collaborative responses, and sharing with and without teacher guidance. Groupings will change depending on students' interests and instructional needs. Different activities and goals, of course, will require different groupings. For example, when students are working on the computers they work in pairs or individually, but when they are reading and discussing books in literature circles, they are in small groups.

Ideally, teachers use flexible grouping to provide many different learning arrangements and opportunities. Grouping patterns include large and small groups, student pairs, individual student and teacher, and individuals. Grouping patterns are described in the following sections and summarized in Exhibit 2.13.

Large Group Instruction

Large group arrangements are used for all types of instruction, but certain specific activities are very successful if the entire class is involved. Discussions, enrichment activities, genre introductions, reading aloud, sharing writing, and explicit instruction are best accomplished with a whole class. It is an efficient way to present information, and the discussions provide students opportunities to hear various opinions and observe differing abilities. One of the most important activities that occurs during whole-class instruction is sharing new and exciting books. Teachers or students read book selections to the class and discuss why they are enjoying a particular book. Positive whole-class interactions resulting from reading books together build a strong community environment.

Whole-class grouping is an excellent arrangement for presenting routines for discussing literature, ways to monitor reading and writing, and different responses to literature. Author and genre studies may be introduced to the entire group at one time. Small group and individual work

		Grouping patterns.	*exhibit* **2.13**

GROUP SIZE	DESCRIPTION	ADVANTAGES	DISADVANTAGES
Whole Class	Teacher works with whole class; everyone participates in the same activity.	▪ Builds community ▪ Provides a common knowledge base for all students	▪ Some students get frustrated or bored depending on the level of instruction ▪ Some students may not participate ▪ Difficult to keep all students on task
Small Group	Groups of three to five students work together to accomplish a specific task.	▪ Provides focused instruction ▪ Engages students ▪ Helps students learn to work with their peers	▪ Creates a higher noise level ▪ Students may have difficulty working with their peers
Partners/Pairs	Students work with a partner to read, write, or complete a specific task.	▪ Promotes student involvement ▪ Encourages engaged learning so teacher can help those who need it	▪ A student may become too dependent on his or her partner ▪ One partner may dominate activity
Individual	Students work alone to read, write, or complete an assignment or task at their level or based on their interests.	▪ Allows students to work at their own level ▪ Enables teacher to determine what students can do on their own	▪ Students may be off task or lack motivation ▪ Requires extensive teacher planning and monitoring

Adapted from Opitz, M. F. & Ford, M. P. (2001). *Reaching readers: Flexible and innovative strategies for guided reading.* Portsmouth, NH: Heinemann.

follows whole-class instruction and provides opportunities to practice and apply the material and strategies that were presented to the whole class.

Whole-class approaches avoid labeling and offer an opportunity for a wide range of interests and abilities to be recognized. Children at all levels are capable of participating in whole-class sharing and instruction. Even if all children do not participate in discussions, they learn a great deal by listening to their peers.

It may be tempting to do a great deal of teaching in whole-class settings, but working in large groups does have limitations and disadvantages. Most young students do not have the attention span for the extensive listening that often occurs during whole-class instruction; without activities that promote student participation, off-task behavior is likely (Graves, Watts-Taffe, & Graves, 1999) and results in classroom management difficulties. Some

students do not interact well in a large group setting, will not feel comfortable speaking up in large group settings, and may be overlooked in whole-group instruction. Students who are learning English and do not feel comfortable with verbal interactions can have a difficult time keeping up and may find it difficult to contribute because of the pace of the discussions.

AMANDA, PRESERVICE TEACHER ▶ I remember being in the low group in reading when I was in first and second grade. It was terrible. I felt stupid and embarrassed. When I decided to become a teacher, I promised myself I would never use ability grouping.

XAVIER, NEW TEACHER ▶ I've been teaching for two years, and I feel so much more prepared to use different types of groups in my teaching now that I have some experience. In the beginning I think I did too much whole group instruction, and some kids would end up daydreaming or causing trouble because they got bored. I learned quickly that I needed to use different types of groups to keep everyone involved, interested, and on task.

EMILY, VETERAN TEACHER ▶ I've been a teacher for over 20 years, and I always tell the new teachers at my school how important it is to create a classroom environment where everyone feels comfortable. The physical layout of the classroom, the teacher's attitude, and the use of different types of groups all contribute to creating a positive classroom environment. Once students (and the teacher, too) feel comfortable, the real learning can begin! As a beginning teacher a lot of this is learned by trial and error, by watching other teachers, by observing students closely, and by reflecting on what is and is not working and why.

Grouping and Classroom Organization

Divide into groups of three. Have each group member choose one of the Teacher Viewpoints above. Discuss grouping and classroom organization, using the viewpoint as a starting place. List questions or concerns you have about grouping and organizing your classroom for language arts instruction. Discuss your questions and concerns with your peers, methods course instructor, and mentor teacher.

Small Groups

Small group work may be teacher led, such as in guided reading, or student led, such as in cooperative groups or literature circles. In teacher-led small groups, the teacher is able to interact with a small number of students. It is usually easier to keep small groups on task, and small group arrangements allow the teacher to focus on the specific needs of students (Flood, Lapp, & Nagel, 1992). Student-led small groups allow for maximum student involvement and student ownership of learning; however, students must understand the rules, processes, and routines before they can assume leadership. If teachers expect students to discuss books in small student-led groups, they should teach questioning and discussion skills, routines, and expectations in advance.

Grouping for literacy instruction has been a topic of disagreement among education experts. Historically, language arts instruction, and specifically reading instruction, has implemented some form of ability or homogeneous grouping strategy. In the past, children were typically grouped together based on test results or the grade level of reading material they could read and understand. However, a great deal of evidence supports the view that ability grouping does not benefit children's learning (Mills, 1997), and educators are beginning to realize that low-achieving children are usually at the greatest disadvantage in ability groups (Allington, 1995; Cunningham & Allington, 1999). This is true for several reasons. Teachers react differently to children in low-ability reading groups. Low-ability groups typically receive less motivating instruction and spend less time reading and writing.

Independent and collaborative activities form the basis for daily language arts instructional activities.

Ability grouping has also given rise to concerns about harmful effects on self-esteem, motivation, and attitudes toward language arts (Fuligni, Eccles, & Barber, 1995). Most troubling is that once children are placed in a low-ability group, they tend to stay in that group throughout their schooling (Cunningham & Allington, 1999).

Another way to group students is in heterogeneous, flexible groups. When flexible grouping is used, the process of forming groups in the classroom is continual; groups are frequently reorganized based on the students' needs and the teacher's instructional goals (Opitz, 1999). In flexible grouping, membership in a group terminates when the specific goal for which the group was established is reached.

One way to think about the variety of flexible grouping arrangements is to consider three possible arrangements: informal, formal, and base groups (Johnson & Johnson, 1999).

- *Informal groupings* occur when and where teachers need them. They might occur when students quickly find a partner to share their writing, explain a portion of a text they have just read, check punctuation during the writing process, or share journal assignments.

- *Formal groups* are formed for extended times, for example to conduct research on a particular topic or participate in an extended book discussion.

- *Base groups* are long-term groups that may last an entire year or grading period, designed to encourage teamwork and camaraderie. Base groups form the seating arrangement in many classrooms where teachers cluster student desks together or seat students at a large table as their "home base" during the school day. Base-group arrangements allow the class to work in small group settings in a quick, routine manner without the teacher having to call names or take time to organize the students.

Student Pairs

Partner learning may involve same-age students or older and younger pairs coming from different classrooms. Students with similar abilities work in pairs on such activities as oral reading and responding to discussion questions after reading.

Peer tutoring involves pairing a student who has mastered a particular strategy or skill with a student who is still mastering the skill. Usually students watch the teacher model the tutoring process, then the student who has mastered the strategy acts as a tutor for the other student. One of the benefits of peer tutoring is extra practice in a one-on-one setting. Students of all abilities benefit, resulting in initial learning on the part of the tutee and reinforced learning and sense of accomplishment on the part of the tutor. It is important to remember, however, that higher-ability students should not be overused as peer tutors. While the peer tutoring experience benefits all students involved, higher-ability students should also have opportunities to participate in other language arts activities and groups that present new and challenging materials and tasks.

Individual Student and Teacher

An important language arts instructional opportunity occurs when a teacher meets with an individual student to talk about reading and writing. Often called a reading or writing conference, a meeting between a teacher and a student helps the student focus on reading and writing, set goals and monitor progress, interact one-on-one with the teacher, and share what he or she has learned (Ministry of Education, 1996). Conferences provide opportunities to encourage, monitor, evaluate, and guide students during language arts instruction. Students are the focus during conferencing, and they do most of the talking. It is an excellent time for the teacher to demonstrate listening and questioning skills. Once students become familiar with the logistics of conferencing, they are capable of conducting *peer conferences*. Teachers generally schedule several conferences each day while the other students participate in self-selected reading, literacy centers, or other student-directed activities. Conferences are generally no more than five to ten minutes in length, depending on the age of the student and the goal of the conference. Questions to guide a conference and other organizational considerations are suggested in Chapter 4, Article II.

Seeking Balance in Grouping Patterns

Language arts instruction should provide opportunities for students to work independently and complete an assignment, read a book, write a journal entry, or work on a special-interest project. As you consider the various grouping patterns, it is best to seek balance in the types of groups used throughout each day or week. Instructional time should be spent in whole-group settings, allow students to share common experiences, and promote interaction with a wide range of peers; time should also be devoted to small group work, both teacher led to allow for targeted instruction and student led to promote engagement and ownership of learning; and time should be provided for students to work independently. By providing regular opportunities for students to participate in different types of groups, you will be able to reach, support, and motivate the many different learners in your classroom.

Meetings between teacher and students provide opportunities to focus on individual writing processes and products.

Observing the Impact of Grouping on Classroom Behaviors

field note
2.5

Observe in your classroom to note the impact of grouping on classroom behaviors of the teacher and the students. Note the role of the teacher in each grouping pattern. What does the teacher do in particular groupings? How do the students interact? Does everyone talk in each type of group? Is there a grouping arrangement that seems to support a great deal of sharing about reading and writing? Record your observations and be prepared to share them with your classmates in small group discussions. Discuss your findings with your teacher, and ask her to talk about your observations.

CLASSROOM LAYOUT

Classroom arrangements reflect teachers' philosophies, encourage children's work (Wood, 1999), promote the growth of literacy development, and support classroom routines and instruction. The room's size, space, and shape are relatively constant in most elementary schools, but teachers typically arrange the furniture and equipment to suggest an emphasis on communication and language–related activities. In general, a classroom provides spaces for whole-class instruction and sharing, small group or individual work, display areas, bookshelves, computer tables, and language learning centers.

Whole-Group Instruction Area

A large area of the room is usually devoted to whole-group instruction. The arrangement of the whole-group instruction area suggests a certain approach to teaching. Rows of desks suggest a formal, teacher-directed classroom, whereas rugs and pillows suggest an informal, flexible classroom. In the area designated for whole-group instruction, desks are arranged in view of the board, chart paper, computer screens, or projection screen. Teachers who allow students to sit on the floor during group discussions should provide a clear designation of seating areas so students will know where to sit and how to behave. Open space, rugs, and pillows are designated as places where the entire class meets together. Teachers refer to the area for the whole class to meet as "home base," "the rug," or other names that students can immediately recognize. It becomes the central information area for classroom events, often with a calendar, birthday list, comfortable chair for reading literature, and classroom schedule conveniently located and easy for everyone to see.

Small-Group Work Areas

At least one table should be devoted to small-group work. Here, the teacher may work with three or four students on teacher-directed lessons, set up sharing activities, or hold reading and writing conferences with students. In a large classroom, additional work areas may be set up for small-group work. If space or furniture is not available, individual student desks are arranged to make areas where groups of two to five children can work on projects or share reading and writing materials.

Individual Work Areas

Areas of the classroom should be arranged so children can pull away from the group and engage in quiet time to read and write. Individual work areas should have the space and materials necessary to complete specific types of activities. Spaces bounded by file cabinets, bookcases, or other classroom furniture are natural places for individual activity. When space is not abundant, special lofts or quiet corners can provide individual reading and writing niches. Children enjoy crawling into corners, cubbyholes, and special places to read favorite books. Some teachers have room for a comfortable chair or sofa that is to be used only for reading. Even large cardboard boxes can provide special hideouts where children may read during their independent reading time.

Display Areas

Space for displaying children's work is an important feature of a language arts classroom. Typically, bulletin boards become an important part of the classroom environment. Teachers develop their own attractive, neat ways of displaying children's work to focus attention on the work. Writing and artwork may be hung from the ceiling to make up for lack of bulletin boards, and school hallways provide gallery space for displaying students' work. If bulletin board space is limited, writing, graphics, and other language arts products can be hung with clothespins on strings draped across a section of the room.

Child-centered displays are organized and maintained by students. Some teachers select a "student of the week" who organizes the bulletin board in a way that reflects his or her life. Other teachers arrange the bulletin boards so that individuals or groups of students take responsibility for a portion of the display. Spaces can be designated with student names and pictures.

Books and other literature should be prominently displayed and easily accessible. Bookcases, shelves, and other display areas are available in most classrooms. If the room lacks shelves and bookcases, wooden or plastic shelves or cartons may serve instead. Folders, boxes, drawers, plastic tubs, or other containers may be used to organize and collect student work.

Centers

Materials related to a specific topic, skill, or interest can be gathered in one place, a center, so that students can work on their own to accomplish an identified task. Some centers, such as library and reading centers, are established permanently. Centers that include rugs, beanbag chairs, sofas, and rocking chairs add character to the permanent arrangement of the classroom and invite children to read. Writing and publishing centers that offer implements for writing stories, poems, and letters make important contributions to language arts instruction.

Centers may be flexible. Occasionally, teachers devote space in the room to a particular emphasis, such as a current event, an activity related to a particular skill needed for reading and writing, or a story related to other activities in the classroom. Furniture is rearranged, and books, equipment, and other props are gathered to support a theme or unit. Motivational devices often accompany teacher-suggested activities that children accomplish independently. Centers that include exhibits, pictures, and artifacts brought in from children's homes and communities are excellent opportunities for focusing on different cultures represented by students' diverse backgrounds. When a theme or unit of study is completed, the room is returned to its familiar order until new centers are established.

field note

2.6

Classroom Maps

Sketch a map of the elementary classroom where you are observing or teaching. Observe other classrooms in your building. Describe how different arrangements in the classroom encourage language arts activities. Share the various arrangements with your classmates, and discuss the effect of class arrangements on language arts instruction.

CREATING A COMMUNITY OF LANGUAGE LEARNERS

Language arts instruction is more than the physical room arrangement and student groupings—it includes intangible aspects as well. Planning and organizing for instruction includes thinking about the emotional environment of the classroom. *Creating a community of learners* is a term often used to describe the intangible content of a classroom. Most teachers recognize when their classrooms become a community—when students work well together, they care about each other, and they listen to each other's ideas and opinions. A community of learners has an important relationship to literacy (Nathan, 1995). When literacy is viewed as "a social activity, essential for living in a literate society" (Teale, 1993, p. 628), the idea of a community of learners collaboratively engaged in learning and working together seems like a natural context for language arts instruction.

Developing a community of learners involves aspects such as sharing class projects, recognizing and honoring students' cultures and language, and involving families and communities (Nathan, 1995). Teachers use some basic strategies to promote the development of a classroom community.

Teachers' Roles in Creating a Learning Community

It is primarily up to the teacher to establish and create a learning environment that says, "We are all in this together." In a community of learners, the teacher's role is one in which she talks about, displays, and models the behaviors she expects students to acquire. Teachers talk about books they are reading and classes they attend, or they show excitement about what the class is studying. Thus a major responsibility of teachers in a community of learners is to engage actively in their own literacy learning, to make their literacy learning visible to students in the classroom, to enjoy and celebrate literacy learning, and to sustain it over time—even (especially) when swamped by the demands of their work (Barth, 1997).

Sharing together is an important component of classroom community building. Classrooms in which students successfully discuss, collaborate, and participate in a variety of ways throughout the curriculum will experience shared events. Teachers facilitate community building with regular classroom meetings where students discuss upcoming events, units of study, and challenges in the classroom. Such classroom meetings allow children to feel part of the group and participate in decision making about the classroom. To promote productive classroom meetings and sharing times, teachers talk about and model respect for all viewpoints, and they encourage students to talk openly, listen carefully, and participate fully in classroom discussions and activities. Rules and expectations that focus on respect of others' ideas establish a classroom where students feel safe, valued, and important. Rules, expectations, and consequences are more meaningful when established collaboratively between the teacher and students. See Exhibit 2.14 for a sample list of classroom rules based on respect.

At the beginning of the year students may need modeling and reminders to interact in a collaborative manner. Such efforts are very important to creating a safe, caring classroom environment. Teachers help all children feel valued and important by getting to know each child on an individual basis and celebrating each child's unique gifts and talents, through strategies such as student-of-the-week activities, student-interest projects, and sharing times like Show and Tell or Daily News (when students and teacher share important events that have happened to them verbally or through shared writing).

Parents and the Community Outside the Classroom

Attitudes about school, the teacher, reading, and language evolve from the talk and actions of adults who are important in children's lives. Most parents are willing to foster values and positive ways of thinking about school, but the learning behaviors of the family are steeped in cultural values and beliefs about schooling (Moll, 1992; Wan, 2000). Different cultural values suggest multiple ways parents may contribute to the classroom community. Traditional contributions include teacher/parent conferences, open houses, and class presentations. Teachers, however, should also be alert for nontraditional opportunities for parental involvement, such as serving as an interpreter to a child who has recently arrived to this country or showing off native artifacts during a social studies lesson, so that everyone will feel wel-

Classroom rules that focus on respect.   *exhibit* **2.14**

1. Respect yourself, your teacher, and your classmates.

2. Do your best, and help others do their best, too.

3. Listen when others are speaking, and respect what they say.

4. Be a good friend.

5. Help your classmates when they need help.

come in the classroom. Even with a wide range of ways for parents to be involved in the classroom, teachers should understand that family situations vary and some parents will have valid reasons for not taking part. Getting to know parents on a personal level will contribute to community spirit in the language arts classroom (Nathan, 1995). The link to parents will help students feel accepted and recognized as members of the classroom community.

Classroom literacy experiences are most effective when they are connected with the uses of literacy in the community outside of school (Rogers, 2000). Community members outside the classroom may share books, make class presentations, or become involved in the classroom in a number of ways. Two teachers in an urban setting included community connections in an innovative way: They invited a local poet into their classrooms, and he motivated students to write about their own lives. Once a month, parents and other guests gathered in the early evening and, with the poet and teachers serving as hosts, shared the children's poetry and conducted workshops that encouraged collaborative writing between parents and students.

Another teacher created a "guest reader" program to invite members of the community into the classroom each week to share a favorite story, poem, or passage with the children. She included community members such as the mayor, police chief, and librarian; parents and grandparents; business owners and employees; coaches, bus drivers, and letter carriers. The children looked forward to hearing the different readers each week, and community members became more involved in the classroom. Each time the classroom and children's neighborhoods connect, it provides an important link to home and family and illustrates the value of children's experiences outside the educational environment.

FINAL REFLECTIONS

Organizing the classroom for language arts instruction involves a wide range of decisions. A teacher should consider grouping patterns and methods for creating a classroom community. However, much like the familiar adage "A house does not make a home," a classroom does not necessarily mean that a community of learners will emerge. The teacher must consciously plan to create a classroom community where all children learn. By using a variety of grouping patterns to allow children to interact and participate in different ways and by building a strong classroom community, you will be well on your way to creating a classroom environment that supports meaningful language arts instruction for all students.

Language Arts Texts, Resources, and Materials

As Debra discovered in the Window to the Classroom at the beginning of this chapter, an empty classroom is a lonely place. Desks, textbooks, a computer or two, and a teacher's desk usually occupy a new teacher's classroom. The bare walls, empty bookcases, and blank bulletin boards that Debra found when she first entered her classroom seem sterile in contrast to the lively, interactive classroom that a new teacher envisions. One of the first jobs you will need to accomplish before the students arrive at the beginning of the school year is to create a classroom that encourages, supports, and motivates students to expand their abilities to read, write, speak, and listen about all subjects.

The materials and resources you will use for language arts instruction are affected by what is provided by your school district and in great part by your own ingenuity. Some teachers will find themselves working in a school that provides many materials, while others will struggle to establish classrooms with the basic instructional supplies. When necessary classroom materials are unavailable, teachers have been known to take it upon themselves to collect materials and resources that enhance their teaching. Elementary teachers are notorious for acquiring materials from the district, through donations and personal efforts. Shopping at library thrift book sales, sharing personal collections of children's literature, and applying for grants that support book purchases are ways teachers add books to empty classroom shelves.

The basic resources needed for language arts instruction include a variety of text-related materials such as children's literature, basal readers and textbooks, student-authored texts, and magazines and newspapers, but non-print materials also contribute to language arts instruction. Children usually will bring their own paper and pencils to school, but teachers or schools may have art materials, computers, and other items available for instructional support. By providing a range of texts and instructional materials in your classroom, you will ensure that students have access to appropriate, engaging, motivating materials that will support their learning (Moore, Moore, Cunningham, & Cunningham, 2003).

JEANNIE, VETERAN TEACHER ▶ I've found that one of the best ways to continue building a book collection is to participate in one of the book ordering companies, such as Scholastic or Troll. Each month, the company sends order sheets for the students to order books. The teacher gets points for each book ordered and can exchange those points for more books! I usually save up my points and order at the end of the year. But sometimes, I use my points to order books for my students as holiday presents.

Viewpoint

TEACHER

At the beginning of every year, I send out a letter asking for a parent volunteer to organize the book orders. The volunteer organizes the order forms, writes a letter telling when they are due, and then sends in the money. When the orders come in, she picks them up and organizes them by the individual child's order. It was really helpful to have a parent assist me with this. It was a good way for a parent to be involved who wasn't able to stay during the school day!

CHILDREN'S LITERATURE

Books are necessary resources for learning about print and serve as the basis for language arts activities. Language arts instruction is embedded in discussions of fiction and nonfiction text selections. Children write, speak, listen, and expand their reading based on children's literature. You simply cannot teach language arts without making books available to children. Most of the books that you will use in your classroom will be classified as picture books or chapter books, and they will represent many styles, media, genres, and creative presentations. Picture and chapter books cover almost any topic and represent many genres and types.

Picture Books

Picture books are illustrated stories, poems, and nonfiction texts that rely on a balance between words and pictures to convey the meaning. The pictures can't tell the story alone, nor would the text tell the story as completely without the pictures. But even the acknowledgment that words and pictures work together will fail to delineate picture books fully. One special case is wordless picture books, which tell their stories entirely with pictures. Picture books include a wide range of formats, content, and artwork that offer a great many options for language arts instruction. Making up stories to go with the pictures, using favorite repetitive stories as modes for their own writing, and developing explanations about what happened before or after the story narrative are just a few of the ways students can use picture books to motivate their own storytelling and writing.

Picture books are designed to encourage young children to read, and traditionally we think of Mother Goose, ABC books, counting books, and concept books as picture books. Books such as *Ducky* (Bunting, 1997) are definitely written for very young children. However, picture books may include complex themes and ideas that are appropriate for older children and even adult readers who are intrigued by the beautiful artwork and multiple levels of meaning and interest presented in picture-book format. Picture books, such as *The Mysteries of Harris Burdick* by Chris Van Allsburg (1984), are often used with students in middle school for creative writing inspiration. And many picture books, such as *Fly Away Home* (1993) by Eve Bunting, deal with serious issues such as homelessness and are appropriate and interesting for upper elementary and middle school students.

Certain picture books have been honored for their excellence. The Caldecott Award and several honor books are announced at the first of each year to recognize the outstanding picture book published in the previous year. A review of the Caldecott medal winners reveals a wide and diverse range of lovely picture books that may be used effectively at many grade levels. A comparison of two of the winners illustrated by David Wisniewski demonstrates the choices offered by the Caldecott winners list. His 1997 Caldecott winner, *Golem* (1996), presents a Jewish legend about a giant man of clay who was given life in order to vanquish those who persecuted Jews. The art is done entirely in cut paper illustrations and matches the darkness and seriousness of the topic. *Golem* is an example of a picture book that is appropriate for older students in upper elementary and middle school. In 1998, Wisniewski illustrated an award-winning book, *Ducky* (1997), written by Eve Bunting, that tells the story of a floating yellow plastic duck that is released in the ocean. The differences between the two picture books with pictures by the same illustrator could not be greater. Comparing *Golem* and *Ducky* reveals the range of possibilities in picture book topics, style, and mood.

Chapter Books

Books that do not have pictures to match each line of text and are longer than picture books are generally referred to as novels or chapter books. Usually we think of chapter books as appropriate for experienced, older readers, and many chapter books are written for upper grades and more experienced readers, but they represent many reading levels, and some novels are enjoyed by the youngest readers. When students do not have the reading ability to read chapter books independently, they may enjoy listening to the teacher read them aloud.

Some wonderful chapter books are recognized for their excellence. The Newbery Medal is presented each year to the author of a novel-length book that makes the most significant contribution to children's literature. The Newbery winners include such well-known books as *Bridge to Terabithia* (Paterson, 1987), with a strong theme of friendship and tragedy; *Bud, Not Buddy* (Curtis, 1999), a story of a homeless boy who searches for his family; and *Lincoln: A Photobiography* (Freedman, 1987), an in-depth study of the president. The annual list of Newbery honor books should not be overlooked as you pick books for your classroom.

Other significant awards are given to books written for children and adolescents. Each year the Coretta Scott King award honors an African American illustrator whose books published during the preceding year made outstanding contributions to literature for children and adolescents. Hoffman's *Amazing Grace* (1991) has won this award. This picture book tells the story of Grace, who wants to play Peter Pan in the school play and is discouraged by her classmates since she is not only Black, but also female.

The Caldecott and Newbery are awarded by a panel of librarians and are not always recognized as students' favorite books. The awards provide one source for identifying good books, but other sources for selection of children's books are book lists. IRA publishes an annual list of Teacher's Choice books and Children's Choice books, and each year NCTE publishes a list of 30 books that are specifically chosen for the contribution they make to language arts instruction and language learning (see the November issues of *Language Arts*). Several states allow children to vote for favorite books. Texas has the Bluebonnet Award, whose winner is selected by a statewide poll of fifth graders. Michigan's Young Reader's Award provides an opportunity for teachers and children to collaborate on selecting favorite books. Ask your methods instructors or mentor teacher if your state has a similar program for children to select their favorite books.

JALONDA, NEW TEACHER ▶ I love children's books, and I'm always looking for good books to share with my students. I talk to our school librarian often to find out if new books are being added to the library. I also talk with the children's librarians at my public library for their recommendations and ideas. I visit bookstores to see what the newest books are that might be good for my students. And I use Internet sites with book reviews like **www.amazon.com, www.bn.com,** and **www.carolhurst.com** to learn about books. It's a lot of work to stay current on books, but it's fun and helps me be a better teacher!

Selecting Children's Literature for Language Arts Instruction

Forty thousand children's books are in print, and 4,000 more are published each year. Keeping up requires a great deal of reading! Teachers discover favorite books to read and use during instruction in several ways. They read many books each month, making sure they are reading what their students are reading, or they identify and read the books of a favorite author. Although it is beyond the scope of this textbook to provide a complete children's literature background, a language arts teacher should be familiar with a wide range of literature for elementary and middle school students. The most important thing is to develop an interest and a willingness to stay aware of good children's literature. Once you make that commitment, the rest is easy. It is a very enjoyable process.

There are just too many books to know each one, but many resources, methods, and approaches to becoming knowledgeable in children's literature are available. Developing skill in selecting appropriate and interesting books for classroom use is important, and is something that teachers should have fun with. You will find, however, that certain considerations usually guide teachers' selection of classroom books. Book selections start with knowledge about students and their needs. Teachers also base selection on curricular requirements, multicultural representation, professional reference recommendations, book award status, and student preferences.

Student Knowledge

Students' developmental levels, interests, motivations, and abilities provide guidelines for determining what books and printed material should be selected for instruction. Observations, informal discussions, and interest inventories inform teachers about students' interests and suggest topics that may motivate young readers. The interest inventory in Exhibit 2.15 is one example of how a teacher can collect information that helps in book selection and in determining a student's level of interest in reading and other areas of literacy.

Students' responses to open-ended sentences can provide insights about their reading interests. exhibit 2.15

1. I am very good at _____

2. I would like to learn more about _____

3. The best book I ever read is _____

4. My favorite author is _____

5. My favorite CD or song is _____

6. In my spare time I like to _____

7. Reading is _____

8. My favorite television show is _____

9. My favorite movie is _____

10. If I spend time on the Internet I search for _____

11. If I could meet anyone in the world, it would be _____

12. I usually read _____

13. Good stories are about _____

14. I like it when people read aloud stories about _____

Scoring

"Scoring" is subjective. Award one point for responses that indicate the reader enjoys reading and has identifiable reading, listening, and viewing interests. Responses left blank or those that seem vague or insincere are not counted as positive.

11 – 14 Student has a positive attitude toward reading, writing, listening, and other literacy activities.

7 – 10 Student has an average interest in these activities.

1 – 6 Student needs guidance and support to develop an interest in literacy activities.

Classroom libraries will need to accommodate a wide range of reading abilities. A collection for early elementary students ranges from picture books such as the classic *Frog and Toad Are Friends* (Lobel, 1987) to novels such as *Charlotte's Web* (White, 1974) or *Shiloh* (Naylor, 1991) that are appropriate for younger readers. Collections for older readers may include picture books by author/illustrators such as Van Allsburg, who illustrates rather sophisticated wordless picture books such as *Ben's Dream* (1997), and David Wiesner, whose wordless picture book *Free Fall* (1991) is a Caldecott Honor Book. Upper-grade collections should also include classics like *Bridge to Terabithia* (Paterson, 1987) and the enormously popular Harry Potter series (Rowling, 1998, 1999a, 1999b, 2000, 2003).

Curricular Requirements

Teachers must also consider state and local curriculum requirements and their own instructional goals when selecting classroom texts. As you gain more experience in teaching you will know which books support your lessons and units and meet the instructional goals of the curriculum. Use your curriculum topics to drive your selection of classroom books. For example, if students are studying the weather, they may enjoy reading *Cloudy with a Chance of Meatballs* by Judi and Ron Barrett (1982) or *The Cloud Book* by Tomie dePaola (1985). Many books are related to history and are easily integrated with social studies instruction. If students are studying colonial times, interesting choices abound, such as *Eating the Plates: A Pilgrim's Book of Food and Manners* (Penner, 1997) and *Sarah Morton's Day* (Waters, 1993). Some school districts provide extensive lists of book suggestions for use at different grade levels or for teaching certain topics, often correlating the lists with lessons, strategies, or standards. The district lists should not be your only consideration, but simply another source to guide your book selections.

Multicultural Representation

Traditionally, minorities have been inadequately represented in books for children (Tomlinson & Lynch-Brown, 2002). In the last decade, however, the quality and selection of African American children's literature have improved. It is becoming easier to find high-quality literature that depicts the Hispanic culture, although available books do not fully represent the wide range of diversity and experiences within cultural groups from Spanish-speaking countries. Literature reflecting cultures such as Arabic, South Pacific Islander, and Vietnamese people are also limited. As classrooms continue to increase in diversity, it may be necessary to seek out publishing companies that focus on increasing the proportion of multicultural and international books among their lists. As librarians, teachers, and parents work together, they will be able to meet some of the classroom needs of multicultural literature by being aware of the issues and considering the backgrounds of children in their classes. For all classrooms, it is important to select books that treat cultural differences fairly and realistically. Exhibit 2.16 provides guidance for selecting books that represent cultural and language differences.

References for Book Selection

Several professional references are available to help teachers keep up to date with children's literature. One of the best magazines for this purpose is *Booklinks,* found in your local library and possibly in your school library. This magazine features articles that group children's books by theme, which is very helpful if you are searching for sources to complement curriculum. *The Horn Book* provides current information about recently published children's picture books. Information about current children's books can also be found in professional journals such as *Language Arts* and *The Reading Teacher.*

Many textbooks and popular texts contain extensive lists of books appropriate to read to children and use in classroom instruction. Nancie Atwell has written several books that discuss language arts instruction and list books to go with specific strategies or lessons. *In the Middle* (Atwell, 1998) and *Coming to Know* (Atwell, 1990) include excellent literature selections for middle school and upper elementary grade levels. In *The Potential of Picture Books,* Barbara Kiefer (1994) not only lists children's books, but also describes the artwork and suggests instructional strategies. Of course, the Internet offers a great deal of support to teachers who are selecting books. The Children's Literature Web Guide, at **www.ucalgary.ca/~dkbrown/index.html,** is an extensive resource for parents, teachers, and discussion groups about children's literature.

Selecting culturally diverse material.   **exhibit 2.16**

Range	Include books that convey the diversity and range of cultural and language groups in the United States.
	Focus on materials that illustrate the cultures in the classroom.
Avoidance of Stereotyping	Depictions of characters recognize differences among groups of people.
	Characters are well rounded.
	Characters and their actions are not generalized.
	Differentiation is made among groups (e.g., Asian Americans come from Japan, China, Korea, and other cultures that are very different).
	Cultural details are accurate.
Perspective	Depiction of social and cultural traditions is realistic.
	Positive images of characters are evident.
Writing	The development of theme, plots, and characters is of high quality.

Learning About Children's Literature

Complete one of the following activities and share with a group of students or your classmates:

- Visit a bookstore and talk with a clerk in the children's area. Come back with a list and brief descriptions of five recent, highly recommended books. Share at least one of the books.

- Visit a public library and talk with the children's librarian. Come back with a list and brief descriptions of five recent, highly recommended books. Share at least one of the books.

KAITLYN, BEGINNING TEACHER ▶ I like to use my students as resources for learning about picture books. Whenever we have a few spare moments, I have students share with the class a book they have read. It can be a library book, a book from the class collection, or a book from their home. They have a structured format for sharing. They begin by reading the title and author and then give a summary about the book. Then they tell their favorite part and show one or two of the pictures. Finally, they recommend the book to specific students or people with a certain interest. This seems to work well to get other students interested in a book!

BASAL READERS

Basal readers—collections of graded texts appropriate for readers in kindergarten to grade eight—are one of the most frequently used instructional materials in the elementary classroom. They are a major source for reading instruction; however, they offer a number of instructional options for the entire language arts program. Selections are usually organized by themes and include portions of popular and classic children's literature. In addition to the graded texts, basals include resources that assist in planning, instructing, and evaluating language arts instruction. Basal series' supplements include teacher's manuals, workbooks and worksheets, texts, and other aids.

The basal reader's teacher's manual includes developmentally appropriate suggestions and activities, such as ways to facilitate class and small group experiences with a particular genre and practice using a reading or writing skill. Basal reader selections represent a wide variety of genres (e.g., science fiction, historical fiction, contemporary realism, biography, and fantasy). Activities include writing, drama, puppetry, choral reading, and multimedia responses.

Basal readers have endured a great deal of criticism. Often basal approaches are associated with homogeneous grouping practices, which resulted in decades of instruction in which children were organized for reading instruction into three groups based on their reading ability. Other criticisms are directed at the amount of time spent on skills development at the exclusion of supporting the comprehension and enjoyment of reading. Basals are also criticized for using very controlled vocabulary and sentence structure so that young readers focus on specific reading skills as they read the stories. Basals are taken to task for including only portions of stories, preventing the reader from experiencing the complete story as intended by the author.

In recent years basal readers have changed for the better. They now include selections of children's literature and informational articles, and they are written with natural vocabulary. Even so, many still believe that the basals offer too little guidance in comprehension development (Ryder & Graves, 1994) and fail to acknowledge close connections among all language arts. Those who support the use of basals suggest that the techniques and instructional procedures promote an organized approach, particularly to reading instruction. Basal readers provide a framework for reading instruction and suggestions for language arts instruction, but as with all the resources and materials available to support language arts instruction, it would be a mistake to rely exclusively on basal readers in instructional situations. Still, they are one resource that is useful during language arts instruction.

Basal readers support language arts instruction in several ways. They provide multiple copies of one story and allow students and teachers to read and share common material. Teachers select well-written basal stories that are interesting to children and meet the criteria for acceptable reading material. When basal readers present only a part of the story, students can be encouraged or directed to read the entire selection. In addition, basals provide a good source of instructional suggestions and strategies. The criticisms of using basal readers are often a result of teachers relying too heavily on the basal reader's prescriptive skill pages and limited literature selections. A more complete description of instructional strategies related to basal readers will be included in your reading methods text.

Social studies, science, and mathematics textbooks are similar to basal readers. They offer non-fictional reading material and suggestions for instructional activities in their content areas. They are an important tool for teachers who are developing a cohesive curriculum in various subject areas and an additional resource for planning and implementing integrated instruction. Like basal readers, textbooks allow students to learn the language arts while they are also engaged in content area learning.

JOO-HEE, BEGINNING TEACHER ▶ I was so excited about implementing a literature-based reading program when I graduated from school and had my first classroom. At first, however, I was frustrated with how to implement all the new ideas I had learned about. Plus, my school didn't have a lot of resources. It took some time to find the books I wanted to use.

I never thought I would use basal readers. But, out of desperation, one day I followed a lesson from the textbook. I was really glad to have that structure. It gave me the opportunity to gradually introduce my own literature-based program, such as book clubs and readers' workshop. I had the chance to learn how to integrate books and strategies into my curriculum slowly, and I think it was more effective this way.

Several years later, the school district initiated a requirement that we use basal readers. I was able to integrate basal reader activities and still maintain my literature-based reading program.

ADDITIONAL TEXTS AND RESOURCES

Books form the foundation for language arts instruction, but other print and non-print materials are necessary for language arts instruction, too. Student-authored texts, magazines, newspapers, technology tools, and various non-print resources enrich the reading, writing, speaking, and listening activities in the classroom.

Student-Authored Texts

Children's original stories are a valuable source of classroom reading material. In a literate classroom, students produce a great many manuscripts that become classroom resources. The student-authored stories are collected, bound, and displayed as regular reading material with a respected position in the classroom library. Students use bound versions of their classmates' stories just as they do children's literature by adult authors. The entire class may contribute to a collection of student-authored anthologies. Student-authored texts are one obvious representative of the link between reading and writing, and their presence in the room is a source of pride for young readers and writers. Chapter 4, Article II presents a more thorough discussion of student-authored texts.

Magazines and Newspapers

Materials for language arts instruction include printed materials regularly read in the home and workplace, such as newspapers, magazines, and other periodicals. Certain magazines and newspapers are designed for classroom use and are appropriate for different grade levels. Two examples of such newspapers are *Time for Kids* (available at **www.timeforkids.com**) and *Scholastic News* (available at **http://teacher.scholastic.com/scholasticnews**). These two publications feature current events and classroom activities related to foreign and domestic news, as well as science and historical topics. Both of these periodicals offer different versions of their magazines geared for upper or lower elementary grade levels. Teachers may subscribe to newspapers for their classes for a few dollars per student per year, and the newspapers are delivered to the classroom. Many teachers put the cost of these periodicals on the supply list for students and have the students bring in money at the beginning of the year to cover their subscription. Often, these periodicals must be ordered prior to the beginning of the school year. Several magazines popular with children, including *Ladybug* and *Cricket* (nature; available at **www.cricketmag.com**), *Sports Illustrated for Kids* (sports; available at **www.sikids.com**), and *Cobblestones* (history; available at **www.cobble-stonepub.com**), provide additional reading material for classroom collections.

Selected newspapers have daily sections written for young readers. They focus on presenting current events in language that elementary-age students can read. One example is the section called "Kids Post" published in the *Washington Post*. It is available at **www.washingtonpost.com/kidspost**. Some local papers publish curriculum guides for using the newspapers. As with the news periodicals described above, students subscribe to these papers, which are delivered once a week with suggestions for activities. Some newspapers have a staff member who will model how to use the newspaper in instructional settings. Instruction using newspapers is usually most appropriate for upper elementary and middle school students, since newspapers require a higher reading level. Local newspapers often provide materials for teachers and students known as Newspapers in Education (NiE) (**www.nieonline.com**). Lists of local papers that have NiE programs are available at **www.pilotonline.com/nie/index2.html** and **www.appeal-democrat.com/features/nie/index.shtml**.

Technology Tools

Language arts classes of the 21st century must include experiences with technology. Integration of technology and language arts instruction will provide students with relevant learning opportunities and a chance to devel-op skills and abilities they will need in the workplace of the future. Technological resources such as computer equipment, software, and the Internet are among many tools that contribute to language arts instruction (Bruce, 2003). However, computers are not the only technology tools—the radio, VCRs or DVDs, handheld PDAs, smart boards, television, and electronic games all play important roles in language arts instruction. Technology and the media are major out-of-school influences on children (Valmont & Wepner, 2000) and should be part of formal language arts instruction. By sharing a popular song to learn rhyming patterns or get in the mood for a new unit of study, rewriting a familiar song with new lyrics to review a concept, or watching a video and comparing it to the book version, children interact with familiar media while enhancing their language arts skills.

Integration of technology and language arts instruction motivates students and expands their communication opportunities.

Computer technology has made its way into the schools slowly and steadily (Wepner, Valmont, & Thurlow, 2000), and many children accept computers as a way of life. Computer equipment is expensive and has a short lifespan, and most schools provide classrooms with the most up-to-date technology that the district can afford. Language arts teachers may have opportunities to request equipment, software, and Internet access or contribute to schoolwide planning for future technology purchases.

Equipment

The basic and most common technological tool placed in classrooms is, of course, the computer. Some teachers have only one computer for all their students; others have an entire computer lab at their disposal. When only a few computers are available for many students, teachers must plan creatively to involve students in high-tech collaborative communication processes. Strategies that encourage children to work together increase their opportunities for language usage. Some teachers find that using a single classroom computer as a learning center also provides a manageable way of integrating the computer into the classroom. Appropriate connections are needed to access learning resources on the Internet (discussed further below). Many exciting strategies and possibilities in language arts instruction are possible only with computers and the Internet.

If your school has limited resources, then encourage your administrators to take advantage of a governmental program that underwrites the costs of Internet connections and hardware. The Telecommunications Act of 1996 established the Universal Service Fund Education Rate (E-Rate) to support educational use of the Internet (Kamp, 1999). This large fund is expanding student access to the Internet in many schools across the nation.

Software

Technology is more than computers and related technology tools. A wide range of software tools is available to enhance language arts instruction. Many programs help students read stories, write stories, add artwork to their own writing, and produce presentations to share what they are learning. Students may also experience good stories on CD-ROM. Professional publications such as the International Reading Association's *Linking Literacy and Technology* (Wepner, Valmont, & Thurlow, 2000) suggest and review software resources for language arts instruction. The Internet can also provide information about software. Chapter 5, Article V, gives additional suggestions.

Word processing and graphics programs are becoming important tools in language arts instruction. Language arts classrooms should include basic applications such as the latest versions of Microsoft Word, a word processing program; Excel, a spreadsheet program, or Access, a database program; and PowerPoint, a presentation program. Some students may use Adobe PageMaker or KidPix to develop illustrations for stories and presentations.

Some software products are designed to enhance multicultural education (Balajthy, 1999). These programs, representing many multicultural texts and supporting students who speak a language other than English, may be valuable additions to language arts classroom. Some software publishers are also attempting to develop software of special interest to girls (Balajthy, 2000). Teachers should watch for innovations that will help them respond to classroom diversity.

The Internet

The Internet is a great resource for language arts instruction. Most obviously, e-mail has become an accepted way to communicate, playing an increasingly important role in communication and literacy. But the Internet also opens new doors to language arts curriculum (Leu & Leu, 2000). Students may participate in an electronic discussion about Harry Potter or view a video of a favorite author explaining the writing process. They can read reviews of books and movies, use an online thesaurus, complete research, or interact with other children in different parts of the world.

Technology Observations

Ask the librarian or principal to tell you which teachers integrate technology into the language arts classroom. Arrange to visit these classrooms. List the hardware and software that are available for language arts instruction. Note how the teacher and students use technology in their daily routines. How are these uses similar to or different from your own access to technology when you were in elementary school, and how do your present technology skills compare to what children know?

field note
2.8

NON-PRINT MATERIALS USED IN LANGUAGE ARTS INSTRUCTION

Non-print materials make valuable contributions to children's engagement in literacy activities. These materials are definitely not high tech, but they are important to encouraging children to take part in activities that help them talk, read, listen, and write about their ideas, experiences, and dreams. Many traditional non-print materials are considered necessary back-to-school materials. Basics include:

- Paper of all kinds: lined, unlined, and specialty papers for making booklets
- Writing implements: pencils, pens, gel pens, crayons, markers, paint, colored chalk, and letter stamps or stickers
- Cutting and pasting tools: scissors, erasers, correction tape, tape, glue, glue sticks, and staples

- Recordkeeping and portfolio tools, such as folders and storage boxes
- Toys and games, including puppetry and role-playing props
- Bookbinding machines and supplies
- Art supplies: construction paper, needles and thread, yarn, string, paint, smocks, butcher paper, and so forth

A new teacher's classroom is rarely fully equipped when the first year begins. It will take some time for you to learn what materials and resources are provided and what you must do to acquire the materials for your classroom. Some materials and resources will be necessary for teaching right away; you can add others to the classroom later—sometimes as a result of long-term efforts.

FINAL REFLECTIONS

When Debra entered her new classroom, she realized she had a great deal of work to do to get ready for language arts instruction. Important tasks include selecting an instructional approach, determining flexible grouping patterns, building a classroom community, and selecting classroom materials and resources to support instruction. While the list of choices may seem overwhelming, it can also be exciting—an opportunity for you and your students to create a classroom environment that works for you. And, you'll likely feel the way Debra did at the end of her first year of teaching, when she exclaimed, "It was so much work, but it's amazing how much our classroom library and sharing times helped us become a community of learners. I can't wait to get started on planning for next year!"

PROFESSIONAL REFLECTIONS

Review the Field Notes from this chapter and develop one or more into a component of your portfolio. To continue to reflect on your Field Note responses, consider these suggestions:

- Create a record of children's literature that you have read. Include the title, author, awards received, and your general reaction to the book. You may want to think of ways to incorporate the book into classroom instruction. Consider maintaining your reading records in a journal, on index cards, or with computer technology.
- Create a map of your future classroom. Include seating arrangements, placements of materials and learning centers, classroom library, and technology resources. What does this arrangement say about you as a language arts teacher?
- Observe an experienced teacher presenting a language arts lesson. Use the lesson plan format in Exhibit 2.10 to record the components of the lesson.

Professional Readings

Textbooks used in children's literature courses are excellent resources for helping you design language arts instruction. They provide descriptions of various genres, ways to analyze the quality of books, and methods for integrating them into instruction.

The following are good examples of concise texts about children's literature:

Jacobs, J. S., & Tunnell, M. O. (2003). *Children's literature, briefly* (3rd ed.). Englewood Cliffs, NJ: Merrill.

Tomlinson, C. M., & Lynch-Brown, C. (2002). *Essentials of children's literature* (4th ed.). Boston: Allyn & Bacon.

The next example is a textbook with elaborate descriptions and extensive explanations of all aspects of children's literature:

Huck, C. S., Kiefer, B., Hepler, S., & Hickman, J. (2003). *Children's literature in the elementary school*. New York: McGraw-Hill.

The following book is an excellent reference for language arts teachers. Among other things, it includes lists of books, descriptions of ways to organize the classroom, and sample lesson plans.

Routman, R. (1988). *Transitions from literature to literacy*. Portsmouth, NH: Heinemann.

Select one of the following children's literature books, read it, and reflect on the lessons it offers about creating a classroom environment and learning community. Share your book and insights with a small group of your peers.

Children's Books

The following examples of children's literature provide insights into the content of this chapter:

Danneberg, J., & Love, J. D. (2000). *First day jitters*. Watertown, MA: Charlesbridge Publishing.

This is a humorous tale of Sarah Jane's worries about going to a new school. The twist is that Sarah Jane is the teacher!

Henkes, K. (1996). *Chrysanthemum*. New York: Greenwillow.

When Chrysanthemum starts school and is teased about her unusual name, a teacher helps her and her classmates realize just how special a name is.

Henkes, K. (1996). *Lilly's purple plastic purse*. New York: Greenwillow.

Lilly and her teacher learn the importance of the teacher–student relationship and a caring classroom environment through a humorous series of events.

Marshall, J. (1985). *Miss Nelson is missing*. Boston: Houghton Mifflin.

Students cause havoc and disobey the rules, then find they must suffer the consequences of losing their supportive teacher. It is a humorous look at the importance of classroom management.

Medina, J., & Vanden Broeck, F. (1999). *My name is Jorge: On both sides of the river*. Honesdale, PA: Boyds Mills Press.

This collection of poems reflects on a Mexican American boy's school experiences in the United States.

Numeroff, L. (2002). *If you take a mouse to school*. New York: Laura Geringer.

The rambunctious little mouse ends up at school in his human friend's lunchbox. Mouse enjoys the school day by spelling, doing a science experiment, and writing his own book.

Rathman, P. (1995). *Officer Buckle and Gloria*. New York: G. P. Putnam.

This favorite book deals with the importance of establishing routines and rules in school settings. It also deals with important friendships and acceptance.

Robinson, B. (1997). *The best school year ever*. New York: Harper Trophy.

In this chapter book, the six Herdman kids are back and causing trouble at school and in their town.

Wells, R. (2000). *Emily's first 100 days of school*. New York: Hyperion Books for Children.

Wells writes about the first 100 days of school and counting activities related to each day. Not only is this an effective beginning of the year book, it is a nice integration of math and language arts. For younger readers.

Other children's books mentioned in this chapter are:

Barrett, J. (1982). *Cloudy with a chance of meatballs.* Illustrated by R. Barrett. Aladdin Library.

Bunting, E. (1997). *Ducky.* Illustrated by D. Wisniewski. New York: Clarion.

Bunting, E. (1993). *Fly away home.* Illustrated by R. Himler. New York: Clarion.

Curtis, C. P. (1999). *Bud, Not Buddy.* New York: Delacorte.

DePaola, T. (1985). *The cloud book.* New York: Holiday House.

DePaola, T. (1975, 1999). *Strega Nona.* New York: Little Simon.

Freedman, R. (1987). *Lincoln: A photobiography.* Boston: Houghton Mifflin.

Galdone, P. (1986). *The magic porridge pot.* London: Egmont Children's Books.

Hoffman, M. (1991). *Amazing Grace.* Illustrated by C. Binch. New York: Dial.

Lobel, A. (1987). *Frog and toad are friends.* New York: HarperCollins Children's Books.

Naylor, P. R. (1991). *Shiloh.* New York: Macmillan.

Paterson, K. (1987). *Bridge to Terabithia.* Illustrated by D. Diamond. New York: HarperTrophy.

Penner, L. R. (1997). *Eating the plates: A pilgrim's book of food and manners.* New York: Aladdin Library.

Rowling, J. K. (1998). *Harry Potter and the Sorcerer's Stone* (Book 1). Illustrated by M. Grandpre. New York: Scholastic.

Rowling, J. K. (1999). *Harry Potter and the Chamber of Secrets* (Book 2). Illustrated by M. Grandpre. New York: Scholastic.

Rowling, J. K. (1999). *Harry Potter and the Prisoner of Azkaban* (Book 3). Illustrated by M. Grandpre. New York: Scholastic.

Rowling, J. K. (2000). *Harry Potter and the Goblet of Fire* (Book 4). Illustrated by M. Grandpre. New York: Scholastic.

Rowling, J. K. (2003). *Harry Potter and the Order of the Phoenix* (Book 5). Illustrated by M. Grandpre. New York: Scholastic.

Van Allsburg, C. (1997). *Ben's dream.* Boston: Houghton Mifflin.

Van Allsburg, C. (1984). *The mysteries of Harris Burdick.* Boston: Houghton Mifflin.

Waters, K. (1993). *Sarah Morton's day: A day in the life of a Pilgrim girl.* Photography by R. Kendall. New York: Scholastic.

White, E. B. (1974). *Charlotte's web.* Illustrated by R. Wells and G. Williams. New York: HarperCollins Juvenile Books.

Wiesner, D. (1991). *Free fall.* New York: HarperCollins Children's Books.

Wisniewski, D. (1996). *Golem.* Illustrated by D. Wisniewski. New York: Clarion.

REFERENCES

Allington, R. L. (1995). Literacy lessons in the elementary schools: Yesterday, today, and tomorrow. In R. L. Allington & S. A. Walmsley (Eds.), *No quick fix: Rethinking literacy programs in America's elementary schools.* New York: Teachers College Press.

Atwell, N. (1990). *Coming to know: Writing to learn in the intermediate grades.* Portsmouth, NH: Heinemann.

Atwell, N. (1998). *In the middle: New understandings about writing, reading, and learning.* Portsmouth, NH: Boyton/Cook.

Au, K. H., Carroll, J. H., & Scheu, J. A. (2001). *Balanced literacy instruction: A teacher's resource book* (2nd ed.). Norwood, MA: Christopher-Gordon.

Balajthy, E. (1999). *Trends in literacy software publication and marketing: Multicultural themes.* Paper presented at the National Reading Research Center Conference on Literacy and Technology for the 21st Century, Atlanta, GA.

Balajthy, E. (2000). Is technology worth my professional time, resources, and efforts? In S. B. Wepner, W. J. Valmont, & R. Thurlow (Eds.). *Linking literacy and technology: A guide for K–8 classrooms* (pp. 203–219). Newark, DE: International Reading Association.

Barth, R. (1997). Building a community of learners. *Theories and Practices in Curriculum and Learning, 8,* 100–118.

Bruce, B. C. (Ed.). (2003). *Literacy in the information age: Inquiries into making meaning with new technologies.* Newark, DE: International Reading Association.

Calkins, L. M. (1994). *The art of teaching writing.* Portsmouth, NH: Heinemann.

Cunningham, P. M., & Allington, R. (1999). *Classrooms that work: They can all read and write* (2nd ed.). New York: Longman.

Cunningham, P. M., Hall, D. P., & Sigmon, C. (1999). *The teacher's guide to the four blocks.* Greensboro, NC: Carson-Dellosa.

Elmore, R. F., & Fuhrman, S. H. (1995, Spring). Opportunity-to-learn standards and the state role in education. *Teachers College Record, 96*(3), 433–458.

Flood, J., Lapp, D., & Nagel, G. (1992). Am I allowed to group? Using flexible patterns for effective instruction. *The Reading Teacher, 45,* 608–616.

Fountas, I. C., & Pinnell, G. S. (1996). *Guided reading: Good first teaching for all children.* Portsmouth, NH: Heinemann.

Fountas, I. C., & Pinnell, G. S. (1999). *Matching books to readers: A book list for guided reading K–3.* Portsmouth, NH: Heinemann Educational.

Fuligni, A. J., Eccles, J. S., & Barber, B. L. (1995). The long-term effects of seventh-grade ability grouping in mathematics. *The Journal of Early Adolescence, 15*(1), 58–89.

Graves, M. F., Watts-Taffe, S. M., & Graves, B. B. (1999). *Essentials of elementary reading.* Boston: Allyn & Bacon.

Hammer, D. (1998). *The standards teacher.* Washington: Council for Basic Education.

Illinois State Board of Education. (1997). *Illinois learning standards.* Springfield: Illinois State Board of Education.

Johnson, D. W., & Johnson, R. T. (1999). *Learning together and alone: Cooperative, competitive and individualistic learning.* Boston: Allyn & Bacon.

Kamp, S. (1999). *1999 education market report, K–12.* Washington, DC: Software and Information Industry Association.

Kiefer, B. Z. (1994). *The potential of picture books: From visual literacy to aesthetic understanding.* Upper Saddle River, NJ: Prentice Hall.

Klein, D. (1999). Big business, race, and gender in mathematics reform. In S. Kravitz (Ed.), *How to Teach Mathematics* (2nd ed.). Reston, VA: American Mathematics Society.

Leu, D. J., & Leu, D. D. (2000). *Teaching with the Internet: Lessons from the classroom* (3rd ed.). Norwood, MA: Christopher-Gordon.

Lipson, M. Y., Valencia, S., Wixson, K. K., & Peters, C. W. (1993). Integration and thematic teaching: Integration to improve teaching and learning. *Language Arts, 70,* 252–255.

Mills, R. (1997). Grouping students for instruction: Issues of equity and effectiveness. In J. I. Irvin (Ed.), *What current research says to the middle level practitioner* (pp. 87–94). Columbus, OH: National Middle School Association.

Ministry of Education. (1996). *Dancing with the pen: The learners as a writer.* Wellington, New Zealand: Learning Media.

Moll, L. (1992). Funds of knowledge for teaching: Using a qualitative approach to connect homes and classrooms. *Theory into Practice, 31*(2), 132–141.

Moore, D. W., Moore, S. A., Cunningham, P. A., & Cunningham, J. W. (2003). *Developing readers and writers in the content areas* (4th ed.). Boston: Allyn & Bacon.

Nathan, R. (1995). Parents, projects, and portfolios: Round and about community building in room 14. *Language Arts, 72,* 82–87.

Opitz, M. F. (1999). *Flexible grouping in reading.* New York: Scholastic.

Opitz, M. F., & Ford, M P. (2001). *Reaching readers: Flexible and innovative strategies for guided reading.* Portsmouth, NH: Heinemann.

Rogers, R. L. (2000). It's not really writing, it's just answering the questions. *Language Arts, 77,* 398–405.

Ryder, R. J., & Graves, M. F. (1994). Vocabulary instruction presented prior to reading in two basal readers. *Elementary School Journal, 95,* 139–153.

Seely, A. E. (1996). *Integrated thematic units.* Westminister, CA: Teacher Created Materials.

Smith, J., & Johnson, H. (1994). Models for implementing literature in content studies. *The Reading Teacher, 48,* 198–209.

Teale, W. (1993). Dear readers. *Language Arts, 70,* 628–629.

Tomlinson, C. M., & Lynch-Brown, C. (2002). *Essentials of children's literature* (4th ed.). Boston: Allyn & Bacon.

Valmont, W., & Wepner, S. (2000). Using technology to support literacy learning. In S. B. Wepner, W. J. Valmont, & R. Thurlow (Eds.), *Linking literacy and technology: A guide for K–8 classrooms* (pp. 2–18). Newark, DE: International Reading Association.

Wan, G. (2000). A Chinese girl's storybook experience at home. *Language Arts, 77,* 398–405.

Wepner, S. B., Valmont, W. J., & Thurlow, R. (Eds.). (2000). *Linking literacy and technology: A guide for K–8 classrooms.* Newark, DE: International Reading Association.

Wood, M. (1999). *Essentials of elementary language arts* (2nd ed.). Boston: Allyn & Bacon.

For some time, Mrs. Gonzales has noticed some of her fifth-grade students are not participating in her lively classroom discussions. She isn't surprised, since five of her students are English language learners—although she observes them interacting with others in a small group or speaking one on one, she knows they are still hesitant to speak in front of the entire class. Others in the classroom who speak English as their first language don't always speak in groups either. They respond when she asks questions, but she wants all students in her class to be more comfortable in a variety of speaking and listening situations. She decides to work on increasing participation in classroom discussions as well as increasing the quality of the discussions. Her class has been reading the

Chapter 3
SPEAKING AND LISTENING

Newbery Award winner *A Single Shard* (Park, 2001) and is intrigued by the story of the 12th-century Korean orphan boy who loves pottery. The story is the perfect vehicle to increase her students' involvement and encourage everyone to express their opinions and ideas about the story.

Mrs. Gonzales starts the discussion process by dividing her class into groups of four. She asks the small groups to give each group member time to share favorite parts of the story and explain why they selected sections as their favorites. This provides everyone time to talk and listen to others. Then, she brings the class together and asks the entire class the same question. As individuals volunteer to share their favorite parts, she asks others who have selected similar sections to share and explain why it is their favorite part too. This process encourages students who normally don't speak in class to share sections of the story.

At one point, one of the students mentions how bad he felt for the main character of the story, Tree-ear, when he breaks a piece of pottery and is required to work and pay for the damage. "It seems as if he is a slave," Kim says.

Before Mrs. Gonzales can respond, Libby says, "Oh, no, he wasn't a slave, he wanted to learn more about pottery."

"But he was so disappointed again, when the Master Potter didn't recognize him or his work," says Ian. "I think the Master Potter was mean to Tree-ear."

"He had his reasons for being mean to others—he was disappointed," said Juan.

"But that still didn't give him a good reason for being mean to Tree-ear, and I don't think he was nice to his wife either," said Nikki.

Mrs. Gonzales let the conversation continue on its own momentum until everyone had their say about the Master Potter. Then she asked, "How did the author develop Tree-ear's and the Master Potter's personalities? What happened in the book that made you feel like the Master Potter was unfair to Tree-ear?" Descriptions of what happened, the way the Master Potter talked, and how Tree-ear felt helped the class know about the Master Potter character. "Can someone read some of the sections that make us not like the Master Potter?" It didn't take much to get her students to talk about their feelings related to the main characters of the story.

The conversation did not end when language arts instruction was over. As Mrs. Gonzales lined up her students after recess, she overheard two of her students talking about the book. They were still talking about how the Master Potter treated Tree-ear. The conversation was continuing in less formal settings and without her assistance. Mrs. Gonzales realized that she was able to incorporate good children's literature, encourage discussion, and rely on her students' interest to encourage speaking and listening opportunities for everyone in her classroom.

INTRODUCTION

Children come to school using language they have developed through interactions in their homes and communities. A major goal of language arts instruction is to provide speaking and listening opportunities that allow children to use language for different purposes and in ways that will expand their ability to communicate. Teachers help their students develop listening and speaking skills by planning for informal and formal classroom oral language activities. Mrs. Gonzales set up a formal setting that provided her students opportunities to talk and be listened to with interest. Not only did they talk about the book, but they also talked about their reading process. Her students were learning good listening and speaking skills throughout their exchanges about *A Single Shard* (Park, 2001). The discussion in her classroom was so relevant and interesting to her students that it continued in an informal setting, too. This chapter will consider how teachers capitalize and build on language skills and how instruction plays an important role in students' continuing oral language development.

GUIDING QUESTIONS

Consider these questions as you read this chapter. Jot down your initial responses to each question. After reading the articles, revisit your responses. Would you make any changes to them? If so, what would those changes be? Discuss your responses with one or more of your classmates, your professor, or your mentor teacher.

1. What impact do the home and community have on oral language development?
2. What speaking and listening behaviors are expected of children?
3. What is the teacher's role during oral language activities?
4. What role does dramatic oral language expression play in developing communicative competence?
5. Can listening be taught?

Speaking and Listening Outside the Classroom

Students arrive at school with a wide range of oral language experiences and capabilities. Their ways of talking reflect what has served them well when interacting in their environments and helped them communicate with their families and in their communities. Most speakers, including children who do not speak English, have developed complex oral language communication patterns (Gallas et al., 1996) during their preschool years.

Children develop various speech patterns depending on how adults interact, ask questions, and talk to them during daily activities (Heath, 1983). Some children regularly listen to books being read, ask questions and provide answers, and interact with a variety of adults and young people. Their oral language development parallels what is expected in most early elementary classrooms. However, many children grow up in environments and cultures where language is used in various ways. Children who live in homes where family members share by telling stories with great flourish and elaboration may bring well-developed storytelling capabilities. Still others will come to school speaking several languages very well or with a primary language other than English. Children's development of oral language, whatever forms it takes, is a natural and impressive accomplishment.

EARLY ORAL LANGUAGE DEVELOPMENT

One amazing aspect of human development is that most children without special language needs (such as hearing loss) learn to speak and listen at an early age without formal instruction. Although humans have some innate abilities that help them learn to speak, children are not born with the ability to use oral language. The abilities involved in speaking develop naturally as children interact with the environment, long before they come to school. In fact, as soon as children are born they begin interacting with their surroundings, learning about communication, and building a foundation to communicate. Just as when they learn to walk, learning to talk requires time and progresses through developmental phases.

The developmental stages are rather predictable, but they may vary from child to child. Newborn babies are startled by noise and cry to convey their discomfort. By the time babies are one to two months old, they are communicating with smiles and crying noises, and, by the time they are three months old, they respond differently to different sounds. Eight- to twelve-month-old children respond to some words, such as "no," and they recognize words from games and routines such as "peek-a-boo" and "bye-bye."

In general children say their first words between 12 and 18 months of age. They soon begin to combine words and use words to communicate their needs. At two years, they display an emerging use of grammar and begin to generate sentences. The length of the sentences increases. When children are almost ready for kindergarten, they have mastered most grammatical conventions, have begun to use complex sentences and polite terms, and are learning to interact in social settings. By the time most children start kindergarten, they know most of the fundamentals of speech and are able to talk to someone who speaks as they do. As with all types of development, language acquisition is different for different children. One child may say a first word at 13 months while another doesn't say a first word until 20 months. One child may use complex sentences at five years of age, while another may have command over the complexities of language when she is three. Language learning is somewhat dependent on developmental maturity of the child; however, a great deal of language development depends on children's involvement with language.

Oral language evolves as children try to understand what others are communicating and to construct language while interacting with other language users (Morrow, 2001). When children actively construct ways to make meaning, the processes they use take on many of the characteristics they observe. They imitate and use words they hear, mimic some behaviors and personal traits that others in their environments exhibit, and in general are greatly influenced by adults who talk with them. But language learning is much more than imitation.

Children learn language when they interact socially and when their environment requires them to communicate in order to meet their needs (Bruner, 1977; Halliday, 1975). Children immersed in rich language environments will develop more complex oral language skills than those who do not have the same opportunities (Halliday, 1975; Morrow, 2001). Children's ability to communicate continues to grow as they encounter the need to use language for different reasons or functions. Exhibit 3.1 lists specific functions

Halliday's functions of language.   *exhibit* **3.1**

FUNCTION OF LANGUAGE	DESCRIPTION	EXAMPLE
Instrumental	Using language to get things done	"I want"
Regulatory	Using language to regulate others	"Do as I tell you."
Interactional	Using language to talk about you and me	"You and me"
Personal	Using language to talk about myself	"Here I come."
Heuristic	Using language to learn about things	"Tell me why."
Imaginative	Using language to create a new environment	"Let's tell a story and pretend."
Representational	Using language to communicate and express propositions	"I've got something to tell you."

Adapted from Halliday, M. A. K. (1969–70). Relevant models of language. *Educational Review, 22,* 26–37.

identified by linguist M. A. K. Halliday to describe children's language development. Children learn about what language is by learning what language does. They communicate to tell people about their personal needs, persuade others to do things, develop interpersonal relationships, express self-awareness, explore, imagine, and inform (Halliday, 1969–1970).

Children as young as two years old will use language that illustrates all the functions Halliday describes. The functions do not evolve linearly, however, and instrumental, regulatory, interactional, and personal functions of language may be used by very young language users before the heuristic, imaginative, and representational functions. As language usage becomes more sophisticated, Halliday's functions can still be identified, but speakers may use more than one function in an utterance, and the functions overlap and merge together, making them more difficult to recognize.

field note

3.1

Observing Halliday's Functions in Young Language Learners

Visit a preschool or a young family member who is learning to talk. Shadow one child as she or he plays and interacts with others. Use Halliday's functions in Exhibit 3.1 to guide your observations about the functions of language young children display. Check off the functions that you hear, and note some actual examples of what they say. Do the same with the adults who interact with the children. Note which functions of language adults use when talking to young children. Share what you find with a small group of classmates. Discuss the implications of differences in language usage of adults and children.

Home and Community Influences

Home and community have a great influence upon children's oral communication processes. Children speak different languages and experience a variety of communication situations that influence the ways they express themselves. If a teacher is not aware of home and community influences, students, especially those from non-native English-speaking or low socioeconomic backgrounds, may experience a divide between the communication patterns they know at home and the "classroom talk" they are expected to use at school (Voss, 1993). For example, students may not have experiences with organized question-and-answer discussion techniques used in schools. On the other hand, these same students may have language skills that serve them well at home or in the community but that are not recognized in traditional classroom experiences (Delpit, 1992). They may be able to speak two or more languages, sing complicated raps and rhythms, chant religious texts, tell elaborate stories, or explain complex hobbies. As you think about your future teaching, it is important to consider and recognize differences between home and school language uses and seek ways to build on the rich oral language skills all children bring to school. Ideas for making connections between home and school are suggested throughout this textbook.

Family Talk

Families impart the "curriculum of the home" (Heath, 1983) starting as soon as very young children learn their first lessons about using language. Family talk and conversations provide models for communication patterns and establish the foundation for language patterns that impact all communication processes. Family members respond to children's early attempts at using language, answer questions formed by young speakers, and help them learn to communicate messages.

Reading aloud to young children is a common language learning activity in many homes; however, even home read-aloud experiences vary. Some children are read to by parents who sit close to them, cuddling and interacting as they read children's literature together. Some children may be encouraged to sit quietly and listen, while others may be expected to join in, reading repeated lines with dramatic flair and enthusiasm. Some families may see read-alouds as a time to "teach" children about the reading topic or the process itself, while read-alouds in other families could be pure fun and enjoyment (Wan, 2000). In some homes stories are shared orally, reflecting an oral tradition. Children may listen to stories told and songs sung by their parents or other caregivers as they work around the house and care for other family members. In other families, story reading or storytelling may not be present, but listening and speaking may be fostered through other activities such as dinner conversations, recitations, or other interactions.

All children have experiences with language that contribute to the development of their communication skills, but they will come to school with very different ideas about how to engage in language activities. For many years the language patterns of the white middle class have dominated classroom talking and listening. Children may have been considered as deficient if they started school without knowing and using the formats and patterns expected in school settings. The richness of different ethnic and cultural speech patterns and literate behaviors is often unrecognized and undervalued at school (Voss, 1993), putting some children at a disadvantage.

One teacher, after making a home visit, described what she learned from observing her student at home (Voss, 1993). Other than a family album, no books were available. However, her student knew a great deal about building things, and he demonstrated his knowledge when explaining his project. He used the appropriate words to share what he was doing, describing a variety of tools and materials. He did more than understand the terminology; he used building tools in creative ways and was able to describe his process. Teachers looking for mainstream examples of literacy might view this home as deficient, since few books were available for reading; however, different does not always equal deficient. The parents of the child in this home obviously provided opportunities to develop language and thinking skills in ways not dependent on interactions with books.

Unfortunately some teachers hold stereotypes about the language skills of children who come from families who speak languages other than English or who are poor or nonwhite. An "educational" blindness to the richness of language and literacy practice present in non–middle class families sometimes leads to a view that both the children and parents from poor or minority families are deficient. This deficit view applied to children who have different oral language patterns results in differentiated instruction and overrepresented placement in remedial classrooms. Some classroom practices deny "poor and minority students the opportunity to make a space for their language and literacy practices within the curriculum" (Murphy & Dudley-Marling, 2000, p. 381). Classroom practices often fail to recognize the knowledge about language that children bring from their homes (Moll, 1994). Effective teachers of the language arts must be aware of these differences and consider how to address them so these children are not limited in the opportunities, encouragement, and support they receive in the classroom. Teachers develop an awareness of what their students know about language by

- talking with them individually
- observing how they respond to assignments
- talking about their home and community
- observing them talking in small groups
- watching their interactions with their peers

Teachers can learn a great deal about oral language, literacy, and the children themselves by interacting with their students in a variety of classroom settings.

Community Talk

In the community in which the child grows up, communication occurs in a variety of forms and for many purposes: to establish and maintain friendships, mark events, control access to community events and institutions, and influence participation in ongoing community activities (Honeyghan, 2000; McGinley & Kamberelis, 1996). Different cultures may rely on specific uses of language, including definite ways of interacting with people and certain uses of words and sentences. Houses of worship, cultural groups, and daycare centers within the communities all expect and use certain patterns of interaction that teach children about language and communication. Religious communities, for example, vary widely in how individuals listen and respond to sermons or services. Some houses of worship are highly ritualistic and require order and quiet attention; others invite their members to respond spontaneously with emotion. As they interact within various community groups, children learn from the modeling by significant adults and from interacting with others. Community values suggest ways to behave and interpret behavior that help children understand the oral language of their community and guide their own communication (Bloome, Harris, & Ludlum, 1991). J. Gee writes,

Thinking and speaking are functions of social groups and their specific discourses; literacy is a social skill involving discourses, attained through guided participation and built on trust; a good part of knowledge resides not in their minds but in the social practices of the group to which they belong. (1992, p. 41)

BRIAN, VETERAN TEACHER ▶ José came to my classroom reading a year and a half below the third-grade level that was expected. I heard stories about him before he reached my room. He hardly spoke English and when he did it was heavy with the Mexican accent reflecting his first language and the language spoken in his home and community. He was often absent, missing important classroom experiences that would improve his English and help him succeed in school.

After school started and I got to know him, I was taken aback by his willingness to learn and his attempts to understand what was happening in the classroom, but I was concerned about his absenteeism and the difficulty he was having, especially during language arts. I finally planned a visit to his home to find out about his literacy background. Accompanied by an interpreter so I could converse with his parents, I found them very concerned about his school work and eager to help him in any way that they could. When I mentioned classroom attendance, I saw a troubled look pass before both his parents' eyes. They began to describe José's importance to the family existence. As the only English speaker in the house, he often accompanied family members to the doctor, the immigration office, and even the bank. He served as the interpreter, helping the adults in the family understand about forms, taxes, and their bank accounts. And this responsible young boy was not succeeding at school. As I began to understand his literacy skills, I realized he was regularly accomplishing complex oral and written communication tasks, but in very different ways than how language was used in the classroom. I understood that it was my responsibility to recognize his skills for interpreting English documentation and help him apply that to school texts.

Reflecting on José's Language Experiences

Consider José's language experiences described in the Teacher Viewpoint. Respond in writing to the following questions:

What assumptions did his teacher make about José's language competence?

About his family's commitment to education?

How did the teacher's home visit help him to understand José's language experiences better?

What implications does this perspective have for your future work with diverse students and their families?

Discuss your responses and insights with your classmates.

Observing Community Language

Attend a community event in the neighborhood surrounding your school. The event may be a religious service, Saturday morning farmer's market, festival, parade, political event, meeting sponsored by a community organization, or any other gathering where you may listen and observe the use of oral language. Use the following questions to guide your observations:

1. What languages or dialects are spoken? Are multiple languages or dialects spoken?
2. What cultures are represented?
3. How does the event reflect the culture(s) of the community?
4. What are some characteristics of the culture(s) and the language(s)?
5. How does the language use compare with your own experiences with language and culture?

Record your observations and discuss your experiences with your classmates. Discuss important insights you gained that you feel will influence your future work with students from diverse settings.

LANGUAGE DIFFERENCES

Over one-third of all students come to school speaking a language other than English (Pang, 2001). Even so, it remains a challenge to implement instructional strategies with students whose English proficiency is limited and whose background and experiences are very different from their teachers' (Freeman & Freeman, 2000).

English Language Learners (ELLs)

Every student in the United States needs to learn how to speak English. Being an English language learner does not cause school failure. It is certainly possible for children who speak a different language to succeed at school, but school failure often occurs when there is a lack of congruence between the language of the home environment and the language expected at school (Anderson & Irvine, 1993; Vogt, 1996). Students' first language helps them communicate during their early years, connects them to their homes, and allows them to interact with friends and family members. If the first language is not recognized or valued during teaching and learning opportunities, then it will be difficult for children to feel the confidence they need to develop English language proficiency.

All children who come to school speaking a language other than English are not the same. Even children from different parts of the world who speak the same language can vary widely in their language use. For example, children from Mexico and Spain will use different forms of Spanish. Among ELLs, ability levels also vary. Some students barely speak, read, or write their first language; others may speak and read fluently and have already begun to acquire English communication skills. Often, children who speak a language other than English are grouped together, but teachers need to recognize that each ELL child possesses different levels of fluency and literacy.

A solid foundation in any first language supports academic achievement in a second language. Children who speak English as a second language can be very successful in school. However, research is beginning to show that it is difficult for children to overcome language differences when this is combined with the effects of poverty. Among other subtle differences, children who grow up in poverty may understand basic concepts differently and fail to possess the cognitive processes expected of children entering school (Payne, 1996). Most noticeably, the combination of language differences and poverty often results in children lacking experiences with the formal language used in school, putting them at a disadvantage. Positive relationships with teachers provide students who are struggling with poverty and learning a new language the motivation for academic achievement.

Dialectical Differences

Children also demonstrate dialectical differences in their language development patterns. Although African American dialects are prevalent, today's classrooms reflect a myriad of language patterns and codes. Regardless of the fact that the dialectical differences have complex rules and structures, students who speak with heavy dialectal characteristics are typically viewed as deficient in language skills (Delgado-Gaitan, 1990). Teachers' lack of understanding of the complexities involved in various dialects leads to the perception that children are not equipped with necessary knowledge.

Teachers who are successful in encouraging students with different dialects make language rules explicit, respectfully draw attention to differences between standard English and dialects, and encourage children to recognize the time and place to use different forms of language. Children's dialectical differences should be accepted in the classroom, and instruction should help them develop Standard English proficiency. Teachers need not be concerned when they hear students use dialects, unusual word combinations, or mixtures of language. Effective language users are able to *code switch*—change from one dialect or language to another to another, based on the context and purpose of communication. Code switching regularly happens in communities where individuals are familiar with two languages. One example is the mixture of Spanish and English, known as Spanglish, illustrated when speakers move from one language to another in normal conversations and produce statements such as, "It's very important to honor your abuelitas (grandparents)." Code switching also occurs in a single language. We speak differently to our minister, to our friends at a bar, and to a three-year-old child, using more formal or less formal speech without even thinking about it. "Classroom learning should be structured so not only are these children able to acquire the verbal patterns they lack, but they will also be able to strengthen their proficiencies, and to share these with class-mates and teachers. We will then all be enriched" (Delpit, 1995, p. 57).

Children's Code Switching

Observe students talking in different school contexts, including the classroom, play-grounds, lunchroom, and hallways. Listen carefully to their interactions and note examples of language differences, code switching, and dialectical influences. Discuss with your mentor teacher, professor, or classmates how these language differences affect classroom instruction.

FINAL REFLECTIONS

Oral language is a major component of who students are and how they view and negotiate the world. Differences in languages and language patterns will be evident in diverse classrooms. If teachers embrace all languages, dialects, and language experiences, accept their students' use of various language patterns, respond to what students are saying and not how it is stated, and provide opportunities for students to expand their language range, students will feel comfortable in the learning situation. By doing so, teachers begin to help children enhance their oral language skills and gain experiences that will help them succeed in today's world.

The remaining articles in this chapter offer practical suggestions and dis-cussions about how language arts instruction can be organized to foster oral language development for all children.

Classroom Talk

Classroom discussions and conversations occur throughout the day. Sometimes the discussions are informal, and other times they are purposely structured. Saying hello in the morning; giving and listening to instructions; asking and answering questions; developing and providing explanations; engaging in differences of opinions; participating in small talk, science talk, or book talk; discussing writing; talking about a television show; sharing a poem; telling a story—all are ways that speaking and listening take place in the classroom. Oral interactions provide numerous opportunities for learning, but the processes are often taken for granted. Teachers typically place a great deal of emphasis on reading and writing, but speaking and listening are often left to chance or allowed to develop naturally through curricular activities and day-to-day communication needs. In fact, oral language use is an important instructional activity that should permeate the language arts curriculum.

THE TEACHER'S ROLE

Traditional notions of class discussion usually involve the teacher eliciting specific responses from students (Almasi, 1995). The teacher makes presentations, asks questions, and probes for answers. This type of classroom talk has been the accepted model for such a long time that teachers often think that they are using discussion methods when they are really asking questions of students and expecting specific answers. Transcripts of classroom discussions show that teachers use an initiate–respond–evaluate pattern during 85 percent of classroom discussions (Almasi, 1995). This pattern results in teacher-dominated classroom conversations, as well as judgmental feedback to students depending on whether a particular comment was "valuable" or not (Gambrell & Almasi, 1996; Wray & Medwell, 1991).

The classroom discussion described in the Window to the Classroom that opened this chapter would have been very different had Mrs. Gonzales followed an initiate–respond–evaluate pattern. Mrs. Gonzales would have initiated the conversation by asking questions, the students would have responded, and Mrs. Gonzales would have given an evaluative response. The conversation might have gone something like this:

Mrs. Gonzales: How would you describe the Master Potter? What type of person was he?

Student 1: He was sort of mean and acted mad all the time.

Mrs. Gonzales: Yes, how did you know he was mean? How did the author characterize him?

Student 2: One way was how he talked.

Mrs. Gonzales: Can you read a section that illustrates how he talked?

Student 2: [reads from the text]

Mrs. Gonzales: Good example. Now can anyone else read a section that illustrates something about what kind of person the Master Potter was?

Notice in this example that Mrs. Gonzales is in control of the topic, and when students add to the discussion, their responses are followed by an evaluative comment. Comments such as "I like that answer," or "pretty close" send messages to students about what the teacher thinks about their responses. This type of interaction between the teacher and students suggests that students are expected to guess what's in the teacher's head and offer the "correct" response.

Instead, Mrs. Gonzales shared the responsibility for classroom discussion and interactions. For example, she let the discussion of the Master Potter continue until everyone had a say. Together she and her students were responsible for discussing, posing questions, finding evidence for answers, and connecting with and elaborating on fellow students' ideas (Jewell & Pratt, 1999). Teachers such as Mrs. Gonzales see their role as providing guidance, facilitating students' discussions, and providing an opportunity to talk about the discussion processes. See Exhibit 3.2 for a list of effective behaviors for teachers during discussion.

Scaffolding

Instructional scaffolding is an effective strategy to use throughout the language arts curriculum. Scaffolding recognizes that students can often perform a task with adult guidance or peer collaboration that they could not achieve alone. Vygotsky (1978) called the difference between what children do with help and what they do without guidance the "zone of

 3.2 *Effective behaviors for teachers during discussion.*

- Present open-ended comments in which the teacher guides rather than directs.

- Listen in order to respond sensitively to students' comments.

- Overlap conversations so that each individual's contribution is connected and builds toward a cohesive understanding.

- Establish a collaborative environment where students are free to experiment with their ideas.

- Encourage extensive engagement by all participants.

- Scaffold conversations, providing a great deal of support when needed and allowing students to take their own lead when appropriate.

- Model appropriate responses during discussion.

Adapted from B. J. Walker. Discussions that focus on strategies and self-assessment. In L. B. Gambrell & J. F. Almasi (Eds.), *Lively discussions! Fostering engaged reading* (pp. 286–296). Newark, DE: International Reading Association.

proximal development" (ZPD). The ZPD is the gap between what *is* understood and what *can be* understood with support, and it represents an
excellent opportunity for learning to take place. Scaffolding helps students
navigate through the ZPD and extend their current knowledge and skills.
Teachers scaffold when they begin instruction at a level that encourages student success, then provide the right amount of support to move students
from their current level of understanding to a higher level of understanding.
Verbal prompting—such as asking questions or elaborating on students'
responses—and providing students with an outline of the material or other
such academic supports are two ways teachers scaffold discussion processes. As students become more skilled at participating in classroom
discussions, unnecessary support is withdrawn and more responsibility is
transferred to them.

Modeling

Another role for teachers is to model appropriate speaking behaviors.
Modeling expected speech behaviors is particularly important for children
who have not had a great deal of experience in group settings. Teachers
should model appropriate responses during discussions, including

- restating students' ideas
- asking for further clarification
- validating a contribution or comment
- pointing out effective discussion techniques
- providing guidance about effective oral language behavior (Jewell &
  Pratt, 1999).

Teachers serve as the classroom's model for good oral language behaviors, but in effective classroom discussions, the teacher and students share
this role.

Observing Classroom Instructional Talk

Observe in your school classroom to learn about how spoken skills are used and
taught. Focus your observations in the following areas:

1. What is the role of the teacher during classroom discussions? What roles do the
   students take on?

2. What patterns of interactions between the teacher and students do you observe?
   Do you see examples of facilitating, questioning, and evaluating by the teacher?
   By the students?

3. What techniques does the teacher use to encourage classroom discussion?

CLASSROOM DISCUSSION CONSIDERATIONS

Discussions are effective teaching techniques, but before teachers make decisions about classroom discussion activities, they should consider some important factors. Students' experiences with discussion, the choice of topic, group size, and cultural/language background all contribute to the nature and quality of classroom discussions (Gambrell & Almasi, 1996).

Experience

Not all students are familiar with classroom discussion processes. It may be necessary to build a bridge from what students understand about sharing in large groups to what they need to know to be successful in school and other settings. Students who have talked only in family situations may not understand how to take turns or listen during classroom discussions. Students who attend a great many religious services may be quite familiar with listening to someone deliver prepared speeches, but they may not be prepared for the give and take of a classroom discussion. Students who are accustomed to classrooms where they are expected to listen to the teacher as an authority may not be prepared to take responsibility for classroom discussions. While the differences may not seem great, the experiences that children have with language before they get to your classroom will affect discussion processes.

One of the first things a teacher will want to do when meeting a new group of students is to understand the skills that students bring and begin establishing the logistics, protocol, and expected behaviors for discussions. Taking turns, raising their hands when they have something to share, and not interrupting others are all important classroom behaviors that students should be taught early. Students learn more readily about expected behaviors if the teacher discusses expectations and allows the students to help establish the processes for classroom discussions.

The topic selected for discussion will affect students' involvement and enjoyment.

Topic

The topic selected for discussion will affect students' involvement (Brookfield & Preskill, 1999; Templeton, 1991). Think about how little you contribute to conversations in which you have no experience related to the topic. Suppose your friends are discussing stock car racing, and you are not interested, nor do you care about the sport. You might find it difficult to listen as they talk about celebrities and share stories about certain races. Your mind wanders and you might feel bored. However, suppose your friends convinced you to attend a stock car race. While you still aren't terribly interested in the sport, you will probably become more involved in a discussion of the topic. Students experience the same kind of response when classroom topics that they do not understand are being discussed. The chances of student-led discussions being productive are not great if a large number of the students are not prepared or interested in the topic. In this situation, the teacher will have to maintain greater control. On the other hand, students will need less teacher support when they are interested in the discussion topic.

Teachers who keep up with what is important to their students, such as current events, pop culture, video games, after-school activities, recent fads, and toys, show that they are willing to respond to students' interests and needs (Larson, 1999). This is an important step in providing for students' participation in classroom oral language activities. When topics are predetermined and it is in the students' best interest to be engaged in conversations, teachers must build the students' background and increase their motivation. A student may not be extremely interested in the formula for calculating the radius of a circle, but that student must be motivated to engage in productive listening and speaking about the topic. If students do not express interest, the teacher will need to take more responsibility for motivating students to take part in the discussion, building the background so that students will discuss the topic, and asking questions to guide the discussion.

Group Size

Students must learn to participate in small and large group discussions. Most children, even those who hesitate to talk in whole-class settings, will talk in small groups. Opportunities for everyone in the classroom to participate in smaller group discussions are instructionally effective. Numerous small discussion group formats (such as pairs or individual conferences) may be adapted to almost any topic or instructional setting. (See Chapter 2, Article II, for a full description of small group arrangements.)

Whole-class discussions may frequently be an effective venue for teaching and learning oral language strategies, but not everyone speaks up during large group discussions. It is often difficult to involve all students in large group discussions, and sometimes several students dominate the conversation. Because teachers usually have 20 to 30 students in their classroom, students who are shy or do not feel comfortable talking in front of groups may be overlooked during whole-class discussions. In the opening Window to the Classroom, Mrs. Gonzales provided small group time for students to talk about a topic before it was discussed in a large group setting. This method could be particularly important for students who are not confident speaking English or who do not understand the topic. Starting the discussion in small groups before introducing the same topic in a large group setting provides all students the opportunity to share in small groups and probably increases the chance that more students will have something to say during whole-class discussions. It is important to provide a variety of group sizes so that all students have an opportunity to share their ideas.

Culture and Language

Different cultures have different oral language interaction patterns. In her famous anthropological study, Shirley Brice Heath (1983) described the language development of children in two Appalachian communities that were less than 10 miles apart. Among other things, she found great differences in the ways parents talked with their children. In one town, children were included in community activities, taking part in lively discussions with adults. From a very young age they participated in the animated talk in the town square. In the other town, the children were carefully coached at home about proper ways to speak in public. They were not expected to talk with adults until they were older. Heath's study of children's language patterns revealed that early cultural interactions affected responses in school to questions with "known" or factual answers. She also found that children who responded actively to question-and-answer patterns in their home may not necessarily respond or talk in the classroom. Given the varied cultures represented in today's classrooms, it should be accepted that children will come to school understanding different patterns of speaking.

Classroom discussions may be particularly difficult for children who speak a language other than English, but it is important that these students nevertheless feel a part of the classroom and interact with their classmates. In order to learn how to speak English effectively, they must be involved in informal and formal conversations and classroom discussions. Effective teacher support offered during instruction can draw English language learners into classroom discussions, even when their English skills are limited. Exhibit 3.3 introduces a few ways teachers can encourage everyone to participate in classroom discussions.

exhibit **3.3**   *Instructional modifications to encourage English language learners to participate in class discussions.*

Build background	Build students' background before and during discussions. Teachers may need to provide experiences that help students build their background. Films, supplemental readings, guest speakers, pictures, and field trips build an understanding of the topic for all students and will be particularly important for ELLs.
Make personal connections	Ask students to connect the conversation with their own lives.
Interpret and explain	Be prepared to assist students in understanding critical aspects of the conversation. When necessary, stop the class discussion, explain a concept in depth, show pictures, or provide translations.

ORAL LANGUAGE STANDARDS AND GOALS

Oral language instruction is generally expected to cover language use for a variety of different functions and contexts, focus on effective communication, and develop collaborative communication skills and the ability to work in groups. National and state language arts standards provide some guidance about what behaviors students should develop as a result of instruction. The NCTE/IRA (1996) standards provide the following general guidelines:

> Students adjust their use of spoken, written, and visual language (e.g., conventions, style, vocabulary) to communicate effectively with a variety of audiences and for different purposes.

> Students whose first language is not English make use of their first language to develop competency in the English language arts and to develop understanding of content across the curriculum.

> Students participate as knowledgeable, reflective, creative, and critical members of a variety of literacy communities.

> Students use spoken, written, and visual language to accomplish their own purposes (e.g., for learning, enjoyment, persuasion, and the exchange of information).

Teachers gain additional guidance about oral language instruction from state and local curriculum standards. The Virginia Standards of Learning provide an explicit example of state curriculum standards related to oral language behaviors (see Exhibit 3.4). Standards from grades 1, 3, and 5 provide an overview of the scope and developmental nature of classroom talk.

Notice that many of the Virginia standards focus on the interpersonal nature of oral language, reflecting oral language usage in and out of school. For example, Standard 3.1 states that the student will use communication skills effectively by asking and responding to questions. Asking and responding to questions are important language skills in many settings. Other goals are more directly associated with academic subjects. Standard 5.1 focuses on subject-related learning by promoting participation in and contributions to discussions across content areas. Another important aspect of communication reflected in the Virginia State Standards is the close connection between speaking and listening (see Standard 3.1).

Standards provide guidelines and assist in the development of cohesive instructional approaches, but they are only one component in good planning. The first consideration for teachers as they determine how to approach oral language instruction is students' interests, needs, and abilities. Lessons guided only by standards are incomplete and miss an important aspect of language learning—the need to be relevant and meaningful.

exhibit 3.4 *Virginia Standards of Learning for oral language behaviors.*

GRADE 1

1.1 The student will continue to demonstrate growth in the use of oral language.
- Listen and respond to a variety of media, including books, audiotapes, videos, and other age-appropriate publications.
- Tell and retell stories and events in logical order.
- Participate in a variety of oral language activities.
- Be able to express ideas orally in complete sentences.

1.2 The student will continue to expand and use listening and speaking vocabularies.
- Increase oral descriptive vocabulary.
- Begin to ask for clarification and explanation of words and ideas.
- Give and follow simple two-step oral directions.
- Use singular and plural nouns.
- Begin to use compound words in oral communication.

1.3 The student will adapt or change oral language to fit the situation.
- Initiate conversation with peers and adults.
- Follow rules for conversation.
- Use appropriate voice level in small-group settings.
- Ask and respond to questions in small-group settings.

1.4 The student will orally identify and manipulate phonemes (small units of sound) in syllables and multisyllable words.
- Count phonemes (sounds) in syllables or words with a maximum of three syllables.
- Add or delete phonemes (sounds) orally to change syllables or words.
- Create rhyming words orally.
- Blend sounds to make word parts and words with one to three syllables.

GRADE 3

3.1 The student will use effective communication skills in group activities.

- Listen attentively by making eye contact, facing the speaker, asking questions, and paraphrasing what is said.
- Ask and respond to questions from teachers and other group members.
- Explain what has been learned.

3.2 The student will present brief oral reports.
- Speak clearly.
- Use appropriate volume and pitch.
- Speak at an understandable rate.
- Organize ideas sequentially or around major points of information.
- Use clear and specific vocabulary to communicate ideas.

GRADE 5

5.1 The student will listen, draw conclusions, and share responses in subject-related group learning activities.
- Participate in and contribute to discussions across content areas.
- Organize information to present reports of group activities.
- Summarize information gathered in group activities.

5.2 The student will use effective nonverbal communication skills.
- Maintain eye contact with listeners.
- Use gestures to support, accentuate, or dramatize verbal message.
- Use facial expressions to support or dramatize verbal message.
- Use posture appropriate for communication setting.

5.3 The student will make planned oral presentations.
- Determine appropriate content for audience.
- Organize content sequentially or around major ideas.
- Summarize main points before or after presentation.
- Incorporate visual aids to support the presentation.

Standards for Speaking

A number of states have identified standards related to spoken language. Investigate whether your state has one or more standards related to spoken language. The Internet will be a good resource for this investigation. If your state does have standards for spoken language, discuss with your peers how the standards are incorporated into the classroom. If your state does not have such standards, discuss why that may be so, based on ideas presented in Chapter 3, Articles I and II, as well as your own experiences. Observe regular classroom routines and note which activities meet the standards. Do the teachers specifically plan to meet the standards, or do they meet them less frequently by speaking throughout the instructional day? Discuss with your classmates how day-to-day activities in the classroom may be organized to meet the oral language standards.

A CONTINUUM OF TALK

Oral language standards may be met through a wide range of instructional possibilities in a variety of classroom settings that engage students in oral language at different levels of complexity. The range of oral language instructional activities is graphically displayed in the "continuum of talk" (Gambrell & Almasi, 1996), shown in Exhibit 3.5.

The continuum of talk characterizes oral language as informal or formal and identifies inner speech, conversations, small group discussions, recita-

A model of the continuum of talk. **exhibit 3.5**

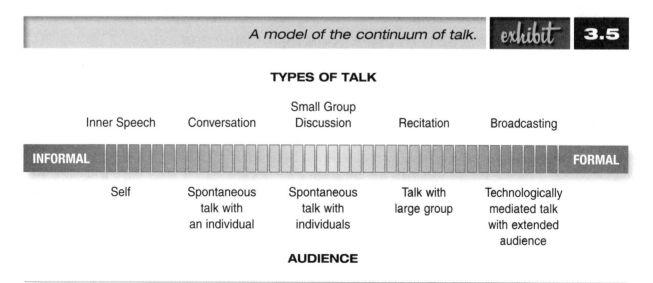

tion, and broadcasting as types of talk. Informal talk would include those instances when neither guidance nor a specific goal directs the interactions. Students discussing what happened on the bus as they traveled to school, playground arguments, and discussions of weekend events are all examples of informal talk. Other oral language activities have a structured format, and participation is predictable. The organized choral reading of a poem and the timed presentation of a debate are examples of formal classroom talk.

The continuum also recognizes the importance of the audience (or the listener), which in all but a few instances is crucial to the talking process. Inner speech is an independent activity almost synonymous with private thoughts; conversation, according to the model, occurs when a person talks with one individual; small group discussions happen with several individuals; recitation occurs in front of large groups of individuals; broadcasting occurs with an extended audience. The continuum illustrated in the model suggests an almost unending range of activities that teachers may implement to meet the standards that guide oral language development.

Understanding the Continuum of Talk

Make a photocopy of Exhibit 3.5 and use it to guide classroom observations in which you focus on the types of talk that occur during daily language arts instructional periods. Where on the continuum does most of the classroom talk occur? Who is participating in oral language activities? Compare what you find with your classmates' observations. Do you see differences among classrooms? What are the implications of the differences you observe?

CLASSROOM DISCUSSION AS INSTRUCTION

Successful classroom discussions take place in many formats and on a variety of topics and subject areas. Different subjects or topics might be best suited for different discussion formats or structures. For example, science and social studies discussions might benefit from small grouping arrangements, whereas mathematics instruction might benefit from students working in pairs. Grand conversations, read-alouds, and literature circles are recognized discussion formats that many language arts teachers use during their language arts instructional times. Structured formats serve as examples of how language arts teachers organize and manage classroom discussions.

Grand Conversations

Grand conversations are discussions in which students talk about a book or poem (Peterson & Eeds, 1990; Tompkins & McGee, 1993). These conversations go beyond question-and-answer sessions and encourage children to express their opinions and ideas. Grand conversations may be accomplished in small groups or whole-class settings. They have two phases.

The first phase of a grand conversation begins when a student leader asks the question, "What did you think?" or "What did you like?" about the book. The teacher responds to the book, modeling the type of sharing that enriches the conversations, but quickly turns the discussion over to the students, who are encouraged to answer the question. Students share the parts of the story or poem they liked and talk about why specific sections are their favorites.

The second phase of a grand conversation is more teacher directed. The teacher asks one or two literary questions—questions that focus on interpretation, attention to literary elements, or discussion of an author's technique. The conversation asks, "What does the story mean?" The conversation should go beyond stating the sequence of events or understanding vocabulary. Often the teacher facilitates and guides the discussion, providing scaffolding for students until they learn strategies for conducting student-centered discussions. Together, the teacher and students engage in interpretation of the work. Grand conversations are student centered, providing a chance for all viewpoints to be heard and different opinions to be discussed. True grand conversations result in a high level of understanding on the part of the students.

Interactive Read-Alouds

Discussion about books can be encouraged with an interactive read-aloud (Barrentine, 1996), outlined in Exhibit 3.6. The teacher encourages responses during the reading process and "lingers" on each page, allowing students to respond to the pictures and words. Interactive read-alouds allow for student-led discussion in a structured format, providing some scaffolding as teachers turn more responsibilities over to the students. As the teacher elicits the students' comments and reactions, she fills in conceptual gaps. This technique may be particularly helpful when English language learners are present in the classroom.

Literature Circles

A popular and effective way to promote discussion about literature is literature circles. Students are arranged in groups of four to six, and the members of each group read the same book or books with similar topics, in similar genres, or written by the same author. An important aspect of literature circles is that readers select their own reading materials and read at their own pace. The literature circles meet regularly as the children are reading their books, and before each meeting, students prepare for discussion time (Daniels, 1994). Students use written or drawn notes, sometimes kept in reading journals, to guide their own reading and discussions.

exhibit 3.6 *Format of interactive read-alouds.*

Goal: As the teacher reads a story aloud, students will be able to lead a discussion about the story, commenting on content and pictures and making connections to their own experiences.

- Teacher reads aloud.

- Teacher stops and encourages children to talk about what was read or discuss pictures.

- If children appear hesitant to discuss, teacher may model comments about the story or pictures.

- Once children begin interacting about the story, teacher asks questions about concepts omitted from the discussion.

Readers are assigned certain roles during the literature discussions (see Exhibit 3.7), with the jobs changing after each discussion. At first the teacher models and monitors the process carefully, being sure that each student understands the different roles during discussion. The process requires some scaffolding by the teacher until students are comfortable enough with the discussion format to take on responsibilities for producing discussion topics on their own.

Constant monitoring of the discussion process is important during literature circles. Teachers and students talk together about what is being

exhibit 3.7 *Roles in literature circle discussions.*

- **Discussion Director:** Compiles a list of questions that will be asked in group discussion.

- **Literary Luminary:** Finds selections from the book that are interesting, powerful, significant, or confusing. Reads the selections or selects someone else to do so. The group discusses the passages.

- **Connector:** Makes connections between the book that is being read and events that occur in students' own lives, their community, or other contexts.

- **Vocabulary Enricher:** Finds confusing or interesting words and gets the definition for them. The vocabulary enricher also looks for words that are used repeatedly throughout the text.

- **Illustrator:** Draws a picture related to the reading. In addition to the picture, the illustrator creates a graphic organizer such as a web, Venn diagram, or story sequence to provide a visual representation of the story.

- **Summarizer:** Prepares a summary of the reading and presents it to the literature circle.

accomplished and assess the effectiveness of group discussions. Teachers take notes and use a checklist or other observation tools to capture what is happening during discussions, modifying the process based on the needs of their students. Students monitor their own process by discussing processes with the teacher and filling out evaluation forms or checklists that provide teachers with additional information.

Many teachers find that when they first begin to use literature circles they stick closely to the format and roles discussed above. As students gain more experience in literature circles, teachers move toward more open-ended literature circle discussions and allow students to make more decisions about their groups and the format for the discussions. The literature circle format should be considered flexible and subject to change based on students' needs and teachers' goals.

Discussion Observations

Select four children to observe during a classroom discussion. (You may want to ask your mentor teacher to help you identify students who represent a range of discussion skills.) Take notes on the children's behaviors. Note when and if they volunteer to talk, their responses to the teacher, the kinds of questions they ask, their level of engagement, and other behaviors. Write up your descriptions, comparing and contrasting the behaviors of the children. Share your information with your mentor teacher and discuss your impressions of the students as speakers.

FINAL REFLECTIONS

Classroom discussions and conversations allow students to share their ideas, insights, and observations. Oral discussion skills are important tools that students will use throughout their lives. Their ability to communicate through spoken language will help them succeed at education, work, and play. Given the wide range of language skills and patterns in classrooms and the diversity of cultural factors that influence how we talk to each other, classroom discussions and conversations are important components of language arts instruction.

Presentations and Drama

Oral presentations and dramatic productions provide opportunities to develop students' formal communication abilities and skills. Presentations and drama are structured oral language activities with a definite format, usually presented before groups of people. Certain children will perform or recite in front of a large group with ease. Others will never feel totally comfortable performing and reciting in front of an audience. However, everyone who participates in presentations and drama will benefit. Students employ physical, emotional, and thinking skills when they present a report or dramatize a story or poem. They can experiment with nonverbal communication (body language, gestures, and facial expressions) as well as verbal communication (intonation, rhythm, stress, slang, and idiomatic expressions) (Gasparro & Falletta, 1994). Additionally, performing before a group can help students build self-confidence and gain positive attention. For all these reasons, oral presentations and drama are important aspects of language arts instruction.

THE TEACHER'S ROLE

As the teacher introduces children to oral presentation, the tone for the level of involvement by the students is established. It will be up to the teacher to maintain a comfortable atmosphere where students feel able to experiment with performing in front of a group. Oral presentations require pre-planning. Resources that help teachers implement oral presentations are available in language arts texts, in school curriculum guides, and on the Internet. Many teachers become involved and excited about dramatic performance, and once teachers perfect one of these routines in the classroom, it usually remains a staple that they use and re-use from year to year. Making a dramatic presentation to other classmates, engaging in choral reading presentations, or developing and performing a script from a favorite story may become an expected event in the school year.

One way the teacher sets the tone for oral language activities is to become involved in the presentations. Showing eagerness to participate sends a message to students about how they should approach the activities. Teachers' involvement and enjoyment of oral presentations will serve as a model for student involvement. The more willing teachers are to perform, the more motivated students will be to be involved in oral presentations.

Standards and Goals of Classroom Presentations and Performance

The standards for language arts recommend that oral performance skills become an important aspect of language arts instruction. The NCTE/IRA (1996) standards provide the following general guidelines, suggesting the role of oral performance as a source of learning and enjoyment:

Students use spoken, written, and visual language to accomplish their own purposes (e.g., for learning, enjoyment, persuasion, and the exchange of information).

The Virginia Standards of Learning for English provide an example of how state guidelines may delineate oral performance skills. The grade 5 standards reveal an emphasis on the nonverbal communication skills necessary for making formal oral presentations (see Exhibit 3.8).

State standards related to oral performance are usually general and require interpretation by the teacher. Because they are offered as general guidelines, teachers have many options, allowing them to consider students' abilities when planning oral presentation activities. Plans for oral language activities should always take into account students' unique skills, abilities, and needs.

| Excerpt from Virginia Learning Standards for grade 5 delineating oral performance behaviors. | **3.8** |

5.2 The student will use effective nonverbal communication skills.

- Maintain eye contact with listeners.
- Use gestures to support, accentuate, or dramatize verbal message.
- Use facial expressions to support or dramatize verbal message.
- Use posture appropriate for communication setting.

ORAL PERFORMANCE CONSIDERATIONS

The primary elements of oral performance are voice and emotion. The voice of the student is the instrument of performance. Expression with the voice requires musicality: tones, pauses, inflections, and rhythms. Students will learn that changing the rhythm, tempo, or pitch of their voice can change the meaning of what they say (Forest, 1995). Emotional engagement increases comprehension, helping listeners—as well as the reader—understand the characters and events in a story. A student who is reading aloud and attempts to capture the emotion of a character such as Gilly in *The Great Gilly Hopkins* (Paterson, 1978) will develop a new understanding of the character and comprehend the story at a deeper level. Learning the impact of voice and the importance of empathizing with others' emotions during oral presentations can improve students' day-to-day communication.

Getting Started

Students who do not have experience with presenting, reciting, or drama may need some "warm-up" activities to help them be comfortable and less inhibited. A simple way to get started is to play a game of charades, either

Students who read aloud will learn that changing the rhythm, tempo, or pitch of their voice can change the meaning of what they say.

individually or as a class. Give the students an animal, emotion, or action and have them show what sounds and motions it would make. Another way to ease students into oral presentations is to read a poem and act it out together. *We're Going on a Bear Hunt* is one example of a poem whose movement, repetitive phrases, and emotions lend it to dramatic interpretation.

Role-playing is another way to get started with oral presentation. Teachers can introduce a problem or a situation, assign students roles, and let them play out how they might solve the problem or react in a certain situation. For example, the teacher introduces the problem of dealing with a bully on the playground by describing their actions. Two class members enact the confrontation. The drama is followed by class discussion, or new actors may perform different interactions to demonstrate other ways to solve the problem. Role-playing doesn't need to be practiced; it is best when performers are extemporaneous. Role-playing helps students solve problems and promotes class discussion.

Reading in unison (see description of choral reading later in this article) is another method for helping students feel comfortable performing in front of large groups. Students can experience being in front of groups, supported by their classmates, without the pressure of individual attention.

Accommodating Cultural and Language Differences

Oral performance has the potential to integrate the various forms of communication from a variety of cultures (Heath, 1982). For example, some students may have grown up in families that tell stories as a means of communication; others may be more comfortable with reading from a book with a great deal of expression. Providing numerous and varied opportunities for oral language performance gives students a chance to use forms of expression that may be more familiar and comfortable to them than traditional classroom interactions.

Performance provides relevant and compelling reasons for attending to vocabulary, idioms, cultural aspects, and plot. Modeling pronunciation, intonation, stress, rhythm, and oral expression may be especially important for ELLs. Opportunities to talk about pronunciation emerge naturally in the context of oral performance and presentations. It may be especially important for the teacher to establish a casual atmosphere that invites ELLs to use their language skills without fear of failure or ridicule. Texts representing different cultures can easily be used for oral language performances and presentations and may help ELLs feel at ease. A lovely picture book entitled *Family Pictures* (Garza, 1990) provides glimpses into an extended family in South Texas. The English and Spanish languages are presented side by side on each page, and the text is easily adapted into an oral presentation when the English and Spanish versions are read aloud in two or more voices. The same technique can be used for reading nursery rhymes from *Tortillitas Para Mama* (translated by Griego, Bucks, Gilbert, & Kimball, 1981). Oral language activities based on these two books offer obvious opportunities to focus on language and cultural diversity.

ORAL LANGUAGE PERFORMANCE AND PRESENTATION ACTIVITIES

Several basic instructional presentation and performance activities traditionally associated with language arts instruction are literature based. Dramatic performance, such as choral reading, readers theatre, storytelling, puppetry, formal plays, and stage productions are usually based on narratives originating from literature or student-authored texts. Formal presentations, on the other hand—such as reports, debates, or panel discussions—are information based. Formal presentations require research in subject areas or current events with a goal of helping others learn or persuading others to accept a point of view. This article discusses both literature-based and information-based presentation activities.

Literature-Based Oral Presentations: Dramatic Performance

Students may experience dramatic oral presentations in the classic language of Shakespeare or the modern, urban rhythms of rap. A drama may be presented to a close friend or a very large audience of strangers—at home, on the street, or in the classroom. As Shakespeare acknowledged, "The world is a stage."

Classroom oral performance can include more than the traditional staging of a play and need not involve acting (Flynn & Carr, 1994). Teachers and students do not have to undertake time-consuming, tedious preparation for high-profile performances in front of large audiences. Classroom drama may be as simple as changing familiar activities into exciting events by reading aloud, dramatizing a text, or chanting in unison. Oral presentations can rejuvenate the reading of a favorite picture book as children read familiar lines with expressions of joy, sorrow, anger, or concern. The range of classroom performance is broad and adaptable. Some examples of dramatic performance that easily adapt to language arts instruction are choral reading, readers theatre, storytelling, and puppetry. Plays and stage productions are another possibility—demanding but rewarding.

Choral Reading

Choral reading is one of the simplest forms of classroom drama. It gives students an opportunity to engage in dramatic readings with minimal stage or prop preparation. Choral reading provides support and a level of comfort to students who have not had a great deal of experience with oral presentations. Choral readings may be performed simply for the joy of expression within the classroom or shared with other classrooms or large audiences.

The first step in choral reading is to select a poem or story, considering student interests, vocabulary that is relevant to their learning, and rhyme and rhythm that would be interesting (see Exhibit 3.9 for suggestions). Pieces may be student selected. Student input builds ownership and interest in the activity, and they will select text that will keep them involved. The list of suitable texts is almost unending, but certain resources are already pre-

exhibit **3.9** *Suggested books for choral reading.*

This list is not comprehensive, but it will get you started thinking about the range of books that would adapt to choral reading activities. Use this list to start your own, adding books that you have tried with students, ones that your classmates, mentor teachers, and university professors recommend, and others you learn about in children's literature classes.

FOR YOUNGER STUDENTS:

Cowley, J. (1990). *Meanies.* Bothell, WA: Wright Group.

De Regniers, M. (1988). *Sing a song of popcorn.* New York: Scholastic.

Emberly, B. (1967). *Drummer Hoff.* Illustrated by E. Emberly. New York: Prentice Hall.

Fleming, D. (1993). *In the small, small pond.* New York: Henry Holt.

Kennedy, J. (1992). *The teddy bears' picnic.* Illustrated by M. Hague. New York: Henry Holt.

Martin, B. (1992). *Brown bear, brown bear, what do you see?* Illustrated by Eric Carle. New York: Henry Holt.

Sendak, M. (1963). *Where the wild things are.* New York: Harper & Row.

Wells, R. (1973). *Noisy Nora.* New York: Dial.

Williams, V. B. (1990). *More, more, more, said the baby.* New York: Greenwillow.

FOR OLDER STUDENTS:

Fleischmann, P. (1985). *I am Phoenix: Poems for two voices.* New York: Harper & Row.

Fleischmann, P. (1988). *Joyful noise: Poems for two voices.* New York: Harper & Row.

Frost, R. (1978). *Stopping by the woods on a snowy evening.* Illustrated by S. Jefferers. New York: Dutton.

Raschk, C. (1993). *Yo! Yes?* New York: Orchard.

Viorst, J. (1972). *Alexander and the terrible, horrible, no good very bad day.* Illustrated by R. Cruz. New York: Atheneum.

Yolen, J. (1987). *Owl moon.* Illustrated by J. Schoenherr. New York: Philomel.

pared for choral reading activities. Most notably, the Newbery medal winner *Joyful Noise: Poems for Two Voices* (Fleischmann, 1988) is an excellent example of the fine literature available especially for choral reading. Fleischmann's collection encourages creative choral readings that mimic the drone of insects. He writes in the foreword:

> The following poems were written to be read aloud by two readers at once, one taking the left-hand part, the other taking the right-hand part. The poems should be read from top to bottom, the two parts meshing as in a musical duet. When both readers have lines at the same horizontal level, those lines are to be spoken simultaneously. (1988, p. iii)

The next step is to determine the order of readers. Choral reading is much like choral singing: students speak as one voice, either in pairs or in small groups. Their voices work as instruments, and meaning is communicated through tone, pitch, and tempo, as well as language. Children should be encouraged to use their voices in different ways to produce effects. They can alternate the reading between various groups, producing different sounds, talking softly, increasing volume, or gradually adding student voices to increase volume and intensity.

Students should discuss how to produce sounds and how certain effects may be achieved. As suggested above, important aspects include volume, tempo, pitch, and reading in unison. Video- or audiotaping the performance can help students evaluate their performance. A few props or instruments that produce sound effects will enhance choral reading, and integrating music, dance, movement, and sound will further enhance the performance.

DOMINIQUE, BEGINNING TEACHER ▶ Recently, while working with some elementary school students with the objective of exposing them to a variety of multicultural poetry, we selected poetry from Native American, African, Chinese, Central American, and Scandinavian cultures. Students were given scarves, musical instruments such as tambourines, drums, wooden blocks, and cymbals to use in their performance. Each group went to an area in the rooms we were working with and practiced their performance for about 30 minutes. They practiced reading their poem together, experimenting with different groups of voices reading different stanzas of the poem. They used the musical instruments to punctuate their words and add excitement to their readings. They recorded their performance, listened to the recording, and made changes before presenting. When the groups finally came back together to perform for each other, we were amazed at the range of interpretation and expression!

Readers Theatre

Readers theatre is an oral reading and performance activity in which students read a narrative text aloud without acting, but showing emotion through their voices. Performing readers theatre differs from staging a play in that students do not memorize lines, do not use props, and usually sit on chairs and read directly from the script. Readers theatre encourages students to transform written literature into oral performances (Hoyt, 1992). As they enact the story, students use vocal expression to develop the characters and enhance the mood of the story. Students can perform individual parts, or groups of children can create a "chorus" of voices. When choruses of children are involved, more children can be included and the benefits of readers theatre extended to the entire classroom.

The first important step in readers theatre is to select or create a script. Any story or portion of a story can be adapted to readers theatre. Although many scripts can be purchased or found on the Internet (see Exhibit 3.10), teachers might want to create the composition themselves or with the help of students. When composing, keep in mind that the role of the narrator and characters can be altered for the needs of the class.

If you want your students to produce their own scripts, it is helpful to model the process by writing a script as a class and then to monitor groups closely as they prepare scripts. After the script is prepared, groups practice the story to perfect their dramatic reading and interpretation. Participants have support from the written text since the parts are not memorized and the dialogue is dramatized through reading, not acting. Each reader should have a copy of the script. Highlighter markings help readers focus on the appropriate lines. After the parts have been distributed, students should have repeated opportunities to practice the selection.

Preparing for readers theatre performances gives students opportunities to practice good oral reading strategies and to increase their reading fluency, comprehension, and engagement (Martinez, Roser, & Strecker, 1998/1999). Often students must work on slowing down as they read, projecting their voices, and enunciating their words. Tape recording or videotaping can help students become more aware of their vocal skills and characteristics.

exhibit **3.10** *Sources for readers theatre scripts.*

PRINT SOURCE

Dixon, N., Davies, A., & Politano, C. (1996). *Learning with Readers Theatre.* Winnipeg, AB: Peguis.

ONLINE SOURCE

http://scriptsforschools.com

www.readingonline.org/electronic

www.readinglady.com/Readers_Theater/Scripts/scripts.html

http://loiswalker.com/catalog/guidesamples.html

http://suzyred.com/readertheater.html

The performance of readers theatre is less complicated than other dramatic productions (Shepard, 1993). Readers sit or stand in a row in front of the audience. They hold the scripts in front of their bodies, much like choir music, or place them on stands. Readers look out to the audience instead of at each other. Unlike in a play, the setting and costumes are only suggested, through minimal movement, gestures, and narration. For example, if two of the characters go into another room, the readers can actually move their chairs to a corner of the stage to indicate that they now have distance from the rest of the readers. While the actions of the readers are significant, they should be simple and subtle. If a character sleeps in the story, the reader might hold her two hands next to her face and pretend to sleep while remaining sitting up. Or if a reader is knocking on a door, he might simply tap his stand or chair to make the knocking noise.

Oral Performance

In small groups, work with your classmates to develop and perform a choral reading or readers theatre selection. Identify a selection from a favorite piece of literature, a teachers' book of resources, or a website. As you prepare for your performance, consider what instructional support students would need to present a choral reading or readers theatre. After you have completed the performance, work with your small group and write a lesson plan for classroom implementation. If possible, arrange to deliver the lesson in your mentor teacher's classroom.

Storytelling

Storytelling is a wonderful skill that comes from the traditions of oral cultures, including African, Native American, and Caribbean. Many cultures passed their history and folklore from generation to generation by retelling stories instead of producing a written text. Storytellers in some cultures hold distinctions of great honor, and both the stories and storytellers are respected for their historical and cultural importance. Many children experience storytelling as part of the home and community life, and they may engage in storytelling at school in a variety of informal ways, such as by sharing personal experiences or retelling tales they know. Because storytelling serves different purposes in different cultures, teachers should become familiar with the role of storytelling in the cultures represented in their classrooms before including it in instruction.

Classroom storytelling may originate from personal experiences. Family stories show how drama can emerge out of personal experiences, and students may be encouraged to collect and perform these stories. Students might interview adults about important events in their family's history (e.g., immigration to the United States, family occupations, how holidays are celebrated) or even have them tell about artifacts such as special mementos or pictures that hold stories. A wonderful book to introduce the importance of family storytelling is *Tell Me a Story, Mama* (Johnson, 1989), in which bedtime stories about two generations of family are shared by a mother and daughter. Possible prompts to encourage the collection and sharing of family stories are provided in Exhibit 3.11.

Formal storytelling festivals or performances are exciting for students and allow them to display their strengths, interests, artistic styles, and favorite literature. Storytelling presentations require preparation and practice. The first step is to select a story. Students can write their own or find one that has been already written or told, but it should be one the storyteller enjoys. In addition to family stories, folktales are natural choices since they reflect the oral tradition of storytelling, having been told many times before they were written down. Other stories that are appropriate for telling include picture books, familiar stories such as fairytales and nursery rhymes, and repetitive stories that give opportunities to include the audience.

The next step in preparing for storytelling is to outline or map the story. One method is storyboarding: Have students divide their paper into three sections and fill in the beginning, middle, and end. This may be done individually or as a class, and students may be encouraged to include details in their own sketches. Writing out the plot on a story map is also a good way for students to show a basic understanding of the story. Instead of sketching out the plot, students could write down a synopsis of the events. The outline or map will help students prepare to tell the story.

A storyteller uses voice, gestures, props, and language to convey a story to others. Performing a story for an audience is a lot like having a black and white sketch in your mind and creating a brilliant portrait for the audience. The design of the story guides what you say during the performance, but the

---

exhibit **3.11** *Prompts to help collect family stories.*

A funny thing that happened to me when I was little . . .

A favorite holiday memory I have is . . .

A sad memory I have is . . .

You'll never believe what happened to me when . . .

I was so embarrassed when . . .

I was so happy when . . .

I was so surprised when . . .

details can change depending on the audience. One of the best ways to introduce storytelling to the classroom is for the teacher to prepare a story to tell her students. Not only will the modeling motivate and encourage children to tell stories, it will also provide a great deal of pleasure to the performing teacher.

MANUEL, VETERAN TEACHER ▶ One way to encourage cultural connections and recognize family history is to encourage students to use literature from their own culture when they tell stories. In my own experience, I have found that students often enjoy selecting stories from their own culture when they choose a story to perform. While I never choose a certain story or even culture for a story for a child, their selections often reflect cultural values or personal interests. I am also careful to recognize that some groups, such as Native American, incorporate stories into their spiritual lives and use them for specific ceremonial purposes. My students and I must honor these traditions.

I invite parents, teachers, administrators, and community members to tell a story to the classroom. Not only do their fresh faces provide a different perspective to the curriculum, students learn from their performance strategies. After observing a guest perform, I encourage students to ask questions and discuss the performance with the guest. Often students are astute at noticing new methods of performing or complimenting guests on their storytelling techniques.

Puppetry

Puppetry combines elements of storytelling and readers theatre. The performance is enhanced through the dramatic voices and expressions of puppets. Puppets can play the role of a character or tell the entire story. Some teachers collect puppets to be used during storytelling, role playing, and other classroom oral presentations. Children enjoy creating their own puppets, too, from socks, felt, foam, fabric, Styrofoam, clay, paper, paper bags, papier-mâché, Popsicle sticks, and many other materials.

Puppetry is a particularly effective strategy for children who do not feel comfortable speaking in front of groups. The act of speaking through a puppet provides some assurance that voice and emotion are appropriate, since they come from a toy or an object. Students may be more comfortable engaging in drama through a puppet.

Plays and Stage Productions

Formal plays and stage productions are rewarding but time consuming. Multiple classrooms or the entire school often collaborate to present a production at special holidays. Be sure you know how your school is choosing to celebrate holidays and that these choices are acceptable to the community. Plays and stage productions require the collaboration of classroom, art, drama, music, and other specialists in the school. Many commercial plays, artistic scripts, and other supports can help teachers who wish to produce more elaborate productions outside the classroom. Plays and theatrical productions form lifelong memories for students and may encourage them to become involved in oral productions as a hobby or profession.

Information-Based Oral Presentations: Formal Presentations

In a formal presentation, the speaker conveys ideas and information to a small or large group. More formally structured formats require special speaking and listening skills that students will use in many situations throughout their lives. The skills that student speakers may use during formal presentations include answering questions, clarifying descriptions, and offering explanations. Organization of information is very important in formal presentations.

Oral presentations can easily be incorporated into content area instruction such as science, social studies, and health. A presentation allows students to demonstrate their knowledge on a specific topic or process, perhaps as a concluding activity after reading a book or completing a research project. Students will need guidance in the special skills required for preparing and presenting. Preparing for a formal presentation requires many of the same skills as writing a formal report and is more often required of students in upper elementary grades or higher. However, any student can share through a presentation and benefit by learning new information and developing public-speaking skills.

When using oral presentations, keep in mind that some children may be shy and uncomfortable speaking in front of the class. By providing a great deal of modeling, supporting their preparation, allowing student-selected topics, and giving ample practice time, teachers can help students feel more comfortable making oral presentations. Working with partners or small groups helps children gain valuable experience and confidence so eventually they will be ready to do individual oral presentations.

Individual Oral Reports

Teachers often guide students to select a specific topic related to a unit of study and prepare an oral report. For example, in connection with a science unit on mammals, a teacher may ask each student to select a mammal and prepare a short oral presentation about it. Students conduct research by using books or Internet resources, then share what they have learned by preparing and presenting an oral report. For those who are listening, the reports may become dull and monotonous; in this case, teachers need to help students incorporate the characteristics of good oral presentations. Such instruction generally focuses on eye contact, voice level, pace, clarity of ideas, and use of visuals to support the presentation. Additionally, students will need explicit instruction on how to prepare, including how to choose and focus their topic, gather and organize their information, create visuals, and give the presentation. They may support their oral presentations with aids such as pictures, posters, charts, diagrams, models, timelines, or slides produced with presentation software such as PowerPoint.

A simple format for informational oral presentations is the "how-to" approach. Students select a specific task, such as brushing their teeth, making a sandwich, riding a bike, or logging on to the Internet, and then orally present "how to" do it. This approach requires students to be very focused on details and the correct sequence of information.

Debates

An interesting way to present different perspectives is to stage a debate. Debating requires specialized skills that students will find valuable in many situations; it also teaches them to see different sides of issues and anticipate responses to their arguments. One of the best ways for students to prepare for debate is to list the pros and cons for a particular issue and take turns offering different points of views.

Formal debates have strict rules and may be reserved for middle and high school students, but a less formal debate activity, called *North–South–East–West,* is appropriate for younger students. This activity will introduce them to debate and illustrate the importance of listening to a variety of ideas. First, select a topic to debate and ask students to share different perspectives. Place four chairs in different corners of a space and have students sit in the four chairs. Each chair represents a different perspective. The students debate the issue from the perspective of the chair they occupy. For example, the topic may be the role of television in students' lives and the attitudes that different people have toward television. The student in one chair would present the student perspective and talk about the role of television as entertainment during free time. The student in the second chair could represent parents' views and establish the importance of doing other activities besides watching television. The student in the third chair might convey the interests of television producers, and the one in the fourth chair could represent the attitudes of people who develop the commercials. Students then change their chairs and take on the role of the new chair. Switching chairs creates opportunities for students to develop an understanding of multiple viewpoints.

Panel Discussions

This activity combines reporting and debating. Four or five students form a panel that will present a topic to the rest of the class. Each panel member prepares in advance by completing research, organizing information, reading books, or interviewing others about a topic. The discussion begins with panel members summarizing their information and making a short presentation about the information they have researched. After they have presented their information, the panel members discuss their topic, sharing their ideas and opinions. Finally, the rest of the class joins the discussion, making comments, offering their opinions, and sharing additional information.

CONNECTING ORAL EXPRESSION AND OTHER LANGUAGE ARTS

Classroom oral performance activities provide opportunities for creativity, spark an interest in a topic, extend students' knowledge base, and develop self-confidence. The many purposes, functions, and contexts of oral presentation provide natural connections with all language arts processes.

Writing About Oral Expressions

Oral language presentations provide many opportunities for writing. Students can write new endings to plays, songs, or rhymes. If they are focusing on a particular character, they might want to write a letter or journal entry based on that person's experience. They can write a different version of a story to include characters they would like to add or settings that are familiar to them. Students may write pieces specifically for performance, such as scripts of their favorite children's literature or family stories. Writing about oral presentations broadens student understanding of written and oral communication and will appeal to children who enjoy the performance aspect of literacy.

Discussion About Oral Presentations

Discussion is a natural accompaniment to oral presentations. Presentations often require making comparisons and evaluations—both of which require different analytical and problem-solving techniques—and form the basis of a post-presentation discussion. Students can discuss how voice, emotion, word choice, and body language affect meaning and understanding in any oral language situation. The fact that versions often change from performance to performance may lead to a discussion of how fairytales and folktales vary from culture to culture.

Discussions may also focus on the characteristics of language. Making oral presentations helps students develop an understanding of rhyme, rhythm, and language sounds and expand their vocabulary. A dramatic presentation is often a good way to begin or end a discussion in class and may deepen and enrich discussions about character or plot. Acting out a scene or story can help children empathize with characters and lead to a deeper understanding of the story.

Reading and Literature

Oral language activities allow teachers to bring a broad range of literature into the classroom. Literature that encourages oral performance may be included in a classroom library, or students may seek resources in the school library that will help in their performances.

Drama and performance activities encourage students to become more engaged and involved in literature (Flynn & Carr, 1994). Students are required to do more than read a story—they must also portray characters to an audience by participating in their actions and words. By trying to communicate a more believable character to the audience, students become involved in the story.

Performances provide opportunities to discuss plot, story structure, character perspectives, and settings. It is important to talk about character development as you rehearse a piece; it is also important to recognize the role of the narrator in the story. Discussions about performances may encompass a wide range of literary aspects.

The repetitive preparation required for performances offers opportunities for students to develop reading abilities. Dramatic oral presentations contribute to increased fluency, comprehension, and expressive ability as students play with communicating in creative and unique ways (Hoyt, 1992). Since oral language activities require retelling and reconstructing the story, students will come to understand the concept of story variations. Rereading and performance of a text also reinforces the vocabulary and concepts in the text.

FINAL REFLECTIONS

Oral language presentations help students to better understand communicative processes. The wide range of possible activities makes oral presentations a particularly adaptable strategy for language arts instruction. Using the classroom as a stage—a place for informational and dramatic oral presentations—enhances all aspects of the language arts curriculum (Wolf, Edmiston, & Enciso, 1996).

Listening in the Classroom

article

IV

A classroom is a cacophonous environment. Voices interact and join together in many ways. Students gather in small groups and work cooperatively with each other on a science experiment. Teachers give instruction about how to divide numbers. Students attend an assembly where an opera singer demonstrates how she uses her voice to create emotion and meaning. The ways that groups of children make noise are endless. But for the talking and noise to make sense, someone must be listening. Where there is learning there is listening.

Students take in a great deal of information by listening to others (Brent & Anderson, 1993; Funk & Funk, 1989). By some estimates, students spend 50 to 75 percent of school time listening to the teacher, other students, or media. They listen across the curriculum, and during games, recordings, films, and writers workshop (Moffett & Wagner, 1992). Listening is the basis for communicating with others and receiving information in day-to-day life.

THE TEACHER'S ROLE

In the best listening lessons, teachers and other adults listen with interest, attention, and patience, providing a model. Students learn a great deal about listening from the examples that teachers set and explanations of what was modeled. If teachers listen closely, watch the speaker intently, ask questions, and explain how they listen, students will observe and learn from these behaviors. The adage "Actions speak louder than words" is quite appropriate for teaching listening skills. Not only should teachers exemplify effective listening behaviors, they should also recognize good listening skills in their classroom, make them explicit, explain how students can listen as they engage in activities, and encourage students to recognize good listening skills in themselves.

Paraphrasing students' ideas not only models good listening behavior but also provides labels, terms, or words for feelings that a child cannot express verbally (Brookfield & Preskill, 1999). When a teacher listens intently to what a student is saying and responds to her ideas by saying, "Here's what I hear you saying . . ." students learn how their ideas sound. Teachers may also respond by asking questions that lead children to solutions or to ideas they haven't considered. Feedback in the form of questions helps students understand what is involved in listening.

Restating students' feelings, such as by commenting, "It sounds as if you had a hard time on the playground at recess," demonstrates that a teacher is listening and helps students clarify what they are feeling. Another way for teachers to respond to what they hear is to share feelings or circumstances that teachers have in common with the speaker. Sharing personal connections to what is being conveyed is an excellent conversational tactic. A teacher who responds, "I felt the same way you did when that happened to me . . ." illustrates how students connect with others. Books, movies, and other shared experiences can provide common ground for sharing feelings about events or experiences.

ABIR, VETERAN TEACHER ▶ I noticed that my second graders were not listening during our social studies time. So, before we started talking about the topic, I explained that we were going to focus on listening. I knew that I was going to talk about the role of police officers in today's lesson, so I began to predict what we might talk about. I predicted that we would discuss the job of a police officer and how the police officer helped second graders. As the social studies lesson evolved, I would occasionally interject a "think-aloud" about my own listening in the class conversations. I would say things like, "Oh, so I was right, we are talking about a police officer's job," or, "I didn't think that we would talk about police dogs today." I continued making predictions and restating the purpose for listening. Before the lesson ended, I asked the children to help me make predictions. After we finished our social studies lesson, the class and I talked about the listening process that occurred. I will be interested to see if my students begin using the same strategies I modeled in my think-aloud.

FACILITATING CLASSROOM LISTENING

Listening is often left to chance in language arts instruction, and the skills associated with the process may not be as familiar as reading and writing skills. Listening skills are difficult to observe and measure, which may explain why they are often omitted in language arts instructional planning. Most of us learn how to be competent listeners without instructional assistance. However, students' listening skills may be improved through instructional approaches. Despite the fact that so much information is transmitted through listening, teachers rarely teach listening skills (Hyslop & Tone, 1988). Although teachers value listening and frequently ask students to "be good listeners" or "listen carefully," the practices of effective listening are not regularly addressed in the language arts classroom. Teachers may assume that since children arrive at school able to *hear,* the process of *listening* does not need to be taught. The skills of attending when someone else is talking and effectively processing information that is heard are paramount to almost everything we do in our lives. Basic considerations in listening are the *relevance* of the message to the listener and the *purpose* for listening (Funk & Funk, 1989). Keeping these two elements in mind can help teachers establish an environment where students listen effectively.

Relevance

Assessing and ensuring the relevance of any listening experience is crucial when providing students with active listening opportunities. Before you plan an event where you expect children to listen to messages, ask yourself: Is this related to what they already know? Does the topic have to do with their interests? Will the speaker communicate in a way that is developmentally appropriate for this group? Children's background knowledge, their interests, and developmental appropriateness are all-important to planning relevant classroom listening activities.

The topic being discussed or the message being delivered has a great deal of impact on how students listen. Think about how important the message topic is to you when you are engaged in a listening activity. You become bored with a topic when you have heard the information over and over again. You may not listen well when no one has related the topic to your own interests or established a need for you to hear the message. A listener will listen best when the material being conveyed is clearly important, relevant, interesting, or entertaining.

When students are required to listen, the length of the message should be appropriate to its relevance and the students' level of development. Students often spend more time listening in school than is developmentally appropriate. For very young children, listening for 10 or 15 minutes may be the best they can do. Older children listen longer depending on their interest in a topic and the level of importance they give it. Often children do not need to listen more, they need to listen better. Establishing the relevance of messages will encourage them to do so.

Listening activities should be directly linked to other learning experiences where students interact with information in a variety of ways. Reading intriguing literature aloud or showing videos about important concepts taught in subject areas are relevant opportunities to focus on listening skills. Listening activities will be more relevant if students can expect to use the information in their day-to-day activities. In other words, when students talk, read, and write about what they hear, then the relevance of what they hear increases.

Purpose

Relevance and purpose for listening are closely linked. Messages in learning contexts may communicate a variety of pieces of information, understandings, and values (Gallas et al., 1996), so learners attend to messages for many reasons. Helping students recognize the multiple purposes for listening will help them attend to and use what they hear.

Listening to music for enjoyment, for example, is quite different from listening to directions for completion of an assignment. The objectives and strategies for listening differ depending on its purposes. One of the basic skills of an effective listener is to identify the purpose of a message and of listening to it. Some of the various listening purposes found in language arts instruction are described below.

Enjoyment

Students listen for creative, appreciative, and artistic reasons. Listening for enjoyment means attending and responding to events such as poetry, plays, or music. Students hear music, poetry, or other audible art, enjoy it as they listen, relate it to other experiences, and consider what they liked or did not like about the experience.

When listening for enjoyment, the listener relies on personal experience and emotional responses. One of the most relevant skills for listening for enjoyment is being able to relate the creative experience to one's own life. When students are active listeners while listening to music or poetry, their understanding is very personal. By making a personal connection, they will remember and understand the art form. It will become a part of their personal experiences that they can build upon.

Information

Informational listening is at the heart of school learning and a common listening purpose in the classroom (Funk & Funk, 1989). Students are expected to listen to and understand information related to subject matter or school activities. They listen to school announcements, research presentations, lectures, television programs, or films and are expected to remember at least some of what they have heard. Discussion is usually interspersed with listening, and older students are often required to take notes. Students' ability to listen to and learn information is crucial to their success in school.

Critical Analysis

In addition to listening and remembers, students must also engage in critical analysis of information that they hear (Funk & Funk, 1989). Critical analysis skills are vital for thinking about information and making judgments about what has been heard. Printed material is often the subject of critical analysis, but the same skills should be applied in listening situations. For children, one of the most important uses of critical analysis is to focus on the media and make critical and informed judgments about advertisements, commercials, and television shows.

Critical analysis requires students to realize that messages convey the biases and interests of their source. The idea of biases, which is vitally important in our daily lives, may be new to children. An easy way to demonstrate the importance of biases is to review a number of sources on the same topic and allow them to identify how messages vary from source to source. National and state elections are excellent opportunities to apply critical listening skills. Students can listen to different candidates talk about the same topics and analyze the biases they communicate. Students should also be asked to think about why certain messages would be conveyed in certain ways.

Informational listening, whether the speaker is the teacher or a student, is at the heart of school learning.

Procedure

Students must listen to and understand procedures. Procedural listening, also called listening to follow directions, is an important function related to instruction and communication. Listening to follow directions is almost always included in state and school language arts goals and standards. The best way to teach children to listen to follow directions is to give directions and have children repeat them, ask questions, and talk about what they are to do.

LISTENING FOR ELLs

Sitting in a classroom where the language is unfamiliar makes listening very difficult. Students who do not know English well may tune out conversations, explanations, and other interactions. Sometimes native speakers talk too fast or use too many idioms for ELLs to keep up with the conversation. Particularly when several languages are represented in one classroom, teachers may find it difficult to find resources or support for ELLs. Supporting English learners in classrooms where so many needs must be met is a challenge for any teacher. Some instructional strategies, outlined below, can help teachers meet the needs of students who are learning English as their second language.

One approach, known as sheltered instruction (Echevarria & Graves, 2004; Freeman & Freeman, 2000), uses specific strategies to present content to students in ways that promote English language development. Sheltered instruction employs high-quality instruction, integrates content area objectives, and gives careful attention to English language learners' needs. Teachers use the class curriculum but modify instructional approaches to meet the language development needs of English language learners.

Sheltered instruction supports ELLs by building their background knowledge. Activities such as looking at pictures, viewing videos and Internet sites, and making field trips help ELLs understand unfamiliar topics. Oral introduction of vocabulary and concepts is supported through pictures, concrete examples, and supportive translations by other students or parent volunteers. ELLs connect classroom learning to their own experiences by speaking and listening or by drawing pictures. Small group discussions provide an opportunity for teachers to work closely with ELLs and encourage students to experiment with listening to English presentations in a supportive environment.

To develop student confidence and promote understanding, teachers may also arrange for supplementary activities related to important topics or engage the support of specialized ESL teachers. Occasionally, it is necessary to slow down classroom discussion and instruction or to provide translation and interpretation for ELLs. Although instructional support for ELLs is not so different from what all students need when they encounter new topics and concepts, ELLs may need more concrete examples to develop concepts and additional opportunities to practice the vocabulary and language associated with the topic.

MARIA GONZALES, VETERAN TEACHER ▶ When Mrs. Gonzales, the teacher we met in the Window to the Classroom, was planning for her class to read the book *A Single Shard* (Park, 2001), she decided to try something different with the four ELLs in her classroom. Several days before she introduced the book to the class, she planned several additional activities to help the ELLs build their backgrounds and vocabularies. She met with them in a small group and together they read an informational book on pottery. They all worked on the English vocabulary associated with pottery, and she made sure that all of them were able to pronounce and understand "shard," "potter," and "clay." The group discussed pictures and read simple material that included the words. Over the next few days the small group drew pictures, wrote short sentences, and reread the informational book. Together Mrs. Gonzales and the four students developed questions to ask the guest speaker who visited their classroom to talk about making pottery. She also asked the teacher who worked regularly with her ELLs to talk with the students about Korea and pottery making. The ESL teacher found some Spanish-language websites about Korea and shared them with the three students who spoke Spanish. The student from West Africa labeled some pictures in French and English. Mrs. Gonzales felt that the students, while not totally fluent in the topic, were certainly supported by the extra work in small groups and the activities provided by the ESL teacher. They were ready to listen as she presented the book to the entire class.

Supporting ELLs

Observe how classroom teachers encourage and prepare ELLs to participate in the day-to-day activities that require listening comprehension. How do the ELLs respond? As you observe the ELLs, can you identify different language needs and abilities? Are the ELLs eager to participate in classroom activities? How can you tell? See if your teacher will allow you to work with at least one ELL to provide some additional experiences before the student begins to study a new topic, read a new book, or embark upon a new unit of study. Focus on the student's listening behaviors as you work together. How do you know the student is listening? Keep track of your experiences in a journal.

LISTENING STANDARDS AND GOALS

The importance of listening is apparent in standards for language arts instruction. The NCTE/IRA standards suggest the seamless integration of listening within the total communicative process. While they do not delineate separate listening skills, they do include some general guidelines that relate to listening. Examples of references to listening in the standards are:

> Students participate as knowledgeable, reflective, creative, and critical members of a variety of literacy communities.

> Students use spoken, written, and visual language to accomplish their own purposes (e.g., for learning, enjoyment, persuasion, and the exchange of information). (NCTE/IRA, 1996)

State and local standards frequently offer specific descriptions of listening skills. The language arts standards from the Virginia Standards of Learning provide one example of how a state has delineated listening skills in language arts instruction. The standards for grades 2, 4, and 6 illustrate the range of listening skills across the elementary curriculum (see Exhibit 3.12). It is important to note that listening skills are so closely related to speaking skills that the Virginia Standards of Learning present them within the same list.

Standards alone are not enough to guide instruction; an understanding of how students listen is also necessary. Students' ability to meet listening standards depends on their prior experiences with language. Because listening is closely related to thinking processes and is not observable, instructional needs related to listening are difficult to determine. However, children's listening processes and attitudes are evident when they interact and respond to others, and teachers must come to know their students well enough to plan appropriate listening instruction.

CLASSROOM LISTENING ACTIVITIES

Listening skills, especially those associated with learning processes, are enhanced by focusing on related language processes. Read-alouds and oral presentations *exhibit* **3.12**   *Excerpt from Virginia Standards of Learning for grades 2, 4, and 6.*

GRADE 2

The student will continue to expand listening and speaking vocabularies.

- Use words that reflect a growing range of interests and knowledge.
- Clarify and explain words and ideas orally.
- Give and follow oral directions with three or four steps.
- Identify and use synonyms and antonyms in oral communication.

GRADE 4

The student will use effective oral communication skills in a variety of settings.

- Present accurate directions to individuals and small groups.
- Contribute to group discussions.
- Seek the ideas and opinions of others.
- Begin to use evidence to support opinions.

The student will make and listen to oral presentations and reports.

- Use subject-related information and vocabulary.
- Listen to and record information.
- Organize information for clarity.

GRADE 6

The student will analyze oral participation in small-group activities.

- Communicate as leader and contributor.
- Evaluate own contributions to discussions.
- Summarize and evaluate group activities.
- Analyze the effectiveness of participant interactions.

The student will listen critically and express opinions in oral presentations.

- Distinguish between facts and opinions.
- Compare and contrast points of view.
- Present a convincing argument.

are excellent times to help students practice effective listening behaviors. Writing, drama, speaking, and sharing in small and large groups provide many opportunities for students to talk about good listening processes. Several specific activities—talking about listening, modified reading activities, and listening centers—provide opportunities to focus directly on classroom listening processes.

Talking About Listening

One way to focus on listening skills is to develop students' awareness of the listening process. It is similar to the technique used in reading instruction when readers are taught to understand and be able to explain the reading process. The teacher encourages metacognitive strategies by allowing students to talk about the listening process. Teachers focus student attention by discussing characteristics of good listeners. Concepts related to good listening should be revisited, especially if children are having a difficult time listening in certain contexts. Some teachers post rules for listening (see Exhibit 3.13 for examples).

Students are capable of evaluating their own listening experiences when teachers guide them to consider how they listen and what would improve their listening process. Discussions may also include evaluating the class's abil-

What do good listeners do?	**exhibit 3.13**

Watch the speaker.

Block distractions around them or move to where it is easier to listen.

Make connections between what the speaker is saying and their own experiences.

Predict what the message will convey.

Think of questions they might ask the speaker.

Take notes as the speaker is talking.

Summarize information as they listen.

ity to listen and setting individual and class goals for improving listening skills. Discussions such as the one Field Note 3.10 presents help students identify the situations where they listen best, become aware of their distractions, and begin to understand how they can become better listeners.

Exhibit 3.14 gives a checklist to guide discussions about listening and help children reflect on their own listening processes. As children learn about effective listening processes, and become aware of their own behavior, they establish and monitor personal listening processes. The suggestions in this exhibit serve as a scaffold for students as they learn to take more and more responsibility for monitoring their own listening processes. Short lessons, think-aloud activities, and class discussions help students learn more about listening.

Monitoring Listening Behaviors

field note 3.10

Monitor your own listening process. Keep notes in the margin of your notebook while listening in a class. Indicate when you listen the best, when you are distracted, and what the speaker does that captures your attention. Note your process of predicting, confirming, and revising. If possible, write what you first predicted and how you confirmed or revised your first predictions by continuing to listen. Make observations in a class you enjoy and in one that is less enjoyable. How are your listening behaviors different in each class? Be prepared to share your monitoring experience in class and use what you have learned to develop descriptions of effective listening contexts.

Work with a small group of students after they have taken part in a class activity in which they were expected to listen. Ask the questions in Exhibit 3.14. What conditions distracted their listening, and what encouraged them to listen? Think about the implications for classroom listening; share your thoughts with your peers.

exhibit 3.14 *A checklist for monitoring the listening process.*

☐ Did I listen to what was being said? If I didn't, it was because

   ☐ I heard it before.

   ☐ it wasn't interesting.

   ☐ I didn't understand it.

   ☐ I was sleepy or I didn't feel well.

   ☐ I couldn't see the speaker.

   ☐ I was uncomfortable. It was too hot or too cold.

   ☐ I needed to move around.

☐ I was very interested in the topic because

   ☐ the information was exciting.

   ☐ I can use the information to do something I want to do.

   ☐ I understood most of what I heard.

   ☐ I enjoyed listening.

   ☐ I asked questions and responded to what I heard.

☐ I was distracted because

   ☐ something was happening at home that bothered me.

   ☐ there was noise in the classroom.

   ☐ my school work kept me from listening.

   ☐ I was hungry or sleepy.

☐ Sometimes I am an effective listener,

   ☐ when I have complete silence except for what I'm listening to.

   ☐ even when there is other noise around.

   ☐ when I am listening to enjoy, follow directions, hear new information, or make some judgments.

What can I do to improve listening the next time?

_____

_____

_____

Role-playing is one way to get children to talk about listening. The teacher describes a situation, such as disruptive behavior during a class discussion, and selects students to act it out for the rest of the class. Students might take turns in each role, either mimicking poor listening behavior or responding to it. After children have role-played the situation and considered several options to solve the problem, the teacher discusses alternatives with the class and points out how the class can improve on their listening skills.

Modified Reading Activities

Listening is embedded in most language arts teaching and learning activities. It is difficult to find ready-made, structured activities that focus explicitly on listening, but modifying reading activities is one way to create guided listening instruction. It is relatively easy to substitute listening for reading and present an effective instructional structure that improves listening comprehension. Two traditional reading comprehension strategies, the directed listening–thinking activity (DL–TA) and KWL, are easily adapted to focus on listening comprehension.

Directed Listening–Thinking Activity

The directed listening–thinking activity (DL–TA) introduces new listening topics, helps students comprehend what is presented, and provides follow-up to oral texts. In the DL–TA, the listener (1) determines the purpose for listening, (2) extracts, comprehends, and assimilates information during the process, (3) examines listening material based on the purpose for listening, (4) suspends judgments, and (5) makes decisions based on information gleaned from listening. The DL–TA is an effective process to use while listening to a speaker, listening to a read-aloud, or watching a film or multimedia presentation. The structure of the DL–TA provides a great deal of support to the listener before, during, and after the listening event. Note that it requires the speaker or presentation to be stopped at several points. The example below is from a read-aloud, but the same process would apply to other kinds of listening activities.

Before the listening activity. The teacher begins by asking students what the story or presentation they are going to hear is about and recording students' predictions. The students and teacher make connections between their predictions and their own experiences. When Mrs. Gonzales first introduced the book *A Single Shard* (Park, 2001), she read the title of the book, showed her students the front cover, and asked them to predict what the book would be about. The cover showed a large, green vase with a crane and the face of an Asian boy looking through bamboo. Students predicted that the story would be about a Japanese boy who loved cranes. They also thought the boy looked sad and predicted the story would talk about why he was sad. As they continued to make predictions, Mrs. Gonzales wrote their ideas on chart paper. After she and the class listed five or six predictions, she asked them about the word "shard." One student predicted that shard was a Japanese word, and someone else predicted it meant something was burned. After discussing the possible meanings of "shard" and writing the students' predicted definitions on chart paper, Mrs. Gonzales began reading the first chapter of the book aloud.

During the listening activity. Next, students listen to the beginning of a read-aloud story or a presentation. They confirm, reject, or modify their original predictions based on the additional information they hear. The read-aloud continues with the students predicting, listening, and reacting to predictions.

The first sentence that Mrs. Gonzales read was the opening of Chapter 1: "A small village on the west coast of Korea, mid to late twelfth century." This excerpt provided important information related to the class's predictions. Mrs. Gonzales stopped reading, and her students amended their predictions and developed new ones. Mrs. Gonzales wrote down three new predictions about the remainder of the chapter and started reading again, and the class listened to find out if their predictions were right. She stopped reading two more times, each time asking about the predictions, clarifying concepts, and discussing important vocabulary. Occasionally when her students made a prediction, she would ask, "What makes you think that will happen?" or "What happened in the story so far that provides you evidence that this is a good prediction?"

After the listening activity. After listening to the story or presentation, students talk about the information presented, focusing on vocabulary and phrases that puzzle or intrigue them. They also take time to discuss the listening process.

After students listened to the first chapter of *A Single Shard* (Park, 2001), Mrs. Gonzales led a discussion about their initial predictions to confirm, amend, or clarify them. As students developed new predictions about the remainder of the story, she asked them to describe what is was about the chapter that led them to make those predictions. She also introduced some of the vocabulary, including the word *shard,* and began clarifying the concepts behind the word. After determining that most of her students had listened well to the reading and had developed an interest in continuing the story, she gave a copy of the book to each student. By using the DL–TA structure and reading the first chapter, Mrs. Gonzales had succeeded in introducing the book, developing some basic concepts, and creating interest in continuing to read the book.

KWL

A common classroom instructional strategy, KWL, guides listening behavior by helping students focus on their prior knowledge, their interest, and the information they are learning as they listen to a book read aloud or watch a speaker, film, television show, or other production. To develop a KWL chart, students divide a sheet of paper into three columns, using the column headings shown in Exhibit 3.15. Under the heading *K,* students write about what they already *know* about the topic. Under *W,* they write about what they *want or need* to learn during the listening opportunity. After they participate in a lesson, complete research, or read materials, they complete the *L* column and reflect on what they have *learned.* As students fill out the chart, they discuss the topic, listen to each other, and establish purposes for listening. As they listen to find out the answers to their ques-

exhibit 3.15   *KWL chart.*

What do I **KNOW** about this topic?	What do I **WANT** to know?	What have I **LEARNED**?

tions, they monitor and evaluate their own listening process. KWL was designed primarily as a strategy to guide reading and research, but it works well to guide classroom listening processes, too.

Let's consider how Mrs. Gonzales facilitated comprehension through a listening process related to the reading of *A Single Shard* (Park, 2001). The day after reading the first chapter of the book to her class, she shared an informational book with them about Korea. Before she read the book to them, she asked her students to brainstorm what they knew about Korea, and she listed everything they said, including misconceptions. Next she asked her students, "What are some questions you want to ask about Korea?" Her students listed several things, such as, "What do people who live in Korea eat? What are they called? Do their children go to school? Does everyone make pottery?" After the students listened to the informational text read aloud, they listed what they learned during the reading. Mrs. Gonzales was particularly careful to discuss some of the misconceptions her students held at the beginning of the activity.

The DL–TA and KWL provided structures to guide Mrs. Gonzales' students' listening and helped her gauge what her students knew about the topic and their level of interest in the story. The DL–TA and KWL share some common traits. They both involve children in establishing the reasons for listening, and they both provide a format for teachers to check students' understanding after a listening activity. The DL–TA, however, provides more opportunities for teacher support throughout the listening activity, whereas the KWL activity depends more on student input and ideas. The DL–TA would be particularly effective with ELLs and students who do not have a great deal of experience or background with the listening topic. The KWL is a good way to begin a unit of study whereby students will continue to research and learn about the listening topic. Both activities are flexible, and teachers will find that they are easily modified.

Listening Centers

The listening center is a valuable instructional strategy that engages students in independent listening opportunities. Headsets, tape recorders, video cassette recorders, and other audiovisual equipment are placed in a corner of the room designated as a listening center. Students may explore books through audiovisual materials or listen to taped stories repeatedly. If more sophisticated audiovisual equipment is available, movies and television clips may be included in the listening center. Listening centers allow students to listen to supplemental materials that build their background of experiences. They are an especially valuable resource for ELLs, who benefit from multiple readings of books, exposure to information prior to whole-class presentations, and viewing films that provide visuals and sound as an introduction to a topic. A listening center provides opportunities for listening for enjoyment, or it can focus on helping children listen for information or other purposes.

field note

3.11

Listening Center

Design a listening center relevant to the curriculum that's being taught in your classroom. Consult with your mentor teacher to get ideas for your center. Plan several listening activities that children can do independently. Activities might include listening to a book on tape, following verbal directions, or responding to music. Collect student responses to the activities you planned and use them to reflect on the effectiveness of the activities.

FINAL REFLECTIONS

Listening is a process that is individual and unique. The best instructional activities provide ample opportunities for students to listen and take part in meaningful interactions. Students should listen for a variety of purposes and respond in various ways. In addition to providing times for students to talk and listen and practice effective listening strategies, teachers should encourage students to monitor their own listening behavior. At first teachers will want to play a guiding role in the process, but as children understand more and more about the process, they should be given more independence in setting purposes, responding to messages, and analyzing their listening processes.

Promoting active listening in the classroom will result in better learning. Not only should students be engaged in what is said, they should also have opportunities to apply the information that they hear in a variety of activities. Linking oral communication to students' learning reflects the fact that the listening process is central to how students learn, think, and develop in your classroom.

PROFESSIONAL REFLECTIONS

Review the Field Notes from this chapter and develop one or more into a component of your portfolio. To continue to reflect on your Field Note responses, consider the following suggestions:

- Create a representation of what you have learned about the culture and the language in the community where your school is located. The representation might be a collection of photographs, a video, a painting, a set of poems, or a collage.
- Evaluate each of the instructional activities that you designed and presented in your classroom. Make changes based on the feedback you received from children, your cooperating teachers, your university professor, and your classmates and on your own reflections. Include the revised lesson plan in your portfolio.

Professional Readings

The following books can expand your understanding of the content of this chapter.

Cooper, P., & Morreale, S. (Eds.). (2003). *Creating competent communicators: Activities for teaching speaking, listening, and media literacy in K–6 classrooms.* Scottsdale, AZ: Holcomb Hathaway.

The teaching activities in this resource have been tested in communication classrooms and found to be successful in helping students develop competencies in the fundamentals of communication, speaking, listening, and media literacy. The activities involve students in sending and receiving messages in a variety of contexts for a variety of purposes and provide for student interaction and involvement—important components of oral communication skill development. In addition, these activities make it easy for a teacher to integrate oral communication instruction across the curriculum.

Gambrell, L. B., & Almasi, J. F. (Eds.). (1996). *Lively discussions! Fostering engaged reading.* Newark, DE: International Reading Association.

The authors of this helpful text provide classroom strategies that integrate discussion with other language arts activities. It includes many descriptions of how teachers can increase comprehension and interpretation skills through discussion. You will not find a more thorough discussion of classroom discussion techniques.

 Select one of the following children's literature books, read it, and reflect on the lessons it offers you as a future teacher about creating a classroom environment and learning community. Share your book and insights with a small group of your peers.

Children's Books

Ackerman, K. (1988). *Song and dance man.* Illustrated by S. Gammel. New York: Alfred A. Knopf.

This book talks about oral performance and expression within a family context. A grandfather who is an old vaudeville performer tells about his experiences on stage. He coordinates a performance involving his grandchildren.

Feelings, M. (1974). *Jambo means hello.* Illustrated by T. Feelings. New York: Dial.

This award-winning counting book has words in both Swahili and English. It introduces adults and children to the music of different languages.

Jacobs, H. (Ed.). (1992). *Cajun Night Before Christmas.* Illustrated by J. Rice. Gretna, LA: Pelican.

In this book a series of versions of "Night Before Christmas" present the dialects of different parts of our country. The book serves as a good example of how the same story may be expressed in different ways. It would also be a good book for discussing dialects and language codes.

Other children's books mentioned in this chapter are:

Fleischmann, P. (1988). *Joyful noise: Poems for two voices.* Illustrated by E. Beddows. New York: Harper Collins.

Garza, C. L. (1990). *Family pictures: Cuadros de familia.* San Francisco: Children's Book Press.

Griego, M. C., Bucks, B. L., Gilbert, S. S. & Kimball, L. H. (1981). *Tortillitas para mama and other nursery rhymes.* Illustrated by B. Cooney. New York: Henry Holt.

Johnson, A. (1989). *Tell me a story, Mama.* New York: Orchard Books.

Park, L. S. (2001). *A single shard.* New York: Dell Yearling.

Paterson, K. (1978). *The great Gilly Hopkins.* New York: Avon.

Rosen, M. (1989). *We're going on a bear hunt.* Illustrated by H. Oxenbury. New York: Margaret K. McElderry Books.

REFERENCES

Almasi, J. F. (1995). *The nature of fourth graders' socio-cognitive conflicts in peer-led discussions of literature* (Research Report No. 12). Athens, GA: University of Maryland and Georgia, National Reading Research Center.

Anderson, G. L., & Irvine, P. (1993). Informing critical literacy with ethnography. In C. Lankshear & P. McLaren (Eds.), *Critical literacy: Politics, praxis, and the postmodern* (pp. 81–104). Albany, NY: SUNY Press.

Baker, C. (2001). *Foundations of bilingual education and bilingualism* (3rd ed.). Clevedon, UK: Multicultural Matters Ltd.

Barrentine, S. J. (1996). Engaging with reading through interactive read-alouds. *Reading Teacher, 50,* 36–43.

Bloome, D., Harris, L. H., & Ludlum, D. E. (1991). Reading and writing as sociocultural activities: Politics and pedagogy in the classroom. *Topics in Language Disorders, 11,* 14–27.

Brent, R., & Anderson, P. (1993). Developing children's classroom listening strategies. *Reading Teacher, 47,* 122–126.

Brisk, M. E. (1998). *Bilingual education: From compensatory to quality schooling.* Mahwah, NJ: Lawrence Erlbaum Associates.

Brookfield, S. D., & Preskill, S. (1999). *Discussion as a way of learning: Tools and techniques for democratic classrooms.* San Francisco: Jossey-Bass.

Bruner, J. (1974). *Beyond the information given: Studies in the psychology of knowing.* London: George Allen & Unwin.

Bruner, J. S. (1977). *The process of education.* Cambridge, MA: Harvard University Press.

Compton-Lilly, C. (2000). "Staying on children": Challenging stereotypes about urban parents. *Language Arts, 77,* 420–428.

Daniels, H. (1994). *Literature circles: Voice and choice in a student-centered classroom.* Portland, ME: Stenhouse.

Delgado-Gaitan, C. (1990). *Literacy for empowerment: The role of parents in children's education.* New York: Falmer Press.

Delpit, L. (1992). Education in a multicultural society: Our future's greatest challenge. *Journal of Negro Education, 61,* 237–249.

Delpit, L. (1995). *Other people's children: Cultural conflict in the classroom.* New York: New Press.

Dugan, J. (1997). Transactional literature discussions: Engaging students in the appreciation and understanding of literature. *Reading Teacher, 51,* 86–96.

Echevarria, J., & Graves, A. (1997). *Sheltered content instruction: Teaching English language learners with diverse abilities.* Upper Saddle River, NJ: Pearson Allyn & Bacon.

Flynn, R. M., & Carr, G. (1994). Exploring classroom literature through drama: A specialist and teacher collaborate. *Language Arts, 71,* 38–43.

Forest, J. (1997). Music technology helps students succeed. *Music Educators Journal 81,* 35–38.

Freeman, D. E., & Freeman, Y. S. (2000). *Teaching reading in multilingual classrooms.* Portsmouth, NH: Heinemann.

Funk, H. D., & Funk, G. D. (1989). Guidelines for developing listening skills. *Reading Teacher, 42,* 660–663.

Gallas, K., Anton-Oldenburg, M., Ballenger, C., Beseler, C., Griffin, S., Papperheimer, R., & Swaim, J. (1996). Talking the talk and walking the walk: Researching oral language in the classroom. *Language Arts, 73,* 608–617.

Gambrell, L. B., & Almasi, J. F. (Eds.). (1996). *Lively discussions! Fostering engaged reading.* Newark, DE: International Reading Association.

Gasparro, M., & Falletta, B. (1994). *Creating drama with poetry: Teaching English as a second language through dramatization and improvisation* (Eric Identifier ED368214). Washington, DC: ERIC Clearinghouse on Language and Linguistics.

Gee, J. (1992). Social cultural approach to literacy (literacies). In W. Grabe (Ed.), *Annual review of applied linguistics* (pp. 31–48). Cambridge: Cambridge University Press.

Halliday, M. A. K. (1969–1970). Relevant models of language. *Educational Review, 22,* 26–37.

Halliday, M. A. K. (1975). *Learning how to mean: Explorations in the development of language.* New York: Elsevier.

Heath, S. B. (1983). *Ways with words: Language, life, and work in communities and classrooms.* New York: Cambridge.

Heath, S. B. (1982). What no bedtime story means: Narrative skills at home and school. *Language in Society, 11*(1), 49–76.

Honeyghan, G. (2000). Rhythm of the Caribbean: Connecting oral history and literacy. *Language Arts, 77,* 406–413.

Hoyt, L. (1992). Many ways of knowing: Using drama, oral interactions, and the visual arts to enhance reading comprehension. *Reading Teacher, 45,* 580–584.

Hyslop, N. B., & Tone, B. (1988). *Listening: Are we teaching it, and if so, how?* (ERIC Identifier ED295132). East Lansing, MI: National Center for Research on Teacher Learning.

Jewell, T. A., & Pratt, D. (1999). Literature discussions in the primary grades: Children's thoughtful discourse about books and what teachers do to make it happen. *Reading Teacher, 52,* 842–850.

Larson, B. E. (1999). Influences on social studies teachers' use of classroom discussion. *Social Studies, 9,* 125–132.

Leal, D. J. (1996). Transforming grand creations: Using different types of texts to influence student discussion. In L. B. Gambrell & J. F. Almasi (Eds.), *Lively discussions* (pp. 149–168). Newark, DE: International Reading Association.

Martinez, M., Roser, N. L., & Strecker, S. (1998/1999). "I never thought I could be a star": A readers theater ticket to fluency. *Reading Teacher, 52,* 326–334.

McGinley, W., & Kamberelis, G. (1996). "Maniac Magee" and "Ragtime Tumpie": Children negotiating self and world through reading and writing. *Research in the Teaching of English, 30*(1), 75–113.

Mead, N. A., & Rubin, D. L. (1985). *Assessing listening and speaking skills.* (ERIC Identifier ED263626). East Lansing, MI: National Center for Research on Teacher Learning.

Meier, D. R. (2000). *Scribble Scrabble—learning to read and write: Success with diverse teachers, children, and families.* New York: Teachers College Press.

Minami, M., & Ovando, C. (1995). Language issues in multicultural contexts. In J. A. Banks & C. M. Banks (Eds.), *Handbook of research on multicultural education.* New York: Macmillan.

Moffett, J., & Wagner, B. J. (1992). *Student-centered language arts, K–12.* Portsmouth, NH: Boynton/Cook.

Moll, L. (1992). Funds of knowledge for teaching: Using a qualitative approach to connect homes and classrooms. *Theory into Practice, 31*(2), 132–141.

Moll, L. C., & Gonzales, N. (1994). Critical issues: Lessons learned from research with language-minority children. *Journal of Literacy Research, 26,* 429–456.

Morrow, L. (2001, 2005 in progress). *Literacy development in the early years* (3rd/4th ed.). Boston: Allyn & Bacon.

Murphy, S., & Dudley-Marling, C. (2000). Editors' pages. *Language Arts, 77,* 380–381.

National Council of Teachers of English/IRA. (1996). *Guidelines for the preparation of teachers of English/language arts.* Urbana, IL: Author.

Pang, V. O. (2001). *Multicultural education: A caring-centered, reflective approach.* Boston: McGraw-Hill.

Payne, R. K. (1996). *A framework for understanding poverty.* Highlands, TX: aha! Process.

Patthey-Chavez, G. G., et al. (1995). *Creating a community of scholarship with instructional conversations in a transitional bilingual classroom* (Educational Practice Report 15). Washington, DC: National Center for Research on Cultural Diversity and Second Language Learning.

Peterson, R., & Eeds, M. (1990). *Grand conversations: Literature groups in action.* Toronto, ON: Scholastic-TAB.

Purcell-Gates, V. (1995). *Other people's words: The cycle of low literacy.* Cambridge, MA: Harvard University Press.

Shepard, A. (Ed.). (1993). *Stories on stage: scripts for reader's theater.* Bronx, NY: H. W. Wilson.

Simich-Dudgeon, C. (1998). Classroom strategies for encouraging collaborative discussion. *Directions in Language and Education, 12,* 1–13.

Taylor, D. (1983). *Family literacy: Young children learning to read and write.* Exeter, NH: Heinemann.

Taylor, D., & Dorsey-Gaines, C. (1988). *Growing up literate: Learning from inner-city families.* Portsmouth, NH: Heinemann.

Templeton, S. (1991). *Teaching the integrated language arts.* Boston: Houghton Mifflin.

Tompkins, G. E., & McGee, L. M. (1993). *Teaching reading with literature: Case studies to action plans.* New York: Merrill.

Vacca, R. T., Vacca, J. L., & Bruneau, B. (1997). Teachers reflecting on practice. In J. Flood, S. B. Heath, & D. Lapp (Eds.), *Handbook of research on teaching literacy through the communicative and visual arts* (pp. 445–450). New York: Macmillan.

Vogt, M. E. (Ed.). (1996). *Creating a response-centered curriculum with literature discussion groups.* Newark, DE: International Reading Association.

Voss, M. M. (1993). "I just watched": Family influences on one child's learning. *Language Arts, 70,* 632–641.

Vygotsky, L. S. (1978). *Mind in society: The development of higher psychological processes.* Cambridge, MA: Harvard University Press.

Wan, G. (2000). A Chinese girl's storybook experience at home. *Language Arts, 77,* 398–405.

Wax, W. (Ed.). (1993). *Hanukkah, oh Hanukkah!: A treasury of stories, songs, and games to share.* Illustrated by J. Speirs. New York: Bantam Doubleday Dell.

Wells, G. (1986). *The meaning makers, children learning language and using language to learn.* Portsmouth, NH: Heinemann.

Wolf, S., Edmiston, B., & Enciso, P. (1996). Drama worlds: Places on the heart, head, voice, and hand in dramatic interpretation. In J. Flood, S. B. Heath, & D. Lapp (Eds.), *Handbook of research on teaching literacy through the communicative and visual arts* (pp. 492–505). New York: Macmillan.

Wray, D., & Medwell, J. (1991). *Literacy and language in the primary years.* London: Routledge.

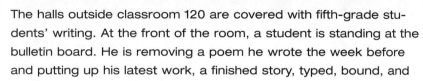
The halls outside classroom 120 are covered with fifth-grade students' writing. At the front of the room, a student is standing at the bulletin board. He is removing a poem he wrote the week before and putting up his latest work, a finished story, typed, bound, and illustrated, ready for others to enjoy. He proudly clips the story next to his picture and name and stands back from his work, admiring his story. The classroom behind him is buzzing with conversations. Small groups and individual students are all around the room.

The teacher is sitting at a round table, guiding a small group of students working on their personal pieces of writing. These students are using dialogue in their stories, and they are talking about how to use quotation marks and how they were used in the novels they have been reading during silent reading time. Some of the students are adding dialogue to their own stories.

At the back of the room, two students are working together. They sit on beanbag chairs and hold clipboards in their laps. One student is reading a draft of his newest composition out loud as his classmate checks off the tasks they have accomplished together on a peer conference sheet. When her partner

WRITING

finishes reading the story aloud, the listener tells her classmate about the parts she liked in the story and asks questions about parts that are not clear.

Students are sitting at their desks and in the quiet space separated from the rest of the classroom by bookshelves, composing the beginnings of their next writing projects. Students share their finished drafts, draw illustrations, and write new stories. One student gets up to pull out a book to read for ideas for her own stories. She leafs through her favorite picture book, *The Relatives Came* (Rylant, 1993), and thinks about how to describe her own family gathering during the holidays.

After the students have worked on their writing projects for half an hour, the teacher calls the students together. Three children have published books and are ready to sit in the author's chair to read their work to their classmates. After

each author reads, the children clap and raise their hands to provide feedback. The author selects three students to give positive feedback on his work. After one person has read and received feedback, the next student gets up to sit in the author's chair.

Everyone in this classroom writes and shares. Those who are confident of their writing process work independently. Students with less experience or those learning English meet often with the teacher. All students prepare to publish their writing and share it with others, regardless of their experience or proficiency with English and writing. As a result, every student receives feedback and gains a feeling of pride and achievement.

INTRODUCTION

Writing is an integral component of communication and learning. It is an important measure of a literate person and the focus of much attention in language arts instruction. Language arts instruction supports and builds on the development of written expression that begins during the preschool years. Writing instruction constantly balances teacher-guided and student-centered activities. On the one hand, writing skills improve when students choose relevant topics, produce text, edit their work, and share it with audiences. On the other hand, students also respond to explicit instruction in the skills and knowledge—such as spelling, grammar, and vocabulary—that make their writing meaningful to others. Students also need to know how to use the wide variety of tools and technology that can help them produce written texts.

GUIDING QUESTIONS

Consider these questions as you read this chapter. Jot down your initial responses to each question. After reading the articles, revisit your responses. Would you make any changes to them? If so, what would those changes be? Discuss your responses with one or more of your classmates, your professor, or your mentor teacher.

1. What behaviors do children exhibit as they are learning how to write? How are writing behaviors supported in the classroom?

2. What processes do students use to produce meaningful and relevant written communication?

3. What instructional strategies encourage authentic classroom writing?

4. How do students learn writing conventions and skills in a language arts curriculum?

5. How is technology used to enhance the writing process?

Early Writing

In a literate society, most children have opportunities to observe how print is used and to participate and interact with others during literacy activities (Lu, 2000). Children learn from the print they encounter in their daily routines, including street signs, food labels, and commercial advertisements (McGee & Richgels, 1990). They learn a great deal about writing from being read to, experimenting with paper and pencil, interacting with media, and observing how their parents and others use print. Their exposure to print starts them on the road to learning many aspects of literacy, including writing. In most cases, a growth in print awareness and the acquisition of writing occur so naturally that many adults are surprised once they realize how much children know and understand about print and related concepts.

WRITING ACQUISITION

We expect students to come to school with a literacy foundation that supports and values learning about print. In most areas of our society, families and communities hold a certain view of the role of print which is transferred to young writers. Children come to school with definite ideas about writing (Glazer & Burke, 1994) based on how language is used at home, in their communities, and among their friends (Taylor, 1998). When the family and the community value writing, writing development can start long before formal school instruction (Morrow, 2001). Not only do students have ideas about writing, but they also use print in various ways and arrive at school ready to make literary attempts that express their ideas. Even so, teachers should be prepared for a wide range of acceptance, knowledge, and ideas about print and know that some children will need to begin at different places on the continuum of learning to write.

Talking and drawing accompany early writing attempts as children experiment with print and engage in a type of literate play (Wiseman, 2003). Experimentation and play provide opportunities for young children to test their hypotheses about how language is produced and used. Children continue their own development by inventing ways of making letters, words, and meaning (Graves, 1994). Most important, they intend for their early attempts at print production to make sense and convey their thoughts and ideas. Continued experiences with producing, observing, and interacting with others about print contribute to an ever-evolving knowledge of print and print production (Templeton, 1995).

A teacher who understands how children progress through early writing development can more accurately perceive what a young student knows and understands about print and determine what instruction is appropriate. This article outlines research on the stages of writing development during the early childhood years.

Patterns of Writing Development

From a very early age, children want and need to communicate, and their attempts to use language arise from the need and intention to make their thoughts and wishes known to others. Children learn language to get things done—by explaining, imagining, requesting, protesting, or asserting. Children's writing development is part of their process of learning how to mean (Halliday, 1975) by understanding, using, and making various symbols. Children progress through at least five stages as they begin to understand and produce print (Gentry, 1984) and develop an intention for conveying their thoughts and ideas. The stages may emerge differently, but an experienced teacher of young students can generally expect specific types of behaviors as children learn how to write.

Prephonetic

Until they learn the differences between writing and drawing, some young writers express their ideas by drawing pictures (Sulzby, 1986). Young writers who are learning that writing and drawing are different may "read" pictures as if they are reading print. Their pictures are often accompanied by scribbles. Although early attempts or "play" writing may look like make-believe or scribbles, drawings and writing products quickly become attempts to convey a thought, an idea, or a story. Children who scribble often use the same behaviors as do adults who are writing. They hold the pencil and move as if they were producing letters. Eventually, they produce scribbles with the intention of telling a story or conveying a message and may "read" what they have written.

As children learn more about print, their scribbling begins to include letter-like figures (Sulzby, 1986). They produce lines and shapes like those used in conventional letters, but the creative forms look different. It is at this time that young writers are developing an awareness of print. The understanding that ideas are represented by print impacts both reading and writing and is characterized by children's development of several different concepts (Clay, 1979). First, young readers and writers learn that the features making up letters are combined to make new letters. For example, the lines that make an "H" are used with other lines to make a "B" or a "T". They also learn about recurring letters and note that letters are used in messages over and over. Finally, they become aware that letters are combined in various ways to make different words and texts. See Exhibit 4.1 for an example of prephonetic writing, in which some letters appear along with other shapes and scribbles. The teacher has written in the student's "translation" of her words.

Children are capable of creating their own meaning through scribbles, letter-like shapes, and conventional letters and often read to you what they have written. This stage may start when children are as young as 1 to $1^1/_2$ years old and may still be observed during early school ages. As children continue to interact with print, their experimentation continues: they change letter order in familiar words such as their names, repeat known letters, and produce strings of letters learned from familiar sources such as their names. The print

In this example of prephonetic writing, letters begin to appear. (The teacher has added "translations" of the child's writing.)   *exhibit*   **4.1**

In this example of prephonetic writing, letters begin to appear. (The teacher has added "translations" of the child's writing.)

they produce begins to match up with spoken language more systematically, as Ericka demonstrated when she produced the following sentence:

IHRADIKDALSNO (I hate rain and I kind of like snow.)

During the prephonetic stage, children need to develop strong connections between words and print. Children at this stage enjoy listening to stories, looking through books on their own, and using writing implements to scribble unconventional symbols (Bear & Templeton, 1998). Read-aloud sessions and writing down stories dictated by children are two important activities that help young students understand that meaning is conveyed by words and visual representations. They should experience numerous opportunities to convey meaning while experimenting with letters and symbol production.

Adult interaction is important for continued experimentation with print. Young students develop knowledge about words and print when they are encouraged to use their evolving knowledge of letters and letter sounds to write meaningful messages (Rhodes & Dudley-Marling, 1996). Adult interest in what they are doing encourages their experimentation and helps them develop an expectation that their writing has something to say. Talking to children about their writing implies that teachers or others expect them to make sense when they are producing print.

Phonemic

As children continue their experimentation with writing and engage in various literacy activities, their knowledge about writing continues to emerge and can be concretely observed in their print productions. Their attempts at expressing ideas become more conventional. They begin to use the dominant letters in a word they are attempting to spell. For example, a child may write "wt" for *write* or "mr" for *monster*. It is typical for children at this stage to write their names, identify some words, know that words are made up of specific letters, and use letters to represent words in messages they produce (Bear & Templeton, 1998). Some children display this behavior early during their preschool years, but it is also typical to observe phonemic spellings in kindergarten and first graders' writing.

When students produce phonemic spellings, it is important to encourage them to express their ideas and help them make connections between letters and sounds while at the same time responding to the conventional spellings that begin to show up in their printed productions (Rhodes & Dudley-Marling, 1996). They are able to express their ideas, write letters and read them back, print their name, and write words. Adult guidance should continually focus on the ideas children wish to express as well as their knowledge of letters and print. Continued exposure to print through reading aloud, dictated stories, and talking about letters and words is appropriate for students at this stage. Making writing tools available to children often motivates them to try their hand at writing. The changes in young writers' production of print are visible, and children's ideas become more complex as they continue to develop literacy abilities.

Phonetic

When adults and others respond to the messages and intentions of children's early print production, they provide motivation for children's continued exploration. Increasing sophistication in speaking and listening is reflected in the ideas children express with print. Reading also teaches them a more sophisticated understanding of letters and phonetics. Children at the phonetic stage use a letter or group of letters to represent every speech sound that they hear in a word. Although some of their choices do not conform to conventional English spelling, they are systematic and easily understood, and these efforts demonstrate what the children understand about written communication. For example, children might spell the word *write* as "writ," and *train* might be "tran"—representing the sounds they hear as they pronounce the words, and often omitting letters they do not hear. Vowels in major syllables and blends and diagraphs begin to appear in their writing (Bear & Templeton, 1998).

Children do not always think about phonetics as adults do. They will use vowels in their spellings, but they may substitute or slot one vowel for another (Beers, 1980). Vowel slotting is common in printed products of young writers. One first grader substituted vowels as he wrote

I'M rollre skateing vare her so mi Foot is herteen

(I'm roller skating very hard, so my foot is hurting.)

Adults should view beginning spelling attempts as progress and provide guidance and support to encourage young writers' continued development. The words they produce look like conventional spelling, and when adults recognize that children intend to produce meaningful messages, it is possible to interpret what they are writing.

The most obvious way to support young writers at this stage of writing is to focus on what they intend to mean, respond to their messages, and enjoy their development. Playing with magnetic letters and putting words together, identifying known words in printed materials, and continuing to write with conventional and developmental spellings all support the writing development of young children. If children start school during this phase of devel-

Young students develop knowledge about words and print when they are encouraged to use their evolving knowledge of letters and letter sounds to write meaningful messages.

opment, they will receive teacher-directed instruction about phonics and phonemic awareness and become aware of word patterns, combinations of words, and other conventions. Reading aloud, dictated stories, and talking about words and letters also contribute a great deal to children's writing development during the phonetic stage of writing.

One of the interesting behaviors during the phonetic stage is that children often become hesitant to experiment with writing. Once they've learned about traditional spellings and word orders, they develop the desire to spell conventionally and they know that they are not always doing so. They need to be reassured that their own spelling will continue to improve as they continue to read and write (Rhodes & Dudley-Marling, 1996).

LIANNE, VETERAN TEACHER ▶ When students are learning to spell and I want to encourage them to try invented spellings on their own, I talk to them about "kid writing." Students develop an awareness that there is a right way to spell, but I don't want them to stop writing because they are too worried about getting the correct spelling. Kid writing is when the child uses invented spelling. Sometimes I have the class sound out and spell a word together. I accept their spelling and let them know that it is good kid writing. Sometimes I spell the word correctly and tell them that the spelling I am giving them is "conventional."

Viewpoint

TEACHER

Transitional

As literate behaviors continue to emerge, the messages that young writers produce look more and more like what adults produce. Children's ideas become more complex and sophisticated, cover a wider range of purposes and genres, and become more flexible. The way they present their ideas approaches a conventional presentation and becomes easier for adults to translate. Adults must reach a balance between focusing on the non-conventional aspects of young writers' productions and attending to the ideas they want to convey. Young students' writing is best supported when adults seek to find out what they are attempting to communicate and respond appropriately to their thoughts and ideas.

It is very easy to recognize growth in spelling behavior. Spelling that is closer to conventional spelling demonstrates increasing understanding of letter–sound correspondence. As children continue to learn about letters and sounds, they use their understanding of vowel and consonant sounds, but they tend to overgeneralize. For example, a child who has learned that a word like "bake" ends in "e" will not omit the "e" when adding a suffix such as "ing," and the word will be spelled "bakeing." During this time, students develop an understanding of complex letter patterns and begin to spell multisyllabic words in their written work (Bear & Templeton, 1998).

This is a good time to introduce word games and to study word derivations and other relationships between words (Rhodes & Dudley-Marling, 1996). Children need to practice identifying where words came from and observing how prefixes and suffixes are used to change meanings. Vowel and consonant patterns, word structures, and meanings are appropriate topics. However, any focus on language conventions should have meaning-making as its purpose.

Conventional

With support, interaction with adults, and opportunities to write about ideas that are important and relevant, not only does children's ability to convey sophisticated messages and meanings expand, but they also reflect a growing knowledge of conventions of print. At this stage, the writer knows how to deal with such things as prefixes and suffixes, silent consonants, alternative spellings, and irregular spellings. The young speller accumulates a large number of learned words and recognizes incorrect forms. At this stage, children's generalizations about spelling and identification of exceptions are usually correct. When they spell correctly many of the words they use regularly in their writing, then they are ready to study connections among words, use a dictionary, and select among similar words to convey what they are trying to say (Bear & Templeton, 1998).

Continued opportunities to experiment and refine what they are learning are important to young writers. Writing and spelling development are reflexive: even when most words are spelled conventionally, young writers may revert to prior stages as they experiment with new vocabulary words, spelling patterns, and prefixes and suffixes. They may confuse vowels, for example, as they learn to spell new words. This is a natural progression that teachers should observe but not emphasize. It is simply part of the learning process!

During the elementary school years, writers continue to develop their abilities in other ways, too. They become more aware of audience. At first they only write for themselves. Then they write for a specific audience, such as a parent, teacher, or friend. As their writing matures, they realize that it is possible to communicate with and entertain others through their writing (Lu, 2000). With practice, guidance, and engagement, their writing becomes more coherent and organized. Writers also become more flexible and comfortable producing multiple forms and genres of writing. They use stories, reports, letters, notes, and e-mails to tell their stories, communicate their feelings, and maintain contact with others.

Learning About "Making Meaning"

Young students' ability to tell stories is closely related to their ability to write (Martens, 1996). Beginning readers and writers choose to interact repeatedly with stories that they enjoy. They may reread a book, memorizing parts of the story, illustrating the story, copying the text, or dramatizing the story. Adults provide support for this important aspect of literacy by encouraging such activities. Repeated readings may be provided by audio-taped versions of favorite stories. Older children have repeated reading opportunities when they are recruited to read stories to younger children. They enjoy talking about and retelling the stories they have read. One way to encourage retellings is through the use of felt boards. Characters made from paper or cloth with a piece of felt on the back can be attached to a felt board and used as a visual aid to help children re-tell stories. Students can also use the felt pieces to create new adventures for the characters.

Students who are beginning the writing and reading process typically learn through verbalizing and interacting with others during their reading and composing process. Many students use verbal "think-alouds" and may be highly social as they begin writing (Wiseman, 2003). For example, Steven, a kindergarten student who has decided to write during center time, sits at a table with paper and crayons while he draws a picture and writes letters on his paper. As he works on his story, he speaks to the characters and talks to himself about what will happen next. Then he begins to tell his friend who has joined him about what he is writing and drawing. His friend interacts, picks up paper and pencil, and begins to produce a parallel story. As the writing process becomes more fluent for Steven, his thoughts will become inner speech and his verbalizations will decrease.

Young writers use their print awareness to write about ideas that are important to them. Although they may not use traditional methods, they should be encouraged to express their ideas and communicate their thoughts. As adults respond to and interact about what they are trying to convey, young writers are motivated to continue to learn how to use print more effectively.

Written Conversations

Written conversations are snapshots of students' writing abilities and provide an opportunity to teach about communicating through writing. At your school, arrange to conduct a written conversation with a student. The steps are as follows:

1. You and a young child should be seated together with one piece of paper and a pencil for each of you.
2. Explain that you both are going to talk on paper, taking turns to write or draw.
3. Begin by writing a simple question or comment that will require a response from the child.
4. Encourage the child to "write back" and verbalize in response.
5. If the child says that he or she cannot write, explain that he or she can pretend to write. This is an important step to make children comfortable with their developmental level and encourage them to write at their level.
6. Continue to take turns as long as the child remains interested.
7. After you have collected some samples of children's writing, analyze them and identify the stages of spelling demonstrated in their written communication processes.

Note: Older children are typically able to engage in written conversations without verbalization.

WRITING STANDARDS AND GOALS

Good preschool programs provide young students with many opportunities to play with print, but by the time children reach kindergarten, most state and school curriculum guides suggest that a structured approach to writing and spelling development is appropriate. Standards associated with kindergarten and first-grade writing describe some of the behaviors expected by the time students complete first grade. Many students will come to school ready to reach goals such as the ones stated in Exhibit 4.2, Virginia Standards of Learning Writing, but others will need to achieve some of the basic benchmarks of development reflecting emerging writing behaviors before the writing standards may be applied to their learning processes. Teachers need to assess the knowledge about writing (what kind and how much) children bring to the classroom, use the standards as guidelines, and plan appropriate instruction.

The writing standards illustrated in the example do not necessarily reflect the complexity of early writing behavior. In particular, the Virginia standards fail to describe explicitly some of the aspects of idea and thought development during the writing process. However, young writers will meet the basic standards more readily if teachers and other adults help them focus on conveying their ideas and thoughts during the writing process.

| *Virginia Standards of Learning Writing for kindergarten and first grade.* | *exhibit* **4.2** |

KINDERGARTEN STANDARDS OF LEARNING WRITING

K.9   The student will print the uppercase and lowercase letters of the alphabet independently.

K.10   The student will print his/her first and last names.

K.11   The student will write to communicate ideas.
   a)   Draw pictures and/or use letters and phonetically spelled words to write about experiences, stories, people, objects, or events.
   b)   Write left to right and top to bottom.

K.12   The student will explore the uses of available technology for reading and writing.

FIRST GRADE STANDARDS OF LEARNING WRITING

1.11   The student will print legibly.
   a)   Form letters.
   b)   Space words and sentences.

1.12   The student will write to communicate ideas.
   a)   Generate ideas.
   b)   Focus on one topic.
   c)   Use descriptive words when writing about people, places, things, and events.
   d)   Use complete sentences in final copies.
   e)   Begin each sentence with a capital letter and use ending punctuation in final copies.
   f)   Use correct spelling for high-frequency sight words and phonetically regular words in final copies.
   g)   Share writing with others.
   h)   Use available technology.

BEGINNING WRITING INSTRUCTION

Formal introduction of writing during language arts instruction should engage children in a variety of ways of expressing themselves. Individual children differ, of course, in how they read, write, draw, and speak in the early ages (Maehr, 1989). Some students use drawings to tell stories, some are comfortable with writing letters, others prefer to tell their stories and have others write for them. Again, teachers need to assess the knowledge about writing that children bring to the classroom. Once teachers know what their students know, they are ready to plan appropriate instructional activities.

In this time of emphasis on specific skills development even for very young children, it is helpful to remember that enjoyable associations with reading and writing are important at an early age. Overemphasis on skills, spelling, and mechanics could discourage students from freely expressing their thoughts on paper. "Children's early writings are to be enjoyed, valued, and understood. . . . They should not usually be made the occasion for the hunting and correcting of errors or for excessive direct instruction" (Morrow, 1996, p. 273). Teachers who want to encourage young children's writing development should relax and enjoy the process with their students and not give a great deal of attention to the fact that their writing attempts are non-traditional. Below we discuss some effective approaches to beginning writing instruction: modeling, writing centers, and dictated stories and journal entries.

Collecting Writing Samples

Ask your mentor teacher to identify students at the lower end, near the middle, and at the high end of writing development in the classroom. Collect a writing sample from each of the three students and tape the "average" student work around your university classroom. Use the descriptions of children's writing in this chapter to analyze the developmental level of their products. Group the low-end student writing with the average writing that looks most similar to it. Do the same with the high-end student writing. What ranges do you see in one classroom? Note the developmental changes and progressions young writers experience. What aspects of the writing products tell you that students are learning about writing?

Modeling

One way a teacher can encourage writing development is by modeling the process. As teachers model different writing behaviors, they talk through the writing process (Sulzby, 1992). The talk might progress like this: "I think I'll write, 'I watched Arthur on television.'" The teacher writes as she talks. She may even spell the words as she writes and make decisions aloud that indicate correct word choice and punctuation. After writing the text, she reads it to her students, pointing to the words as she reads. As teachers model the writing process and talk through the writing, they may describe how they get their ideas for writing, mention literature that contributes to their products, and help their students think about the content.

Writing Centers

Setting up a writing center in the classroom encourages young writers to experiment with print and is an important instructional approach in some literacy programs. Designate a corner of the classroom as the writing center, and arrange tables and chairs for individual activity or small group work. Young writers must be taught the expectations for the center, the rules they are to follow when working at the center, how to store materials, where to file their writing, and how they should work with others. Review expectations periodically so that students' time spent at the center will be productive.

Writing materials such as crayons, large and small pencils, markers, and chalk should be accessible. A variety of sizes and colors of lined and unlined paper, notepads, sticky notes, and blank books encourage young writers to experiment with print. Inclusion of manipulative letters of the alphabet in the writing center encourages children to experiment with different letter arrangements and shows them correct formation of letters. Of course, books and other printed material should be close at hand to provide students with examples of print.

Dictated Stories and Journal Entries

Young writers are capable of dictating journal entries to their teacher. In dictated stories, students keep track of their daily routines, record their experiences on a field trip, or write about their weekend adventures. They react to stories they have read or respond to their favorite movies or television shows. Almost any event or happening may serve as the motivation to write a story. Either individuals or small groups of children dictate entire stories or adventures to the teacher, who types the stories on a computer or writes them on chart paper. While writing each word, the teacher reads back what the children have dictated. The completed stories are displayed in prominent locations around the classroom or bound and used as reading material during instruction or free time.

Some students use drawings to tell stories, some are comfortable with writing letters, others prefer to tell their stories and have others write for them.

The dictated stories, also referred to as language experience activities (LEA), are important language activities that value children's own language and involve all ability levels. As young children dictate their ideas and thoughts and observe the teacher writing what they say, they begin to make important connections among thinking, reading, and writing. They recognize that what they say can be written, that what is written down can be read by themselves and others, and that they can read what is written by others (Templeton, 1995). The act of dictating stories reinforces reading–writing connections, shows young writers that thoughts and ideas can be represented with print, and provides opportunities for young writers to observe letter formation, spelling patterns, sentence structure, and punctuation usage. Children may illustrate their dictated products as another way to make meaning. The dictated stories are also an excellent way to engage ELLs in classroom activities.

Journals teach young writers how to write about topics that interest them. Young students may engage in journal writing (see Exhibit 4.3) either through dictated stories or by producing their own text. Regular class entries may be dictated to the teacher, who writes as children talk about the day's events. This class journal will serve as a model for students to keep their own personal journals. Students should be encouraged to draw and use their own spellings. Children in the early stages of writing development may want to read or interpret their text to the teacher, who produces conventional spellings to represent their ideas. A teacher's more conventional

exhibit   4.3   *A student's journal entry, with teacher response.*

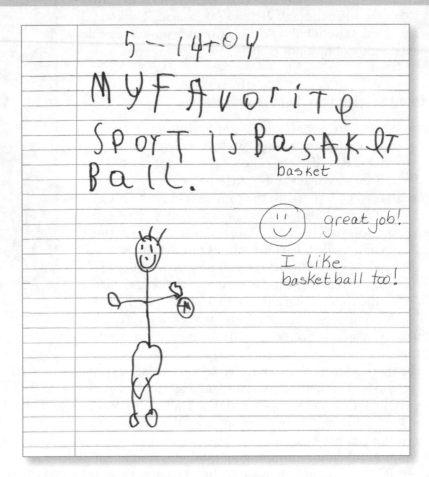

representation written underneath the child's print production provides a model and an important lesson in letter formation and spelling.

FINAL REFLECTIONS

Young children come to school with developed knowledge and attitudes about print that reflect how language is used in their homes and communities. These attitudes and knowledge are evident in their early writing attempts. Opportunities for children to expand their knowledge of print and print production are important in instruction for beginning writers. Through continued experimentation, teacher guidance and interactions, and instructional opportunities, children expand their knowledge of print and print production, progressing from non-conventional expressive writing to more conventional writing. An environment that recognizes the developmental process and facilitates experimentation with writing and other language activities will produce prolific young writers.

Teaching the Writing Process

In the classroom depicted at the beginning of the chapter, students are engaged in different aspects of the writing process. The classroom is set up to involve students in prewriting, drafting, rewriting, editing, and sharing activities. Some students are establishing plans for writing by talking and reading about subjects that are meaningful and relevant, engaging in needed research, establishing the purpose for writing, and identifying the audience. Other students are drafting portions or entire writing products, occasionally editing ideas and grammar and checking for legibility and other technical aspects. Students are also making their writing available to audiences by reading what they wrote, allowing someone to read the writing, or publishing their composition. This entire series of events occurs repeatedly as students engage in the writing process, reflecting the processes used by "real" authors.

STAGES IN THE WRITING PROCESS

One of the primary goals of writing instruction is to help students understand and "live the writerly life" (Calkins, 1994). Every student should think of herself or himself as an author, someone who has something important to write. Classroom instruction should contribute to students' realization that ordinary life suggests writing opportunities and is worth writing about. Recounting a caterpillar's trip across the sidewalk, describing the shadows on the wall of a tall building, or reliving what it is like to arrive home after school are all legitimate writing topics.

Almost all authors progress through several stages when producing written products (Graves, 2003). The stages are fairly identifiable, but not all writers move through the stages in a linear, methodical way. Writers may begin at different stages, take varying amounts of time to complete a stage, progress through stages in unique sequences, and repeatedly revisit stages throughout the writing process. The stages provide a framework for a series of activities that help students understand how writers write.

Prewriting and Planning

Writers plan what they will write during the *prewriting* or *planning* stage. They determine what is interesting and important, decide what content will be included, and organize their ideas in a way that will be clear to others. Some writers plan by engaging in a mental process of visualization and thinking through what they want to write. Others benefit from putting their thoughts on paper, perhaps in a graphic format. They use their own knowledge and experiences, choosing interesting, relevant, meaningful content that motivates them to experiment with writing. Students should be encouraged to do the same and write on topics that reflect their experiences and abilities.

When planning to write about a topic, writers use language arts processes in addition to writing. Oral discussion is an important aspect of planning because children may wish to talk out their ideas and receive feedback from their peers or the teacher. As classmates listen and make contributions, writers identify and clarify topics. Reading literature or other texts also supports the planning stage of the writing process. Writing is a natural way to respond after reading both fiction and nonfiction material. Students' reading may furnish content, and it may suggest a structure or a format.

Interacting with books provides students with a framework and knowledge about what an author does. Discussions and instructional activities that help students understand how authors make decisions as they write books will increase students' knowledge of their own writing process. Visually representing ideas through drawings, graphs, or computer-assisted graphics may also help students prepare for writing. Calling on all the language arts during writing time encourages, organizes, and motivates students who are planning to write.

personal reflection

Understanding Your Personal Writing Process

Take note of how you prepare to write a letter, a class assignment, or another written product. What do you do to prepare? Do you research, scribble on a notepad, read similar materials? Or do you start writing whatever comes into your head, knowing that you will need to rewrite later? Is it easier for you to write if you are using your own computer, jotting thoughts down in a special notebook, or sitting in a familiar place? Can you write in a public location, such as a bookstore, coffeehouse, or all-night restaurant? Describe your prewriting behaviors and needs to a small group of your classmates. Compare behaviors within your group.

Drafting

After prewriting or planning, it's time to "put pencil to paper" and begin to write. Most writers produce a draft—not a final copy—with their first efforts. Writers of different ages and abilities may use drafting for different purposes. Young students do not always understand the concept of drafting and feel that once their ideas are on paper, their job is finished. Older students understand that real authors write and rewrite, attending to content and conventions differently each time they revise. When students create a *rough draft* of their work, they focus on getting their ideas down on paper—forming the big ideas and concepts they wish to present—without being overly concerned about the mechanics of writing. Worrying over mechanics at this stage may prevent students from developing their best ideas and slow the entire process.

Revision

The *revision* process repeats throughout the entire writing process. Depending on the maturity of writers, they revise paragraphs or sentences as they write or spend time after producing an entire text to make sure that they have written what they intended. Revising allows students to discover more about what they know, change what they think, change what they feel, make connections between experiences or facts, and change their point of view (Murray, 1998). The goal of revision is to provide greater clarity, organization, word fluency, and understanding (Routman, 1994). Students should know that professional authors use this stage to expand, clarify, and illustrate their ideas. Students need to be taught how to revise. The revision stage is probably the most difficult part of the writing process for elementary school writers to grasp. Revisiting text and making changes to it once they have produced a draft may be a challenge for them.

By observing as young writers revise, teachers can plan for needed instruction and support. When teachers see that children need help developing ideas, organizing the presentation, rewriting paragraphs and sentences to clarify them, or selecting interesting words and phrases, they can schedule appropriate small or large group instruction to provide needed learning opportunities.

Editing

While revising is related to changing content to enhance expression, *editing* focuses on punctuation, mechanics, and spelling. Editing is directed at making the writing easier to read. Working with the text that children have produced and preparing it for publication is an excellent way to help students understand the importance of conventions. Although the revising and editing processes often occur simultaneously, it is important to differentiate them and teach the distinction to children. After they have formulated their ideas and presented and organized them clearly, students check spelling, punctuation, and grammatical structures. Some teachers model editing and revising skills during morning meetings or other shared writing experiences. Brief discussions about word choice or spelling patterns are helpful in assisting students with editing skills.

Learning from Authors

Attend an author's presentation at a local library or bookstore. Notice how the author talks about his or her writing experiences. Describe the author's writing techniques, strategies, and methods. Ask questions about the person's writing process—how does he or she proceed through the writing process, what happens if he or she gets stuck and cannot write, and how does he or she edit and revise?

personal reflection

Conferencing

Conferences are an important aspect of the classroom writing process, providing opportunities for feedback in writing instruction. The goal of conferences is to support and encourage the writer. Teachers use conferences to share what students have written, encourage new ideas, teach skills, and scaffold learning. Conferences may be as short as one minute or be more involved and last five to ten minutes. Some conferences are spontaneous, taking place as a teacher walks by a student's desk or overhears the student talking to classmates. Other conferences are scheduled, so that children know they will have an opportunity to talk about and reflect on their writing.

Many teachers have developed a system of peer conferences to allow writers to share what they have written and receive feedback. In the vignette that opened this chapter, two students were working together, checking off tasks on a teacher-prepared worksheet that led them though a conferencing process. One student talked to another about what he was writing. The teacher had communicated and modeled what was expected during the conferencing.

Successful peer conferencing requires a great deal of teacher guidance. The teacher should establish specific procedures and expectations and make them well known to students. Through modeling, role-playing, and descriptions, students learn what processes to follow during the writing conference (Elbow, 1998). For example, after reading a piece, a teacher or student can guide the conference with the author by engaging in the following:

1. Discussing words or phrases that were strong or weak in the piece. This discussion begins with asking the writer, "Which part of the story makes you the most proud?" "Which part of the story doesn't seem organized?"

2. Having the writer summarize the story. The writer could be asked to tell about the story in three to five short sentences.

3. Reacting to the writing. The reader might comment, for example, "I felt confused by . . ." or "I was happy that . . ." or "I really like the section where you . . . ." These comments should be directly related to the actual writing.

4. Asking questions to encourage the writer to think about the story. The basic activities require a teacher or peer to read carefully and listen well. It may be difficult to respond to another's writing tactfully, so students will need to learn how to question proud writers gently. A series of probing questions such as these will help peers to help each other.

   - Read your favorite part to me. Why do you like it?

   - Are there any parts of your writing that you don't like? Why?

   - Here's a part that I would like you to explain to me.

   - What do you want to do next with this story or text?

| *Checklist to guide student conferences.* | *exhibit* | **4.4** |

☐ The author reads a selection.

☐ The partner listens carefully while the author reads.

☐ The partner responds to the selection. Some ways to respond:

   My favorite section was . . .

   I really liked how the character . . .

   Would you reread the part when . . .

☐ The partner asks questions about the selection. Some questions could be:

   I didn't understand what happened when . . .

   Why did . . . happen?

   What are your next steps?

   What if this event happened differently?

☐ Switch roles. The person who was the author listens, and the partner becomes the author.

Checklists such as the one in Exhibit 4.4 help students navigate the process and reinforce the structure established by the teacher.

The author also has some responsibility during conferences. He or she should listen to the responses without rejecting or arguing. One teacher's class talked about the idea of "taking it or leaving it" as a response to suggestions. Students listened to suggestions about their writing and decided for themselves whether they would use them in the revisions—without having to explain why. The author must be allowed to retain ownership in decision making during the writing process.

Peer conferences are a most rewarding instructional approach, but when students do not understand the process, neither they or their teachers will be motivated to continue the process. Hence it is important that teachers prepare and support students for conferencing.

Publishing

Publishing happens in many ways. Desktop publishing allows student writers to produce stories with typed print, graphics, picture art, and other sophisticated production features. Students type up their stories (or the teacher or a parent volunteer does so) and the authors

Students enjoy reading student-authored books that have been bound and are accessible in classroom displays.

illustrate each page with a picture. Books may be bound with binding machines found in many schools or hand-sewn together. One teacher provided drawers of binding supplies, including large needles (without sharp points) and yarn. Students punched holes at the spine and sewed their books together. Students loved learning how to sew, it was good for their motor skills, and it added to the artistry of the final product.

Publishing books is a great opportunity to talk to students about the structure of a book. Books have a title page, copyright page, and dedication page. Students often enjoy creating their own dedications and title pages. Publishing teaches students about the structure of literature while also giving them artistic freedom to create their own books.

Publishing may be the most gratifying step of the writing process as students produce a final copy suitable to put on display or share with others. Selections should be published for authentic audiences, because identifying authentic audiences is an important component of providing relevant writing opportunities for students. Students are motivated by the idea of being able to share a final product with authentic audiences—others both in and out of their classroom. When they finish the final copy and publish the book, stories, reports, letters, or poems, they experience great satisfaction in allowing other students, family members, and adults to read their books. When their work is published and actually communicates the author's intent to others, students gain a sense of the validity of their process of writing and of their identity as authors.

This student is reading aloud from his own book, which the class published.

Developing a writing community is an important aspect of writing instruction. Reading each other's writing and sharing interests, family backgrounds, cultural attributes, and special talents connects students and helps them identify common interests. While not every piece of writing needs to be read by another person or published, students should have opportunities to select writing for sharing and feedback. Letting them know that others will read their stories and texts is one way to motivate students to attend to form, word choice, and spelling, once they understand the importance of communication.

It is possible for students to engage in the process of writing from an early point in their educational experience. Young writers may not spend a great deal of time on any one stage, and revision may not be as crucial while they are learning to spell and form letters. Eventually, as learners gain more control over their writing, they are guided through the entire process.

WRITING PROCESS STANDARDS AND GOALS

Planning writing instruction in language arts classrooms depends on your understanding of the writing process and your students' writing abilities and connecting that knowledge with state and local standards. The examples given in this section illustrate that standards support the teaching of writing as a process and provide teachers with guidelines for effective planning. The general NCTE/IRA standards specifically refer to the writing process as an important aspect of language arts instruction. Along with acknowledging the importance of different audiences, the standards refer directly to "writing process." Standard 5 states:

> Students employ a wide range of strategies as they write and use different writing process elements appropriately to communicate with different audiences for a variety of purposes.

Some state standards reflect the writing process stages; see Exhibit 4.5, for example. The Texas Essential Knowledge and Skills for Language Arts,

| | *Ohio Academic Content Standards for Writing, grade 3.* | *exhibit* **4.5** |

Prewriting	1. Generate writing ideas through discussions with others and from printed material.
	2. Develop a clear main idea for writing.
	3. Develop a purpose and audience for writing.
	4. Use organizational strategies (e.g., brainstorming, lists, webs, and Venn diagrams) to plan writing.
Drafting, Revising and Editing	5. Organize writing by providing a simple introduction, a body, and a clear sense of closure.
	6. Use a wide range of simple, compound, and complex sentences.
	7. Create paragraphs with topic sentences and supporting sentences that are marked by indentation and are linked by transitional words and phrases.
	8. Use language for writing that is different from oral language, mimicking the writing style of books when appropriate.
	9. Use available technology to compose text.
	10. Reread and assess writing for clarity, using a variety of methods (e.g., writer's circle or author's chair).
	11. Add descriptive words and details, and delete extraneous information.
	12. Rearrange words, sentences, and paragraphs to clarify meaning.
	13. Use resources and reference materials, including dictionaries, to select more effective vocabulary.
	14. Proofread writing and edit to improve conventions (e.g., grammar, spelling, punctuation, and capitalization) and identify and correct fragments and run-ons.
	15. Apply tools (e.g., rubric, checklist, and feedback) to judge the quality of writing.
Publishing	16. Rewrite and illustrate writing samples for display and for sharing with others.

shown in Exhibit 4.6, also refer directly to the stages. The writing process goals are not the only writing instruction standards but are presented in the standards along with other goals related to purpose, grammar skills, penmanship, and research skills.

The Texas Essential Knowledge and Skills identify the writing process as important as early as in the first grade. The Texas standards also emphasize the importance of others in the writing process. Standard 19B focuses on the importance of responding to others' writing, indicating the assumption that students read their work to each other. Many of the standards listed in the writing/evaluation section are accomplished during the stages of the writing process. Other state standards deal with the writing process in one way or another. Unfortunately, in most cases more state standards focus on writing skills than on the writing process.

---

exhibit **4.6** *Texas Essential Knowledge and Skills for Language Arts, grade 3.*

(18) **Writing/writing processes.** The student selects and uses writing processes for self-initiated and assigned writing. The student is expected to:

   (A) generate ideas for writing by using prewriting techniques such as drawing and listing key thoughts (2–3);

   (B) develop drafts (1–3);

   (C) revise selected drafts for varied purposes, including to achieve a sense of audience, precise word choices, and vivid images (1–3);

   (D) edit for appropriate grammar, spelling, punctuation, and features of polished writing (2–3);

   (E) use available technology for aspects of writing such as word processing, spell checking, and printing (2–3); and

   (F) demonstrate understanding of language use and spelling by bringing selected pieces frequently to final form, "publishing" them for audiences (2–3).

(19) **Writing/evaluation.** The student evaluates his/her own writing and the writing of others. The student is expected to:

   (A) identify the most effective features of a piece of writing using criteria generated by the teacher and class (1–3);

   (B) respond constructively to others' writing (1–3);

   (C) determine how his/her own writing achieves its purposes (1–3);

   (D) use published pieces as models for writing (2–3); and

   (E) review a collection of his/her own written work to monitor growth as a writer (2–3).

Personal Writing

Take a piece of your own writing through the writing process, from prewriting activities to publication.

1. Begin by brainstorming possible topics, and select ones that you are interested in developing. Topic ideas may come from literature, imagination, memories, or day-to-day events. Some topics may emerge from journal entries.

2. Produce a first draft. Don't be too concerned about the conventions; just get your ideas on paper. You can write using any genre or form.

3. Revise and edit your product. Share your writing with a partner as you draft and revise. Your partner will provide feedback that will help you communicate your ideas clearly.

4. Select a method of publishing your work, such as in a typed version incorporating graphics, in picture book format, or as a hypertext.

5. Share your work with others. You may choose to have someone else read your work or read it aloud to a partner, a small group, or the entire class. Allow time and opportunity for feedback and response.

WRITING INSTRUCTION

Regularly scheduled writing helps students think like writers and encourages them to gather topics and think about the writing process. The amount of time a teacher schedules for writing will depend on the age and developmental levels of the students and the scheduling restrictions of the classroom. Ideally writing should be taught in 45- to 60-minute blocks of time, at least three times per week. There are many strategies and approaches to teaching writing. To introduce you to important aspects of teaching writing, we will describe writers' workshop, a widely used instructional approach.

Writers' Workshop

Nancie Atwell (1998) is a New England teacher who wanted to replicate in her classrooms the discussions that she and her children had about children's literature around the dinner table. What emerged as she attempted to embed the sharing and writing into her classroom instruction was writers' workshop, a framework for teaching writing that has been implemented in many classrooms. The purpose of writers' workshop is to provide daily time for students to write, work through the writing process, and share their texts with others. When these workshops are successfully integrated into classroom instructional routines, students begin thinking of themselves as authors who are writing about important ideas.

The schedule and routine of writers' workshop (Atwell, 1998; Calkins, 1994) must be explicitly demonstrated to students. Teachers often spend the first few weeks of school teaching students how to do each of the steps. Writers' workshop consists of writing, sharing, and mini-lessons (Atwell, 1998). The workshop approach is described in Chapter 2, Article I.

Classroom Writing

In a workshop classroom, writers write on their own during nearly two-thirds of the time scheduled for writing instruction. The time differs depending on students' ability to engage in prolonged writing activity. Younger students need less time; older students who have experience with writing can engage in independent writing for a longer period of time. Time to write should be scheduled on a regular basis. The teacher writes along with the students at selected times. Eventually, the teacher stops writing and begins moving around the room, quietly discussing students' writing as they engage in the process.

Students progress through the stages of writing in unique ways, some stopping to share what they are writing with others, engage in research, or illustrate their work. Providing blocks of time in which children are expected to write is crucial to their development as writers. As they write, they learn about writing and their own writing processes. The more they understand about their own processes, the more effective they will be as writers.

Time to write should be scheduled on a regular basis.

Sharing

An important part of the workshop occurs when the students gather together and read some of what they have been writing. Sharing helps writers improve their writing, reading, and listening skills and allows them to see how others respond to their ideas. The sharing time allows children to showcase what they wrote about during their writing time and provides closure for daily workshops.

TEACHER *Viewpoint*

LAKESHA, BEGINNING TEACHER ▶ The important idea for me when I plan writers' workshop is that writing is creative. An interesting connection occurred in one language arts classroom where students met an artist during Career Day. He was showing how he thought about what he was going to draw and then created drafts on a piece of paper. As he held up his drafts next to his final product, he described changing things in the pictures and adding details to make his painting. As the artist explained his creative process, a fourth grader raised her hand and said, "I do the same thing when I write!" This student had the right idea about her own writing process, comparing it to art. It is this idea that I want my students to understand about the writing process.

Mini-lessons

Mini-lessons, an essential aspect of writers' workshop, should take place continually during the writing process (Atwell, 2002). They are a great opportunity to consider how authors progress through the writing process, to model the thought processes necessary for writing, and to connect the writing process to examples of writing, including literature (Lunsford, 1997). Many teachers typically begin their writers' workshop with a mini-lesson, but the middle and the end of the workshop are also appropriate times for mini-lessons.

Teachers design mini-lessons to meet the needs of the writers in the classroom community. As teachers conference with their students, read papers, and listen to students talk about their writing, they note how they might support and assist students' development as writers. Once a particular need is identified, then the teacher presents an appropriate lesson or demonstration.

Mini-lessons may be five to 15 minutes long and provide time to share short sections of text, discuss an aspect of organization, or provide support in numerous ways. A variation is to expand the time and address the lesson to small groups or individuals (Atwell, 2002). A combination of whole-class, small group, and individual instruction is appropriate for mini-lessons, depending on the skills and support students need.

The planning of mini-lessons is linked to informal assessment practices. The best way to determine what mini-lessons to teach is to be aware of what and how students are writing. During conferences with students, teachers note what needs the students demonstrate. Some teachers carry a clipboard and note observations as they interact with their students. For example, if you notice that several students need assistance on how to edit their papers, you might conduct a mini-lesson on proofreading marks and highlight a few of the editing skills that are most important to your writers. It is important to decide on a few key points to teach during a mini-lesson and not overwhelm students with multiple instructional goals. Exhibit 4.7 shows the focus of a mini-lesson, which may be procedural, literary, or mechanical:

- *Procedural.* Initial mini-lessons are procedural, including information about the writing process and stages. Topics might include peer conferencing, topic selection, and publishing options.
- *Literary.* These mini-lessons cover improving content and thinking of ideas. Examples include using description to develop strong characters, writing strong beginnings and endings, and using dialogue.
- *Mechanical.* These lessons focus on skills and mechanics. Examples include paragraph formation, capitalization, incomplete and complete sentences, and quotation marks. See Article III in this chapter for information on teaching writing conventions.

exhibit   **4.7**   *The focus of mini-lessons.*

TYPE OF MINI-LESSON	PURPOSE	EXAMPLES
Procedural	Understanding the writing process	Modeling ways of brainstorming Demonstrating different methods of publishing books
Literary	Focusing on the content or story types	Using different literary forms (nonfiction, poetry, science fiction, etc.) Discussing how to begin and end stories
Mechanical	Learning about writing skills and mechanics	Punctuation Spelling Dialogue/quotation marks

Mini-lessons

With the guidance of your classroom teacher, observe one or two students or a small group. Identify some area where a mini-lesson would provide support, help students develop an idea, or introduce a needed skill. Use feedback and suggestions from the students and your mentor teacher and design a mini-lesson that teaches students some aspect of the writing process. For example, you may design a mini-lesson about selecting a topic, reading from other sources to use in your own writing, asking questions that help the writer organize, or revising content to use interesting words. The lesson format given earlier in Exhibit 2.10 may help you develop the mini-lesson. Present the mini-lesson to the students and take notes about their responses. Were you able to keep the students' attention? Did the students seem to need what you presented? Did you notice that they applied what you taught to what they were writing? What would you change about the mini-lesson if you were to present it again?

By implementing writers' workshop as a way to teach writing, teachers recognize individual differences in the classroom. Students who have a great deal of experience writing move quickly into the process. Others, including those who are learning English, need more support during the writing process. Writers find support in informal and formal small group instructional meetings based on students' needs as well as in whole-class mini-lessons and individual conferences.

Strategies for Facilitating Writing Growth

As with most language arts instruction, reading, listening, speaking, and visual interpretation play a role in supporting writing growth. In order to learn how to write, students must read, talk, listen, and respond to images. The language arts strategies described below help students work through the writing process and are effectively embedded in the writers' workshop structure.

Reading Aloud

No matter what format is used during instruction, reading together is an important element of learning to write. Reading aloud works well in conjunction with writers' workshop. Selecting children's literature that is relevant to mini-lessons or that encourages children to try new things in writing gives teachers the opportunity to discuss how writers learn from other authors. Read-alouds may also include examples of genres discussed in class.

Think-Alouds

Demonstrating the thought processes that a writer uses in creating a story helps children understand the writing process. To model these processes, the teacher "thinks aloud" as he develops his own ideas or follows the writing process. An example of a think-aloud in which a teacher demonstrates how to select a topic is presented in the Teacher Viewpoint from Jan, a veteran teacher.

JAN, VETERAN TEACHER ▶ Sometimes I forget how valuable it is to my students to let them see how a writer would think though a part of the writing process. I'm also usually surprised what an impact a demonstration makes on my class. I was encouraging my students to select their own topics for writing and decided to show them how I would select a topic. I started a mini-lesson in the following way:

Okay students, today during writers' workshop I would like you to experiment with choosing your own topic. When I was driving to work today, I began thinking about what I wanted to write about next. I thought about a couple of ideas. First of all, I always like writing about my brother and my summer adventures, especially when we vacationed on the beach. I also like to write about special holidays with my family. But today, I have decided that I would like to write about my favorite pet, a Scottish terrier named Tosh. Tomorrow I am going to bring in a picture of her so it will help me write. In fact, if you want to bring in something that would help you write your story, go ahead and do it.

Today I am going to brainstorm what I would like to tell in my story. I am going to make a list of things I loved about my dog and some of the stories I would like to tell about her.

I demonstrated the process using a think-aloud. I wrote my topic choices on chart paper, made notes as I decided which topic I would write about, and began to list ideas about the selected topic. The next day I asked my students to use the same process I had demonstrated to select a topic for writing during the workshop. I was amused to see how closely they modeled my topics. Most all the students listed topics about their summer vacations and pets. What really surprised me was that their lists looked very similar to mine. They had produced check marks, discussion points, and notes that resembled my chart page from the day before. The think-aloud helped establish a process for completing the activity as I had described.

Collective Writing

During collective writing several students or an entire classroom create a written piece together. Writing together is a good way to promote enthusiasm for writing, model the writing process, and develop classroom community. Either the teacher or a student composes as the class gives ideas and direction. Current events, fads, a classroom happening, content area learning, or a modification of an existing story or text are some of the many topics that work well for collective writing. Starting with a familiar story (such as a fairytale or fable) and guiding the students to write a revised classroom version by changing the setting (perhaps set it in the classroom or school) or the perspective (such as telling the story from the villain's point of view) is one way to begin a collective story.

Collective writing is a sophisticated version of dictated stories, a language experience activity in which the teacher acts as the scribe for very young students as they tell stories or talk about events (see Article I in this chapter). Depending on the writing skills of the students, the teacher may write the story as students dictate, or a student may be selected for this role. The writing should be visible to all students; either an overhead projector or a large projected image of a word-processing screen is best. As she writes, the teacher discusses ideas, language usage, and skills. Because the whole class is working together as the teacher guides them, collective writing allows the teacher to model the writing process, focus students on important ideas, teach spelling and grammar skills in context, and invite students' participation in a non-threatening activity while building a sense of a writing community in the classroom. Collective writing is an excellent writing strategy in classrooms with a wide range of writing and language abilities. Students look forward to the times when they write together, and they often refer to the collective writing as "our story."

Writer's Notebooks

A writer's notebook is a place for each student to record thoughts and brainstorm ideas in a risk-free location. Students are encouraged to draw, jot down ideas, and keep lists of favorite words, phrases, and potential writing topics. The notebook serves as a resource and provides ideas for writing. Students should feel free to experiment and develop a strong sense of ownership in their notebooks (Calkins, 1992).

Notebooks may be organized in many ways and used with all subjects. Elementary teachers who are planning to use journals in different subject areas may ask students to bring multi-subject notebooks and designate a section for each subject. Multiple spiral notebooks can serve the same purpose. The writer's notebook helps students develop stories and discover interests, and it serves as a record of progress during the year. By looking at the writer's notebook entries from throughout the school year, students and teachers see how their writing develops over time.

LYNETTE, BEGINNING TEACHER ▶ My students and I used our writer's notebooks to create collages of life experiences. We pasted movie ticket stubs, pictures, postcards, and even dried flowers and used these as a springboard for our writing. Students' writings were quite descriptive and imaginative when they referred to visual objects. I have also found that student drawings, scribbles, and doodles inspire writing.

FINAL REFLECTIONS

Teachers can encourage students to progress through the writing process by allowing them to select their own topics, write at their own pace, and share and receive feedback from others. Writers' workshop suggests a framework that focuses on the writing process, incorporates standards, integrates all the language processes, and allows students to experience the joy of writing and sharing their work. The workshop framework includes mini-lessons, brief teacher-directed instruction aimed at the needs of students as they are writing.

Teaching Writing Conventions

Young writers need to see a link between communicating in writing and using the conventions associated with writing. When they understand that writing conventions help others to understand their ideas, then learning about handwriting, punctuation, grammar, and spelling becomes meaningful and relevant. Language arts instruction offers many opportunities to teach grammar, spelling, and other writing conventions because they are best taught and applied as students communicate with their peers, parents, friends, and others. Writing conventions must sometimes be taught directly, but often they may be taught in an integrated fashion and applied through writing experiences.

Teachers who understand writing development can gauge and monitor students' emerging knowledge of conventions by carefully analyzing their work and noting errors or deviations from what is expected during writing tasks. Because students experiment at the same time as they are learning rules, writing growth and non-standard writing behaviors often occur together (Weaver, 1996). The role of experimentation and unconventional usage is an important consideration of language arts instruction. Providing thoughtful and appropriate feedback is essential to help students learn about writing conventions.

WRITING CONVENTIONS

Critics of recent approaches to language arts instruction have expressed concern that the conventions of writing—punctuation, handwriting, grammar, and spelling—are sacrificed when instruction is based on the writing process and integrated skills development. This criticism is made even though integrated language arts instruction teaches these conventions in the context of language and literacy experiences. We refer to such a method as *integrated skills instruction* because the instruction in and use of conventions (and other skills) are usually based on evaluation of students' current writing development and needs.

Integrated skills instruction involves a shift from an emphasis of conventions to a concern with thought processes and idea development, but it does not mean that skills development is ignored. Development of ideas and use of writing conventions are developed simultaneously. The balancing act involved in integrated skills instruction can be tricky. Attention to conventions is often de-emphasized during instruction that focuses on the process, and teachers may wrongly assume that students will learn the skills they need without direct teacher-led instruction. Neglecting the teaching of writing conventions can be particularly detrimental to students who do not have the same cultural, linguistic, or educational background as the teacher (Delpit, 1995) or who come to school with varying literacy backgrounds (including those who are learning to speak English). Writing conventions should be presented when the need to use them arises or when young writers understand that applying the appropriate conventions will enhance their communication processes (Pang, 2000). Teaching conventions when they are needed provides an immediate opportunity for students to use and practice them.

Punctuation

Periods, apostrophes, question marks, exclamation marks, quotation marks, and other punctuation marks are used in various ways, making usage seem difficult and abstract (Wilde, 1992) to young writers. The apostrophe, for example, is used in contractions but also shows possession. Periods are used in abbreviations and at the end of sentences. Students learn punctuation best when they have opportunities to experiment with its use, make predictions about how and when to use certain marks, and see how their own writing is clarified with proper usage.

Discussions about punctuation begin very early in language arts instruction. When kindergarten students dictate stories to their teachers or read big books together or talk about the stories they read and write, punctuation is discussed. Once students learn about punctuation, it won't be long before teachers observe their rudimentary attempts to use punctuation as they experiment with writing. As students continue their writing development, they participate in more formal, structured instructional processes. When a teacher notices that young writers are experimenting with periods, question marks, or other punctuation throughout their writing, this is a good time to plan explicit instruction that helps them understand appropriate usage.

Students first demonstrate their awareness of punctuation by overgeneralizing. They begin using punctuation marks, but not necessarily in a conventional manner. During the early stages of writing development, young writers may use periods at the end of each line instead of at the end of each sentence, or they may put quotation marks around all sentences. Overgeneralizations of this nature illustrate that the students have learned to use periods or quotation marks but are in the process of learning the specifics of punctuation conventions.

Teachers can teach punctuation in an interesting and relevant manner by presenting it as a series of systems in our language with certain rules and logic. Studying punctuation then becomes a "scientific" process where students learn about conventions and test them within their writing (Wilde, 1992). Exhibit 4.8 lists some examples of punctuation-related knowledge and instructional strategies that will help students learn conventional usage.

Learning about punctuation may be difficult for students who have not had extended experiences with print before school or who are learning English as a second language. Consider how difficult it would be to learn to use punctuation before learning how to form sentences, use vocabulary, and express ideas completely, or if a student is transitioning from a language that uses some punctuation elements differently (for example, marks used to show certain pronunciations in Spanish). Teachers should consider what students already know about language when implementing instructional strategies.

Handwriting

Handwriting is a crucial component of language arts instruction during the early years of schools. Walk into any kindergarten or first-grade classroom and you will observe models of letter formation and other aids to help students with their handwriting. About the third grade, you will see excited young writers who are changing from writing manuscript letters to using cursive forms of handwriting. Both students and parents value the achievement of learning correct formation of letters and transitioning to cursive.

exhibit **4.8**   *Punctuation and instructional strategies.*

Sentence boundaries:	Students should know how sentences begin and end and whether a sentence is complete or not. Teachers may cover this during language experience activities and by using specific examples from books and students' work. Writing conferences and mini-lessons are excellent opportunities to teach sentence boundaries.
Commas:	Commas have defined uses, such as for geographical names, quotations, letter formats, dates, and dividing units within a sentence. Students should learn these rules. Books they are reading and their own writing can provide examples.
Capital letters:	It is important to teach students that the first letter of proper nouns and of sentences should be capitalized. Students quickly catch on to the idea of proper nouns as they learn to recognize their own names and the name of their teacher, school, or city.
Quotation marks:	Students should learn where the quotation marks go and how to punctuate different spoken phrases. After direct instruction, they may use their own reading and writing to find examples. Editing and publishing processes are excellent times to hone quotation mark usage.
Apostrophes:	Apostrophes occur with possessives and contractions. The concepts should be taught directly to students, and they should have plenty of time to experiment, discuss, and clarify apostrophe rules in their writing.
Colons, dashes, and semicolons:	More sophisticated or advanced punctuation marks become necessary when students produce more complex sentences and are best taught as students need to use them in their writing.

Adapted from Wilde, S. (1992). *You kan red this! Spelling and punctuation for whole language classrooms, K–6.* Portsmouth, NH: Heinemann.

The computer and other technology tools are beginning to change views of handwriting. Advances in technology that make it easy for students to write and compose on the computer affect instruction related to writing. As it becomes more and more common for students to type assignments and stories with word processors, keyboarding skills become more relevant than handwriting. However, language arts curriculum in most states still designates letter formation as an important skill, and it should be formally presented to students.

An important handwriting instructional strategy is to demonstrate the formation of letters (Routman, 1994). Writers' workshop mini-lessons and small group settings are appropriate for encouraging legible and correct letter formation and helping individual students who have problems with forming letters, developing a consistent slant, and dealing with spacing. For very young writers, demonstrations are appropriate as long as mastery is not the goal. Familiarizing students with the forms of letter production through modeling and discussion is the first step to teaching correct formation.

Some students have more difficulty with forming letters than do others. Some who write illegibly may have delayed motor development skills. Students who are learning English as their second language may be familiar with other alphabetic principles or different print symbols (such as Asian and Middle Eastern languages). Trying to form letters is very frustrating for some students, especially when they are under pressure to produce correctly formed letters. Even the brightest students may be frustrated when asked to form letters that they are unable to create because of developmental lags. Those who find letter formation difficult often labor over their writing, working slowly, producing smeared, messy lines and many erasures. These students are often relieved to learn cursive or use computers. Parent volunteers and teacher assistants can help by writing down stories and practicing letter formation with young writers. Motor skills frequently improve with practice and age (Rhodes & Dudley-Marling, 1996). The same is true of letter reversals; unless a child has been writing for a long period of time and is in third or fourth grade, occasional reversals should not be considered a serious handwriting problem.

Three elements determine the legibility of handwriting and letter formation: correct formation, consistent slant, and spacing. Teachers may analyze students' handwriting to see which of these factors are reducing its legibility and then group students for lessons and discussions about those factors. Exhibit 4.9 suggests strategies for helping students with letter formation, slant, and spacing.

Some writers continue to find it very difficult to produce legible written products. Often they are not interested in writing and become frustrated when they are told repeatedly to write neatly. Some teachers find it necessary to set standards for neatness and work with students to rewrite their work so it is

---

Suggestions for helping students with handwriting.   *exhibit*   **4.9**

- If letter formation is labored and slow, use timed writing events where students see how many words they can write in one minute or five minutes (Rhodes & Dudley-Marling, 1996).

- If letters are poorly formed, make sure that the model letters are in clear view of the writers. Students should be able to view a large wall chart and a smaller chart at their desk so they can compare their writing with models.

- Check the slant of letters by moving a straight-edge ruler along the line of their writing. If writing slant is not consistent, draw lines that represent the correct slant and let students practice forming letters between the slants.

- Use a ruler or finger spacing to analyze spaces between letters. If letter spacing is unequal, have students use the ruler or their fingers to measure spaces between the letters and adjust subsequent writing.

legible (Morrow, Gambrell, & Pressley, 2003). Different levels of writing quality on drafts and final copies may be acceptable and appropriate. Students may be asked to self-assess their own handwriting, using colored pencils, pens, correction fluid or tape, and other tools to improve their handwriting form.

Sloppy writing may indicate a lack of interest in the topic or the writing process itself. One way to counteract the problem is to assign writing topics that students find relevant and meaningful. When the writing assignment is something students want to write about, they take more care with their handwriting. By learning students' interests and needs and using this knowledge to identify important and interesting writing topics and activities, teachers help students to produce writing products they care about and want others to read. When students feel proud of their work and ready to share it with others, they are more readily convinced that legibility is important.

Grammar

Grammar describes how the parts of speech fit together. The rules of grammar are established by repeated usage, and when grammar is correct, it is barely noticed (Elbow, 1998). On the other hand, mistakes in grammar may distract a reader or, even worse, cause readers to misunderstand or disregard the writing. Some students find grammar complex and difficult to understand because of the range of acceptable ways to organize words and sentences. The thought, "The cat and dog played together all afternoon" is a little different when it is expressed by, "Together, the cat and dog played all afternoon," or "All afternoon, the dog and cat played together." Each of these sentences is grammatically correct, but they are not all equally comfortable. To make matters more difficult, grammar rules have many nuances, and the rules may change over time. Grammar can be particularly difficult for students who speak with a different dialect and those who are learning English as a second language.

Attention to grammar begins very early during language arts instruction. Grammar instruction involves teaching the parts of speech, diagramming or analyzing sentence construction, understanding syntax, and studying punctuation. Traditional instruction in grammar focused on teaching individual, discrete skills and in some cases the rules of grammar. Learning the rules of grammar does not assure flawless writing, as Barr and Johnson report: "As early as 1935, the National Council of Teachers of English notes that research clearly indicated that instruction in traditional grammar is ineffective in eradicating errors in written composition" (1997, p. 232).

The most important activity in teaching grammar is to have students communicate their feelings and thoughts regularly. Writing process activities are considered one of the best ways to teach grammar. As students become more and more committed to conveying their ideas, they become interested in understanding grammar and correcting their papers. The editing and publishing stages of the writing process are opportune times to focus on grammar instruction.

Students who are learning English should receive special consideration, especially with regard to their writing process. The focus of their writing should be to convey their ideas and communicate with others. Students who are learning basic English communication skills need plenty of practice applying grammar rules.

Analyzing Writing Conventions

Select a piece of writing from a student. You may want to use one of the writing samples from Field Note 4.2, or ask your mentor teacher if it is possible to review a recent writing assignment. Analyze the writer's use of conventions. Try to find writing samples from students who have had a great deal of experience with writing in English and from those who are just learning English. In each group, which conventions do they use with the most confidence? Which conventions seem to be absent from their writing? Which conventions do they use with mixed effectiveness? Meet with three or four of your classmates and describe your young writers' punctuation, handwriting, spelling, and grammar.

An activity for teaching the parts of speech is *cloze,* in which words in a text are deleted (usually every fifth or seventh) and readers are encouraged to fill in the blanks with appropriate, new words. The cloze procedure was developed to measure reading ability or determine if a reader was capable of comprehending certain reading material. When readers place meaningful words in the blanks, then they are considered to be reading at an appropriate reading level. When readers cannot fill in the missing words, this indicates that the text is too difficult for them. Depending upon the way in which it is used, cloze can be a flexible instructional tool to teach grammar.

Instructional cloze focuses students on particular parts of speech and developing grammar concepts. One way to use instructional cloze is to copy the text of a story or poem, omitting all instances of one part of speech. For example, in the following excerpt from *A River Ran Wild* (Cherry, 1992), all of the adjectives have been replaced by blanks:

> Long ago a river ran wild through a land of _____ forests. Bears, moose, and herds of deer, hawks, and owls all made their homes in the _____ river valley. Geese paused on their _____ migration and rested on its banks. Beavers, turtles, and schools of fish swam in its _____ waters.
>
> (The missing words are *towering, peaceful, long,* and *warm.*)

Encourage students to suggest words to fill in the blanks, and write their suggestions on chart paper, an overhead, or a chalkboard. After the students think of several words that make sense in the blanks, share the text from the book and ask the students to discuss and compare their choices with the author's choices of adjectives. The discussion helps to define grammatical structures and clarify the role that adjectives and other parts of speech play.

A Web version of the cloze procedure may be found at **www.smilesand grins.com/cgi-bin/weblibs2.pl.**

Spelling

Effective instructional programs will encourage behaviors associated with good spellers. Good spellers show interest in word meanings, develop visual memory for new words, and notice word patterns (Hughes & Searle, 2000). They see spelling as problem solving and have a range of strategies to help them spell correctly. They use visual cues or rules, check their reading material, depend on knowledge of patterns, and spell words several ways to see which spelling looks right. Good spellers are confident that they can independently figure out spellings by using word families, dictionaries, and experimentation. They are active readers and writers who are continually exposed to print. They remember and use the words they know how to spell.

Spelling Development

Students' ability to spell is developmental (Fresch, 2000). Article I of this chapter outlined print awareness and writing development. Exhibit 4.10 expands on these developmental characteristics. The descriptors in this exhibit identify behaviors associated with spelling stages. Although the descriptors offer a developmental framework, students focus on spelling knowledge in different ways and may display characteristics in different ways. Spelling behaviors may develop differently with each young writer (Fresch, 2000).

The overall goal of spelling instruction is to help students continue their spelling development. Correct spelling requires a variety of skills, including reading, writing, memorization, and phonetic awareness (Turbill, 2000). Students acquire competence through reading, writing, and instruction that focuses students' attention on how words are spelled. Word games, pattern identification, and analysis of spelling errors also bring children's attention to words, sounds, and spelling.

Regular writing routines contribute to spelling development. Students often begin utilizing spelling strategies when they see the importance of conventional spelling in their written communication (Hughes & Searle, 2000). When students recognize the significance of being clear to an audience, their spelling improves. For example, if a relative that a student writes to expresses confusion about some of the student's invented spellings, the student will likely become motivated to study and learn spelling patterns.

Spelling Instruction

Developing an effective spelling program is a complex process. Spelling instruction should be explicit—it cannot be left to chance. Lessons should be short and readily applied to writing, avoiding overloading students with instructions or information (Rhodes & Dudley-Marling, 1996). A rule of

| Characteristics of stages of developmental spelling knowledge. | *exhibit* **4.10** |

Preliterate/prephonetic	Scribbles Imitates reading and writing Is aware of print
Preliterate/phonetic	Learns alphabet Strings letters to create message
Letter name	Attempts at spelling become more logical as relationships between letters and sounds begin to be used Develops sight vocabulary for reading and writing. Uses obvious strategies to spell (such as use of the letter *c* for *sea, u* for *you*) Exchanges short vowel for closest long (*a* for short *e; e* for short *i*) Common errors include affrications ("jriv" for *drive*), nasal ("bop" for *bump*), exaggerated sounding ("palena" for *plane*)
Within word	Develops larger reading and writing sight vocabulary Correctly uses short vowels Marks long vowels (sometimes incorrectly) Uses -d for past tense, adds -ing Understands that words have two elements (beginning consonant pattern and a vowel plus ending) Begins to internalize rules May overgeneralize newly learned patterns and rules
Syllable juncture	Begins to correctly double consonant before adding endings Invents at the juncture or schwa position Spellings show orthographic awareness available for word attack
Derivational constancy	Reads efficiently, fluently Attends less to words as literacy processing quickens

Note: These stages are meant to describe a continuum of development. Typically, students do not completely leave one stage before entering the next. When characteristics of two stages are observed simultaneously, the student generally is described as "late" or "early" stage (e.g., a student who strings letters but is also beginning to use knowledge of letter sounds and writes a few sight words is said to be "late preliterate/early letter name"). Such descriptions allow us to see remnants of an earlier stage the student must work through, yet indicate a moving on in understanding.

Figure and excerpt from Fresch, M.J. (2000/2001, December/January). Using think-alouds to analyze decision making during spelling word sorts. *Reading Online, 4*(6). Available: www.readingonline.org/articles/art_index.asp?HREF=/articles/fresch/index.html. Reprinted with permission of Mary Jo Fresch and International Reading Association. All rights reserved.

thumb is to allow about 60 to 75 minutes per week for formal spelling instruction (Gentry, 1984).

The traditional instructional method of teaching weekly lists and skills in isolation, which teachers still use in many classrooms, is not consistent with how learners acquire an understanding of letter and sound correspondence. Yet many school districts provide instructional materials based on rote memorization that ignore important aspects of how children learn phonemic patterns and word structure. In particular, for very young writers spelling tests and skills pages are not developmentally appropriate and could be stressful (Gentry, 1984).

Many interesting games and instructional strategies are available that encourage young writers to attend to spelling. In general, good spelling programs include daily reading, models for conventional spellings, opportunities for discussing word patterns and spelling strategies, a risk-free environment that encourages experimentation, and a de-emphasis of correctness in rough drafts (Bolton & Snowball, 1992). Another feature of good spelling programs is assessment that encourages the teacher and young writers to examine and analyze spelling behavior within the writing process. (For more information on assessment strategies, see Chapter 7.)

Phonics. Phonics instruction in reading and language arts enhances spelling achievement (Gentry, 1984). Phonics capabilities that children learn during beginning reading acquisition contribute to spelling and grammar knowledge and will usually be applied during the writing process. As students increase their print awareness, add more words to their vocabulary, and express more complex ideas, their knowledge about spelling and phonics increases. Phonics and spelling are interrelated, and instructional activities that integrate these areas help young spellers make connections between reading and writing. When students learn to spell the "ph" sound, they should also have the opportunity to read text that includes that sound. The strongest encouragement for using phonic knowledge in writing is regular involvement in reading and writing activities that are meaningful to the young writer.

Spelling textbooks. Almost every school district has some form of spelling textbooks. They may be hardcover or consumable workbooks with lists of words and activities that use the words. Some textbooks group their word lists by specific skills or spelling patterns. The *Spell It—Write!* series (Gentry, 1984) of textbooks is based on spelling developmental stages that many students progress through. Although textbooks that present spelling lists based on word study and phonemic patterns are valuable, they alone cannot provide a complete spelling program. Students learn spelling while engaging in language activities across the curriculum.

Spelling lists. Spelling lists are developed in several ways. Many spelling texts include lists of words for students to spell, teachers compile lists of words that are used in content areas, or students are guided to develop self-selected spelling lists from their writing. New lists of words are usually introduced each week with a series of activities designed to help students learn how to spell them. Typically the weekly activities culminate with a spelling test that is scored by the teacher. Teachers are often dismayed when students misspell words from lists that were the focus of study during recent weeks. Students often successfully memorize a spelling list in order to make an A on a spelling test, but fail to retain the knowledge, and the same words they spelled correctly on Friday's test may be misspelled in their writing on Monday. Students who have difficulty spelling usually fail to transfer what they learn for spelling tests to their writing. Another reason why students misspell words they "know" is that while writing a composition, the writer is focused on many things, including formulating ideas and communicating thoughts. It is not surprising that spelling performance differs from one context to another.

Even so, spelling lists can be used in positive ways, as long as they do not make up the entire spelling program. Spelling lists help students focus on a set of words, and teachers can make them more relevant by keeping in mind that words on spelling lists will be retained longer if students use them in writing. Words that are used with great frequency in writing, as well as words that are spelled with similar patterns, should be selected for the spelling program (Rogers, 1999).

If students are expected to learn lists of words, then they should be taught some of the best ways to study their lists. The steps in Exhibit 4.11 are introduced in the *Spell It—Write!* program (Gentry, 1984). Many other spelling programs include similar strategies for students who must study for spelling tests. Although study skills may help many students, others will continue to struggle even after exposure to these skills.

Spelling notebooks. The spelling notebook, an innovative instructional technique, is a place where students are encouraged to record words they want to learn (Wright, 2000). Students date their entries, select words they would like to know how to spell, and explain why they included the words in their notebook. They may find words in their writing and reading, or select words from televi-

---

Steps for learning spelling words.   **exhibit** **4.11**

1. Look at the word.

2. Say the word.

3. See it in your mind.

4. Write the word from memory.

5. Check the word by comparing to your word list.

6. If you need to, repeat the steps until you know how to spell the word.

sion, signs, or postings around the classroom. Students may wish to designate a section of a writing notebook to keep track of spelling words they would like to discuss and think about (Rhodes & Dudley-Marling, 1996; Gentry, 1984; Wright, 2000). Students' active involvement in selecting words for their notebook increases their word awareness and helps them attend to spellings.

In turn, teachers use students' notes to plan organized discussions about words (Wright, 2000). Teachers may select common word patterns from students' notes for discussion and study.

Spelling meetings. Another interesting strategy is to hold spelling meetings (Wright, 2000). Students discuss new words they are using in their writing, ways they self-correct their spellings, and strategies they use to spell words. Students chart words that are difficult to spell and use dictionaries to identify letter combinations. They may be encouraged to take notes from the meetings in their spelling notebooks. Spelling meetings offer an opportunity to engage students in meaningful discussions about how they deal with spelling and also focus their attention on the importance of spelling words accurately.

Analogies. Teachers can enhance students' spelling development by making them aware of word patterns. One way to do this is spelling by analogy, which involves studying rimes and onsets, as shown in Exhibit 4.12 (Johnston, 1999). A rime comprises a vowel and the letters that follow it in the syllable. For example, if students were studying the rime -at, they might come up with the words cat, sat, mat, that, and so forth. The onset is the initial consonant or cluster. Teaching word families using rimes and onsets is an effective way to teach spelling and decoding. Students will learn to break apart the onset and rime of a word as they are spelling it, rather than focusing on individual phonemes. Teaching words by analogy is effective because pronunciations and spelling patterns are relatively consistent within word families.

exhibit 4.12 *Onsets and rimes (Johnston, 1999).*

ONSETS

b c d f g h j
k l m n p r s
t v w y z ch sh
wh th ph wr kn qu bl
br cl cr dr fl fr gl
pl pr sc scr sk sl sm
sn sp spr st str sw tr

RIMES

ack ail ain ake ale ame
an ank ap ash at ate
aw ay eat ell est ice
ick ide ight ill in ine
ing ink it ock oke op
ore ot uck ug ump unk

WORD SORT GUIDELINES

- Select words that students know. Words may be gathered from reading and writing material, writing and spelling notebooks, or content area vocabulary.
- Ask students to put the words that have something in common in groups. If the word sort has an explicit goal, such as learning "ie" spellings, then provide the category label for them.
- Examples of category headings include:
  - Short vowel sounds
  - Long vowel sounds
  - One-syllable words
  - Verbs ending in "ing"
  - Past tense verbs
  - Words with prefixes
  - Words carrying the same meaning

Once students categorize the words, ask the following questions to guide students' discussions:

- Why did you put these words together?
- What do you find similar in these words?
- What do you find different in these words? Why do you think they are different?
- Why is this a useful category for grouping words?

Word sorts. Playing with and discussing words contribute greatly to students' spelling development. Word sorts (see the box above) provide a framework for the analysis of words. When students are involved in the word sort process, they tend to discuss spelling, grammar, and meanings related to the words.

STANDARDS AND GOALS RELATED TO WRITING CONVENTIONS

Writing conventions are so closely aligned with learning standards, standardized testing, and assessments that teachers tend to pay particular attention to which writing conventions should be taught and when. Academic standards usually reflect the importance placed on students' learning of conventions. See, for example, item 14 in the Ohio Academic Standards (refer back to Exhibit 4.5) and item 18(D) in Exhibit 4.6. Writing standards are presented in a manner that reflects the drafting, revising, and editing stages of the writing process and are based on students' abilities to adhere to and manipulate the conventions of writing. Not all state standards for conventions focus solely on the writing process. For example, California's English Language Arts Content Standards (see Exhibit 4.13) integrate speaking and listening conventions. The introduction to the California standards indicates the importance of conventions to both speaking and writing and notes the overlapping nature of language arts skills.

Ohio, California, and other state standards encourage teachers to devote a great deal of time to teaching the skills and conventions of writing. Some state standards, such as Ohio's, embed writing convention standards (or benchmarks) within the writing process, while the California standards *exhibit* **4.13** *Written and oral English language conventions.*

STATE OF CALIFORNIA (THIRD GRADE)

The standards for written and oral English language conventions have been placed between those for writing and for listening and speaking because these conventions are essential to both sets of skills.

1.0 Written and Oral English Language Conventions

Students write and speak with a command of standard English conventions appropriate to this grade level.

Sentence Structure

1.1 Understand and be able to use complete and correct declarative, interrogative, imperative, and exclamatory sentences in writing and speaking.

Grammar

1.2 Identify subjects and verbs that are in agreement and identify and use pronouns, adjectives, compound words, and articles correctly in writing and speaking.

1.3 Identify and use past, present, and future verb tenses properly in writing and speaking.

1.4 Identify and use subjects and verbs correctly in speaking and writing simple sentences.

Punctuation

1.5 Punctuate dates, city and state, and titles of books correctly.

1.6 Use commas in dates, locations, and addresses and for items in a series.

Capitalization

1.7 Capitalize geographical names, holidays, historical periods, and special events correctly.

Spelling

1.8 Spell correctly one-syllable words that have blends, contractions, compounds, orthographic patterns (e.g., *qu,* consonant doubling, changing the ending of a word from -y to -ies when forming the plural), and common homophones (e.g., *hair–hare*).

1.9 Arrange words in alphabetic order.

Source: California Dept. of Education, www.cde.ca.gov.

connect speaking and listening. In both cases, the standards suggest that conventions are best learned while students are involved in relevant and meaningful communication.

The focus on accountability and standards tends to direct teachers' attention to teaching writing conventions without offering relevant and authentic writing practices (Strickland et al., 2001). In the worst-case scenario, attention to writing standards related to conventions reduces time spent on classroom writing. Good writers need opportunities to engage in the writing process while learning about writing conventions (Morrow, Gambrell, & Pressley, 2003). During a time of increased accountability such as we are currently experiencing, it may require a delicate balance to remember that standards only provide instructional guidelines and are not effective if teachers do not consider students' interests and needs, the stages of writing development, and effective ways to implement curriculum.

Writing Standards

Review the standards for your state or local school related to writing. Consider how the standards related to writing skills are presented. Are they closely connected to the writing process, as in the Ohio standards presented in Exhibit 4.5, or are they presented without reference to other language arts or writing processes? Now, observe writing instruction for a week or more to see how teachers are integrating the state standards. Are you able to identify the components of the writing process during writing instruction? Discuss with your mentor teacher how standards affect their presentation of skills during writing instruction. In a small group, discuss your state's writing standards related to conventions and skills and how teachers are implementing the standards.

JACKI, BEGINNING TEACHER ▶ Sometimes I let my students tell me when it is time to present a teacher-directed lesson. For example, one time during independent writing time, after I had written in my journal for a while, I began to walk around their desks to observe my first graders as they were writing independently. As I surveyed my students engaging in the writing process, I took notes about the topics they were developing and the skills they were using as they wrote. I walked by Chris's desk and observed him writing a description to accompany a picture he had drawn of a bathtub filled to the brim with soap bubbles. He was drafting a sentence that read, "This sope [sic] will keep you clean, too." As I walked away, I noticed a frown on his face. "What's the matter?" I asked him. "I need to know how to spell soap," he said. I didn't want to interfere with his creative composing process, so I replied, "I know what you mean with the spelling you are using. You can just leave it the way it is for now." "No," he said adamantly, "soap is not spelled right and I need to know how to spell it." I wrote the correct spelling on a yellow sticky note and stuck it on his desk. Then I noted on my clipboard all that I had learned about Chris's spelling development in that short interchange. Chris understood about the silent "e" in the vowel–consonant–e pattern, but he knew there were other ways to spell the same sound. I made a note in my anecdotal records about Chris's growth and reminded myself that it was time for a teacher-directed lesson about spelling patterns.

FINAL REFLECTIONS

Writing skills are best taught when students need to use them for conveying messages and expressing their ideas. At times, therefore, teachers will embed skills instruction into the writing process. At other times, teachers will design instruction that focuses directly on specific skill development. In both cases, students should come to understand how their use of conventions affects their overall message and the role that skills play in written language and communication processes.

article IV

Technology and Writing

Every stage of the writing process can be supported or enhanced by computer software and other technological assistance. Technology, however, will never take the place of good writing behaviors. To use technology effectively during the writing process, students must possess strong writing skills as well as an understanding of the many options in software available to help them communicate their ideas.

THE TEACHER'S ROLE

Teachers influence how computer technology affects classroom writing activities. Like their students, teachers reflect various levels and abilities in working with computers. Some come to their university studies knowing a great deal about computers. Their course work provides additional learning opportunities as they rely upon computers to research topics in general education courses and learn to integrate computers into instructional procedures during methods courses. They find that once they are employed as teachers, school districts provide ongoing in-service activities to help them learn about additional ways to use computers in the classroom.

Even when teachers are familiar with computers and other technological innovations, lack of experience or support often makes them reluctant to use computers as an instructional tool. Teachers who are trained to use computers during instructional activities frequently abandon their efforts to use new tools if something does not work when they try to apply the tools in the classroom. Adding to their hesitancy, classroom computer setups are not always convenient or accessible. Teachers may have only one computer for 25 students, find it necessary to reserve a cart or computer laboratory, or discover that the computers and software in the classroom are different from the ones they use at home.

TEACHER Viewpoint

ROSA, BEGINNING TEACHER ▶ I have used computers since I was in elementary school and feel very comfortable using all the tools associated with them in my day-to-day life. However, I realized my own limitations when I participated in a project sponsored by a local university that collaborates with my school. Teams of university professors and teachers spent a week during the summer learning how to use a tool called the Mimeo. The Mimeo adapted any white board in my classroom to become a "smart board." There are several advantages to a smart board. First, it serves as a large computer projection device, making it possible to display anything on my computer screen to an entire class. But it had another advantage: my class and I could write notes, draw diagrams, or keep track of brainstorming sessions; save our handwritten notes to the computer; and have immediate access to printed copies of our classroom notes and activities. The school–university project provided me with a laptop computer, a projector, the white board, and software that would help me integrate the process into my teaching. The summer training session provided valuable time to plan lessons that could be immediately integrated into my existing curriculum. I was psyched! And ready to use my new knowledge as soon as school started the next year. When school started, I found that my white board had not been hung, the Internet access was not compatible with my computer, and the password on my computer had to be changed from a university code to one that would work in my school district. About a month into the school year, the bugs were worked out of the first set of problems and I was ready to set up my computer and use it to teach language arts. The first day I tried it during instruction, it took over 20 minutes to set it up and get it going. My students were restless but polite while I struggled to make it work. I was doing something wrong, so I decided to go on and teach the lesson without the technology. I tried it the next day and I couldn't save the notes the class made to the computer. I was more than a little bit frustrated. It's almost January and I haven't picked up the equipment again. I know it would work, but there are so many other important things to do that I can't make myself take the time to work out all the kinks.

Using computers as classroom writing tools requires a certain acceptance of the role technology plays as a communicative tool. Obviously, using computers during the writing process is an opportunity for teachers and students to learn more about computers and writing. Teachers do not have to be experts to use the computer, and students appreciate teachers who approach instructional integration of the computer as a challenge, admitting that they have a great deal to learn. Teachers learn along with their students and often find that the students surpass them in knowledge. The acceptance and willingness to consider technology as an important tool in students' lives goes a long way.

STANDARDS AND GOALS RELATED TO TECHNOLOGY AND WRITING

States' standards differ in the ways they connect technology and writing. Technology is not mentioned at all in California's writing standards. Ohio's mention technology briefly (see Exhibit 4.14) as the last of eight benchmarks associated with the writing process. The Texas Essential Knowledge and Skills for Language Arts and Reading are similar to the Ohio standards, listing technology as one of several sub-goals related to the writing process. Additionally, the Texas writing standards focus on technology in the writing research section as a way to present information.

In the examples provided in Exhibit 4.14, the writing standards use technology as a general term and do not suggest what type of technology should be used during the writing process. Although pencils and typewriters are considered technology, when educators refer to technology in the classroom, they are usually making a specific reference to computers and the Internet.

Even when technology references are omitted in state writing standards, teachers cannot ignore the impact of computers on their students' writing processes. In one way or another, technology plays an important part in

exhibit 4.14 *References to technology in Ohio and Texas learning standards.*

OHIO ACADEMIC CONTENT STANDARDS (GRADE 3)

Drafting, Revising and Editing   Use available technology to compose text.

TEXAS ESSENTIAL KNOWLEDGE AND SKILLS (GRADES 4–8)

(19) **Writing/writing processes.** The student selects and uses writing processes for self-initiated and assigned writing. The student is expected to:

(F) use available technology to support aspects of creating, revising, editing, and publishing texts (4–8) . . .

(21) **Writing/inquiry/research.** The student uses writing as a tool for learning and research. The student is expected to:

(E) present information in various forms using available technology (4–8) . . .

almost everyone's daily lives, and many students come to school familiar with word processors and other software applications. Additionally, computer programs tend to be highly motivating for young writers. Young writers use computer tools to write, and computer applications are the topic of various writing activities. Since computers are used in so many ways to communicate and are such an important aspect of popular media, it seems only natural to incorporate computers in language arts teaching and learning.

CLASSROOM TECHNOLOGY-BASED WRITING TOOLS AND ACTIVITIES

The computer supports every stage of the writing process. Characteristics of individual students' writing processes, however, affect the manner in which they use computers. Some students progress through the writing process using the computer at the planning, writing, revising, and editing stages. Other students write their first ideas on paper before using the computer later in the process. Just as students use pencil and paper in different ways during the writing process, they should be encouraged to use computers in ways that reflect their individual writing preferences.

Almost any instructional strategy is enhanced when the appropriate technological tools are available, but the computer setup and software available in the classroom dictate their instructional applications. Classroom strategies differ depending on whether teachers have access to one computer, multiple networked computers, or sophisticated tools such as the one described in the Teacher Viewpoint on page 182. Some basic computer applications directly enhance and extend common strategies associated with writing instruction. These include tools for word processing and desktop publishing, brainstorming and organizing, drafting, multimedia publishing, and reference and research.

Word Processing and Desktop Publishing

Word processing is as familiar to some writers as paper and pencils. Word processing is available to elementary students on most school computers and allows them to add a wide range of printed, graphic, and audio enhancements to their written products. Students' knowledge of software programs depends on the resources available in their homes and on previous classroom experiences. Students are usually eager to begin exploring and using the software, requiring minimal encouragement and direction. Most word processors have tutoring programs that introduce children to basic operating procedures, characteristics, and features unique to the specific program. Even so, teachers who have the technological resources for their students to use word processing at school may find that basic instructional assistance to students about how to use the software is necessary.

There are various methods to acquaint students with word processing tools. A teacher or a child who is familiar with a word processing program can demonstrate its tools by working with small groups gathered around a computer. Small group instruction is very effective, but word processing text projected on a large screen, if available, can serve as an example for the entire class.

Word processing and desktop publishing are easily adapted to independent work, but they also lend themselves to collaborative work. If students work together on a report, for example, they can easily cut and paste

Teachers influence how technology affects classroom writing activities.

paragraphs each of them have written into one document and print out multiple copies to read and discuss. It is important to model group collaboration methods at the computer so that students know how to work together.

Word processing tools are useful at each stage of the writing process (see Exhibit 4.15). Word processing programs assist writers by providing ways to revise on the screen, save their work, find synonyms and definitions, and check spelling and grammar. Word processing software often includes desktop publishing tools that allow students to produce a finished product. These tools allow students to select a typeface, arrange their text, and add graphics with relative ease.

Overview of the writing process, selected instructional strategies, and example software.

WRITING PROCESS	SELECTED INSTRUCTIONAL STRATEGIES	EXAMPLE SOFTWARE
Prewriting/planning	Brainstorming Organizing ideas Developing graphic outlines	ClarisWorks for Kids Microsoft Word Inspiration Storybook Weave Deluxe Imagination Express Kid Pix
Drafting/writing	Journaling Letter writing Outlining stories Framing poetry	The Amazing Writing Machine Storybook Weaver Deluxe Creativity Workshop for Kids Imagination Express
Publishing/revising and editing	Arranging print Including graphics Creating multimedia productions	Kid Pix Studio ClarisWorks for Kids
Research and referencing	Dictionaries Encyclopedias Atlases	Encarta Encyclopedia Grolier Multimedia

Brainstorming and Organizing

Most word processing programs have the capability to create some form of graphic organizer. Charts, graphs, webs, and tables are effective brainstorming or organizational tools to use during writers' workshop, research, or other writing activities. Microsoft Word, for example, has drawing tools, preformatted tables, and templates for charts that teachers or students can use to produce visual representations. These graphic organizers help writers gather their thoughts during the writing process or convey their ideas in the final product.

The program Inspiration is particularly helpful for organizing stories. It produces lists, outlines, and graphic organizers designed to link information and develop ideas for writing. It does offer word processing capabilities, but its strength is in the organization of ideas and thoughts. Students find it a very effective aid when they are preparing to write.

Databases provide ways for writers to collect, store, and organize information. Students can use databases such as Excel to report, organize, and sort information, at every step of the writing process. Another program that makes it easy to manipulate, format, and organize data is FileMaker Pro. With this program, students create fields, sort in a variety of ways, and print out information in different forms. One classroom researched endangered animals and created a database that included data such as where the animals lived, what they ate, and other habits. The classification of the animals became an excellent lesson in organizing content.

Drafting

Some programs incorporate a wide range of visual and auditory features that are excellent tools for creating or drafting written documents. A program called The Amazing Writing Machine encourages students to write journals, letters, stories, and poems with a pre-designed page format or template. Students can create a private journal with a password so that only the writer can access the file. Storybook Weaver Deluxe features graphics, drawing, and text-to-speech functions (the computer will read the text back to the user). In addition, the program allows students to record their own voices in Spanish or English. Creativity Workshop for Kids features text-to-speech options as well as graphics and formatted pages. Imagination Express is like a storybook construction kit, inviting students to create background scenes, use clip art, animate, and add music as they create their own electronic books. The program allows adults to customize the options that are available for each child based on the child's needs and ability.

Multimedia Publishing

Software programs that allow the user to incorporate visual, sound, and written symbols permit students to publish multimedia "documents." Computer programs and websites offer an array of graphic displays that can be integrated into published texts, and software is available for expressing writing in different forms. One of the most sophisticated software programs is Kid Pix Studio, featuring multimedia art and animation within a publishing program. Kid Pix Studio software integrates video, special effects, slide shows, QuickTime movies, stamps, drawings, and photos into a publishing program. The software extends visual expression by allowing users to create movies and use digital puppets that can be manipulated and given voices.

Software Review

Select some software used in your classroom. Focus on software that is particularly useful in teaching language and communicative arts. Perhaps some of the software suggested in this section or software that accomplishes similar tasks is available for you to review. Have a student show you how to use it. How do students use it, and how does it assist in their writing?

Many word processing programs include features that support rather sophisticated desktop printing processes. Students can create original art with software tools and print their text in almost any form they desire. Some desktop publishing programs even support audio recording of students' stories. ClarisWorks for Kids provides templates that allow students to create books, letters, and graphs incorporating writing and art. It also features a text-to-speech option.

Reference and Research

Software allows students to access the most up-to-date information available as they research topics and explore new ideas. Documents and other information can be stored on a CD-ROM in electronic form. In the near future, many reference materials—such as dictionaries, encyclopedias, and atlases—will likely be available *only* on CD-ROM. The various types of encyclopedia CD-ROMs are very useful sources of information. Both Encarta Encyclopedia and Grolier Multimedia are good references for students who want to find out about a variety of topics. They feature maps, photos, sound clips, QuickTime movies, and textual information that can be found either alphabetically, through a search, or through links from related topics. These encyclopedias tend to be more up to date than print versions, because releasing an updated CD-ROM is much less expensive than reprinting entire sets of volumes. Many schools have a library of CD-ROMs that can be checked out for use in the classroom.

Software programs continually advance. New products and new features added to existing programs constantly improve the capabilities and utility of computers. School districts purchase software in much the same way they purchase textbooks, updating their materials every few years. Occasionally, special programs offer opportunities for individual teachers to order software for their classrooms. In any case, informed language arts teachers need to keep abreast of the most current software available to support their teaching.

KEYBOARDING SKILLS

Students must be comfortable and skilled with computer keyboards in order to write and accomplish all the other processes that computers perform. Teaching keyboarding in elementary school has lately become an important issue because of the increasing presence of computers in the classroom. Some debate surrounds the question of when keyboarding should be taught. Some experts believe that it should be introduced as soon as children demonstrate manual dexterity and interest in working on a keyboard, even as early as kindergarten. Ideally, by the time children are in third grade, they should be able to type as fast as they can write (Lockard, Abrams, & Many, 1997). Although the debate about when keyboarding should be taught may continue, more agreement exists about the keyboarding skills that children need to learn.

Correct finger placement on the computer keyboard is a technical skill necessary for writing with the computer. Students who are comfortable on the keyboard will use the Web, play games, and develop graphics with greater facility than those with lesser keyboard skills. Any individual who works on the computer, whether it is to use a word processor or surf the Web, benefits from understanding the basics of keyboarding. Keyboard skills should be introduced early, before students become hunt-and-peck typists (Ubelacker, 1992). Once bad habits are developed they may be difficult to replace with more efficient ones.

After children learn correct finger placement on the keys, they need a great deal of meaningful practice to develop the ability to type by touch. Each time a young writer sits at the computer, he or she should be encouraged to use correct posture and hand position. As with any psychomotor skill, repetitions of identical movements will result in their eventually becoming automatic. Typing speed should increase with children's continued use of the keyboard. Any focus on typing accuracy and speed should be developmentally appropriate for the young writer.

The most logical approach to keyboard instruction is to let the computer teach the students. Motivating instructional tools are available on the Internet. Graphics associated with the tools illustrate the correct placement of hands on the keyboard, provide practice to increase speed, and explain how to type difficult letter sequences. Internet-based programs are adaptable to individual differences and are particularly helpful for teachers who will be facilitating the keyboarding skills of children with various typing abilities. Internet resources for teaching keyboarding include:

www.bytesoflearning.com/UltraKey/Activities.htm

www.thelearningstudio.com/index.html

www.schdist42.bc.ca/ProjectInfo/Reviews/KeyboardingSoftware.html

www.education-world.com/a_curr/curr006.shtml

TECHNOLOGY AND ENGLISH LANGUAGE LEARNERS

In the past, students who were learning to write English as their second language often engaged in computer-based vocabulary exercises, grammar drills, and spelling practice (Warschauer & Healey, 1998). Many drills and exercises are still available, and practice is valuable for students who are learning English; however, newer programs include multimedia options, games, and visual clues that provide more motivation and incentives for student participation. Warschauer and Healey write, "Those who do need extra help with those aspects of language that improve with practice can use small, focused programs to give them additional time and assistance outside of regular classroom time" (1998, p. 59).

UNDERSTANDING THE IMPACT OF TECHNOLOGY ON WRITING INSTRUCTION

A Classroom Example

Russell is a third grader who is very interested in airplanes. He dreams of being a pilot and can identify any plane that flies overhead. Russell is excited when his teacher explains that students will create their own research papers on something related to science. Finding out about the type of training that pilots go through and what their job is like seems very interesting to Russell. Russell is also interested in learning some aviation history, especially after visiting the National Air & Space Museum last year and watching the movie *October Sky.*

His teacher, Ms. Jones, assists students with selecting their topics. After each child has discussed her or his interests, she has students write an online journal entry where they list what they already know and what they want to find out by conducting their research. She uses this as a basis for a conversation in which students discuss their interests in small groups and suggest further questions about one another's topics. Students add questions that come up during the discussion to their online journal.

Ms. Jones's class has done some research prior to this project, but her students are at different levels of comfort regarding computer research and publication. She begins by scheduling a session at the computer lab where students work with Grolier's Encyclopedia on CD-ROM. Each child has a disk to save information on, and she demonstrates how they can take notes, cut and paste graphics, and pull quotes from the encyclopedia. She takes time to remind students about plagiarism and the rules for using information from the Internet. As always, she reminds her students to reference material they have used from other sources.

During the next few days, Ms. Jones sets up a learning center that is monitored by a teaching assistant. At the center, students conduct searches on the Internet using **www.yahooligans.com.** They continue with their note taking and information gathering.

One of the students has a question that provides Ms. Jones with a "teachable moment" that is both relevant and significant to the class's research. Tammy, who is researching the planets, encounters information on a website that conflicts with information on the encyclopedia CD-ROM. Ms. Jones realizes the importance of this discovery and uses it to illustrate that students may encounter outdated or incorrect information from sources. She reiterates the importance of citing references, checking information, and interacting critically with information. Her students point out other examples of inconsistent information they have encountered in their research projects. Ms. Jones makes a note to continue talking about biases and sources in their future projects.

As students continue gathering information, they begin to design a presentation on Hyperstudio. A few of the students are familiar with the Hyperstudio software, which helps them write stories, add artwork and audio accompaniment, and produce presentations to share with other students. Some students integrate pictures that they scanned on the computer, videos they downloaded from the Internet, and sounds they recorded. The computer lab assistant supports this project by continuing instruction during lab time.

Russell is very excited about his research and presentation. He makes one slide about a pilot's job and the training an individual must

UNDERSTANDING THE IMPACT OF TECHNOLOGY ON WRITING INSTRUCTION, cont.

complete to become a pilot. He obtained that information by e-mailing an airline with questions about their requirements. Russell received an answer within a week of sending his questions. Another slide has a timeline of the progression of air transportation. The timeline includes a link to a video replicating the Wright brothers' first flight at Kitty Hawk. Russell decides to use his questions as a format for his research presentation. At the top of each slide is a specific question that he is attempting to answer. He integrates text, graphics, and video into his research presentation to demonstrate his understanding.

Russell utilizes technology to integrate various modes of expression. He is able to access a variety of informational sources in order to understand more about pilots. His quest for information takes him to a variety of sources, including library books, Internet sites, airline personnel, and CD-ROMs. Russell's teacher guides the format for his research writing, but the assignment also allows latitude for his own personal choice in many options. As a result, Russell learns valuable research skills, writing skills, and information that are relevant to his own interests.

English language learners engaged in the writing process benefit from word processing programs in many of the same ways as do those who speak English as their first language. They may use Inspiration or another graphic organizer during the prewriting stage to generate and outline ideas. The spell check feature of word processing software is very helpful to students who are not sure of English pronunciations and spellings. References such as Collins On-Line Dictionaries translate from other languages to English. Many dictionary programs incorporate grammatical help, and some include video clips and graphics that help students with word choices. Text-to-speech software, although it does not sound natural, provides support for pronouncing new and unfamiliar vocabulary. As with all computer-based instruction, the tool will not replace the teacher, but it simply offers support during the writing process.

FINAL REFLECTIONS

Computer technology provides a variety of options for young writers. When students are encouraged to use and are able to integrate technology tools—organizational tools, word processing programs, desktop printing programs, and multimedia publishing programs—their range of expression expands. Computers will continue to grow more powerful and versatile as new innovations appear. Modes of expression in the classroom today are limited only by the type of technology available and the creativity of students and teachers in the learning environment.

PROFESSIONAL REFLECTIONS

Review the Field Notes from this chapter and develop one or more into a component of your portfolio. To continue to reflect on your Field Note responses, consider the following suggestions:

- Review writing samples from a student you've been observing throughout the semester. Meet with the student and discuss some of the writing strategies he or she used. Ask the student if he or she can see any growth or change in his or her writing. After your conference with the student, use the writing samples to identify the strengths that the writer exhibits. Based on your evaluation, identify some instructional goals that would support this writer's development.

- Write a reflection on your own writing process. How can becoming aware of your writing process add to your understanding of teaching?

- Present the mini-lesson you designed in Field Note 4.3 to an individual, a small group, or a whole class. Afterward, evaluate the effectiveness of your methods. Write a reflection on your experience. Note changes that you will make the next time you teach this skill.

Professional Readings

The following books will expand your understanding of the content of this chapter:

Atwell, N. (1998). *In the middle: Writing, reading and learning with adolescents.* Portsmouth, NH: Heinemann.

Although this text is directed at middle school teachers, it is one of the best descriptions of writers' workshop and can be applied to any age level. It's very easy to read and offers many suggestions for writing instruction, including an extensive list of mini-lesson topics. Atwell also presents a long list of books suitable for use in writers' workshops. This is a must-read for any language arts teacher.

Calkins, L. M. (1994). *The art of teaching writing.* Portsmouth, NH: Heinemann.

Calkins begins with the foundations of literacy and describes writing development in the preschool years. She then describes important structures in writing workshops. She emphasizes the idea of using writing both in and out of school. This is another classic text that every elementary language arts teacher should read.

Fletcher, R. (1993). *What a writer needs.* Portsmouth, NH: Heinemann.

This book describes the process of writing from a writer's perspective. It focuses on loving words, developing characters, describing settings, and selecting topics. The information presented from the perspective of a writer suggests that teachers should be writers themselves and understand the process.

Ray, K. W. (1999). *Wondrous words: Writers and writing in the elementary classroom.* Urbana, IL: National Council of Teachers of English.

This book talks about how to teach students from kindergarten to college age to read like a writer. It includes excellent ideas that link children's literature and writing instruction.

Rosencrans, G. (1998). *The spelling book: Teaching children how to spell, not what to spell.* Newark, DE: International Reading Association.

This book outlines a methodology for teaching spelling to students in grades 3 through 6, focusing on helping students become independent spellers who can identify and apply spelling patterns in their writing. Sample spelling lessons and activities are provided.

The following children's books will provide you insights about some of the topics discussed in this chapter. Many of the books feature characters who are writers and may serve as examples for your students. Review these books and identify how they might help you introduce discussions about aspects of the writing process. Talk about one of the books with young writers.

Children's Books

Cleary, B. (2000 reprint). *Dear Mr. Henshaw*. New York: HarperTrophy.

This chapter book depicts a boy's correspondence with his favorite author, Mr. Henshaw. In the process of writing letters, Lee Botts touches on issues common to elementary students. While the book deals with children of divorce, it also presents a description of the writing process as Lee records his feelings in letters to Mr. Henshaw.

Creech, S. (2000). *The wanderer*. New York: Harper-Collins Juvenile Books.

In this adventure, 13-year-old Sophie joins her uncles and cousins on a sailing voyage across the Atlantic. She relays her story in a journal format, reflecting her feelings, emotions, and actions during a risky journey.

Fitzhugh, L. (2001 classic edition). *Harriet the spy*. New York: Yearling Books.

Harriet fills her notebooks with observations of her friends, neighbors, and family. She includes intimate descriptions of her personal feelings. When one of the notebooks is discovered and read by her friends, Harriet has to deal with the repercussions of sharing feelings involuntarily. This book is appropriate for upper elementary grades.

Moss, M. (1996). *Amelia writes again*. Middleton, WI: Pleasant Company.

Amelia keeps a writer's notebook in which she describes her experiences in school, friends, teachers, and lessons. This book provides an excellent model for journal writing.

Williams, V. B. (1986). *Cherries and cherry pits*. New York: Scholastic.

This book is about two friends who write and draw together. It provides a good basis for discussion on how to select topics and write about everyday events.

Other children's books mentioned in this chapter are:

Cherry, L. (1992). *A river ran wild*. San Diego, CA: Harcourt Brace.

Rylant, C. (1993). *The relatives came*. New York: Aladdin.

REFERENCES

Atwell, N. (1987). *In the middle: Writing, reading and learning with adolescents*. Portsmouth, NH: Heinemann.

Atwell, N. (1998). *In the middle*. Portsmouth, NH: Heinemann.

Atwell, N. (2002). *Lessons that change writers*. Portsmouth, NH: Heinemann.

Barr, R., & Johnson, B. (1997). *Teaching reading and writing in elementary classrooms* (2nd ed.). New York: Longman.

Barron, A. E., & Ivers, K. S. (1998). *The Internet and instruction: Activities and ideas*. Englewood, CO: Libraries Unlimited, Inc. and Teachers Ideas Press.

Bear, D., & Templeton, S. (1998). Explorations in developmental spelling: Foundations for teaching phonics, spelling, and vocabulary. *The Reading Teacher, 52*(3).

Beers, J. W. (1980). Developmental spelling strategies of spelling competence in primary school children. In E. H. Henderson & J. W. Beers (Eds.), *Developmental and cognitive aspects of learning to spell: A reflection of word knowledge.* Newark, DE: International Reading Association.

Bolton, F., & Snowball, D. (1993). *Ideas for spelling.* Portsmouth, NH: Heinemann.

Calkins, L. (1994). *The art of teaching writing.* Portsmouth, NH: Heinemann.

Calkins, L. M. (1992). *Living between the lines.* Portsmouth, NH: Heinemann.

Callies, R. (1998). Why grammar matters: Guiding students through revision. In C. Weaver (Ed.), *Lessons to share in teaching grammar in context* (pp. 110–119). Portsmouth, NH: Boynton/Cook.

Carroll, M. (1999). Dancing on the keyboard: A theoretical basis for the use of computers in the classroom. Retrieved August 19, 2004, from www.readingonline.org/articles/carroll.

Chandler, K., & The Mapleton Teacher–Researcher Group. (2000). Squaring up to spelling. *Language Arts, 77,* 224–231.

Clay, M. M. (1979, 1985). *The early detection of reading difficulties.* Auckland, New Zealand: Heinemann.

Crafton, L. K. (1996). *Standards in practice grades K–2.* Urbana, IL: National Council of Teachers of English.

Danielson, K. (1992). Picture books to use with older students. *Journal of Reading, 35,* 652–654.

Davis, B. C., & Shade, D. D. (1994). *Integrate, don't isolate! Computers in the early childhood curriculum* (ERIC Identifier ED376991). Urbana, IL: ERIC Clearinghouse on Elementary and Early Childhood Education. Retrieved August 19, 2004, from www.ed.gov/databases/ERIC_Digests/ed376991.html.

Delpit, L. (1995). *Other people's children.* New York: New Press.

Downes, T., & Fatouros, C. (1995). *Learning in an electronic world.* Portsmouth, NH: Heinemann.

El-Hindi, A. E. (1998). *Beyond classroom boundaries: Constructivist teaching with the Internet* [Electronic version]. *Reading Teacher, 51*(8), 694–700. Retrieved August 19, 2004, from www.reading online.org/electronic/RT/constructivist.html.

Elbow, P. (1981). *Writing with power: Techniques for mastering the writing process.* New York: Oxford University Press.

Elbow, P. (1998). *Writing without teachers.* London: Oxford University Press.

Fox, R. F. (1999). Beating the moon: A reflection on media and literacy. *Language Arts, 76*(6), 479–482.

Fresch, M. J. (2000). What we learned from Josh: Sorting out word sorting. *Language Arts, 77,* 209–217.

Gentry, R. (1984). *Spel . . . is a four-letter word.* Portsmouth, NH: Heinemann.

Glazer, S. M., & Burke, E. M. (1994). *An integrated approach to early literacy.* Boston: Allyn & Bacon.

Graves, D. (1994). *A fresh look at writing.* Portsmouth, NH: Heinemann.

Graves, D. (2003). *Writing: Teachers and children at work* (20th Anniversary ed.). Exeter, NH: Heinemann.

Halliday, M. A. K. (1975). *Learning how to mean: Explorations in the development of language.* New York: Elsevier.

Harper, L. (1997). The writer's toolbox: Five tools for active revision instruction. *Language Arts, 74,* 193–200.

Heath, S. B. (1983). *Ways with words: Language, life and work in community and classrooms.* Cambridge, England: Cambridge University Press.

Hughes, M., & Searle, D. (2000). Spelling and "the second 'R'." *Language Arts, 77,* 203–208.

Iannone, P. V. (1998). *Just beyond the horizon: Writing-centered literacy activities for traditional and electronic contexts* [Electronic version]. *Reading Teacher, 51*(5), 438–443. Retrieved August 19, 2004, www.readingonline.org/electronic/RT/horizon.html.

Invernizzi, M. A., Abouzeid, M. P., & Bloodgood, J. W. (1997). Integrated word study: Spelling, grammar and meaning in the language arts classroom. *Language Arts, 74,* 185–192.

Johnston, F. R. (1999). The timing and teaching of word families. *The Reading Teacher, 5,* 64–75.

Leu, D. J. (1996). *Sarah's secret: Social aspects of literacy and learning in a digital information age* [Electronic version]. *Reading Teacher, 50*(2), 162–165. Retrieved August 19, 2004, from www.reading online.org/electronic/RT/sarah.html.

Lockard, J., Abrams, P. D., & Many, W. A. (1997). *Microcomputers for twenty-first century educators* (4th ed.). New York: Longman.

Lu, M. Y. (2000). *Writing development* (ERIC Identifier ED446341). Bloomington, IN: ERIC Clearinghouse on Reading English and Communication. Retrieved August 21, 2003, from www.ericfacility.net/ericdigests/ed446341.html.

Lunsford, S. H. (1997). And they wrote happily ever after: Literature-based mini-lessons in writing. *Language Arts, 74,* 42–48.

Maehr, J. (1989, December). Right! Young children can write! *Extensions: Newsletter of the High/Scope Curriculum, 4,* 1–4.

Martens, P. (1996). *"I already know how to read": A child's view of literacy*. Portsmouth, NH: Heinemann.

McGee, L. M., & Richgels, D. J. (1990). *Literacy's beginnings: Supporting young readers and writers*. Needham Heights, MA: Allyn & Bacon.

Moffett, J., & Wagner, B. J. (1992). *Student centered language arts, K–12*. Portsmouth, NH: Heinemann.

Morrow, L. (2001, 2005 in press). *Literacy development in the early years* (3rd/4th eds.). Boston: Allyn & Bacon.

Morrow, L. M., Gambrell, L. B., & Pressley, M. (Eds.) (2003). *Best practices in literacy instruction* (2nd ed.). New York: Guilford.

Murray, D. (1998). *Write to learn*. Fort Worth, TX: Harcourt Brace College.

Pang, V. O. (2000). *Multicultural education: A caring-centered, reflective approach*. Boston: McGraw-Hill.

Reinking, D. (1997). Me and my hypertext :) A multiple digression analysis of technology and literacy (sic). *The Reading Teacher, 50,* 626–635.

Rhodes, L., & Dudley-Marling, C. (1996). *Readers and writers with a difference: A holistic approach to teaching struggling readers and writers* (2nd ed.). Portsmouth, NH: Heinemann.

Rogers, L. K. (1999). Spelling cheerleading. *The Reading Teacher, 53,* 110–111.

Routman, R. (1991). *Invitations*. Portsmouth, NH: Heinemann.

Routman, R. (1994). *Invitations: Changing as teachers and learners and K–12*. Portsmouth, NH: Heinemann.

Strickland, D. S., Ganske, K., & Monroe, J. K. (2001). *Supporting struggling readers and writers: Strategies for classroom intervention, 3–6*. Portland, ME: Stenhouse.

Sulzby, E. (1986). Young children's concepts for oral and written texts. In K. Durkin (Ed.), *Language development during the school years* (pp. 95–116). London: Croom Helm.

Sulzby, E. (1992). Research directions: Transitions from emergent to conventional writing. *Language Arts, 69,* 290–297.

Taylor, D. (1998). *Family literacy: Young children learning to read and write*. Portsmouth, NH: Heinemann.

Templeton, S. (1995). *Children's literacy: Contexts for meaningful learning*. Boston: Houghton Mifflin.

Turbill, J. (2000). Developing a spelling conscience. *Language Arts, 77*(3), 209–217.

Ubelacker, S. (1992). Keyboarding, the universal curriculum tool for children. *Proceedings of the 9th International Conference on Technology and Education*. Austin: University of Texas, 808–810.

Warschauer, M., & Healey, D. (1998). Computers and language learning: An overview [Electronic version]. *Language Teaching, 31,* 57–71. Retrieved September 1, 2003, from: www.gse.uci.edu/markw/overview.html.

Weaver, C. (1996). *Teaching grammar in context*. Portsmouth, NH: Heinemann.

Wilde, S. (1992). *You kan red this! Spelling and punctuation for whole language classrooms, K–6*. Portsmouth, NH: Heinemann.

Wiseman, A. (2003). Collaboration, initiation, and rejection: The social construction of stories in a kindergarten class. *Reading Teacher, 56,* 638.

Wright, K. A. (2000). Weekly spelling meetings: Improving spelling instruction through classroom based inquiry. *Language Arts, 77,* 218–223.

Zinn, A. (1998). Ideas in practice: Assessing writing in the developmental classroom. *Journal of Developmental Education, 22,* 29–34, 39.

The entire classroom is totally taken over by the Harry Potter book. Ms. Watson is reading the book aloud, chapter by chapter, and it is only a matter of time before copies of the books begin appearing in the fourth graders' desks. Eventually, the students begin to read the other books in the series even before the teacher finishes the first book. They talk about the book. They pick out aspects of language—how the author makes the book exciting—and they describe the strong characters. Ms. Watson devotes a bulletin board to illustrations and computer graphics that the children produce. Before long, students' writing journals begin to include predictions about what will happen next in the story. Students produce versions of the stories with different endings and plot twists. When the new movie is announced, students rush to the Internet to see pictures of the actors who will play the characters' roles.

Ms. Watson is pleased with how her students are responding to the classroom activities. She had worried about using Harry Potter in the classroom because the books are controversial for their presentation of wizardry and witchcraft. Some schools discourage teachers from using the books, but it was difficult to ignore students' interest in the series. Before she decided to read the book, Ms. Watson wrote an e-mail or talked to each of her students' parents to ask their opinion. No parents objected to the books, so she discussed the issue with her principal. They agreed together that the books could be used in the classroom.

Chapter 5

READING

Ms. Watson is able to capitalize on the excitement of the Harry Potter series. She begins to make connections between the Potter books and other high-quality children's literature. She reads portions of *A Wrinkle in Time* (L'Engle, 1973) to show the fourth graders that other books are just as exciting as the Harry Potter series. She uses literature circles to assign other books. During sharing times, the fourth graders begin to compare the Harry Potter books with other stories they are reading. Soon the students' excitement with

the popular Potter books expands and includes other books. Ms. Watson feels it is time to introduce the genres of fantasy and science fiction. The fourth graders jump into the integrated language arts unit—reading, writing, speaking, and listening together—with enthusiasm and a sense of joy about reading.

Ms. Watson's students reached the point where they were motivated to read as a result of support and encouragement. It took lots of effective instruction, access to wonderful books, and practice! Ms. Watson worked hard to teach the students how to comprehend, use basic reading skills and develop their vocabulary and fluency so they could become confident independent readers. Ms. Watson knows that encouraging a love of reading is important to promoting lifelong learning, but she also knows that teaching reading skills and strategies is critical. She is proud of her students' growth, and she is sure they will continue to improve their reading and writing with ongoing instruction and opportunities to read and respond to great books like the Harry Potter series.

INTRODUCTION

Reading contributes to language development and is a crucial aspect of literacy. Ms. Watson understands that children learn to read by reading, but writing also contributes to their understanding of written language. Although some reading and writing skills may be taught separately, you will be a more effective teacher if you understand the connections between the two processes and how you can link the two processes in instruction. The integrated language arts unit that Ms. Watson designed to focus on the Harry Potter series provided many opportunities to connect reading and writing. This chapter does not present a comprehensive reading program. Instead, it examines the key components of reading instruction, connections between reading and writing, the importance of responding to literature, and reading independently.

GUIDING QUESTIONS

Consider these questions as you read this chapter. Jot down your initial responses to each question. After reading the articles, revisit your responses. Would you make any changes to them? If so, what would those changes be? Discuss your responses with one or more of your classmates, your professor, or your mentor teacher.

1. What is the reading process?
2. What are the key elements of reading, and how are they taught?
3. What is the role of literature in language arts instruction, and what responses and activities encourage continued growth in the language arts?
4. How can language arts instruction foster lifelong independent reading habits?

Understanding Reading

Of all the language processes, the one that receives the most attention in the classroom is reading. Teachers typically devote a large proportion of instructional time to teaching students how to read. They give attention to assessing reading skills, and they spend a great deal of time in professional-development activities related to reading instruction. The focus on reading goes beyond the classroom level. District, state, and national efforts are often directed at improving the reading abilities of students. In fact, reading has become a symbol of success or failure in the education of our nation's children. Evaluation of our nation's entire educational system is often based on reading acquisition rates. You may see the impact of the emphasis on reading in your own preparation program. Chances are your state or certification agency requires you to take more reading courses than any other set of courses.

Reading is an important factor in individual academic success or failure, too. Because it is at the heart of educational achievement, students who do not learn to read well will remain at a disadvantage for the remainder of their academic career. Later, a person's ability to read can affect success at work and happiness in personal life. Needless to say, parents are concerned deeply with the reading success of their children, and elementary teachers view literacy and reading instruction as among their most important responsibilities.

A good understanding of the reading process is a necessity for every elementary teacher. However, the process is complex, and descriptions, explanations, and definitions of the reading process abound. To understand and define reading, one must consider the physical aspects of the eyes, memory mechanisms and attention, anxiety, risk taking, the nature and uses of language, speech, interpersonal interactions, sociocultural differences, learning theory, and child development. Most important, reading is the process of constructing meaning with text. You may have heard your professor or mentor teacher make this statement, but what does it really mean? How do children actually learn to read? This article provides some answers to these questions.

Experiencing the Reading Process

Read the following passage. Reflect on your experiences.

ωϑ′Ω υ′Υˆ ⁺′Υ, ⁺′ΥΥ ′Υφϋ, ¨φφˆζ Φ′Υ″ˆ ⁺′Υ, ′ΩΫϰ″Ωϋ ´ϖ εϖ ´ϖ ϑ′Ω ;′Υ′φζ

1. How did you feel when reading the passage?
2. What made it hard to read the passage?

Now try to read the passage again, using the following information:

> Title: "Going to the Park"
> the = ωϑ′Ω
> was = ⁺′Υ,

(continued)

and = Ῐφῢ

to = ῞ϖ

3. How does this additional information help you "read" the passage? What other information do you need to be able to read and understand the entire passage?

4. What insights can you gain about teaching reading from this experience?

APPROACHES TO READING INSTRUCTION

As we noted above, the reading process is complex, and to describe it one must consider many elements, including the physical aspects of the eyes, memory and cognitive ability, background of experiences, the nature and uses of language, sociocultural differences, learning theory, child development, and political influences. Given this complexity, it is no wonder that reading instruction is the subject of many debates and a variety of approaches.

There are three main theories about the reading process: the top down, bottom up, and interactive theories.

Top Down Theory

The top down theory, also referred to as the *holistic* approach, emphasizes that the reader learns to read by interacting with whole texts, focusing on the pieces or skills as needed. The top down theory places more emphasis on the reader than the text.

Bottom Up Theory

The bottom up theory, sometimes called the *skills-based* approach, emphasizes a systematic movement from learning letters and sounds to learning words and finally to reading complete texts. The bottom up theory places more emphasis on the text than on the reader. However, most educators currently believe that a balanced, interactive approach to reading is appropriate and productive (Blair & Williams, 1999; Fitzgerald, 1999; Gambrell, Morrow, Neuman, & Pressley, 1999; Pressley, 2002). We will use this approach, described below, to frame our discussions in this text.

Interactive Theory

The interactive theory combines aspects of the top down and bottom up theories to reflect what research has shown about how readers actually interact with text. Interactive theory places equal emphasis on the reader and the text. Some educators, parents, or others may advocate a top down or bottom up theory, but most educators currently believe that the interactive (or *balanced*) approach is the most appropriate and productive approach.

Thinking About Learning to Read

Think back to when you learned to read. What do you remember about reading instruction when you were an elementary student? What theory or theories do you think your teachers used to guide the reading instruction you experienced? From your perspective as the student, what did you see as the strengths and limitations of this approach? Share your insights with your peers.

The key characteristics of the interactive reading theory are listed in Exhibit 5.1 and described in the following sections to help you understand the interactive theory of reading more fully.

Prior Knowledge, Culture, and Previous Experiences

Each reader brings a great deal of experience and prior knowledge to a text. This knowledge interacts with what is written when the reader interprets the text. For this reason, no two people read and interpret a text in exactly the same way. For example, read the following:

Marty was on his way to school. He was very worried about the science lesson.

Stop for a minute and think about what these sentences mean. Now read the next sentence to see if your interpretation changes.

He thought he might have classroom management problems because of the hands-on activity he had planned.

Chances are you changed your understanding from the first two sentences to the final sentence as you received more information. You had a great deal of background knowledge about the subject—attending school—to help you understand the first two sentences, but you probably concluded it was a stu-

---

Characteristics of the interactive theory of reading.   **exhibit   5.1**

- During reading and learning to read, readers process language by using features of the print along with prior knowledge, culture, and previous experiences. Reading is the construction of meaning that occurs through the interaction of the text and the reader's prior knowledge.

- Reading consists of a balance of decoding skills, vocabulary knowledge, and comprehension strategies.

- Readers use three types of cueing systems to make meaning while reading: graphophonic, semantic, and syntactic.

Adapted from Pressley, M. (2002). *Reading instruction that works: The case for balanced reading* (2nd ed.). New York: Guilford.

dent who was worried about the science lesson, perhaps because he had not done his homework or the concepts were confusing to him. You likely based these or similar expectations on your previous experiences as a student. When you encountered the third sentence, you likely had an "aha moment" when you realized that Marty was a teacher. You probably based this conclusion on your knowledge of teacher education, identifying Marty's concern about classroom management and the hands-on activity as the concerns of a teacher. You and your peers probably interpreted these sentences in similar ways. However, friends or family members who are not teachers or preservice teachers may not have understood the terms "classroom management" and "hands-on activity" in the same way, because they have different background subject knowledge and previous experiences.

Although experience and subject knowledge are extremely important in understanding a text, the reader must also attend to print and literary conventions. The interactive theory of reading places equal emphasis on the actual text and the reader's background knowledge about textual conventions. For example, when Svetlana, a student in Ms. Watson's fourth-grade class, was reading a fantasy story, she drew on her knowledge of fantasy stories such as *Harry Potter* (Rowling, 1998) and *A Wrinkle in Time* (L'Engle, 1973) to make sense of the story's structure and plot. Svetlana also noticed when the author used an exclamation mark or question mark in the dialogue to help her understand the character's emotions at that time in the story. Finally, Svetlana asked herself questions such as "Does this make sense?" and "Is this what I would expect in a fantasy story?" as she read the story. These are just a few of the ways readers use their knowledge about textual conventions—such as punctuation and genres—to make sense of a story.

Decoding, Vocabulary, and Comprehension

In the interactive theory of reading, skills in decoding, vocabulary, and comprehension are all important. It is only through the application of skills in these three areas that the student can become an independent reader.

Decoding. Decoding skills refer to the ability to figure out words by breaking them into parts. Decoding includes using phonics skills and looking for word parts: prefixes, suffixes, and familiar chunks such as -ip and -tion. A reader must have solid decoding strategies in order to figure out unknown words efficiently while reading.

Vocabulary. Readers must also have strong vocabulary skills, including both sight word vocabulary and meaning vocabulary. Sight vocabulary includes high-frequency and high-function words such as *in, on, before,* and *have.* See Exhibit 5.2 for a list of the 50 most common sight words in reading. If students have a strong sight vocabulary, they can easily read these common words when they encounter them in print and concentrate on understanding the text rather than struggling to decode each word. It is important to note

Fifty most common sight words.			*exhibit*	**5.2**

a*	by	if	said	to*
about	can	in*	she	up
all	for*	is*	so	was*
an	from	it*	some	we
and*	had	not	that*	were
are	have	of*	the*	what
as	he*	on	their	when
at	her	one	there	with
be	his	or	they	would
but	I	out	this	you*

From Johns, J. L. (1981). The development of the revised Dolch list. *Illinois School Research and Development, 17,* 15–24. Reprinted with the permission of Jerry L. Johns.

that 13 words account for nearly 25 percent of the words readers encounter in texts. These 13 words are marked with an asterisk (*) in Exhibit 5.2.

In addition to having a strong sight word vocabulary, readers must possess content vocabularies. Vocabulary words are labels for concepts, and students must understand the concepts behind key vocabulary words in order to understand what they read (Blachowicz & Fisher, 2000). In addition, readers need to develop strong vocabularies for their reading, writing, listening, and speaking. The more words students know, the easier reading becomes for them.

Comprehension. Reading skills are important, but comprehension is the goal of all reading. In other words, the purpose of reading is to understand what one is reading. Comprehension strategies include basic skills such as identifying the main idea and more complex strategies such as making inferences and drawing conclusions. To comprehend texts, readers need to be able to use a variety of comprehension strategies (Harvey & Goudvis, 2000). The most useful comprehension strategies, according to the National Reading Panel report (2000), are monitoring comprehension (knowing when you do or do not understand what you are reading), using graphic and semantic organizers (such as maps or webs) to understand concepts and relationships among concepts in a text, asking and answering questions about a text, recognizing story structure and informational text structure, and summarizing.

In the interactive theory of reading, readers' ability to use decoding, vocabulary, and comprehension skills and strategies to understand what they are reading is of prime importance. Articles II and III of this chapter discuss these areas in greater detail and recommend instructional strategies for the classroom.

Cueing Systems

Readers use the following three cueing systems to help them identify unknown words and make meaning from the texts they read (Ruddell, Ruddell, & Singer, 1994).

- *Graphophonic system.* This system focuses on using sound–symbol correspondences to identify unknown words. An easy way to remember the nature of the graphophonic cueing system is to think of the word "phonics." In other words, readers look at letters in the word and correlate them with the sounds they make to identify unknown words. Sometimes teachers ask students if a word they said while reading aloud "looks right" to get them to attend to the actual letters on the page.
- *Syntactic system.* The syntactic cueing system focuses on using the structure of language to determine if a word "sounds right" or "sounds like language."
- *Semantic system.* This system focuses on meaning and relies on using context clues and background knowledge to determine if a word "makes sense."

Good readers use the three cueing systems to make meaning when they are reading. For example, when Lilliana, a student in Ms. Watson's fourth-grade class, encountered the word "stupendous" in her reading, she asked herself questions such as: "What is the beginning sound?" "Are there chunks I can identify in the word?" (graphophonic cues), "Does it sound right?" (syntactic cue), and "Does it make sense?" (semantic cue). Using the cueing systems in tandem is sometimes called cross checking. When Rasem, another fourth-grade student in Ms. Watson's class, came to the word "appropriate" while reading a novel, he asked himself, "Does it look right?" (graphophonic), "Does it sound right?" (syntactic), and "Does it make sense?" (semantic). Exhibit 5.3 shows how the three cueing systems operate to help the reader make meaning.

T. J., BEGINNING TEACHER ▶ I'm just finishing my first year of teaching, and I have to be honest: I was overwhelmed by teaching reading. I found the basal manual intimidating because it contained so much information. I also had a ton of great reading activities I learned during my teacher education program and student teaching that I wanted to use. When I looked at the manual and all of the activities I wanted to do, I found myself asking "How can I do all of this?!" I talked to my mentor, who teaches next door and has over 15 years of experience. She asked me what theory of reading I used to guide my instruction. I hadn't thought about theories or philosophies since I graduated from my teacher education program. She helped me realize that I believe in a balanced approach to reading instruction, and that helped me figure out what to include and what to leave out when teaching reading. I believe I'll know what works after a few years of teaching. It's amazing how thinking about the theory or the "why" behind my teaching has helped me develop a clearer plan for teaching reading.

Syntactic
"Does it sound right?"
"Does it sound like English?"
"Does it sound like language?"

MAKING MEANING

Graphophonic
"Does it look right?"
"What does it start with?"
"Are there word chunks I know?"

Semantic
"Does it make sense?"
"What do I already know about this?"

READING STAGES

Reading is a complex process, involving more than just looking at the words or letters on a page. Mature readers interact with text during three distinct phases: pre-reading, during reading, and post-reading (Blachowicz & Ogle, 2001). The phases are similar to ones often used to describe the writing process and to guide instructional processes.

During the pre-reading phase, readers get ready to read. They set a purpose for reading, activate background knowledge about the topic, and develop a plan for approaching the text. The during reading phase is when readers actually read the text, monitor understanding, and apply strategies for comprehension. In the post-reading phase, readers focus on summarizing ideas from the text, applying information from the text, and extending their understanding of the text. Let's see how the three phases of the reading process look for Lucas, a student in Ms. Watson's classroom.

- *Pre-reading.* Lucas is going to be reading the novel *Holes* (Sachar, 1998). Before he starts reading, he looks at the cover of the book and reads the description on the book jacket. He predicts what the book will be about. He also thinks about the information his friends who have already read the book have shared with him. He approaches this novel as a fun task that he'll do for recreation.

- *During reading.* As Lucas is reading the short chapters in this novel, he frequently stops and asks himself, "What just happened?" "I wonder what that means for the story?" and "I wonder what will happen next?" When he comes across a part that he does not understand, he stops and thinks about strategies he can use to make sense of his reading. He considers whether he should reread, use a decoding strategy to figure out a word's meaning, or ask someone else for clarification.

- *Post-reading.* After Lucas is done reading the novel, he tells a friend about his favorite parts of the story. He discusses his ideas with several friends who have already read the book. He considers how he would have reacted if he had been Stanley Yelnats, the main character in the novel. He also concludes that he enjoyed the book and is interested in reading other novels by the same author.

The phases of the reading process seem to flow effortlessly for Lucas, but he has received much instruction and guidance from Ms. Watson and his previous teachers to reach this point. Articles II and III in this chapter will provide specific teaching strategies to support pre-reading, during reading, and post-reading processes.

LEARNING HOW TO READ

Children are not born knowing how to read. Language development and learning how to read begin right at birth and continue until a child can read independently. The process is separated into two main stages—the emergent literacy stage and the independent reading stage—each of which also has sub-stages.

Emergent Literacy

As soon as children are born, they begin interacting with their surroundings, learning about communication, and building the foundations for reading. Infants learn a great deal as parents, caregivers, and family members talk to them, read to them, and expose them to print in their daily lives. Children explore books, label pictures, and learn important concepts as they progress from birth through the preschool years (Yaden, Rowe, & MacGillivray, 2000). This stage, often labeled as the emergent literacy phase (Teale & Sulzby, 1986), continues until children can read and write independently. Since so many important changes take place during the emergent literacy phase, some researchers have broken it down into more specific stages. These include the magical stage, self-concepting stage, and bridging stage (Cochrane, Cochrane, Scalena, & Buchanan, 1984).

Magical Stage

The magical stage begins in infancy. During this stage, children show an interest in handling books (although they may mishandle them by chewing on or ripping pages), see reading as a magical process, enjoy listening to stories read to them (often showing a desire to hear the same story read again and again), and enjoy labeling pictures in books.

Self-Concepting Stage

When young children reach the self-concepting stage, they begin to view themselves as readers, although they may not be able to read the text themselves. At this stage, children "pretend read" to their toys, dolls, or others, usually by retelling parts of a very familiar text. They can recognize their names and possibly other common words or names (e.g., McDonald's, Crest) in print, and they can construct meaning for a story told in pictures. Children at this stage also orally rhyme words and understand common story elements and structures such as "Once upon a time" and "They lived happily ever after."

Bridging Stage

During the bridging stage, children can pick out individual words and letters in reading. They can read familiar books and poems, and they use pictures to support their reading. They may be able to read words in one context, such as in a familiar poem or story, but not in another situation. They gain increasing control over the graphophonic cueing system. This stage is often referred to as beginning reading.

Independent Reading

Once children have moved through the magical stage, self-concepting stage, and bridging stage, they are on their way to becoming independent readers. The independent reading process has also been broken down into several specific stages. These are the takeoff stage, independent stage, and skilled reader stage.

Takeoff Stage

During the takeoff stage, children demonstrate great interest in and enthusiasm about reading. They want others to read to them often, and they also want to demonstrate their reading skills for others. Children in this stage understand that print carries the message in reading, and they can identify words in familiar and unfamiliar texts. Oral reading during this stage tends to focus on letters and words, with fluency developing later.

Independent Stage

Students in the independent stage take great pride in reading books by and for themselves. Independent readers have gained control over the three cueing systems (graphophonic, syntactic, and semantic), and they apply them appropriately.

Students in the independent reading stage take great pride in reading books by and for themselves.

Oral reading during this stage is fluent, meaning that it is done smoothly, easily, and with expression. Independent readers have accomplished much in their reading, but they have not yet learned to analyze texts critically. This becomes the focus of the final stage of reading acquisition—the skilled reader phase.

Skilled Reader Stage

The skilled reader not only understands print but also uses print to support and extend thinking. Becoming a skilled reader may begin in the elementary school years, but it continues throughout the lifetime. The skilled reader develops critical reading strategies, including questioning the validity of what is read, drawing conclusions beyond the text, and considering the purposes and limitations of texts. Skilled readers read a wide variety of texts, including those that are far removed from the reader's personal experience and background knowledge. Skilled readers adjust their reading rate according to the type of text and purpose, make inferences from and beyond the text, and consider multiple perspectives on or responses to the text.

Understanding Reading Acquisition

Interview a teacher or parent about children's reading acquisition. If possible, observe and interact with a child or children to gain greater insight into the stages of reading acquisition. Consider the information presented in this article about the magical stage, self-concepting stage, bridging stage, takeoff stage, independent stage, and skilled reader stage during your interview and observation/interaction. What insights can you gain about reading acquisition from this experience? Share your findings and insights with your class colleagues.

Note to instructor: If possible, have preservice teachers target the following levels to gain information about the various stages of reading acquisition: infant/toddler; preschool; grades K–1; grades 2–3; grades 4–5; and grades 6–8.

FINAL REFLECTIONS

Reading is a critical aspect of school and life. This article presented background theories about the reading process and stages of reading acquisition, but it did not examine how teachers can provide appropriate reading instruction in their classrooms. Articles II and III will address the five key elements of reading instruction and recommend teaching strategies in each of these areas. It is likely that you will take an entire course in your teacher education program devoted specifically to reading instruction.

As Ms. Watson and her students demonstrated in the Window to the Classroom for this chapter, reading is a complex process that has many dimensions. Providing students with the necessary skills and strategies to become skilled readers is certainly an important goal for all teachers; however, it is not the only goal. Teachers must also help students develop a love of reading and encourage them to become lifelong readers who not only *can* read but *choose* to read!

Strategies for Teaching Comprehension, Vocabulary, and Reading Fluency

Reading instruction is a critical component of the language arts curriculum. Determining how to teach reading can feel like a daunting challenge. A good way to get started is to reflect on what you know about your students, review your state's curriculum standards, consider the key elements of reading instruction suggested by research, and learn about strategies for incorporating these elements into your reading program. As you begin to organize for reading instruction, you will probably find that it helps to think in terms of the components of reading. These components—phonemic awareness, phonics, vocabulary, fluency, and comprehension—all impact a student's reading ability. Effective readers use all five components without thinking about how they are interacting, but instructional strategies often focus on one or more of them. This article describes some of the instructional strategies that can help readers focus on comprehension, vocabulary, and fluency to become effective readers.

COMPREHENSION

Comprehension, or understanding text, is the purpose of reading; therefore, comprehension instruction is a key component of any reading instructional program (Block & Pressley, 2002; Keene & Zimmermann, 1997). If a student can decode the words correctly but does not understand what she has read, she is not really reading (Pressley, 2000).

Factors in Comprehension

According to *Put Reading First* (Armbruster, Lehr, & Osborn, 2003), good readers must be *purposeful* and *active* in order to comprehend.

Purposeful Reading

When readers have a purpose or reason for reading, they are more likely to understand the text. For example, when reading directions to assemble a toy, the reader has a clear purpose, and this purpose is very different from the purposes for reading a story, an encyclopedia article, or a personal letter. In Ms. Watson's fourth-grade classroom, she works with four students, Joy, Emil, DeMichael, and Grace, in a small group and guides them through reading an informational text on tornadoes. Ms. Watson has her students skim the text, look at the pictures and headings, and predict what they think they will learn about tornadoes as a result of reading the text. Next, she asks the students to pose questions they think will be answered by the text. Finally, she guides her students through the reading with the purpose of answering the questions they generated. When students have a specific purpose for reading a text, they are more focused and their comprehension is stronger.

Active Reading

Being an active reader is an important factor in comprehension. Active readers think as they read (Blachowicz & Ogle, 2001). They use their prior knowledge, understanding of vocabulary and language structure (syntax), and reading strategies to make sense of their reading. They monitor their reading and use strategies to aid their comprehension when they don't understand what they are reading. For example, Nico, a student in Ms. Watson's classroom, is reading a story from the class literature anthology. He comes to a part that reads, "Katrina felt apprehensive and worried. How could she make a quick decision when she was entirely unsure what to do? How she wished her sister were here to help her decide what to choose." Nico stopped here and asked himself, "What's apprehensive? I don't know that word. Is there anything in the sentence that can give me a hint about what it means?" As Nico uses the context from the excerpt, he guesses that "apprehensive" means something like "worried." He decides to reread the section to see if it now makes sense. Nico is thinking, connecting, monitoring, and making sense while he reads. He is an active reader.

Instructional Standards and Goals

In teaching reading comprehension, as in all areas of language arts instruction, the teacher must consider what she knows about her students, including their strengths, needs, and interests, in order to make plans for appropriate instruction. Once the teacher considers where her students are in the area of reading comprehension, she then consults the state curricular standards to determine what comprehension instruction is most appropriate for her students. The examples from the Texas Essential Knowledge and Skills shown in Exhibit 5.4 suggest some of the skills associated with comprehension.

Reading/comprehension standards for grades K–3, from the Texas Essential Knowledge and Skills.	*exhibit* **5.4**

Reading/comprehension. The student uses a variety of strategies to comprehend selections read aloud and selections read independently. The student is expected to:

(A) use prior knowledge to anticipate meaning and make sense of texts (K–3);

(B) establish purposes for reading and listening such as to be informed, to follow directions, and to be entertained (K–3);

(C) retell or act out the order of important events in stories (K–3);

(D) monitor his/her own comprehension and act purposefully when comprehension breaks down using strategies such as rereading, searching for clues, and asking for help (1–3);

(E) draw and discuss visual images based on text descriptions (1–3);

(F) make and explain inferences from texts such as determining important ideas and causes and effects, making predictions, and drawing conclusions (1–3); and

(G) identify similarities and differences across texts such as in topics, characters, and problems (1–2).

Comprehension Teaching Strategies

In a review of research, the National Reading Panel report (2000) concludes that comprehension can be taught and that several general strategies are the most effective routes for teaching students to become purposeful, active readers who understand what they read. The key strategies are:

- monitoring comprehension
- using graphic organizers
- answering and generating questions
- recognizing story structure
- summarizing

You will notice that many of these strategies are evident in the comprehension goals listed in your state standards. For each of these strategies, we will provide a brief description and an instructional activity to support its development.

As you plan instruction of these comprehension strategies, consider the following stages of strategy instruction (Armbruster, Lehr, & Osborn, 2003):

- **Direct explanation:** The teacher explains why the strategy helps comprehension and when to apply it.
- **Modeling:** The teacher demonstrates how to apply the strategy to text, usually by "thinking aloud."
- **Guided practice:** The teacher guides and assists students as they try to apply the strategy to text.

- **Application:** The teacher helps students practice using the strategy until they can do so independently.

By providing students with thorough exposure to and practice applying comprehension strategies to a variety of texts, teachers help students gain control over the strategies and become able to use them independently when reading (Harvey & Goudvis, 2000).

Monitoring Comprehension

While reading, good readers think about what they are reading. They ask themselves questions such as "Does this make sense?" and "What can I do to understand what I'm reading?" Monitoring comprehension helps students become aware of what they understand, what they do not understand, and how to use strategies to aid comprehension problems. This type of "thinking about thinking" is sometimes called *metacognition*.

The easiest and most effective way to teach students to monitor their comprehension is through teacher think-alouds. The teacher selects a passage, story, or other text that contains information or ideas that may be difficult for the children. She places the text on the overhead projector and thinks aloud to show students how to make sense of the text. For example, the teacher might select the following excerpt from *Earthquakes* by Franklyn M. Branley (1990).

> Large sections of the Earth's crust are always moving. Sometimes two sections push against each other. The place where they meet is called a fault. (p. 16)

The teacher has selected this excerpt because she thinks the students will have difficulty with the word "fault," which has a different meaning in this text than the students are used to seeing. The teacher may think aloud for her students in the following manner to help them make sense of this text:

> The word "fault" sounds funny here. It doesn't make sense. I think I need to figure out what "fault" means before I go on reading the book any further.
>
> I know what fault means when it is my brother's fault that the glass got broken. That meaning doesn't make sense here. I will look back at the sentences around "fault" to see if I can get some clues to what it means in this book. The book says a "fault" is the place where sections of the earth meet. Since they are talking about pieces of the earth's crust, that must be what a fault is. It sounds like it is a crack in the earth. If I look back at the picture in the book, I can see if it looks like a crack, too.

Teachers can use think-alouds to model comprehension monitoring and strategies for many aspects of reading. Exhibit 5.5 lists reading processes and teacher think-aloud prompts to use in instruction.

Using Graphic Organizers

Graphic organizers show how concepts are related and organized in a text. Sometimes graphic organizers are called webs, maps, or clusters, but they all serve the same purpose—to help readers see how concepts are related and

Think-aloud prompts for instruction.   **exhibit 5.5**

Pre-reading	■ When I look over this passage, I can see . . . ■ The pictures tell me . . . ■ The headings make me think this will be about . . .
Accessing background knowledge	■ I know some things about . . . ■ This story reminds me of . . .
Setting a purpose	■ I want to find out about . . . ■ I'm reading this because . . .
Predicting	■ From the title I can tell . . . ■ I think . . . will happen because . . .
Visualizing	■ The picture I have in my mind is . . .
Identifying new words	■ If I use the other words in the sentence, this word must be . . . ■ What parts of the word do I know?
Thinking through a confusing point	■ This might mean . . . ■ I'm not sure I understand this because . . .
Checking for understanding	■ So far, this story is about . . . ■ The important parts so far are . . .
Using strategies	■ I need to reread this part about . . . ■ I need help with . . .
Summarizing the story or text	■ The story/text was about . . . ■ The story/text means . . .

From Jerry L. Johns, Susan Davis Lenski, and Laurie Elish-Piper. *Teaching beginning readers: Linking assessment and instruction* (2nd ed.). Copyright © 2002 by Kendall/Hunt Publishing Company (1-800-247-3458, ext. 5). May be reproduced for noncommercial educational purposes.

organized in a text. Graphic organizers can help students understand story structure (story maps), and they are also very useful for understanding informational texts (Blachowicz & Ogle, 2001). Teachers typically model graphic organizers for students first, then engage students in group completion of examples. Eventually students will be able to complete graphic organizers with minimal assistance. It is important that teachers carefully select graphic organizers that match the text closely. A graphic organizer that doesn't match the text can actually impede students' comprehension; therefore, it is important to complete the graphic organizer yourself first before using it with students (Hoyt, Mooney, & Parkes, 2003).

Two sample graphic organizers are provided in Exhibit 5.6. The first is a story map for use with stories, and the second can be used with many informational texts.

exhibit 5.6 *Sample graphic organizers.*

STORY MAP

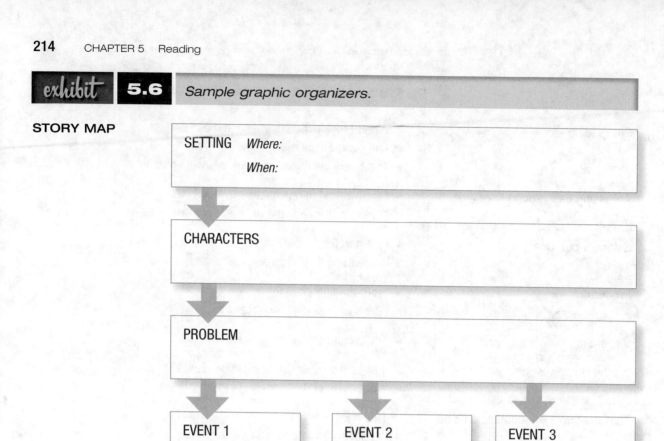

**GRAPHIC ORGANIZER FOR
INFORMATIONAL TEXT**

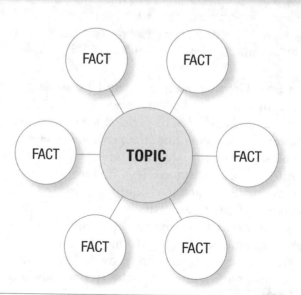

Graphic organizer resources.   **exhibit   5.7**

Bromley, K. D., & Modlo, M. (1996). *Graphic organizers.* New York: Scholastic.

Bromley, K. D., & Irwin-Devitis, L. (1999). *50 graphic organizers.* New York: Scholastic.

SCORE Graphic Organizers (Schools of California Online Resources for Education), www.sdcoe.k12.ca.us/score/actbank/torganiz.htm.

NCREL Graphic Organizers (North Central Regional Educational Laboratory), www.ncrel.org/sdrs/areas/issues/students/learning/lr1grorg.htm.

Many resources are available for finding useful graphic organizers to match the texts you read with your students. Several are listed in Exhibit 5.7.

Generating and Answering Questions

Teachers traditionally use questions to monitor students' comprehension of texts. Questioning helps students to learn while reading. Questions support comprehension because they give students a purpose for reading, they focus students' attention on the text, and they encourage students to monitor their comprehension as they look for answers to questions (Pressley, 2000). To support students' comprehension development, teachers should use a balance of three main types of questions:

1. Text explicit or "right there" (stated explicitly in the text in a single sentence)
2. Text implicit or "think and search" (implied by information in two or more sentences)
3. Scriptal or "on my own" (not found in the text but based on the reader's prior knowledge or experience)

The instructional strategy known as question–answer relationships (QAR) is very helpful in building student comprehension and teaching students how to answer questions (Raphael, 1984). This strategy also helps students figure out the types of questions they are being asked and whether they will find the answer in one place in the text, by connecting several pieces of the text, or by using their background knowledge. This strategy is outlined in Exhibit 5.8.

When students ask their own questions, they become actively engaged with the text (Blachowicz & Ogle, 2001). Students can be taught to ask questions at the three QAR levels—right there, think and search, and on my own. Students can also be taught to ask questions about the main ideas in a text. One approach to doing so is using "W" questions—who, what, where, when, and why?

exhibit   5.8   *Question–answer relationships (Raphael, 1984).*

Excerpt from *Be a Friend to Trees* (Lauber, 1994):

> Trees are green plants, and so they make their own food. Green plants are the only living things that can do this. Other living things depend on green plants for food. Some eat parts of plants. Some eat the plant eaters. Some eat both.
>
> You eat the parts of trees known as fruits and nuts—apples, oranges, pears, cherries, peaches, walnuts, almonds, pecans, hazelnuts, and lots of others. Chocolate also comes from a tree. It is made from the seeds of cacao trees.
>
> Many animals eat parts of trees. Caterpillars eat leaves. So do deer. So do koalas. And so do giraffes and elephants. Porcupines eat the inner bark of trees, as well as buds and twigs.

Text Explicit/Right There: The answer can be found in a single sentence in the text.

Question: What are the only living things that can make their own food?

Answer: Green plants

Text Implicit/Think and Search: The answer can be inferred from reading the text.

Question: Are green plants important?

Answer: Yes, they provide food for animals and people.

Scriptal/On My Own: The answer is not found in the text. There is no right or wrong answer to the question; it must "emanate from the student's imagination or from information he or she already has about the topic" (Cecil & Gipe, 2003, p. 136).

Question: What might happen if green plants were not available in an area?

Answer: Some animals might die since there would be nothing for them to eat.

Recognizing Story Structure

Once students understand the structure or plot organization of a story, they will be better able to understand and remember the story. Story structure includes the elements of a story—the characters, setting, goal, problem, events, and solution. Teachers can teach story structure by using story maps that show how these plot elements connect to form the story. The story map in the graphic organizer section of this chapter works well for teaching story structure. Another tool for teaching story structure is the plot relations chart (Schmidt & Buckley, 1991).

The plot relations chart helps students identify the major elements in a story by completing a chart with columns labeled "Somebody" (character),

| | | | *Plot relations chart for* **Poppleton.** | *exhibit* **5.9** |

SOMEBODY	WANTED	BUT	SO
Poppleton	To live a quiet life in the country	Cherry Sue kept inviting him over every day.	He sprayed her with a hose and told her he needed to be alone. She understood and said she needed to be alone sometimes too!

"Wanted" (goal), "But" (problem), and "So" (solution). These chart labels are helpful prompts to remind students of the elements of stories. A sample plot relations chart for the book *Poppleton* (Rylant, 1997) appears in Exhibit 5.9.

Summarizing

A summary identifies the important ideas from a story or text. Summarizing requires students to determine what is important, how to condense the information, and how to put it into their own words (Block, 2004; Block & Pressley, 2002). By providing instruction in summarizing, teachers can help their students to:

- Identify main ideas
- Connect main ideas
- Eliminate unnecessary information
- Remember what they read (Armbruster, Lehr, & Osborn, 2003)

Teaching students to summarize is challenging but important. Modeling is effective in helping students learn to summarize in writing and orally. Graphic organizers help students visually organize main ideas and supporting details as they prepare summaries. Another strategy that guides students through the process is called GRASP (Hayes, 1989), an acronym for the guided reading and summarizing procedure. The steps in GRASP are outlined in Exhibit 5.10.

Comprehension Strategies

Select one of the comprehension strategies described in this chapter and develop a lesson using the strategy, then teach it in your field experience classroom. Use your state standards to establish a goal for the lesson. After teaching the lesson, reflect on how the lesson went and what changes you would make if you could teach the lesson again. Share your lesson, experiences, and reflections with your peers.

field note 5.2

exhibit 5.10   *GRASP strategy.*

1. Provide students with a short passage at their instructional level. Tell students you will be teaching them how to summarize a text.

2. Ask students to read the text and try to remember all they can.

3. After students have read the text, ask them to tell you what they remember. Write their ideas on the chalkboard.

4. Ask students to reread the text with the purpose of adding or deleting ideas from the list on the chalkboard.

5. Have students suggest revisions to the list based on their second reading of the text.

6. Ask students for suggestions about how to organize or categorize the ideas on the chalkboard. List the categories and divide the ideas into these categories. Guide students to make any necessary revisions to categories.

7. Using the categories, write a summary of the text on an overhead. Ask the students to assist you with making decisions about how to write the summary.

8. Provide multiple opportunities for students to participate in GRASP so they can learn to summarize on their own.

Adapted from Hayes, D. A. (1989). Helping students GRASP the knack of writing summaries, *Journal of Reading, 33*, 96–101.

Supporting English Language Learners

Since comprehension is the purpose of reading, it is important to help English language learners (ELLs) understand the texts they encounter in your classroom. A basic approach to helping make academic texts and concepts accessible to ELLs is to use sheltered English strategies such as the sheltered instruction observation protocol (SIOP) (Echevarria, Vogt, & Short, 2000). Within a sheltered English approach, the teacher prepares instruction to make content comprehensible to ELLs by including visuals, meaningful hands-on experiences, and peer interaction to expand the resources available to ELLs. The teacher builds ELLs' background knowledge by linking new ideas and information to the students' background knowledge and prior experiences. The teacher emphasizes new vocabulary by introducing key words, writing and saying them, and then repeating the words during instructional activities and experiences. The teacher also works to make the instruction comprehensible to ELLs by using speech they understand, explaining academic tasks clearly and completely, and using a variety of techniques to teach concepts (e.g., modeling, visuals, hands-on activities, demonstrations, gestures). In addition, to support ELLs' comprehension, the teacher should provide them many opportunities to use the content and strategies they are learning. They will also need scaffolding from the teacher and their peers in group activities so they can gain control over what they are learning. Exhibit 5.11 provides some basic tips for supporting English language learners.

VOCABULARY

Vocabulary plays an important role in reading. Students must understand the words they encounter so they can construct meaning. Vocabulary knowledge is directly correlated with comprehension, meaning that when students have a strong vocabulary, they tend to have good comprehension (Blachowicz & Fisher, 2000; Pressley, 2000).

Children learn vocabulary words in two main ways. The first is through indirect methods; the second is through instruction. Children learn most words and their meanings indirectly as they converse with others, interact with media such as television and radio, listen to adults read aloud to them, and read on their own. However, explicit instruction of vocabulary is also an important aspect of vocabulary development. When teachers provide specific word instruction, they help students learn new words and deepen their understanding of words they might already have encountered. In addition, teachers help students develop word-learning strategies that help them learn words on their own (Beck, McKeown, & Kucan, 2002).

Since comprehension is the purpose of reading, it is important to help English language learners understand the texts they encounter in your classroom.

Tips for supporting English language learners in the classroom.	*exhibit* **5.11**

- Use graphic organizers to help ELLs see relationships between and among words and concepts.

- Slow down your speech, but not too much! Speak clearly, using key terms repeatedly.

- Use physical representations such as visuals, concrete objects, models, and videos to make learning more concrete.

- Act out processes, use gestures, and role-play to help ELLs grasp concepts.

- Focus on key ideas in depth rather than overwhelming ELLs with too much information at once.

INSTRUCTIONAL RESOURCES FOR COMPREHENSION

Many resources are available to help you plan for teaching comprehension. Following is a list of useful teaching resources related to comprehension:

Blachowicz, C., & Ogle, D. (2001). *Reading comprehension: Strategies for independent learners.* New York: Guilford.

Block, C. C. (2004). *Teaching comprehension: The comprehension process approach.* Boston: Pearson.

Fountas, I., & Pinnell, G. S. (2001). *Guiding readers and writers (grades 3–6): Teaching comprehension, genre, and content literacy.* Portsmouth, NH: Heinemann.

Harvey, S., & Goudvis, A. (2000). *Strategies that work.* York, ME: Stenhouse.

Pinnell, G. S., & Scharer, P. L. (2003). *Teaching comprehension in reading—grades K–2.* New York: Scholastic.

Instructional Goals

Once you know your students and their strengths, needs, and interests, you can develop your instruction so it meets students where they are and guides them to higher levels of achievement in vocabulary. An important consideration for developing vocabulary instruction is your state learning standards. Nearly all state standards include specific recommendations for developing vocabulary during reading instruction. The Texas Essential Knowledge and Skills for fourth through eighth grade, shown in Exhibit 5.12, illustrate that vocabulary development is an important instructional goal throughout the elementary and middle school years.

Strategies for Supporting Indirect Word Learning

Students are like sponges; they soak up words through their daily life experiences. As they talk with their friends, teachers, and family members, they learn new words. As they watch television, listen to the radio, play computer games, and surf the Internet, they expand their vocabularies. As students listen to others read to them and as they engage in independent reading, they encounter and learn more new words. Teachers can support students in learning words indirectly by creating classroom climates that encourage word learning (Blachowicz & Fisher, 2000).

For example, in Ms. Watson's classroom, students participate in many group activities where they discuss books, projects, and topics they are studying. Ms. Watson speaks with her students individually and in small groups about many topics during the day. By creating rich oral language opportunities, she helps her students learn and use new words. Ms. Watson also reads aloud to her students each day. She reads a wide variety of texts, including novels, picture books, informational books, textbooks, newspaper

Texas Essential Knowledge and Skills reading/vocabulary development standards, grades 4–8.	**exhibit 5.12**

Reading/vocabulary development. The student acquires an extensive vocabulary through reading and systematic word study. The student is expected to:

(A) develop vocabulary by listening to selections read aloud (4–8);

(B) draw on experiences to bring meanings to words in context such as interpreting figurative language and multiple-meaning words (4–5);

(C) use multiple reference aids, including a thesaurus, a synonym finder, a dictionary, and software, to clarify meanings and usage (4–8);

(D) determine meanings of derivatives by applying knowledge of the meanings of root words such as *like, pay,* or *happy* and affixes such as *dis-, pre-, un-* (4–8); and

(E) study word meanings systematically such as across curricular content areas and through current events (4–8).

articles, and poetry. When she selects material to read, she considers the content of the read-alouds as well as the richness of the vocabulary. Students in Ms. Watson's class also have daily time to read independently from materials of their choice. Because her students are surrounded by interesting words, they are constantly expanding and deepening their vocabularies.

MARILYN, VETERAN TEACHER ▶ I used to spend class time having students write definitions for long lists of vocabulary words. I also gave weekly vocabulary quizzes. I was so frustrated because the kids could not remember the words after the quiz was over. It wasn't until I started talking to other teachers and reading professional books that I learned that there are other ways to teach vocabulary. Just because I experienced this type of vocabulary instruction when I was a child doesn't mean that I need to use it in my classroom. I have limited the number of words I teach, but I teach them more thoroughly so students really understand them. It's been a great improvement for my students and for me too!

Specific Word Instruction

Explicit instruction of key vocabulary words is another important aspect of acquiring vocabulary. Teachers typically teach words directly when students must understand specific words to learn content or understand a text (Blachowicz & Fisher, 2002). Armbruster, Lehr, and Osborn (2003) urge teachers to consider three general principles to promote effective specific-word vocabulary learning:

1. Teach specific words before reading to help students acquire vocabulary and strengthen comprehension.

2. Provide vocabulary instruction that extends over time and promotes active engagement with words.

3. Expose students to vocabulary many times and in many contexts.

These principles probably seem very logical, but you might wonder what this type of vocabulary instruction looks like in the classroom. Let's visit Ms. Watson's classroom again to get a clearer picture of these vocabulary instruction principles in action.

Ms. Watson has identified four important vocabulary words the students will need to know in order to understand a short story they will be reading. The words are "companion," "weariness," "ignite," and "soot." She plans to introduce the words to the students by writing them on the chalkboard in the sentences in which they appear in the story. She reads each sentence aloud, emphasizing the correct pronunciation of each vocabulary word. She models for students how to use the context of the sentence to figure out the meaning of the word. She also asks students if they have ever heard of the words, and if so what they know about their meaning. In these discussions, Ms. Watson helps students put the meaning of the words into their own language. She also invites students to work with a partner to create their own sentences using the words. Finally, Ms. Watson reminds students to look for these words and think about their meanings as they read the short story silently. When their reading is completed and they are discussing the story, Ms. Watson mentions the vocabulary words and asks students to clarify the meaning of each. Finally, as students write responses to the story in their literature journals, Ms. Watson asks them to use the words in their responses and to share their entries with a partner. Clearly Ms. Watson's instruction follows the three principles that guide instruction. She has introduced words before reading, extended instruction over time while promoting active engagement with words, and provided repeated exposure to the words in multiple contexts. By reading, writing, listening, and speaking in conjunction with these vocabulary words, Ms. Watson has increased the likelihood that her students really understand the words and that they will remember and be able to use them in the future.

The ideas in this example are not the only ways to teach vocabulary; many other instructional strategies promote vocabulary development. Each of the additional vocabulary strategies discussed below addresses the basic principles of vocabulary learning given above.

Knowledge Rating Guide

The knowledge rating guide strategy helps students (and teachers) understand to what degree they know specific words. It is used to promote a class discussion about vocabulary words so students can share their background knowledge related to the words. This strategy can help teachers target their instruction to words that students need to understand better.

PROCEDURE

1. The teacher prepares a list of 5 to 8 vocabulary words from a text the students will be reading.

2. The teacher creates a table containing the words and three columns related to word knowledge. For example:

	Can define	Have seen/heard	Don't know
glacier			
avalanche			
carabineer			
pulley			
ascend			

3. The teacher pronounces each of the words for the students and asks them to rate whether they can define the word, have seen or heard the word, or don't know anything about the word.

4. The teacher engages the students in discussing the words and sharing what they know about each. When necessary, the teacher fills in gaps in understanding by clarifying the words or sharing sentences to illustrate their meanings.

5. The students then read the text.

6. Finally, the teacher asks the students to go back to the knowledge rating chart and rank their knowledge of each word. A brief discussion about the words should also take place to help clarify and review the meanings.

Four-Square Vocabulary

When students make personal connections to new vocabulary words, they understand and remember them better than when the words are taught in isolation. The four-square strategy reinforces vocabulary learning and helps students remember words over time.

PROCEDURE

1. The teacher models how to fill out a four-square grid with a familiar word.

2. Once students understand the process, the teacher models the grid with a vocabulary word the students have been studying.

3. Finally, the teacher invites the students to create their own grids for target vocabulary words.

Word *nervous*	Makes me think of . . . *butterflies in my stomach*
Meaning *anxious, worried*	Opposite *calm*

Word Mapping

Word mapping allows students to create visual frameworks for vocabulary words. The format can be adapted to match the vocabulary words you are teaching. (Note: This strategy works best for key vocabulary words that represent main concepts in your teaching.)

PROCEDURE

1. The teacher displays a blank word map on the overhead projector or the chalkboard.
2. The teacher writes the target vocabulary word in the center of the word map and models the process of filling out the word map.
3. After students understand the process, the teacher asks them to work with a partner to fill out a word map for a vocabulary word they have been studying.

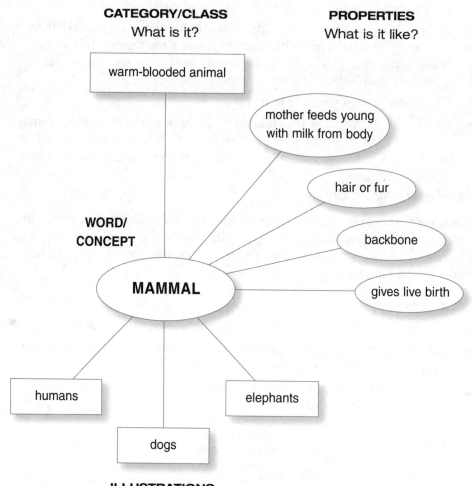

CATEGORY/CLASS
What is it?

PROPERTIES
What is it like?

warm-blooded animal

mother feeds young with milk from body

hair or fur

backbone

gives live birth

WORD/ CONCEPT

MAMMAL

humans

elephants

dogs

ILLUSTRATIONS
What are some examples?

English Language Learners and Vocabulary

English language learners will encounter a great deal of new vocabulary as they work in your language arts classroom. Blachowicz and Fisher (2002) offer several general suggestions for helping ELLs understand and learn new vocabulary. First, they encourage teachers to focus on activating and using ELLs' prior knowledge as a foundation for new word learning. In addition, incorporating tasks that use key vocabulary purposefully and repeatedly will help ELLs gain control over new vocabulary. Teachers can also support ELLs' English vocabulary development by scaffolding, such as by clarifying concepts using gestures or models and using synonyms to link new vocabulary to known concepts and words. English language learners also benefit from vocabulary instruction that focuses on comprehension of key ideas rather than complete mastery of all vocabulary terms. Incorporating various media, such as pictures, charts, videos, and technology, will make vocabulary more concrete and meaningful to ELLs. Finally, having students use multiple modalities, such as dramatization, art, song, and other responses that allow them to show what they know and understand, will build a comfortable classroom environment for vocabulary learning for ELLs.

Vocabulary Strategies

Select a text you will be teaching to your students in your field experience. Identify several important vocabulary words from the text. Choose and apply one of the vocabulary strategies discussed in this chapter or in one of the resource books listed in the box on the following page. Connect your lesson with a standard from your state curriculum. Teach your lesson. Reflect on the lesson and share your experiences and insights with your peers.

If there is an English language learner in your field classroom, incorporate suggestions for supporting ELLs into your lesson and teach the lesson to this student. Reflect on how the lesson went and insights you gained about supporting ELLs in the area of vocabulary instruction.

FLUENCY

Fluency in reading is the ability to read a text accurately and easily. Fluent readers recognize sight words automatically and read with expression. Their oral reading sounds natural, like spontaneous speech. Students who are not fluent readers tend to read slowly, word by word, in a choppy manner (Opitz & Rasinski, 1998).

Fluency is important because it provides a link between word identification and comprehension (Johns & Berglund, 2002). Because fluent readers do not have to devote their attention to figuring out words, they can concentrate on understanding the meaning of the text. Less fluent readers

RESOURCES FOR TEACHING VOCABULARY

In addition to those discussed in this chapter, many other meaningful activities can help you promote vocabulary learning. Following are some useful instructional resources related to vocabulary.

Beck, I., McKeown, M., & Kucan, L. (2002). *Bringing words to life: Robust vocabulary instruction.* New York: Guilford.

Blachowicz, C., & Fisher, P. (2002). *Teaching vocabulary in all classrooms* (2nd ed.). Upper Saddle River, NJ: Merrill.

Bromley, K. D., & Lynch, J. (2002). *Stretching students' vocabulary.* New York: Scholastic.

Hartill, M. (1998). *Fab vocab: 30 creative vocabulary boosting activities for kids.* New York: Scholastic.

Johns, J. L., & Lenski, S. D. (2001). *Improving reading: Strategies and resources* (2nd ed.). Dubuque, IA: Kendall/Hunt.

must focus their attention on decoding words; hence, they have little attention available for making meaning of the text (Pressley, 2000). For example, Mandi, a student in Ms. Watson's fourth-grade class, is trying to read *Harry Potter and the Sorcerer's Stone* (Rowling, 1998), which has become popular in her classroom. Mandi's word identification skills are weak, and she struggles to sound out words. Mandi is also frustrated by the many unusual words in the book such, as "quiddich," "quaffle," "muggle," and the long names of characters. When Mandi tries to read a chapter with a partner, she stumbles over the words and becomes frustrated. She explains to Ms. Watson, "I don't even know what I'm reading about!" Clearly, Mandi is not able to read this book fluently. There are specific strategies that Ms. Watson can use to help Mandi improve her reading fluency. Some of these strategies are described in this article.

Perhaps the term "fluency" is a new one for you. In fact, many classroom teachers have only recently become aware of the role of fluency in reading development. A recent study, the National Assessment of Educational Progress (NAEP) (U. S. Dept. of Education, 2000), found that 44 percent of fourth graders tested were low in reading fluency. These students scored lower in comprehension, suggesting a strong direct correlation between fluency and comprehension. As a result of this study and others like it, more attention is now being paid to fluency development.

Instructional Standards and Goals

As with all aspects of language arts instruction, it is critical that you know your students well and then develop instruction that bridges from where they are to where they can be. In other words, some students in your classroom may be fluent readers, others may demonstrate some aspects of fluency, and others may struggle with fluency in general. By consulting your state language arts standards, you will be able to see the general expectations for reading fluency at your grade level. The next step is to develop instruction that bridges between where your students are now and the state standards (and beyond, in the case of students who have already met the standard). As you can see in the sample standards from the Texas Essential Knowledge and Skills presented in Exhibit 5.13, reading fluency includes reading a wide range of appropriate texts with expression and ease. The standards in Exhibit 5.13 are for grades 1 through 3; however, as the numbers in the parentheses indicate, the first grade is the target for most fluency practice.

Fluency Standards

Using your state standards as a guide, select one of the fluency activities described in this chapter and implement it in the classroom. Afterward, analyze how the lesson went, including what went well and why, what went poorly and why, and what you would change in the future. Also, consider what insights you can draw from this experience about teaching fluency. Share your experiences and findings with your peers.

Approaches to Fluency Instruction

Three approaches to fluency instruction are repeated oral reading, taped reading, and silent reading. According to research by the National Reading Panel (2000), repeated oral reading has the greatest influence on the development of fluency.

Texas Essential Knowledge and Skills reading/fluency standards, grades 1–3.

Reading/fluency. The student reads with fluency and understanding in texts at appropriate difficulty levels. The student is expected to:

(A) read regularly in independent-level materials (texts in which no more than approximately 1 in 20 words is difficult for the reader) (1);

(B) read regularly in instructional-level materials that are challenging but manageable (texts in which no more than approximately 1 in 10 words is difficult for the reader; a "typical" first grader reads approximately 60 wpm) (1);

(C) read orally from familiar texts with fluency (accuracy, expression, appropriate phrasing, and attention to punctuation) (1); and

(D) self-select independent-level reading such as by drawing on personal interest, by relying on knowledge of authors and different types of texts, and/or by estimating text difficulty (1–3).

Repeated Oral Readings

In repeated oral reading, the student reads and rereads a passage orally while receiving guidance on how to improve the oral reading. Repeated oral readings result in improved word recognition, reading speed, and fluency. They also improve comprehension (Opitz & Rasinski, 1998). Repeated reading differs from the most common type of oral reading activity in elementary classrooms, known as round-robin reading. In round-robin reading, students each read a part of a text without preparation while other students listen. This approach lacks educational value for several reasons: (1) it does not allow students to prepare or practice their oral reading, (2) it promotes negative attitudes toward oral reading, and (3) it fails to focus on comprehension. (Opitz & Rasinski, 1998). Repeated readings, on the other hand, support students' fluency and comprehension by allowing them to practice the same passage until they can read it fluently. The students can then transfer these fluency skills to other materials (Johns & Berglund, 2002).

Fluency develops when students practice reading with lots of success (Rasinski, 2003). To promote such a degree of success, students should practice oral reading with texts that are easy for them—independent-level texts (Allington, 2001). See Exhibit 5.14.

For repeated oral readings, the passages should be of reasonably short length—generally 50 to 200 words, depending on the age of the students. In addition, a variety of text types or genres should be used, including fiction, nonfiction, and poetry (Johns & Berglund, 2002). Take some time to review partner reading, reader's theatre, and choral reading to see how these strategies can provide opportunities for repeated reading. (Repeated oral reading strategies are described in Chapter 3.)

Taped Reading

In this approach to developing fluency, a student listens to a tape-recorded version of the text while following along in the book. The text should be at the student's independent reading level and should be read at about 80 to

exhibit 5.14   *Levels of text.*

INDEPENDENT LEVEL	INSTRUCTIONAL LEVEL	FRUSTRATION LEVEL
Easy text for the reader.	Challenging but manageable.	Difficult text.
Can be read with at least 95 percent accuracy in word identification.	Can be read with 90–94 percent accuracy in word identification.	Word identification accuracy is 89 percent or lower.
Can be read independently.	Can be read with teacher support.	Cannot be read even with support.

100 words per minute. Some commercially prepared tapes are read too fast, so many teachers prepare their own or enlist the help of parent volunteers or older students who are fluent readers to make the tapes. For the first reading, the student follows along with the tape, pointing to the words or phrases while listening. Next, the student replays the tape, trying to read aloud with the tape. Students typically repeat this step several times until they are able to read the text independently with good fluency.

Independent Silent Reading

Independent silent reading practice is another way students can improve their reading fluency. According to the National Reading Panel report (2000), there is a strong correlation between the amount of independent silent reading students do and the fluency of their reading. Research, however, has not confirmed that independent silent reading can actually improve reading achievement or fluency. In other words, the question becomes, "Is Michael a good reader because he does a lot of independent silent reading? Or does Michael do a lot of independent silent reading because he is a good reader who enjoys that activity?" Conversely, the question can be posed for a poor reader, "Is Maddie a poor reader because she does little independent silent reading? Or does Maddie do little independent silent reading because she is a poor reader who does not enjoy that activity?" Although common sense indicates that providing children with daily times to read texts of their choice will improve their skills, research has not proven the specific instructional value of this activity. We must note, however, that based on our experiences as elementary, middle school, and special education teachers, such practice does make a difference in students' attitudes toward reading and their confidence in reading, and for these reasons we encourage all teachers to incorporate it into their classroom schedules.

Teacher Modeling

Teacher modeling of fluent reading contributes to the development of fluent reading for students (Johns & Berglund, 2002). The teacher reads the text first, modeling proper phrasing, speed, and expression. Students then reread the text, trying to match the teacher's model of fluent reading. For many students, four rereadings will be necessary to demonstrate fluency. In the primary grades, teachers often model fluent reading using big books, poems, and chart stories. With older students, teachers may model fluency by reading orally from a variety of texts, including passages displayed on the overhead projector or sections of a textbook.

English Language Learners and Fluency

English language learners can best develop fluency by learning to read first in their native language. This is not possible for all students, however. The Center for the Improvement of Early Reading Achievement (CIERA) sug-

RESOURCES FOR TEACHING FLUENCY

Fluency is an important component of reading because it helps readers devote their energy and attention to comprehension (Pressley, 2000). The strategies described in this chapter can be easily implemented in the classroom. For additional teaching strategies for promoting reading fluency, consult the following resources.

Blevins, W., & Lynch, J. (2001). *Building fluency: Lessons and strategies for reading success.* New York: Scholastic.

Johns, J. L., & Berglund, R. L. (2002). *Fluency: Questions, answers, and evidence-based strategies.* Dubuque, IA: Kendall/Hunt.

Opitz, M. F., & Rasinski, T. V. (1998). *Good-bye round robin.* Portsmouth, NH: Heinemann.

Rasinski, T. V. (2003). *The fluent reader.* New York: Scholastic.

gests that ELLs will need to see and hear many books read to them during the school year so that appropriate English reading fluency is modeled for them. Teachers can provide this practice through read-alouds of big books and texts where ELLs can see and hear the text simultaneously, through partner reading, and through listening center activities (Hiebert, Pearson, Taylor, Richardson, & Paris, 1998). It is important to note, however, that oral reading fluency should not be confused with reading without an accent. Most ELLs will speak and read with an accent when they are learning English, and some will maintain an accent throughout their lives. This does not mean they are not fluent readers.

FINAL REFLECTIONS

Reading is a complex and important process, and effective reading instruction is an essential component of the elementary curriculum. Without solid reading skills, students will struggle in many aspects of school. By including in your instruction the components of comprehension, vocabulary, and fluency, along with phonemic awareness and phonics (discussed in Article III), you will ensure that your students have the reading skills and strategies necessary to be successful in school. Although it is difficult to identify individual skills during effective reading processes, at times it is appropriate to focus on reading components during instruction. An effective language arts teacher balances reading instruction so that students learn the basic components, understand how they interact, and use them to make reading a lifelong learning activity. As Ms. Watson demonstrated in the Window to the Classroom at the beginning of the chapter, teaching reading is challenging but rewarding. It opens the world of books and ideas to students.

Strategies for Teaching Phonemic Awareness and Phonics

According to the National Reading Panel report (2000), the key components of reading instruction are phonemic awareness, phonics, fluency, vocabulary, and comprehension. Although the reading components are highly interactive, elementary teachers should understand each reading component individually so that they can better plan for comprehensive reading instruction. Specific instructional strategies can help beginning readers become more effective at using all the tools available to them. This article focuses on instructional strategies for developing phonemic awareness and phonics.

INSTRUCTIONAL STANDARDS AND GOALS

The first years of school provide an opportunity for young readers to learn a great deal about phonemic awareness and phonics. When teachers know their students, the district curriculum, and their state standards well, they are able to develop and implement appropriate instruction that supports all learners. Exhibit 5.15, state standards taken from the Texas Essential Knowledge and Skills, describes the behaviors teachers might expect from young readers and provides guidance for instructional planning in the areas of phonemic awareness and phonics.

The long list of skills associated with phonological awareness in the Texas standards indicates the importance of focusing on the components of phonemic awareness and phonics as children learn to read.

Texas Essential Knowledge and Skills reading/phonological awareness, reading/letter–sound awareness, and reading/word identification standards (grades K–3).		5.15

(6) Reading/phonological awareness. The student orally demonstrates phonological awareness (an understanding that spoken language is composed of sequences of sounds). The student is expected to:

(A) demonstrate the concept of word by dividing spoken sentences into individual words (K–1);

(B) identify, segment, and combine syllables within spoken words such as by clapping syllables and moving manipulatives to represent syllables in words (K–1);

(C) produce rhyming words and distinguish rhyming words from non-rhyming words (K–1);

(continued)

exhibit **5.15**   *Continued.*

(D) identify and isolate the initial and final sound of a spoken word (K–1);

(E) blend sounds to make spoken words, including three and four phoneme words, through ways such as moving manipulatives to blend phonemes in a spoken word (1); and

(F) segment one-syllable spoken words into individual phonemes, including three and four phoneme words, clearly producing beginning, medial, and final sounds (K–1).

(7) Reading/letter–sound relationships. The student uses letter–sound knowledge to decode written language. The student is expected to:

(A) name and identify each letter of the alphabet (K–1);

(B) understand that written words are composed of letters that represent sounds (K–1);

(C) learn and apply letter–sound correspondences of a set of consonants and vowels to begin to read (K–1);

(D) learn and apply the most common letter–sound correspondences, including the sounds represented by single letters (consonants and vowels); consonant blends such as *bl, st, tr;* consonant digraphs such as *th, sh, ck;* and vowel digraphs and diphthongs such as *ea, ie, ee* (1);

(E) blend initial letter–sounds with common vowel spelling patterns to read words (1–3);

(F) decode by using all letter–sound correspondences within regularly spelled words (1–3); and

(G) use letter–sound knowledge to read decodable texts (engaging and coherent texts in which most of the words are composed of an accumulating sequence of letter–sound correspondences being taught) (1).

(8) Reading/word identification. The student uses a variety of word identification strategies. The student is expected to:

(A) decode by using all letter–sound correspondences within a word (1–3);

(B) use common spelling patterns to read words (1);

(C) use structural cues to recognize words such as compounds, base words, and inflections such as *-s, -es, -ed,* and *-ing* (1–2);

(D) identify multisyllabic words by using common syllable patterns (1–3);

(E) recognize high frequency irregular words such as *said, was, where,* and *is* (1–2);

(F) use knowledge of word order (syntax) and context to support word identification and confirm word meaning (1–3); and

(G) read both regular and irregular words automatically such as through multiple opportunities to read and reread (1–3).

PHONEMIC AWARENESS

A phoneme is the smallest unit of sound in a spoken word that affects the meaning of the word. For example, if we change the first phoneme in the word "dog" to a /h/ sound, the word becomes "hog." Phonemic awareness is the ability to identify and manipulate sounds in spoken words.

Phonemic awareness has many dimensions, including phoneme isolation, phoneme identity, phoneme categorization, phoneme blending, phoneme segmentation, phoneme deletion, phoneme addition, and phoneme substitution. Each of these types of phonemic awareness tasks is described in Exhibit 5.16.

Clearly phonemic awareness is a key component in learning to read, but it is not the only or even the most important one (Blachman, 2000). In other

	Phonemic awareness tasks. *exhibit* **5.16**
Phoneme isolation:	Recognizing individual sounds in a word *Teacher:* "What is the first sound in 'dog'?" *Student:* "The first sound in 'dog' is /d/."
Phoneme identity:	Recognizing the same sound in different words *Teacher:* "What sound is the same in 'bat,' 'big,' and 'boy'?" *Student:* "The first sound, /b/, is the same."
Phoneme categorization:	Recognizing the word in a set that has the "odd" sound *Teacher:* "Which word does not belong: 'cat,' 'ball,' 'car'?" *Student:* "'Ball' doesn't belong because it starts with the sound /b/."
Phoneme blending:	Combining separately spoken phonemes into a word *Teacher:* "What word is /c/ /o/ /w/?" *Student:* "The word is 'cow'."
Phoneme segmentation:	Breaking a word into separate sounds *Teacher:* "Think about how many sounds you hear in the word 'top'. Stretch the word out and say the sounds." *Student:* "/t/ /o/ /p/."
Phoneme deletion:	Recognizing the word that remains when a phoneme is removed from another word *Teacher:* "What is 'pat' without the /p/?" *Student:* "At."
Phoneme addition:	Making a new word by adding a phoneme to an existing word *Teacher:* "What word do you get if you add /c/ to the beginning of 'lap'?" *Student:* "Clap."
Phoneme substitution:	Substituting one phoneme to make a new word *Teacher:* "The word is 'cat'. Change the /t/ to /b/." *Student:* "Cab."

Source: Armbruster, B. B., Lehr, F., & Osborn, J. (2003). *Put reading first: The research building blocks for teaching children to read* (2nd ed.). Washington, DC: National Institute for Literacy.

words, phonemic awareness is important, but students also need instruction in and opportunities to learn about the other components of reading—comprehension, vocabulary, fluency, and phonics. State standards reflect the importance of studying words in various ways; however, most of the standards directly relate to the components established in the National Reading Panel report (2000), which identified phonemic awareness as necessary but not sufficient for reading development.

CARISSA, BEGINNING TEACHER ▶ I am teaching kindergarten for the second year, and I was worried about phonemic awareness instruction, since I never experienced this when I was a student. I have found that I only need to spend about 10 minutes on it a day, and it's mostly songs and games. Some of my students already can do all of the phonemic awareness activities, so I try and make instructional decisions that recognize their differing abilities. I pull small groups of children from their center time each day to do some phonemic awareness instruction. Since it's mostly games and songs, they love it! This year I even taught a few of the activities during Open House so the parents can reinforce these skills at home.

Phonemic Awareness Instruction

Phonemic awareness instruction is an important component of the reading program during preschool through grade 1 (Blachman, 2000). It may also be important for older students who struggle with reading. To fully benefit from phonemic awareness instruction, children should be taught to manipulate sounds using letters of the alphabet so they can make the link between phonemic awareness and reading. Here is an example of the link between phonemic awareness, letters, and reading:

Teacher: Listen. I am going to say the sounds in the word **hat**—/h/ /a/ /t/. What is the word?

Children: **Hat.**

Teacher: Children, say the sounds in the word **hat.**

Children: /h/ /a/ /t/.

Teacher: Now let's write the sounds in **hat.** /h/ is "h," /a/ is "a," and /t/ is "t." (Writes **hat** on the board.) Now let's read the word **hat.**

The general approach to phonemic awareness instruction is brief oral activities, songs, and games. Some sample instructional activities for phonemic awareness are provided in Exhibits 5.17 through 5.21.

Phoneme Isolation and Phoneme Identity

Phoneme isolation and phoneme identity tend to develop first and are easiest for children to acquire. The activities in Exhibit 5.17 can be used to teach these aspects of phonemic awareness.

Instructional activities for phoneme isolation and phoneme identity.   **exhibit** **5.17**

PUPPET BEGINNING SOUND ACTIVITY (PHONEME ISOLATION)

Explain to children that you have a special puppet named "Frank" that only likes to say the beginning sound of words. Follow this pattern when doing the activity.

>Teacher: The word is **rat.** Frank, what is the first sound in **rat?**

>Child (using puppet): /r/

LISTENING ACTIVITY FOR BEGINNING SOUNDS (PHONEME IDENTITY)

"Listen to these words: **mom, map, mud.** These words begin with the same sound. What is it?" Continue with other beginning sounds. This activity works well in small groups so all children can participate.

SONG FOR BEGINNING SOUNDS (PHONEME IDENTITY)

Sing the song "What's the Sound?" to the tune of "Old McDonald Had a Farm" (Yopp & Yopp, 1997). Use different sounds each time you sing the song. An example for /b/ is provided below.

>What's the sound that starts these words?
>baby, ball, and bed?
>/b/ is the sound that starts these words:
>baby, ball, and bed.
>With a /b/ /b/ here, and a /b/ /b/ there,
>Here a /b/, there a /b/, everywhere a /b/ /b/.
>/b/ is the sound that starts these words:
>baby, ball, and bed.

Phoneme Categorization

The skill of phoneme categorization allows a child to identify a sound that doesn't match other sounds. The sample activities in Exhibit 5.18 can be implemented easily in the classroom to help children acquire phoneme categorization skills.

Phoneme Blending and Phoneme Segmentation

The skills of phoneme blending and phoneme segmentation tend to develop after the skills of phoneme isolation, phoneme identity, and phoneme categorization. When children have demonstrated the ability to isolate, identify, and categorize phonemes, they are likely ready for instruction in blending and segmentation. Sample activities to teach blending and segmentation are provided in Exhibit 5.19.

5.18   *Instructional activities for phoneme categorization.*

SOUND BAG ACTIVITY

Obtain three objects or pictures. Two of the objects or pictures should begin with the same sound, such as **dog, doll,** and **ring.** Place the objects or pictures in a bag. Pull them out one at a time and ask children to identify each. Stress the beginning sound. For example, say, "What is the first sound in dddd . . . og?" Continue with the second object and the third, asking children, "Do the words have the same first sound?" Continue to use the activity with various phonemes.

ODDBALL ACTIVITY

Present three words to students orally. Two of the words should begin with the same sound and one should begin with a different sound. Guide the children to identify the oddball word that starts with a different sound. For example, "I have three words: **wood, cup, want.** One word is the oddball because it doesn't have the same first sound as the others—**wood, cup, want.** Which is the oddball?"

 5.19   *Instructional activities for phoneme blending and phoneme segmentation.*

RUBBER BAND WORDS

Take a large rubber band and stretch it. Tell the children you are going to say words as you stretch and let go of the rubber band. Say the first word slowly, focusing on the individual phonemes as you stretch the rubber band—**/c/ /a/ /p/.** Stop stretching and let the rubber band go back to its original size as you say the whole word by blending the phonemes together—**cap.** Ask children to stretch their imaginary rubber bands as you stretch and blend words.

SAY IT SLOW, SAY IT FAST CHANT

Teach the children the following chant:

Say the sounds slow.
Now say them fast.
O.K., here we go!

Repeat the chant, and then say a word and model how to say the sounds slow (segmenting) and fast (blending). Continue using different words. Start with words with two phonemes and progress to those with three or more phonemes. For example:

"The word is *no.* Say the sounds slow, /n/ /o/. Say the sounds fast, **no.**"
"The word is **fan.** Say the sounds slow, /f/ /a/ /n/. Say the sounds fast, **fan.**"

Phoneme Deletion and Phoneme Addition

Phoneme deletion is the ability to recognize what remains when a phoneme is deleted from a word. For example,

Teacher: "What is **smart** without the /s/?"
Child: "**Mart.**"

Phoneme addition requires the children to add a phoneme to make a new word. Exhibit 5.20 provides sample activities to teach phoneme deletion and addition.

Phoneme Substitution

Phoneme substitution is the ability to substitute one phoneme for another to make a new word. This task ranges in difficulty depending on the location of the phoneme. It is easiest to substitute phonemes at the beginning

---

Instructional activities for teaching phoneme deletion and phoneme addition.	**5.20**

SIMON SAYS

Use the Simon Says format to demonstrate how phonemes are deleted from or added to words and then have students respond to prompts. For example,

Teacher: Simon says say **bring** without the /b/.
Student: **Ring.**
Teacher: Simon says say **cat** without the /c/.
Student: **At.**
Teacher: Simon says what word do you get if you add /t/ to the beginning of **op?**
Student: **Top.**

WHAT'S MISSING?

The teacher models and then asks students to identify the phoneme(s) missing from the target word. For example:

Teacher: What's missing? **Pat** and **at?**
Child: /p/.

WHAT'S BEEN ADDED?

The teacher models and then asks students to identify the phoneme(s) added to the target word. For example:

Teacher: What's been added to change **park** to **spark?**
Child: /s/.

of the word, next in difficulty is substituting phonemes at the end of the word, and substituting medial (middle) phonemes is the most difficult. Some sample instructional activities for phoneme substitution are provided in Exhibit 5.21.

exhibit 5.21   *Instructional activities for phoneme substitution.*

NAME CHANGE

Select a sound for the day and have children each say their names with the target sound at the beginning (Yopp & Yopp, 1997). For example, the sound might be /m/. Therefore, **Carol** would become **Marol** and **Joe** would become **Moe.**

RIDDLES

Share riddles such as:

"What rhymes with **bunny** but starts with /f/?" Answer: **funny.**

"What word do I get if I start with **game,** I take off the /m/, and add /t/?" Answer: **gate.**

"What word do I get if I start with **big** and I change the /i/ to /a/?" Answer: **bag.**

Phonemic Awareness Activity

Select one of the activities described in this chapter for phonemic awareness. Correlate the activity with your state standards. Implement the activity with an individual child or small group of young children (ages 4 to 6). Reflect on how the activity went. What was easy for the children? What was difficult for the children? What insights about teaching phonemic awareness did you gain? What questions do you have about teaching phonemic awareness? Share your experiences and insights with your peers.

Phonemic Awareness Instruction and English Language Learners

If English phonemes are not present in ELLs' native language, it will be difficult for them to hear, pronounce, and distinguish these phonemes. To help make such phonemes meaningful for ELLs, link target phonemes to words that are familiar to the students (Hiebert, et al., 1998). Research also indicates that activities such as language games, songs, poems, and chants work well with English language learners (Hiebert, et al., 1998).

RESOURCES FOR TEACHING PHONEMIC AWARENESS

Many additional resources are available to help you plan for instruction in phonemic awareness. A few are listed here.

Adams, M. J., Foorman, B. R., Ingyar, L., & Beeler, T. (1997). *Phonemic awareness in young children: A classroom curriculum.* Baltimore, MD: Brookes.

Blevins, W. (1999). *Phonemic awareness activities for early reading success.* New York: Scholastic.

Davis, K. (2000). *Phonemic awareness.* Crandall, TX: Frog Street Press.

Ericson, L., & Juliebo, M. F. (1998). *The phonological awareness handbook for kindergarten and primary teachers.* Newark, DE: International Reading Association.

Gunning, T. G. (2000). *Phonological awareness and primary phonics.* Boston: Allyn & Bacon.

Johns, J. L., Lenski, S. D., & Elish-Piper, L. (2002). *Teaching beginning reading.* Dubuque, IA: Kendall/Hunt.

Yopp, H. K., & Yopp, R. H. (1997). *Oo-pples and boo-noo-noos: Songs and activities for phonemic awareness.* Orlando, FL: Harcourt Brace.

PHONICS

Perhaps you remember learning phonics when you were a student in elementary school, such as by doing worksheets or workbook exercises. On the other hand, you may not remember any phonics instruction during your own schooling. After a great deal of debate in the field of education during the 1990s about the importance and role of phonics instruction in the reading curriculum, there is now general agreement that phonics is an essential component of reading instruction (NRP, 2000).

Phonics instruction focuses on teaching children the relationships between letters (graphemes) and sounds (phonemes). It other words, it helps children "break the code" and connect the written letters on the page with the sounds they make. Understanding the relationships between letters and sounds leads children to develop a grasp of the alphabetic principle—the predictable relationships between letters and sounds. When children have strong phonics skills, they can recognize familiar words easily and decode or break apart new words to figure them out (Johns, Lenski, & Elish-Piper, 2002).

Approaches to Teaching Phonics

There are two basic approaches to teaching phonics. With a systematic approach, instruction is explicit, teaching phonics skills in a carefully designed progression. With an embedded approach, the teacher addresses phonics incidentally as it arises in conjunction with reading, writing, and spelling in the classroom. According to the National Reading Panel (2000), a systematic approach to phonics instruction is more effective for children's reading growth and development because it addresses all aspects of the letter–sound correspondences in the English language. An embedded approach tends to leave certain aspects untaught, resulting in incomplete phonics knowledge. However, teachers use both approaches depending on the needs of their students.

While phonics is an important part of the reading curriculum, it is important to note that it is not the complete curriculum. Children must learn to decode words and they must also learn what the words mean and how they connect in order to make sense of the text (Pressley, 2000).

As a preservice teacher, you may be wondering, what phonics skills should I teach? Do I still need to teach phonics if I'm a fourth-grade or fifth-grade teacher? One way to answer this question is to review your state standards, which will probably be somewhat similar to the Texas standards listed in Exhibit 5.15. In addition, Cindy's Teacher Viewpoint will shed light on some common questions about teaching phonics.

TEACHER *Viewpoint*

CINDY, VETERAN TEACHER ▶ I was assigned as a mentor for our new first-grade teacher, Kristi, this year. She had a lot of questions about teaching phonics, so we talked about this topic often. Kristi told me that several of her friends who were teaching in other schools and districts had some of the same types of questions. She asked me if I would be willing to make a list of important ideas about teaching phonics. I told her I was happy to share my experience and ideas. Here is the list. I hope you find it as helpful as Kristi and her friends did!

Q. When do you teach phonics (in which grades)?

A. Phonics instruction should begin in kindergarten and continue through second grade. After second grade, word study tends to focus more on structural analysis, such as figuring out prefixes, suffixes, root words, compound words, and so on.

Q. How do I know what order to teach the skills in . . . ? There seem to be so many!

A. Our district has a phonics program that lays out the order of the phonics skills for us. That makes it easier, but there is a general approach to sequencing phonics skills that you can use even if your school doesn't have a specific phonics program.

- Teach common consonant sounds first.

- Teach short vowel sounds before long vowel sounds.

- Teach consonants and short vowels in combination so words can be made as soon as possible.

- Use a sequence in which the most words can be generated. Teach higher frequency letter–sound relationships before less common ones.

Here is a breakdown according to grade levels:

Kindergarten: phonemic awareness
alphabet recognition
consonants

Grade 1:   phonemic awareness
blending and word building
short vowels (CVC pattern)
final "e" (CVCe pattern)
long vowel diphthongs (*ai, ay, ae, ee, oa, ow*, etc.)
consonant clusters (*br, cl, st,* etc.)
other vowel combinations (*oo, ou, ow, oi, oy,* etc.)

Grade 2:   grade 1 skill review
more complex vowel spellings
structural analysis (compound words, suffixes, prefixes)
multisyllabic words

Q.   There seem to be so many exceptions to the rules with phonics; is it really necessary to teach phonics to students?

A.   It's true there are some exceptions to the rules with phonics, but there are also lots of words that do follow phonics generalizations. Since decoding, sounding out, or breaking apart words is one of the most effective ways a reader has to figure out an unknown word, it is essential that we teach phonics in the early grades.

Q.   Since phonics is so important should it be the major part of my reading program?

A.   Phonics is important, but it is only a piece of reading! You need to be sure that your students are also reading, learning vocabulary, and developing comprehension strategies. I read that phonics instruction should only be 10 to 15 minutes each day, and that works perfectly for me! (Gunning, 2000).

Note: I based my answers to these questions on my personal teaching experience and professional resources for teaching phonics such as those listed at the end of this section.

Instructional Strategies for Teaching Phonics

The general approach for teaching phonic elements in an explicit manner is described in Exhibit 5.22. The rationale for this approach to teaching phonic elements is that it helps children make clear connections between letters and sounds and it provides ample practice to allow children to relate this new learning to their reading and writing.

In addition to teaching phonic elements explicitly, teachers should provide many opportunities for children to apply their knowledge of letter–sound relationships to reading and writing. During shared writing (see Chapter 4 for more information on shared writing), the teacher can reinforce and apply letter–sound knowledge students have been acquiring through

exhibit 5.22   *Approach for the explicit teaching of phonics elements.*

1. Select a letter, digraph, or other phonic element to be taught.

2. Present the phonic element by writing the letter or letters that represent it (e.g., "b").

3. Tell the children, "The letter 'b' makes the /b/ sound."

4. Ask the children to make the /b/ sound as you point to the letter.

5. Have the children write the letter "b" on their papers. Ask them to say the sound /b/ as they point to the letter "b."

6. Present the children with several words that use the target phonic element. If possible, include a picture with the word to help children understand what the word means. Have the children sound out the target sound as you guide them through the words. For example, you might use the following words for the /b/ sound:

   ball

   boy

   box

7. Depending on the students you are teaching, this lesson can be extended to include writing sentences for the words, reading the words in other materials, brainstorming other words with the target phonic element, or playing a word game.

From Jerry L. Johns, Susan Davis Lenski, and Laurie Elish-Piper. *Teaching beginning readers: Linking assessment and instruction* (2nd ed.). Copyright © 2002 by Kendall/Hunt Publishing Company (1-800-247-3458, ext. 5). May be reproduced for noncommercial educational purposes.

explicit phonics instruction. In addition, during shared reading, the teacher can draw children's attention to phonic elements they have been studying.

Teaching Patterns in Phonics

Looking for patterns is a natural part of learning and reading. In addition to teaching children the sounds of individual letters and common blends, clusters, and diphthongs, it is also helpful to teach students the most common spelling patterns or rimes that appear in the English language. A rime is the part of the word from the vowel to the end of the base word. A list of the 37 most common rimes is provided in Exhibit 5.23. It is important to note that these 37 rimes account for more than 500 primary-level words! By teaching these common rimes (see Exhibit 5.24 for sample activities), you can greatly expand children's competence in reading and writing primary-level words.

Games and Activities for Reinforcing Phonics Instruction

Children need opportunities to practice their phonics skills. They can practice by engaging in reading and writing activities and by playing games that are specifically designed to reinforce phonics instruction. Phonics games can

-ack	-ain	-ake	-ale	-all	-ame	-an	-ank	-ap	-ash
-at	-ate	-aw	-ay	-eat	-ell	-est	-ice	-ick	-ide
-ight	-ill	-in	-ine	-ing	-ink	-ip	-ir	-ock	-oke
-op	-or	-ore	-uck	-ug	-ump	-unk			

Common rimes (Wylie & Durrell, 1970).   **exhibit 5.23**

These rimes can be used in a variety of meaningful phonics activities. First, the teacher should teach the rime explicitly, using the format described in Exhibit 5.22. To extend understanding of the target rime, the teacher can use activities such as Word Ladders or Build It! to provide practice (see Exhibit 5.24).

Instructional activities to extend understanding of rime.   **exhibit 5.24**

WORD LADDERS

1. Draw a ladder on the chalkboard. On the first rung, write a word that contains the target rime.

2. Have students think of other words to add to the ladder using the same rime.

3. For example, if the target rime is **est,** the teacher might provide **best** on the bottom rung. The children could then generate other *est* words, such as **nest, rest, west,** and **pest.**

BUILD IT!

1. Prepare white index cards that contain word beginnings (onsets), such as a consonant, blend, or diagraph.

2. Prepare colored index cards that contain rimes you have been teaching in class, such as those listed in Exhibit 5.23.

3. Have students use one white card (onset) and one colored card (rime) to make words. They can do this independently or with a partner as a game.

be implemented as a learning center, as a small group activity, or as a whole-class activity. Bingo is a flexible game that is useful for teaching individual letter–sound relationships, blends, digraphs, rimes, prefixes, suffixes, and other phonic elements. Sound Spinners can help children apply their phonics knowledge to form words. Word sorting is another activity that reinforces phonics instruction in a hands-on manner. See Exhibit 5.25 for instructions for these activities.

exhibit 5.25 Activities to reinforce phonics skills.

PHONICS BINGO

1. Make copies of bingo cards that have 5 rows and 5 columns of squares.
2. Select target phonic elements to include on the bingo cards (elements you have previously taught to students).
3. Arrange the phonic elements in a different order on each card.
4. Create picture cards that correspond to the target phonic elements (see samples below).
5. Place the picture cards in a bag or box.
6. Play the game just as you would regular bingo, except that the caller (either the teacher or a student) draws one picture card, gives a moment for players to think of the word the picture represents, and then says the word aloud.
7. Players then cover the corresponding initial sound on their cards.
8. A player who has bingo must read the letters and state the corresponding sounds to be declared the winner.
9. The winner becomes the caller for the next game.

p	s	d	m	b
g	c	f	l	n
t	b	s	c	f
p	g	h	b	n
m	d	l	p	f

Continued.

SOUND SPINNERS

For two to four players per set of materials.

1. Cut out three spinners and dials (see drawing below).
2. On the outside edge of the first dial, write target letters, such as **t, b, c, d, f, h, m, p, r,** and **s.**
3. On the outside edge of the second dial, write the target vowels **a, e, i, o,** and **u** two times each (or target vowel diphthongs, if that is what you have been teaching).
4. On the third dial, write target letters such as **m, n, t, b, p, d,** and **g.**
5. Using brass paper fasteners, secure a dial to each spinner.
6. Fasten the spinners to a piece of tag board or a file folder.
7. Have each student spin all three to see if a word can be formed. If the student spins a word, he or she writes it on a piece of paper.
8. Each word is worth 1 point. The goal is to reach a predetermined number of words, such as 5 per player or 10 as a group.

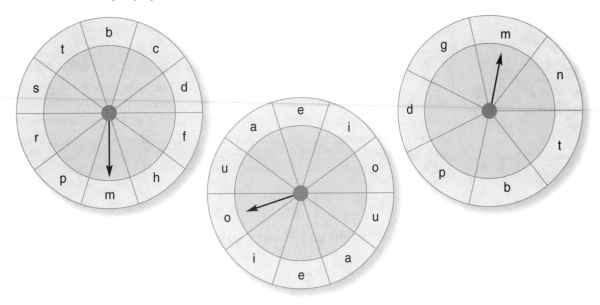

WORD SORTING

1. Provide students with sets of word cards that review phonic elements you have been teaching.
2. Have them sort their word cards individually or with a partner into common sounds, such as long /a/ sound (which can be spelled **a _ e, ai,** and **ay**) and short /a/ sound.
3. The game can be adapted to help students sort for any phonic element.

Testing Your Phonics Skills

How good are your own phonics skills? Take the following online phonics assessments to get a clearer idea of your strengths and weaknesses in phonics.

Phonics Tests for Teachers: **www.departments.dsu.edu/disted/quiz/quiz1.asp? target=quiz1**

Please note there are 10 quizzes. To complete each one, change the final digit from 1 to 2 to 3 and so on up to 10.

If your score is low, consult one of the following self-study guides to help you strengthen your phonics skills.

Eldredge, J. L. (1999). *Phonics for teachers.* Upper Saddle River, NJ: Prentice Hall.

Fox, B. J., & Hull, M. A. (2002). *Phonics for the teacher of reading: Programmed for self instruction* (8th ed.). Upper Saddle River, NJ: Merrill.

State Standards and Phonics Instruction

Review your state standards and use them as a guide to develop a classroom activity. Choose one of the phonics activities described in this chapter and implement it with a small group of children or an individual child. Reflect on how the activity went. Were the children able to demonstrate the skill suggested in the standard that you used to develop your activity? Share your experiences and insights with your peers.

Phonics Instruction and English Language Learners

Students who do not read in their native language or who speak a language that does not have a written alphabetic form may not understand the importance of learning phonics (Peregoy & Boyle, 2001). Such students need opportunities to learn about concepts of print, such as that words carry meaning and that we read from top to bottom and left to right, before they will be ready to begin phonics instruction. Linking phonics instruction to meaningful words will also help ELLs begin to understand the function and importance of phonics in the English language. In addition, repetition, use of graphics and visuals, partner work, games, and other low-risk activities will support ELLs as they develop phonics skills (Peregoy & Boyle, 2001).

RESOURCES FOR TEACHING PHONICS

Helping students develop strong phonics skills is an important component of teaching reading. By providing children with the skills to break apart or decode words, we give them an important tool for making meaning in reading. For additional information on how to teach phonics, consult the following resources.

Bear, D. R., Invernizzi, M., Templeton, S., & Johnston, F. (2000). *Words their way* (2nd ed.). Upper Saddle River, NJ: Prentice Hall.

Blevins, W. (1998). *Phonics from A to Z.* New York: Scholastic.

Cunningham, P. M. (2000). *Phonics they use* (3rd ed.). New York: Longman.

Gunning, T. G. (2000). *Phonological awareness and primary phonics.* Boston: Allyn & Bacon.

Johns, J. L., Lenski, S. D., & Elish-Piper, L. (2002). *Teaching beginning readers.* Dubuque, IA: Kendall/Hunt.

Strickland, D. (1998). *Teaching phonics today: A primer for teachers.* Newark, DE: International Reading Association.

FINAL REFLECTIONS

Classroom reading activities instruction in kindergarten through third grade should include instruction directed at developing phonemic awareness and knowledge about phonics. While reading certainly requires more skills than phonemic awareness and phonics, young readers must have opportunities to develop all skills and integrate them into the reading process. Additional skills, such as comprehension, vocabulary, and fluency (described in Article II), are also crucial components of students' reading processes.

article IV

Reading and Literature

What is your response to the following excerpt from Cynthia Rylant's 1992 Newbery Award winner for fiction, *Missing May*? Take some time to discuss this excerpt with small groups or as an entire class. After you discuss your response to the text, then think about the nature of the responses. Are others' responses different from your own?

I remembered her then. I remembered May.

I began to cry. I had not ever really cried for May. I had tried so hard to bear her loss and had swallowed back the tears that had been building up inside me for two seasons. But nothing could keep them back once that owl disappeared from my eyes and I knew as I had never known before that I would never, ever, see May on this earth again.

I cried and cried and could not stop crying. Then Ob lifted me up and carried me through the door Cletus held open and he took me to my room as he had done so many times when I was a little girl. My stomach and my throat burned and ached with the tears as I curled into a ball on my bed and tried to cry the very life out of my body. But for every bit of life I cried away, Ob held me hard against him and he put more life back in me. He did not ever speak. Just held on to me and wiped away the tears with his strong, wide hands until finally my body was emptied of those tears and I was no more burdened.

From *Missing May* by Cynthia Rylant. Published by Orchard Books/Scholastic, Inc. Copyright © 1992 by Cynthia Rylant. Reprinted by permission of Scholastic, Inc.

Now take some time to read the next excerpt, from a Caldecott Award-winning picture book, *Smoky Night* (Bunting, 1994); it never fails to produce a wide range of responses from readers.

Mama explains about rioting. "It can happen when people get angry. They want to smash and destroy. They don't care anymore what's right and what's wrong."

Below us they are smashing everything. Windows, cars, streetlights.

"They look angry. But they look happy, too," I whisper.

"After a while it's like a game," Mama says.

Two boys are carrying a TV from Morton's Appliances. It's hard for them because the TV is so heavy.

"Are they stealing it?" I ask.

Mama nods.

Someone breaks the window of Fashion Shoes. Two women and a man climb in through the broken glass. They toss out shoes like they're throwing footballs. I've never heard anybody laugh the way they laugh.

Smoke drifts, light as fog. I see the distant flicker of flames.

Excerpt from *Smoky Night,* text copyright © 1994 by Eve Bunting, reprinted by permission of Harcourt, Inc.

What were your responses to this short text? Did you make connections with other things that you have read? Did you think about your own experiences? Did you begin to think about the setting of the story? Does talking with others about the excerpt change your ideas about the text?

READER RESPONSE

At one time, many language arts teachers thought that responses to literature should be based entirely on what a reader gained from the texts. This resulted in the view that there was one "correct" understanding or a "right" way to interpret texts (Langer, 1994). You may have been in classes in which you were asked to share your interpretation of a text's meaning and found that you had come away with a response different from the one your teacher expected. You may have had the feeling that your response was wrong. More recently, it has been asserted that readers understand texts based on how their own background and experiences interact with the ideas set forth in the text. The interpretation of a text is based on the idea that "each reader reads a text uniquely and, therefore, interpretation is an open system" (Lehr, 1991, p. 13). Teachers who recognize this—that because of the varied experiences readers bring to material, they come away from print interactions with different understandings, images, feelings, and ideas (Wiseman, Many, & Altieri, 1997)—usually plan literature strategies that focus on the readers' responses instead of expecting a structured meaning or single interpretation.

All readers bring different understandings to the text and "understand it through their own unique cultural and psychological filters" (Sipe, 2000, p. 256). An approach that encourages unique responses to literature results in various interpretations and many responses to text. Instructional strategies based on such an approach are more student-centered, recognizing that each reader's response is worthwhile. When reader response is the focus of literature instruction, students, regardless of their background or experiences, are encouraged to respond naturally, share their ideas, and listen to others as they consider what they can learn from the texts. A response approach to literature values the diversity and uniqueness of what each student has to say about a text. Classrooms where students' backgrounds are different will benefit a great deal from a reader response approach to literature.

Teachers who use a response-centered approach recognize that the reader has a role in interpreting and determining meaning. The meaning is developed when readers' experiences and backgrounds interact with the author's ideas and thoughts. A reader-response approach to understanding text emphasizes the role of the readers' experiences, values independent interpretations, and consequently accepts various purposes for reading text (Many & Wiseman, 1992).

Reader response puts the reader more in control of the outcome of reading, recognizes that each reader's response is worthwhile, and suggests that the function of the text is to inform and entertain the reader. A response-centered approach discourages the teacher from controlling outcomes, thoughts, and emotions. Students with different backgrounds are encouraged to respond naturally and allow their ideas to be modified after reading new material. This will lead to lively discussions when children share their unique responses to a piece of literature.

JULIE, VETERAN TEACHER ▶ I find that choosing quality children's books makes kids want to get involved with reading and responding to books. When I choose rich, descriptive books with interesting characters and problems, my students get very involved in their reading. I use the book award lists like the Newbery, Caldecott, and Coretta Scott King to find wonderful books. I read the books before I introduce them to my students for instruction. While most award-winning books are wonderful, some may not be appropriate for my students or interesting to them. If you haven't looked at these award lists, I suggest you do! They are wonderful resources.

Award-Winning Books

Select an award-winning children's book (from the Newbery, Caldecott, Coretta Scott King, or other award-winning list—see Exhibit 5.26 for websites). Read it and share it with your peers. Make a list of books your peers shared with you that you want to read for possible use in your future teaching. Consider how you will promote discussion related to the books. Share your ideas with your mentor teacher for feedback. If possible, share one of the books in your field experience classroom.

 5.26   *Websites listing award-winning books.*

Newbery Medal and Honor Books 1922–Present (most distinguished American children's books):   **www.ala.org/ala/alsc/awardsscholarships/literaryawds/ newberymedal/newberyhonors/newberymedal.htm**

Caldecott Medal and Honor Books 1938–Present (most distinguished American picture books for children):   **www.ala.org/ala/alsc/awardsscholarships/ literaryawds/caldecottmedal/caldecotthonors/caldecottmedal.htm**

Coretta Scott King Award (most distinguished books that promote an understanding and appreciation of the "American Dream")   **www.ala.org/ala/srrt/coretta scottking/winners/pastwinners/pastwinners.htm**

A response-centered approach to literature encourages children to use their personal experiences and associations to help them understand what they are reading (Cochran, 1992). Such a focus on personal experiences and associations opens up multiple meanings and encourages a wide range of responses.

One way to think of responses to literature is as a continuum (see Exhibit 5.27). In one case a reader may respond by recognizing only what is mentioned in the text. A straightforward retelling of a story might be considered a text-based response. An evaluation of the writing style, plot, themes, or action of the story would also be considered more text-based. Reader-response theory refers to this acquisition of knowledge or analytical involvement between the reader and the text as an *efferent* approach to literature (Rosenblatt, 1978). For example, after reading the *Smoky Night* excerpt at the beginning of this article, a reader could respond by summarizing. She may say, "This is the story of a riot, in which angry people were smashing windows and stealing from stores. It also appears as if there is a fire." A response of this nature is more efferent and is based on what is presented in the text.

At the other end of the continuum, responses focus more on the reader. Here, a reader interacts with the text and brings into account personal images, feelings, sensations, moods, and ideas that emerge from the interaction (Wiseman, Many, & Altieri, 1996). A response in which the reader lives the experience presented in the book or connects to a personal experience as a result of interactions with the text is referred to as an *aesthetic* response to literature (Rosenblatt, 1978). After reading the *Smoky Night* text, a reader might respond in the following way: "This would be a scary place to be. It seems as if things are out of control and I would be afraid that some terrible type of violence might occur." This reader has responded in a more personal way—almost living the experience. In an aesthetic approach to text, the reader constructs much of the meaning by involving personal experiences.

The way the reader views, uses, and interprets literature is called the reader's stance (Hade, 1992; Rosenblatt, 1978). One type of response or

---

Continuum of reader response to literature.   *exhibit* **5.27**

EFFERENT RESPONSE		AESTHETIC RESPONSE

Text based
Includes acquisition of knowledge or analytical involvement between the reader and the text.
"This is the story of a riot."

Reader based
Emphasizes personal images, feelings, sensations, moods that emerge from interactions with the text.
"This would be a scary place to be."

stance is no better than another, and a well-rounded literature program should allow a great deal of latitude in the ways students may respond to what they read. Expected classroom responses to literature are typically efferent, requiring the reader to recall the story, evaluate literary elements, or sequence the events. More reader-based approaches—ones that result in a wide range of responses—require teachers to plan for a combination of efferent and aesthetic responses. A reader can assume an efferent or aesthetic stance toward a story at any time, and in fact stance may vary for the same reader and the same text at different times. Readers may respond in ways that mingle efferent and aesthetic stances (Cox & Many, 1992). Teachers who encourage a wide range of both text-based and reader-based responses expect a rich variety of reactions, discussions, and sharing.

A reader-response approach to language arts instruction can help students develop their own personal meanings and ways of responding to literature; it can also help students become aware of how groups of readers react to a text. After students respond openly to a text, then they can compare and contrast their responses with other readers. By comparing responses, a group can converge on a socially constructed response. In response-centered classrooms, teachers demonstrate that meaning is constructed socially as well as within each individual reader, as students share interpretations with one another and engage in further analysis of the text (Vacca, Vacca, & Bruneau, 1997). Discussion encourages the sharing of personal responses and a social construction of the story.

Analyzing Responses

Either observe or lead a discussion in a large or small group where elementary students respond to a story. Document responses by taking notes or recording the conversation. Identify examples of aesthetic and efferent responses. Be prepared to share and discuss examples with your classmates. Note the differences in responses among children in early, middle, and upper grades.

INSTRUCTIONAL GOALS AND STANDARDS

State curriculum standards reflect the importance of reading literature in a variety of ways. The Voluntary State Curriculum of Maryland has an elaborate set of standards relating to reading literary texts. Excerpts from the fourth-grade curriculum included in Exhibit 5.28 describe some of the behaviors students are expected to display. Note that the standards are wide ranging, but even this short excerpt suggests the importance given to responding to a wide range of literature in various ways. Be sure to check your own state standards to gather information about how literature is used in the language arts curriculum in your school.

Standards related to language arts and literature from Maryland Voluntary State Curriculum (grade 4).

Comprehension of Literary Text:
Students will read, comprehend, interpret, analyze, and evaluate literary texts.

Indicator Statement:
Develop comprehension skills by reading a variety of self-selected and assigned literary texts

Objective(s):

- Listen to critically, read, and discuss a variety of literary texts representing diverse cultures, perspectives, ethnicities, and time periods
- Listen to critically, read, and discuss a variety of literary forms and genres

Indicator Statement:
Determine important ideas and messages in literary texts

Objective(s):

- Identify and explain main ideas and universal themes
- Identify and explain a similar theme in more than one text
- Paraphrase the text
- Summarize the text
- Identify and explain personal connections to the text

CHOOSING LITERATURE

A vast range of literature is available for use in the classroom. You can choose among them by keeping in mind a few important considerations. These vary depending on whether the literature is fiction or nonfiction. Both types of selections enrich the language arts curriculum and help children learn to read, respond to, and appreciate literature.

Fiction

When selecting fiction books, teachers should consider the five literary elements: characterization, plot, setting (both time and place), theme, and author's style.

Characterization

The development of character is important because it allows the reader to identify and become engaged with the character and book. Authors develop characters through their actions, thoughts, and conversations with other characters; through the thoughts of other characters; and through narration. Well-developed characters seem to "leap off the page," like Ruby, who tries so hard to be like her classmate Angela, in the picture book *Ruby the Copy Cat* (Rathmann, 1997), or like the shy peasant boy, Crispin, who leaves his village after being accused of a crime he did not commit in *Crispin: The Cross of Lead* (Avi, 2003).

Plot

The plot is what happens in the story—the action, conflict, and resolution. Stories such as folktales and fairytales tend to have a specific type of plot that is relatively predictable. To hold children's interest, plots should begin early in the story so the reader can become interested in finding out what will happen next. The novel *Bud, Not Buddy* (Curtis, 1999) has a very engaging plot that draws readers in right from the beginning. The picture book *Amazing Grace* (Hoffman, 1991) provides another example of a well-developed plot that will draw children in. The plot describes Grace's struggle to overcome stereotypical attitudes about gender and race and illustrates how she perseveres in her desire to play an important role in a school play.

Setting

The setting of a story includes both place and time. Setting plays a very important role in some books; it is less important in others. For example, in the novel *George Washington's Socks* (Woodruff, 1993), the setting is the time of the American Revolutionary War, and the location is Valley Forge during the winter. This setting is important to developing both the characters and the plot in this book.

Theme

The theme of a story is the "big idea" that the author leaves with the reader. Some themes may be directly stated, almost like the moral of a fable or the lesson learned at the end of a fairytale. Other books have a theme that requires the reader to think beyond the words for the message the author is trying to convey. For example, the classic novel *Charlotte's Web* (White, 1973) has the theme of friendship, and the picture book *Chrysanthemum* (Henkes, 1991) has self-esteem as its theme.

Both fiction and nonfiction selections enrich the language arts curriculum and help children learn to read, respond to, and appreciate literature.

Style

The author's style includes word choice and sentence structure. Picture books for young children tend to use simple words and techniques, such as cumulative rhyme and rhythm, as in *I Went Walking* (Williams, 1992). Books for older children tend to use more complex language and description. *A Single Shard* (Park, 2001) is an example of a novel with a very specific writing style that adds to the development of the plot. The author, Linda Sue Park, uses very sparse language that is descriptive yet concise. In doing so, she helps the reader understand the character, the plot, and life in ancient Korea. *Holes* (Sachar, 1998), another novel, also uses a distinct style to draw the reader into the book. The author, Louis Sachar, writes short sentences and paragraphs and develops the story through the experiences of the main character, Stanley Yelnats.

Nonfiction or Informational Literature

Informational books for children provide a wide range of literature choices for classroom enjoyment and learning. Some examples of informational literature are biographies, scientific books, descriptions, how-to books, and essays. When selecting informational books, consider their accuracy and authenticity. Is the information accurate and up-to-date? Also consider the language used in the book. Does the author use appropriate language to make the concepts clear and accessible to children? Does the language draw readers into the book, making them want to keep reading? Are the information, text, and illustrations well organized? Also note the use of features such as the table of contents, index, headings, subheadings, and glossary to help students understand the content.

Informational books should contain interesting, attractive visuals such as photographs, drawings, charts, and tables. Visuals draw the reader into the book and enhance the presentation of information. Informative captions should be included where necessary to help the reader understand the visuals.

Understanding Genres

Divide your methods class into groups and assign a genre to each group: picture books, traditional books, modern fantasy, realistic fiction, historical fiction, informational books, and poetry. Identify a book for your genre and read it. Prepare a short presentation to share your book with your peers, and be sure to explain the genre of the book.

Genres

When choosing literature for your language arts classroom, try to include a variety of genres; this will help children learn to read all types of books effectively; it will also help you motivate and interest all students. Exhibit 5.29 lists the main genres. For more information, consider seeking out a course on children's literature at your school.

exhibit **5.29** *Genres of literature for children.*

Picture books: Books in which the illustrations are as important for the story as the text. Wordless picture books do not contain any words; the entire story is told in pictures.

Traditional stories: Folktales, fables, myths, and legends make up the genre of traditional stories.

Modern fantasy: These stories use time and place to make things that are unbelievable become believable.

Realistic fiction: Realistic stories feature characters and events that could really happen.

Historical fiction: In these stories, the characters, events, and settings are historically accurate, but the story is fictional.

Informational/nonfiction: Nonfiction books tell about real events, people, and information. Biographies, autobiographies, how-to books, and reference books are examples of the informational genre.

Poetry: Poetry selectively uses words to celebrate language and evoke emotions. Poets may use rhythm, rhyme, imagery, figurative language, and shaping and spacing in their works.

INCORPORATING LITERATURE IN THE CLASSROOM

Language arts instruction should provide opportunities for students to talk and write—to themselves, to each other, or to adults who are interested in how they feel about the books they read. It should also provide opportunities for students to learn about literary elements and encourage growth and complexity in their responses to literature.

Discussing Literature

Discussion is the basic activity that allows students to respond to what they are reading. Discussion times should be opportunities for students to share their responses to literature and to listen to others' responses. As children talk, they build their own understandings of the literature (Roller & Beed, 1994), and when they hear the responses of their teacher and classmates, they may expand their range of understanding.

Discussions about what students are reading occur during or after read-alouds or independent reading. They may involve small groups or the whole class, partners, or a student talking with the teacher. Discussion does not always have to be planned and facilitated by teachers. It is important to understand that different children respond differently to various discussion venues, and that all discussions do not require teacher guidance and structure. To be personally meaningful, literature discussions should reflect students' interests and ways of talking.

Class meetings allow students to explore possibilities and develop understandings. For example, readers workshop discussions or mini-lessons offer the whole class or small groups opportunities to respond to what they are reading. Reader response can also be encouraged through journals and conferences that take place throughout the language arts curriculum. Classrooms should welcome a wide range of responses, offering thought-provoking literature and encouraging students to negotiate their own meaning by "exploring possibilities, considering understanding from multiple perspectives, sharpening their own interpretations, and learning about features of literary style and analysis through the insights of their own responses. Responses are based as much on readers' own personal and cultural experiences as on the particular text and its author" (Langer, 1994, p. 207).

Personal responses to literature should be structured and organized; they should not be seen as "anything goes" (Wiseman, Many, & Altieri, 1997). Although it is important to encourage responses and development of meaning for each individual reader, teachers should encourage students to regulate their ideas based on the blueprint or framework that the text provides (Smith, 1992). When students' responses are inappropriate or lacking understanding and comprehension, teachers should guide students to fuller understanding. Class discussions where children are exposed to social or group understanding of the literature may help them to do this.

Prompts for Encouraging Discussion

Since most students are familiar with efferent responses to literature, the teacher may want to begin discussions with a prompt that encourages personal responses to the literature. Starting by eliciting their initial impressions will validate their ideas, and it is the most productive place for them to begin to develop their own understandings. The phrasing of the questions can be important in encouraging a wide range of open responses. Some examples are:

- What is your response to this book?
- Does this story remind you of anything that has happened in your own life?
- Have you ever experienced anything that is like an event in this story?
- What feelings did you have as you read this story?

Not only should teachers encourage students to make personal connections, they should also focus on intertextual connections (Cox & Many, 1992) that link the story they are reading to other texts. Questions that encourage intertextual responses include:

- What other stories, movies, or television programs does this text bring to mind? How are they alike?
- Are there characters in other books that resemble this character?

Responding to literature also involves analyzing and interpreting the text. Analysis and interpretation require the reader to take a critical stance.

The teacher can support students' learning by guiding them to refine and sharpen their insights and perceptions of the story (Langer, 1994). Questions that encourage a critical stance include:

- How are the perspectives in this story different from your own? Are they different from what you see on TV, in movies, or in books?
- How do your classmates' views about the story differ from your own?
- Defend your interpretation of the story. What in your experience makes you believe this way?
- What does the story tell you about people and how they experience life?

Encouraging English Language Learners to Join Literature Discussions

Depending on their level of English language proficiency, some ELLs may be very comfortable participating in large group literature discussions, but others may find a large group setting overwhelming. Encourage and validate all responses from ELLs, including those that consist of single words, short phrases, gestures, or a combination of the student's native language and English. Small groups, such as literature circles and reading buddies, may provide a safe environment for ELLs to discuss their responses to literature with their peers (Herrell & Jordan, 2003).

Writing About Literature

Writing about books is a powerful vehicle for motivating student involvement in authentic language processes. One way to respond to literature is in a literature response journal (see Chapter 4, Article I). Not only does such a journal integrate the language processes, but it also provides an opportunity for a wide range of responses. Writing allows students to discuss previously read literature and explore text characteristics (Leal, 1996). There are as many different ways to encourage written responses to literature as there are responses. Almost any instructional writing activity can be used to capture readers' responses to a story they are reading.

Writing is one way to articulate differences of opinion or opposing perspectives (Lehr & Thompson, 2000). Understanding different perspectives is a difficult task for children, and they often need frameworks to help them develop contrasting ideas. For practice, children can be encouraged to take the role of different characters and write about their perspectives. For example, the format of *The True Story of the Three Little Pigs* (Scieska, 1995), which tells the classic story from the wolf's perspective, offers an example of how different perspectives could change the nature of the story. Fairytales are particularly adaptable to different perspectives, and children often enjoy telling or writing a story from the villain's point of view.

If preferences in reading or opinions of a story differ among students, they may be asked to write about their own perspective. Written responses can form the basis of classroom discussions and comparisons.

Learning About Literary Elements

Traditionally, teachers have focused on students' knowledge of literary elements, their ability to identify and critique the use of these elements in a text, and their ability to use their knowledge of elements to interpret texts (Wiseman, Many, & Alteiri, 1997). For example, you may remember being required to describe the characters, settings, plots, and writing styles of books that you read in school. This type of response requires an efferent stance, and it often fails to take into account your experiences as a reader. In contrast, a more balanced reader-response approach recognizes the important contributions of personal experiences and reactions to the reader's understanding. This does not mean that literary elements and other processes related to literature study may be ignored, but that the teacher begins with more aesthetic, personal responses and then scaffolds to the literary elements while students are reading and responding to literature. Beginning with personal responses allows readers to develop personal and deeper understandings of the text before they respond to the text in a more technical manner.

This can be done in several ways. For example, a possible response to the story excerpt from *Missing May* (Rylant, 1991) might be, "This story made me sad. I wanted to cry because it reminded me of when my grandmother went away. I was very sad." To link to the literary elements and encourage growth and understanding about how authors evoke our feelings, a teacher might ask, "What does the author do to make you feel this way?" "What language creates such an emotional response?" or "How was the character of May developed to make you feel sad?" The ensuing discussion could focus on the actions of the character, the dialogue, the choice of words, and the development of the main characters in the story.

Encouraging Growth and Complexity in Readers' Responses

Students' responses to literature are often insightful and thought provoking; at other times they are more difficult to recognize as valuable (Roller & Beed, 1994; Wiseman, Many, & Alteiri, 1997). This textbook and other resources offer advice for using questions to encourage discussions that evoke a wide range of responses and increase students' understandings of the texts they are reading. Still, there may be times when discussions in the classroom are lifeless, nonsubstantive, or content free (Roller & Beed, 1994). With the following strategies, teachers can encourage student growth in responding to literature (Wiseman, Many, & Alteiri, 1997).

- Make a conscious effort to help children read high-quality literature that elicits genuine responses.

- Respond authentically in discussions as a participant, and provide opportunities for student-led discussions.

- Allow student choice in selecting the books they read and the ways in which they may respond.

- Model, define, and exemplify responses to literature.
- Involve students in activities that encourage responses to literature.
- Have students compile their own portfolios of a variety of responses to literature.

ACTIVITIES THAT PROMOTE READER RESPONSES

A response-centered classroom is characterized by collaboration and a high level of participation (Vogt, 1996). Students feel comfortable sharing their responses, recognize that there will be differences in responses, and respect others' responses. To be successful, response-based activities must be planned, organized, and monitored. No one activity or strategy is designed specifically for a reader-response approach. Most of the standard language arts instructional activities can be used to promote a wide range of responses to what students are reading.

Literature Circles

Literature circles, discussed in Chapter 3, Article II, are student-led discussion groups that encourage discussion and responses to books that children have read. They provide an instructional framework that supports literature response. Group members may all read the same book or each select their own book to read. The selection of literature depends on the purpose of the group and the interests of the group members. When a teacher's goal is to develop a reader's response to literature, then all of the children would probably read the same book so they can compare and contrast their responses.

Groups of three to five are appropriate, with smaller groups at the beginning, until students learn to support each others' responses. Group membership may change over the course of a book reading, or the groups may remain together until the book's completion.

Literature circles should function with minimal supervision from the teacher. A regular process, one that students can predict, should be followed. When necessary, the teacher may model, role-play, or work closely with an individual group to demonstrate to the class how members can support each other's responses. Response strategies should be taught throughout the year, in a variety of situations.

To prepare for working in literature circles, a teacher could first demonstrate responding to books in whole-class settings, being careful to show students how to ask a question, request clarification from others, ask for examples, or react to a personal response. Small groups could role-play response sessions for the entire class. Children should be taught to respect each other's responses and to encourage personal and text-based examples. When children are just beginning to work in literature circles, the teacher might provide sample responses or questions on charts so that children can begin with a framework. As soon as they are comfortable with the processes, they can work independently.

Response Journals

One purpose of the literature response journal is to encourage personal responses to literature. Journal responses may be structured or free. Questions such as the ones listed at the beginning of this article can help guide students' responses, but children should also have opportunities to respond freely, without a great deal of guidance from the teacher. Students might write in their literature response journals after read-alouds, independent reading, or class assignments, in response to stories or classroom discussions. At first, the teacher may need to model journal entries, but children should be encouraged to write on their own right away. Prompts such as "What did you think about this story?" "What do you think will happen next?" and "What other stories does this make you think about?" can spark their responses. Readers can be encouraged to illustrate their responses with pictures, computer graphics, or other types of visual representation. Very young children can start writing responses in journals by dictating their ideas to teachers or older children or by using illustrations. Eventually, they should feel confident enough to write with developmental spelling.

Literature journals can be integrated into classroom activities in many ways. The teacher may work with small groups or the entire class, reading to them, facilitating discussion, and exploring alternative kinds of written responses in an effort to help them consider a wider range of responses. Having children discuss the stories before they write independently may inspire more thoughtful journal responses (Wollman-Bonilla & Werchadlo, 1995). Talking about what they read with others can help students see things from a different perspective, ask new questions, and organize their ideas. Teachers should share their own personal responses and talk about the different types of responses they could include in their journal. Older students may use response journals as a tool for gathering ideas that they later might share in class discussions. After students have finished reading and responding on their own, the teacher or other students can react or reply to their entries. Occasionally, children can be encouraged to share their responses with the rest of the class. As teachers respond back to the students, they can ask questions about the responses to encourage more complex responses. The questions might ask students to elaborate, to give examples, or to explain their responses. The students then can respond to these entries. Technology tools can be used in the process, too. Journal entries may be typed and stored on computers. Electronic bulletin boards can serve as interactive journals.

The literature response journal is an instructional activity that can involve all communicative skills. These journals emphasize the interdependence among reading, writing, discussion, and thinking, and they provide a basis for discussion with other readers. Literary response journals can help teachers get to know their students better and assess how they responded to the literature. They can even be used to link home and school—parents and children might read texts together and respond to them in the journal. Journal writing is a flexible instructional activity, one that is meaningful for strong readers and writers as well as for children who need extra support. Good readers will most likely read more texts and have longer responses, while poorer or less motivated readers may need a format or structure for writing in their journals.

personal reflection

Response Journals

For a children's book you have read recently, write a literature response journal entry that answers at least one of the following prompts. Share your response with a peer who has read the same book.

- What is your response to this book? Explain.
- Does this story remind you of anything from your own life? Other books you have read? Movies or television programs you have watched?
- What feelings did you have as you read this story?
- What is your response to the characters in the book?

With a peer who has read the same book, discuss your response and your experience writing in the journal. Share with your classmates your insights for using response journals in your teaching.

Dialogue journals, in which two or more students have an extended discussion about a book, provide opportunities for written interactions and continued discussions about what they are reading. Web board software is available that allows students to hold discussions online, from different computers. Any strategy that encourages students to interact about what they are reading will help them respond to and understand what they are reading.

Visual Representations

Giving students the option to respond to their reading with visual representations can encourage a wide range of responses. Given the importance of the media arts and technology in the lives of children today, teachers should be willing to provide opportunities for children to respond in various ways to what they read. They might develop websites, create graphics, and write and illustrate their responses with the help of technology tools. For example, children might express their responses to the illustrations in *Smoky Night* (Bunting, 1994) by assembling a multimedia production with visuals, sounds, and animation available on the Internet or on CDs. Responding to literature can certainly go beyond writing and speaking. There is almost no end to how children can respond to what they are reading.

Activities That Invite English Language Learners to Respond to Literature

English language learners can respond to texts in a variety of ways, including by writing in literature journals and creating multimedia responses. When using literature journals with ELLs, encourage them to use many methods of responding to text, including writing, drawing, graphic organizers, and so on. ELLs might feel more comfortable responding with art, drama, technology applications, music, and other creative and media resources than in writing. By giving ELLs choice in how they convey their responses, you allow them to focus their attention on the ideas they wish to share (Herrell & Jordan, 2003). If their responses are in writing, focus on the big ideas they wish to share rather than the mechanics of their English language use (Herrell & Jordan, 2003).

Literature Mini-lesson

Design a literature-based lesson that encourages a range of reader responses, both efferent and aesthetic. Consider the following suggestions when developing your lesson.

1. Use high-quality literature for instruction.

2. Use the format from the lesson plan in Exhibit 2.10 for designing your instruction.

3. Modify and adapt activities from this article and others to meet your instructional goals and objectives. Student responses may include writing, reading aloud, discussing, acting, and other forms of expression.

4. Focus on encouraging a wide variety of responses.

If you are able to implement your mini-lesson, reflect on the successes and limitations of your instruction.

FINAL REFLECTIONS

A reader-response approach to literature study implies that each reader is capable of a legitimate response based on experience. A language arts environment that encourages a wide range of responses is one that allows free expression of thoughts, supports young readers and writers, and uses literature that provokes responses (Probst, 1988). In this kind of classroom, students can learn the importance of literary elements while taking a personal perspective and becoming actively involved in the reading process.

Independent Reading

Compared to the many other options that children have during free time, reading a book may not seem to be the most attractive to them. In fact, the past few years have seen a decrease in reading for fun and recreation, and studies find that involvement in recreational reading steadily falls as children move from first to sixth grade (McKenna, Kear, & Ellsworth, 1995; Reinking & Watkins, 2000). Language arts teachers can help children see that books and reading can provide rich and exciting experiences. Instruction that encourages and motivates independent reading can contribute to lifelong learning habits. It is one way teachers can impact children's lives.

Through many strategies, language arts instructors can nurture reading behaviors that lead to independent reading habits. Motivating children to read and demonstrating that they can rely on books for information and entertainment throughout their lives should be an overriding goal of reading and language arts instruction. When teachers make books accessible, read aloud in the classroom, encourage independent reading at school, and allow time to discuss literature, children learn to view reading as a highly valued activity that can be incorporated into all aspects of their lives.

Encouraging independent reading is central to building positive reading habits. Many language arts instructional strategies require that children read independently—on their own, without teacher guidance. Language arts goals should include additional activities to expand independent reading beyond classroom assignments and instructional strategies. Teachers can encourage children to read at home, away from school, in their spare time, and during free time at school.

MARNITA, PRESERVICE TEACHER ▶ My love of reading is one of the reasons I want to be a teacher—so I can share reading and books with my students. I plan to have a big classroom library, daily read-alouds, and SSR each day. I see cooperating teachers use techniques that encourage independent reading, and they really work! I can't wait to get my students excited about reading!

IMPACT OF INDEPENDENT READING

Independent reading is any reading that is done without the teacher directly guiding the process. It happens many times during a school day. Language arts teachers may plan for children to read independently in response to a math, science, or social studies assignment or may require independent reading during reading instruction. A child's desire or motivation to read will also result in independent reading.

Development of Lifetime Readers

When children read simply because they feel it's a good way to spend free time, independent reading becomes recreational. Recreational reading is a highly desired outcome of reading and language arts instruction because there is a payoff when children read on their own. A classic study by the Commission on Reading concluded that "the amount of reading done out of school is consistently related to gains in reading achievement" (Anderson et al., 1985, p. 7). Children who read for recreation tend to be better readers. Readers who read on their own must learn how to do so, and as they continue to read, their reading abilities will increase.

They are also building toward a lifelong habit. Students learn independence by practicing how to be an independent reader (Herber & Nelson-Herber, 1987), and they need this practice—they will not become lifetime readers unless they frequently read for recreation (Sanacore, 1990). Teachers can encourage children to incorporate reading behaviors in their daily lives by including independent reading as an instructional goal.

Reading Achievement

As indicated above, independent reading impacts overall reading achievement (Reinking & Watkins, 2000). By interacting with print, children develop new reading interests, acquire vocabulary, perfect their prediction skills, and begin to make linkages among the texts that they read. They learn where to find books, how to select reading material, and what texts are meaningful and relevant in their own lives.

Independent reading is an important but often overlooked objective of most reading programs. In 1998 the National Research Council (Snow, Burns, & Griffin) recognized the importance of independent reading and recommended that

> time, materials, and resources should be provided to support daily independent reading [and] schools should promote independent reading outside of school by such means as daily at-home reading assignments and expectations, summer reading lists, encouraging parental involvement, and working with community groups, including public librarians, who share this same goal. (p. xx)

Teachers often see themselves as being responsible for reading only inside of school, but a great deal of evidence indicates that they can impact reading *outside* of school as well. Children may read books discussed in class, reflect the reading behaviors of their peers and teachers, and respond to their teachers' encouragement to read on their own. Teachers who recognize the influence they have on children's independent and recreational reading will make a point to plan language arts activities that encourage personal reading.

INSTRUCTIONAL PRACTICES THAT ENCOURAGE INDEPENDENT READING

Independent reading activities can be the basis of discussion, listening, writing, and media connections that often are among the most enjoyable activities associated with language arts instruction. Independent reading that is free of grading, testing procedures, and other academic structures provides reading experiences where children do not need to write formal responses, report on their reading, or share with others. They simply read for their own pleasure.

Providing Access to Books

The first step in encouraging independent and recreational reading is to make sure that plentiful reading material is available. Children are more apt to read when they find themselves surrounded with books (Clary, 1991; Livaudais, 1985). Language arts classrooms should have large collections of hardbacks, paperbacks, magazines, newspapers, and other reading materials. Books from home libraries, community and school libraries, and personal collections can broaden a classroom library. Classroom book clubs such as those sponsored by Scholastic and other publishers offer opportunities to order books at a reduced rate. Secondhand book sales sponsored by libraries and service clubs are also inexpensive ways to stock classroom libraries. Chapter 2, Article III, outlines some additional ways a teacher can establish a classroom library. A classroom filled with books indicates that the teacher values and supports reading.

Providing Time to Read

One of the most effective ways a language arts teacher can encourage independent reading is to provide time during the school day for children to read. Devoting class time to reading without excessive follow-up, such as book reports, worksheets, and other required activities, can become an important motivator for independent reading activities. It also sends a message to students about what the teacher values.

Taking Advantage of School and Community Resources

Establishing a collection of books in the classroom is vital, but school and community libraries are valuable resources, too. Not only do libraries offer a wide range of reading material, but they also often include a media center and other materials that can promote and motivate independent reading. Libraries have attractive displays, computers with books on CD, posters, storytimes, and audio and video books that can motivate even the most reluctant readers.

The librarian's advice and suggestions for book selection are critical to promoting independent reading behaviors. Librarians are usually up to date on current children's literature and can recommend popular books. They are usually available to give book talks and help guide students to books that match their interests. Many librarians develop programs designed to promote independent and recreational reading. Reading books aloud, theater productions, puppetry, and summer reading programs can supplement teachers' plans to promote independent reading activities. Librarians can also lead conversations about authors or genres and discuss illustrators and illustrations in picture books.

Encouraging Children's Book Selection

The ability to select books is necessary to becoming a lifelong independent reader. Children who come from homes where reading is valued will probably have been involved in selecting reading material out of home libraries, community libraries, bookstores, and supermarkets. It is important to invite children to talk about the books they select to read at home and how they choose books in public libraries and stores. Descriptions of how children select books will provide their classmates who have little experience making these decisions on their own. Teachers can occasionally provide time for children to talk about the books they are currently reading and how they came to select the books. They can promote discussion about independent reading or ask students to write about their book selections in their literature response journals.

Another way to help children select books is to develop some system for students to recommend books to one another. A simple file in which children list books that they have read and make comments and recommendations about the books is easy to implement in any classroom. Children can be encouraged to write their opinion of the book and to suggest other students in the classroom who might be interested in reading the book. The file may be electronic, in a computer file, or on paper, in a card file box that is available to the entire classroom.

Reading Interview

Meet with a small group of your classmates and develop a questionnaire designed to find out about children's independent and recreational reading. Questions should elicit information about students' access to books, time spent reading, use of libraries, and book selection processes. Test your questions on each other before asking children. Select at least one child to interview in the classroom where you observe and teach. Document the responses and write a profile of your student's reading behavior.

field note

5.10

Children and teachers can turn to lists of recommended and award-winning books to help in their selections. These vary from local or state choices, such as the Texas Bluebonnet award lists, to national award lists such as the Newbery and Caldecott winners. Many children's magazines offer suggestions, and most major newspapers review children's books in their Sunday book sections. The World Wide Web's sites related to children's choices of literature can become important tools for children selecting books. Students can be asked to bring recommendations from newspapers, the Web, or television to add to classroom lists.

Providing attractive book displays, sharing book videos, and discussing movies or television shows that are based on children's literature will inspire children to select books to read on their own. Children can also encourage others to read their favorite books by developing ads or websites that promote the books. The ads or websites might provide summaries, reviews, and reasons why others should read the book.

Reading Aloud

Most avid readers come from homes where there are books and where parents read aloud to them. Reading aloud can continue to have an important impact on children in elementary years and beyond. Interacting with children during read-aloud sessions promotes engagement and motivates children to read on their own. Reading aloud keeps children involved in reading and interested in reading more on their own (Cullinan, Greene, & Jagger, 1990).

Reading aloud is a beneficial and powerful literary experience (Tomlinson & Lynch-Brown, 1996) that provides opportunities for teachers to share a wide variety of books and texts with the entire class, small groups, or individuals. Teachers may read an entire book to children or read portions of the book to motivate independent reading. Reading aloud is a way to share popular favorites or to introduce new genres or authors. Usually reading aloud by the teacher is a greatly anticipated event that helps to build community in the classroom.

Almost all primary classrooms allow time for reading aloud each day. Although in upper grades time for reading aloud may not be routinely scheduled, reading aloud is valuable no matter what the age of the students (Tomlinson & Lynch-Brown, 1996). It allows children to listen to texts that are too difficult for them to read and exposes them to ideas, concepts, and vocabulary that enrich their language and experiences. Reading aloud builds class spirit and provides a time for common experiences. When children are read to,

- positive attitudes toward reading increase,
- independent reading behaviors develop, and
- comprehension levels improve. (Cosgrove, 1987)

The following suggestions can increase the impact of reading aloud to students before, during, and after the reading event (Tomlinson & Lynch-Brown, 1996; Wiseman, 1992).

Before Reading

The teacher should read a book before sharing it with the class to make certain that it is appropriate for and will be interesting to her students. When it is time to share, children should sit where they can watch the teacher read. This is particularly important if the book is a picture book. Some teachers have a special corner of the room where they gather children for read-aloud time.

The teacher should begin the read-aloud session by introducing the title, author, and illustrator of the book, poem, or other reading material. This is an excellent opportunity to acquaint even the youngest listeners with authors and illustrators who will become their favorites. Next, the teacher should draw children's attention to the endpages of the book, describing how the colors, shapes, and pictures might suggest what the story is about. Children can be asked to predict what they think the book is about and should be encouraged to make connections between their own experiences and the topic of the book. This preparation should invite children to participate in the literary experience.

During Reading

Teachers usually show the pictures of a picture book as they read the pages aloud. Some teachers are comfortable with dramatic reading and embellishments; others will read in a style that is comfortable for them. Body movements and facial expressions can add to the dramatic rendering of a story. Even while reading, a teacher should monitor her students' responses, which may indicate a time to stop for explanations to clarify the story. In most cases, the entire book or chapter should be read without interruptions.

Almost any book can be read aloud, but books that move fast, have dialogue, and can engage multiple readers with different interests and abilities are particularly entertaining. Books with adventurous plots, complex characters, and fast action are particularly adaptable to being read aloud. High-quality books, such as Newbery and Caldecott award winners, are always worth considering, and they provide a great deal of opportunity for discussion and response. Some read-aloud books, such as concept books, interactive books, and informational books, call for students' responses as they are being read, facilitating student interaction with the text.

After Reading

When the read-aloud is a chapter book, the class might follow the reading with activities such as keeping charts of characters, designing a map of the story setting, developing a timeline, or other ways to help students recall events that occur over several days or weeks of reading aloud.

Reading Aloud

Select a book that you would like to share with a student or a class. Prepare for the experience by reading your selection carefully. Follow the routine that your cooperating teacher uses, whether it is reading in a certain location in the classroom, allowing students to sit on the floor, or having them relax at their desks. Use the description in this article to prepare for reading aloud. Afterward, evaluate and reflect on your experience.

field note

5.11

Using Technology

Several technological tools encourage or facilitate independent reading. An important example is CD-ROM talking books, which engage readers in the story through multimedia features such as animation, music, sound effects, highlighted text, and modeled fluent reading (Labbo, 2000). When stories are interactive, children can use the mouse to hear how words are pronounced, animate illustrations, and view special effects that accompany their reading. Teachers should model the use of the software for readers and encourage them to interact with the stories in multiple ways. The stories can be used to promote independent reading, or they can be included in the curriculum in numerous ways.

Evidence suggests that multimedia books can increase independent reading (Reinking & Watson, 2000). Connecting books to "an engaging, challenging use of the computer" (p. 411) proves to be an important mechanism for enhancing independent reading behaviors. For some students, the option to use technological innovations in independent reading will be highly motivational.

Classroom Activities

In addition to the general classroom strategies, such as making books accessible, reading aloud, and utilizing technological innovations, certain specific classroom activities encourage and motivate children to read voluntarily. Many of these activities are routinely included in language arts instruction, and teachers often add their own unique interpretation. You will see many modifications of the following activities in language arts classrooms.

Independent, Silent Reading

Independent reading time in the classroom often takes the form of sustained silent reading (SSR). During a scheduled time, teachers and students read what they want. Children understand that during SSR time, they will read books of their choice for a specific length of time. Five or 10 minutes might be a reasonable time for independent reading for children who have not read on their own before, while avid readers can usually read independently for 30 or 45 minutes. The rules of SSR are simple. Everyone in the class, including the teacher, selects material to read. Children and teacher read silently with no interruptions. Guests, such as parents, the principal, school nurses, or gym teachers, may be invited to join the class in reading their favorite books, providing students with examples of the importance of reading in adult lives.

SSR should follow a routine. For example, readers can make a sign for the door that states, "PLEASE DO NOT DISTURB. WE ARE READING." The beginning of SSR can be signaled by someone placing the sign on the door and end at the sound of a bell. The rules for SSR should be clear and explicit. Some classrooms keep their rules posted for all to see. Readers need a clear understanding of what is expected of them during this time. They should know where to sit, how to get their reading material, and whether and how they are allowed to move around during the silent reading time.

Students should understand that everyone reads during this time and that interruptions should be as few as possible. They should also know that no formal follow-up is necessary after the reading. Many students want to share their reading after SSR, and teachers often provide time for sharing through discussion or journal writing.

To help assure success during SSR, make sure that children have books to read during the scheduled time. Young children should be encouraged to have two or three books in their possession when the SSR time begins. The teacher might provide a basket of books to help students make selections. Older students should be given responsibility for identifying books to read, but the teacher can help them plan for SSR, for example by suggesting titles during conferences, when responding to journals, or during class discussions. The teacher may want to encourage students to make selections themselves, but if children are having a difficult time finding books on their own, the teacher should be prepared to suggest titles.

It is important that the teacher read along with the children during SSR. A teacher's modeling can have a direct impact on the independent reading behaviors of the children in the classroom. Modeling is particularly important if children have not had many opportunities to see adults reading. Adults who engage in recreational reading will send the message that reading is enjoyable and worthwhile.

KENT, VETERAN TEACHER ▶ I have noticed that some students need more structure for their independent reading time. Sometimes, I incorporate ideas from literature circles and have students discuss their independent reading in groups. I also use peer journal writing as a follow-up to their reading time. I enjoy giving students opportunities for independent reading, but there are times I have felt more comfortable with follow-up activities in the classroom.

Book Talks

Book talks are presentations in which teachers, students, librarians, parents, or other readers introduce a favorite book to the class. They are not book reports, critiques, or formal analysis of a story, but a way to share with the class and stimulate interest and motivation to read. Teachers may give book talks to introduce new books, authors, or genres and to entice students to read and experience good literature (Tomlinson & Lynch-Brown, 1996). Important guidelines for presenting a book talk include:

- Select a book that you truly enjoy. Enthusiasm is necessary to encourage others to read the book.

- The book should be on view during the book talk. Some students select books based on cover illustrations, length, size, and shape.

- Book talks should be brief—no longer than two to five minutes. Beginning presenters might find it helpful to write out what they are going to say.

- Describe the topic and something about the action, but not the plot of the story. The presenter may tell about one scene or even read a very short excerpt from the book (Tomlinson & Lynch-Brown, 1996).

- Make connections to other books that the class has read or shared.

Book Talk

Using the suggestions in this article, conduct a book talk for a group of students in your field-experience classroom. Afterward, share your experiences with your peers.

Reader for a Day

Students often enjoy sharing their own written texts or a favorite book, and reader for a day activities offer them the opportunity (Van Horn, 2000). Each student in the classroom is asked to sign up to read aloud to the class on a particular day. They are encouraged to select favorite readings from short pieces of poetry, excerpts from fiction or nonfiction, or articles from newspapers or magazines. On one day a student might read a chapter from a book he is reading independently. Another day, a student could read a short story she has written or an article from the newspaper. The reader is encouraged (but not required) to lead a discussion, and the listeners may ask questions or share their own thoughts about what was read aloud. Reader for a day is an opportunity for students to share some reading they have enjoyed and to encourage others to read the same or similar material on their own. The activity focuses on independent reading and selecting texts and allows readers to play a role in encouraging independent reading.

Summer Reading Programs

Teachers can encourage students to continue their independent reading by stressing the idea of summer reading during the last few weeks prior to the summer vacation. Librarians, teachers, and principals may find the following suggestions helpful:

- Contact the nearest public library to learn about summer reading opportunities.

- Have students who participated in last summer's public library program talk about their experiences.
- Provide suggested reading lists to students and parents.
- Have students produce posters promoting summer reading.
- Provide book talks for a large number of books.

For more information about summer reading programs, visit www2.evansville.edu/mgrnweb/netwdw2000.html.

FINAL REFLECTIONS

Independent reading in language arts instruction can shape students' life-long reading habits. Instilling a love for reading and demonstrating the benefits of interacting with books can make a difference in a child's life. The important message for children is that lifetime reading is valuable. Teachers who are aware of their potential impact on reading behavior and plan activities that encourage independent and recreational reading will have a great influence on the lifelong reading behaviors of their students.

PROFESSIONAL REFLECTIONS

Review the field notes from this chapter and develop one or more into a component of your portfolio. To continue to reflect on your field note responses, consider the following suggestions:

- Teach one of the reading component lessons you developed for the chapter (phonemic awareness, phonics, fluency, vocabulary, or comprehension). Reflect on how the lesson went and what you could improve in the future.
- Teach the literature response mini-lesson that you designed to a group of students. Evaluate your teaching practices and how the children responded to the lesson. Be sure to note successful strategies as well as those that need to be modified.
- Review the interviews suggested as field-based activities in this chapter. Summarize the information you learned from your interviews. What did you learn about the reader's (or readers') strengths and weaknesses? Make suggestions for extending or expanding her independent or recreational reading behaviors. Does the reader need to be provided a reading list, does she need some way to respond to what she has read, or is she unfamiliar with how to gain access to books for independent reading? If you have the opportunity, work with the student to see if your suggestions are helpful. Record your efforts and the child's responses.

Professional Readings

Some books that will expand your understanding of the content of this chapter include:

Atwell, N. (1987). *In the middle: Writing, reading, and learning with adolescents.* Portsmouth, NH: Boynton/Cook Heinemann.

This classic text provides a foundation for readers workshop. Atwell outlines each step of readers workshop and includes examples, book selections, and practical advice for classroom implementation.

Cecil, N. (2004). *Activities for a comprehensive approach to literacy.* Scottsdale, AZ: Holcomb Hathaway.

This compact book of more than 100 classroom activities is an ideal resource for field-based literacy courses and K–8 classrooms. Field-tested and research-based, the activities represent a broad range of methodologies and techniques found to be highly effective in today's diverse classrooms. Each activity features an easy-to-follow organization that includes a professional illustration, suggested grade level, step-by-step directions, an assessment tool, a defined purpose, and needed materials.

Trelease, J. (1995). *The read-aloud handbook* (4th ed.). New York: Penguin.

This perennial favorite of parents provides many suggestions for reading aloud to small children. For classroom teachers, it is a useful source of titles and appropriate age-level material. Teachers may wish to recommend this book to parents who are concerned about helping their children become good readers.

Children's Books

The following examples of children's literature provide insights into the content of this chapter:

Avi. (2002). *Crispin: The cross of lead.* New York: Hyperion Books for Children.

This is the story of an orphaned boy in medieval England who must fight for his life and uncovers his identity in the process.

Curtis, C. P. (1999). *Bud, Not Buddy.* New York: Delacorte Press.

In 1936 in Flint, Michigan, Bud is looking for his father. This is a heartwarming and heartbreaking tale full of humor, wonderful characters, and surprising plot twists.

Park, L. S. (2001). *A single shard.* New York: Clarion.

Tree-Ear is an orphan in ancient Korea. With the support of his friend Crane-man, Tree-Ear strives to become a potter, learning many life lessons in the process.

O'Brien, R. C. (1974). *Mrs. Frisby and the Rats of Nimh.* New York: Atheneum.

In this story, a mouse family escapes from a laboratory where reading skills are taught.

Spinelli, J. (1990). *Maniac Magee.* New York: Little Brown & Co.

A homeless boy takes shelter with others on the street in order to survive. One of his most valued possessions is a suitcase full of books. Although this book includes many important themes, the importance of reading is highlighted.

 **literature LINK**

Select one of the books listed above or below and read it. Reflect on the insights you gained from reading the book. Also, consider how the book could be used in language arts instruction in your field experience classroom.

Other children's books mentioned in this chapter include:

Branley, F. M. (1990). *Earthquakes.* New York: Trumpet.

Bunting, E. (1994). *Smoky night.* New York: Harcourt Brace.

Carle, E. (1995). *Do you want to be my friend?* New York: HarperCollins.

Cherry, L. (1992). *A river runs wild.* New York: Harcourt Brace.

Hoffman, M. (1991). *Amazing Grace.* Illustrated by C. Binch. New York: Dial.

L'Engle, M. (1973). *A wrinkle in time.* New York: Yearling.

Rathmann, M. (1997). *Ruby the copycat.* New York: Blue Ribbon/Scholastic.

Rowling, J. K. (1998). *Harry Potter and the sorcerer's stone*. New York: Scholastic.

Rylant, C. (1991). *Missing May*. New York: Orchard.

Scieska, J. (1995). *The true story of the three little pigs by A. Wolf*. East Rutherford, NJ: Puffin Books.

Van Allsburg, C. (1982). *Ben's dream*. Boston: Houghton Mifflin.

Weisner, D. (1991). *Tuesday*. Boston: Houghton Mifflin.

White, E. B. (1973). *Charlotte's Web*. New York: HarperCollins.

Williams, R. (1992). *I Went Walking*. San Diego: Red Wagon Books/Harcourt.

Woodruff, E. (1993). *George Washington's Socks*. New York: Apple/Scholastic.

REFERENCES

Allington, R. L. (2001). *What really matters for struggling readers: Designing research-based programs*. New York: Longman.

Anderson, R., Hiebert, E., Scott, J., & Wilkinson, I. (1985). *The report of the commission on reading: Becoming a nation of readers*. Urbana, IL: Center for the Study of Reading.

Armbruster, B. B., Lehr, F., & Osborn, J. (2003). *Put reading first: The research building blocks for teaching children to read* (2nd ed.). Washington, DC: Partnership for Reading.

Atwell, N. (1987). *In the middle: Writing, reading, and learning with adolescents*. Portsmouth, NH: Boynton/Cook Heinemann.

Beck, I., McKeown, M., & Kucan, L. (2002). *Teaching vocabulary in all classrooms* (2nd ed.). Upper Saddle River, NJ: Merrill.

Belanger, J. (1987). Theory and research into reading and writing connections: A critical review. *Reading-Canada Lecture, 5*(1), 10–21.

Blachman, B. A. (2000). Phonological awareness. In M. L. Kamil, P. B. Mosenthal, P. D. Pearson, & R. Barr (Eds.), *Handbook of reading research* (Vol. III, pp. 483–502). Mahwah, NJ: Erlbaum.

Blachowicz, C., & Fisher, P. (2000). Vocabulary instruction. In M. L. Kamil, P. B. Mosenthal, P. D. Pearson, & R. Barr (Eds.), *Handbook of reading research* (Vol. III, pp. 503–523). Mahwah, NJ: Erlbaum.

Blachowicz, C., & Fisher, P. J. (2002). *Teaching vocabulary in all classrooms* (2nd ed.). Upper Saddle River, NJ: Merrill.

Blachowicz, C., & Ogle, D. (2001). *Reading comprehension: Strategies for independent learners*. New York: Guilford.

Blair, S. M., & Williams, K. A. (1999). *Balanced reading instruction: Achieving success with every child*. Newark, DE: International Reading Association.

Block, C. C. (2004). *Teaching comprehension: The comprehension process approach*. Boston: Pearson.

Block, C. C., & Pressley, M. (Eds.). (2002). *Comprehension instruction: Research-based best practices*. New York: Guilford.

Brown, J. E., Phillips, L. B., & Stephens, E. C. (1993). *Toward literacy: Theory and applications for teaching writing in the content areas*. Belmont, CA: Wadsworth.

Calkins, L. M. (1994). *The art of teaching writing*. Portsmouth, NH: Heinemann.

Cecil, N., & Gipe, J. (2003). *Literacy in the intermediate grades: Best practices for a comprehensive program*. Scottsdale, AZ: Holcomb Hathaway.

Clary, L. M. (1991). Getting adolescents to read. *Journal of Reading, 34*(5), 340–345.

Cochran, B. (1992). Reader stance: From willed aesthetic to discursive construction. In J. Many & C. Cox (Eds.), *Reader stance and literary understanding: Exploring the theories, research, and practice*. Norwood, NJ: Ablex.

Cochrane, O., Cochrane, D., Scalena, D., & Buchanan, E. (1984). *Reading, writing, and caring*. New York: Owen.

Cosgrove, M. S. (1987). *Reading aloud to children: The effects of listening on the reading comprehension and attitudes of fourth and sixth graders in six communities in Connecticut*. Unpublished doctoral dissertation, University of Connecticut, Storrs, CT.

Cox, C., & Many, J. E. (1992). Beyond choosing: Emergent categories of efferent and aesthetic stance. In J. Many & C. Cox (Eds.), *Reader stance and literary understandings* (pp. 103–126). Norwood, NJ: Ablex.

Cox, C., & Many, J. E. (1992). Toward an understanding of the aesthetic response to literature. *Language Arts, 69*(1), 28–33.

Cullinan, B. E., Greene, E., & Jagger, A. J. (1990). Books, babies, and libraries: The librarian's role in literacy development. *Language Arts, 67*(7), 750–755.

Cunningham, P. M., & Allington, R. L. (1994). *Classrooms that work: They can all read and write*. New York: HarperCollins.

Echevarria, J., Vogt, M. E., & Short, D. (2004). *Making content comprehensible for English language learners: The SIOP model.* Boston: Allyn & Bacon.

Fader, D. N., & McNeil, E. B. (1967). *Hooked on books: Program & proof.* New York: Berkley.

Fitzgerald, J. (1999). What is this thing called "balance"? *The Reading Teacher, 53,* 100–115.

Gambrell, L. B., Morrow, L. M., Neuman, S. B., & Pressley, M. (1999). *Best practices in literacy instruction.* New York: Guilford.

Gaskin, I. W. (1997). Teaching the delayed reader: The Benchmark School model. In J. Flood, S. B. Heath, & D. Lapp (Eds.), *Handbook of research on teaching literacy through the communicative and visual arts* (pp. 677–687). New York: Macmillan.

Gunning, T. G. (2000), *Phonological awareness and primary phonics.* Boston: Allyn & Bacon.

Hade, D. (1992). The reader's stance as event: Transaction in the classroom. In J. Many & C. Cox (Eds.), *Reader stance and literary understandings* (pp. 191–216). Norwood, NJ: Ablex.

Harvey, S., & Goudvis, A. (2000). *Strategies that work: Teaching comprehension to enhance understanding.* Portland, ME: Stenhouse.

Hayes, D. A. (1989). Helping students GRASP the knack of writing summaries. *Journal of Reading, 33,* 96–101.

Herber, H. L., & Nelson-Herber, J. (1987). Developing independent learners. *Journal of Reading, 30*(7), 584–588.

Herrell, A. L. & Jordan, M. (2003). *Fifty strategies for teaching English language learners.* Upper Saddle River, NJ: Prentice Hall.

Hiebert, E. H., Pearson, P. D., Taylor, B. M., Richardson, V., & Paris, S. G. (1998). *Every child a reader: Applying reading research to the classroom.* Center for the Improvement of Early Reading Achievement. Ann Arbor, MI: University of Michigan School of Education.

Holdaway, D. (1979). *The foundations of literacy.* Sydney: Ashton Scholastic.

Hoyt, L., Mooney, M. E., & Parkes, B. (2003). *Exploring informational texts: From theory to practice.* Portsmouth, NH: Heinemann.

Johns, J. L., & Berglund, R. L. (2002). *Fluency: Questions, answers, and evidence-based strategies.* Dubuque, IA: Kendall/Hunt.

Johns, J. L., Lenski, S. D., & Elish-Piper, L. (2002). *Teaching beginning readers: Linking assessment and instruction.* Dubuque, IA: Kendall/Hunt.

Keene, E. O., & Zimmermann, S. (1997). *Mosaic of thought: Teaching comprehension in a reader's workshop.* Portsmouth, NH: Heinemann.

Labbo, L. (2000). 12 things young children can do with a talking book in a classroom computer center. *The Reading Teacher, 53*(7), 542–546.

Langer, J. (1994). A response based approach to reading literature. *Language Arts, 71*(3), 203–211.

Leal, D. J. (1996). Transforming grand conversations into grand creations: Using different types of text to influence student discussion. In L. B. Gambrell & J. F. Almasi (Eds.), *Lively discussions!* (pp. 149–168). Newark, DE: International Reading Association.

Lehr, S. S. (1991). *The child's developing sense of theme: Responses to literature.* New York: Teachers College Press.

Lehr, S. S., & Thompson, D. L. (2000). The dynamic nature of response: Children reading and responding to Maniac Magee and The Friendship. *The Reading Teacher, 53*(6), 480–493.

Livaudais, M. A. (1985). *Survey of secondary (grades 9–12) students' attitudes toward reading motivational activities.* Unpublished doctoral dissertation, University of Houston, Houston, TX.

Many, J. E., & Wiseman, D. L. (1992). The effect of teaching approach on third-grade students' response to literature. *Journal of Reading Behavior, 24*(3), 265–287.

McKenna, M. C., Kear, D. J., & Ellsworth, R. A. (1995). Children's attitudes toward reading: A national survey. *Reading Research Quarterly, 30*(4), 934–956.

Moore, S. R. (1995). Questions for research into reading-writing relationships and text structure knowledge. *Language Arts, 72*(8), 598–606.

Murphy, S., & Dudley-Marling, C. (2000). Editors' pages. *Language Arts, 77*(6), 476–478.

National Reading Panel. (2000). *Teaching children to read: An evidence-based assessment of the scientific research literature on reading and its implications for reading instruction.* Washington, DC: National Institute of Child Health and Human Development.

New Zealand Ministry of Education. (1997). *Reading for life: The learner as a reader.* Wellington, NZ: Learning Media Limited.

Opitz, M. F. & Rasinski, T. V. (1998). *Good-bye round robin.* Portsmouth, NH: Heinemann.

Peregoy, S. F., & Boyle, O. F. (2001). *Reading, writing, and learning in ESL* (3rd ed.). New York: Longman.

Pressley, M. (2000). What should comprehension instruction be the instruction of? In M. L. Kamil, P. B.

Mosenthal, P. D. Pearson, & R. Barr (Eds.), *Handbook of reading research* (Vol. III, pp. 545–661). Mahwah, NJ: Erlbaum.

Pressley, M. (2002). *Reading instruction that works: The case for balanced teaching* (2nd ed.). New York: Guilford.

Probst, R. E. (1988). *Response and analysis: Teaching literature in junior and high school.* Portsmouth, NH: Heinemann.

Raphael, T. E. (1984). Teaching learners about sources of information for answering comprehension questions. *Journal of Reading, 27*(4).

Rasinski, T. V. (2003). *The fluent reader.* New York: Scholastic.

Reinking, D., & Watkins, J. (2000). A formative experiment investigating the use of multimedia book reviews to increase elementary students' independent reading. *Reading Research Quarterly, 35*(3), 384–419.

Resnick, L. B. (1984). Comprehending and learning: Implications for a cognitive theory of instruction. In H. Mandl, N. L. Stein, & T. Trabasso (Eds.), *Learning and comprehension of text* (pp. 431–443). Hillsdale, NJ: Erlbaum.

Roller, C. M., & Beed, P. L. (1994). Sometimes the conversations were grand, and sometimes . . . *Language Arts, 71*(7), 509–515.

Rosenblatt, L. (1978). *The reader, the text, the poem: The transactional theory of the literary work.* Carbondale, IL: Southern Illinois University Press.

Ruddell, R., Ruddell, M., & Singer, H. (Eds.). (1994). *Theoretical models and processes of reading* (4th ed.). Newark, DE: International Reading Association.

Sanacore, J. (1990). Creating the lifetime reading habit in social studies. *The Journal of Reading, 33*(6), 414–418.

Schmidt, B., & Buckley, M. (1991). Plot relationships chart. In J. M. Macon, D. Bewell, & M. Vogt (Eds.), *Response to literature: Grades K–8* (pp. 7–8). Newark, DE: International Reading Association.

Sipe, L. R. (2000). The construction of literary understanding by first and second graders in oral response to picture storybook read-alouds. *Reading Research Quarterly, 35*(2), 252–275.

Smith, M. (1992). Submission versus control in literary transactions. In J. Many & C. Cox (Eds.), *Reader stance and literary understandings* (pp. 143–161). Norwood, NJ: Ablex.

Snow, C. E., Burns, M. S., & Griffin, P. (Eds.). (1998). *Preventing reading difficulties in young children.* Washington, DC: National Research Council.

Stotsky, S. (1984). Research on reading/writing relationships: A synthesis and suggested directions. In J. Jensen (Ed.), *Composing and comprehending* (pp. 7–22). Urbana, IL: ERIC Clearinghouse on Reading and Communication Skills.

Teale, W., & Sulzby, E. (1986). *Emergent literacy: Writing and reading.* Norwood, NJ: Ablex.

Tomlinson, C., & Lynch-Brown, C. (1996). *Essentials of children's literature* (3rd ed.). Boston: Allyn & Bacon.

U.S. Department of Education. (2000). *National Assessment of Educational Progress.* Washington, DC: U.S. Department of Education.

Vacca, R. T., Vacca, J. L., & Bruneau, B. (1997). Teachers reflecting on practice. In J. Flood, S. B. Heath, & D. Lapp (Eds.), *Research on teaching literacy through the communicative and visual arts* (pp. 445–450). New York: Macmillan.

Van Horn, L. (2000). Sharing literature, sharing selves: Students reveal themselves through read-alouds. *Journal of Adolescent & Adult Literacy, 43*(8), 752–763.

Vogt, M. E. (1996). Creating a response-centered curriculum with literature discussion groups. In L. B. Gambrell & J. F. Almasi (Eds.), *Lively discussions!* (pp. 181–193). Newark, DE: International Reading Association.

Wiseman, D. L. (1992). *Learning to read with literature.* Needham Heights, MA: Allyn & Bacon.

Wiseman, D. L., Many, J. E., & Altieri, J. L. (1996). Exploring the influences of literature approaches on children's stance when responding and their response complexity. *Reading Psychology: An International Quarterly, 17*, 1–41.

Wiseman, D. L., Many, J. E., & Altieri, J. (1997). When the literary response is: "I like the book—it is funny." Where do we go from here? *Georgia Journal of Reading, 17*–25.

Wollman-Bonilla, J. E., & Werchadlo, B. (1995). Literature response journals in a first-grade classroom. *Language Arts, 72*(8), 562–570.

Wylie, R., & Durrell, D. D. (1970). Teaching vowels through phonograms. *Elementary English, 47*, 787–791.

Yaden, D. B., Rowe, D. W., & MacGillivray, L. (2000). Emergent literacy: A matter (polyphony) of perspectives. In M. L. Kamil, P. B. Mosenthal, P. D. Pearson, & R. Barr (Eds.), *Handbook of reading research* (Vol. III, pp. 425–454). Mahwah, NJ: Erlbaum.

Yopp, H. K., & Yopp, R. H. (1997). *Oo-pples and boo-noo-noos: Songs and activities for phonemic awareness.* Orlando, FL: Harcourt Brace.

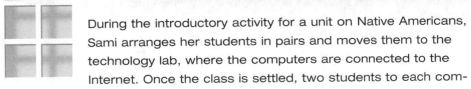

During the introductory activity for a unit on Native Americans, Sami arranges her students in pairs and moves them to the technology lab, where the computers are connected to the Internet. Once the class is settled, two students to each computer, she helps the pairs of students log on to a website that includes extensive picture collections of several Native American tribes. "Class," she says, "please visit this museum site. Look at the pictures the museum has placed on their website." As they find the correct website, Sami begins to show the pairs how to move the pictures to a file for their use. Then she asks each pair to select three or more pictures that are most interesting.

After the partners find the pictures they like and place them in their folders, Sami hands them cards with the following questions:

What do your pictures remind you of? Why?

Have you ever seen any of these images outside of a museum, a gallery, or an art center? Where? Why do you think someone took these pictures?

What story do your pictures tell?

The partners use the questions to talk to each other about their pictures. After a time she stops their discussions and asks them to share some of the

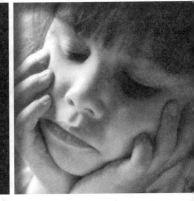

Chapter 6

LITERACY AND VISUAL REPRESENTATION, INTERPRETATION, AND EVALUATION

ideas they have discussed in pairs. After they talk about their pictures, Sami says, "I have another task for you. Find five pictures that help you tell a story about one Native American tribe's clothes, food, families, or other interesting ideas. Look carefully at each picture and write a sentence based on your pictures." It doesn't take long for her students to begin working on their second task. Sami walks around the room, stopping and working with each pair of students while they compose a summary sentence describing what they have learned from the pictures. After her students write a sentence about their pic-

tures, Sami reorganizes the class into groups of four and asks them to share their pictures and sentences with another pair. Her students are eager to share what they have learned by examining the pictures.

She ends the activity by asking, "What did you learn about your Native American tribe, and what else would you like to know?" She types a list of what they learned and the questions they want to know on a large computer screen that allows her to print the lists. She finds that the students have a great deal to share and ask many questions that will guide the activities in her unit. She is very pleased with the results of the introductory activity. Not only has she motivated her students to learn more about Native Americans, she also has been able to evaluate their current knowledge and find out what they would like to learn as the unit progresses. Most important, the opening activity has provided her students the opportunity to discuss, listen, read, and write based on what they have learned from visual representations.

INTRODUCTION

In order to communicate in today's world, language users must be visually literate. Picture books, computers, Web pages, television, and movies share basic visual components and visual symbolism, and students must develop an understanding of these visual elements in order to use these media effectively.

Language arts instruction helps children develop these skills. The integration of visual literacy, technology, popular media, and other school subjects allows students to improve the communication skills they need to use technology tools and popular media. Through instructional strategies, teachers can incorporate visual literacy skills throughout school curriculum.

GUIDING QUESTIONS

Consider these questions as you read this chapter. Jot down your initial responses to each question. After reading the articles, revisit your responses. Would you make any changes to them? If so, what would those changes be? Discuss your responses with one or more of your classmates, your professor, or your mentor teacher.

1. What does it mean to be visually literate?
2. What role can picture books play in facilitating the development of visual literacy?
3. How do visual elements contribute to understanding information presented with electronic media?
4. What skills are necessary for children to be consumers of commercial visual media?
5. What strategies can teachers use to help students develop and expand their knowledge about visual representation, technology, and popular media?

Visual Representation

Hot is hot, right? Well, that may not be the case. It depends on how the meaning is represented and displayed. Below, each visual representation of the concept "hot," using different visual symbols, conveys a slightly different message or idea. The word written in lowercase conveys one idea of "hot." Bold capital letters produce a more powerful impression. Squiggly lines in the background indicate a less serious, more playful attitude. The visual style in the third example depicts a humorous interpretation of the concept. The real-life visual representation of fire danger in the last example may generate fear, anxiety, or sadness, depending on the viewer's personal experiences.

Understanding the world around us requires a complex process involving all sensory systems. For most of us, the most sophisticated sensory system, vision (Jonassen, Peck, & Wilson, 1999), provides us with the largest amount and greatest variety of information about our world. Texts and other visual symbols enrich communication and provide multiple ways to express, interpret, and comprehend. Visual symbolism, and the form, manner, and style in which visuals are presented, contributes a great deal to our understanding of a message. The ways we can communicate and express our ideas multiply when we consider all of the possibilities associated with visual symbolism—graphics, signs, photos, designs, and so forth (Eisner, 1991).

VISUAL SYMBOLS

Visual symbols have always helped people understand the world around them, and a great deal of evidence suggests that our modern culture is becoming more and more dependent upon visual communication. Visual genres and media dominate communication: signs, movies, photographs, television, film, the Internet, and print are part of the visual symbol system that we encounter each day as we learn, communicate, and interpret. A literate person in today's world may indeed be "first and foremost someone who is able to recognize, read, analyze, and communicate using a variety of visual genres and mediums" (Schirato & Yell, 1996, p. 209).

The communication power of visual symbols is complex. Symbols have layers and different aspects of meaning production. The style, color, lines, and context of visual symbols help us understand messages in a particular way. Each aspect of visual representation can be discussed and understood individually, but it is the sum of the whole that conveys meaning. Moreover, visual symbols convey different messages depending on their method of construction or formation—by computer, photo, video, pencil, crayon, or paint. As the "hot" representations suggested, the medium becomes part of the message, conveying a feeling, an emotion, or a concept. For example, one would focus on a formally typed set of symbols differently than the same symbols written with crayon. Or if someone wrote you a note with computer graphics, you might take away a different meaning than if the same message was written with pencil.

CATS

The word "cat" by itself may mean very little, but an image automatically brings further meaning.

The location of visual symbols also affects the meaning that one derives from them. Visual representations in this book, for example, are related to what you are learning in a university course. "Hot" written with squiggly lines and posted in a supermarket or in a factory will be interpreted differently than when the same symbol appears at the beginning of a methods textbook chapter. Visual symbols in a television ad will be interpreted differently than visual symbols at a house of worship, because the person who is interpreting the message has differing associations and expectations for each place.

Personal experiences and beliefs contribute to the interpretation of visual messages. What you know and how you understand concepts are important influences on your understanding of visual symbols. If you have witnessed a forest fire or if your home has burned, your interpretation of "hot" might reflect your experiences. Visual symbols embody the same complexity as any other language processes.

VISUAL LITERACY

Increased awareness of the impact of visual representations and symbols has led to the use of the term *visual literacy*. According to Moore and Dwyer, "Visual literacy involves reading visuals and creating visuals, but most importantly, it is a method or process for thinking. . . . Visual literacy is the ability to understand (read) and use (write and draw) images and to think and learn in terms of images" (1994, p. 25). Visual literacy gains importance as students develop sophistication in their use of technology and media transmissions, both of which depend on visual symbolism. Photographs, television, film, video, electronic games, websites, cartoons, posters, T-shirts, comics, multimedia presentations, and computer simulations are visual genres and media that dominate students' communication processes (Sankey, 2002). Most recently, a new visual medium has emerged: the use of cell phones to send messages, including photographs. A visually literate person understands that graphics, computer and cell phone screens, movie frames, and printed pages convey meaning and messages, and such a person is capable of using visual symbols to convey meaning. Defining communication and literacy skills more broadly to include visual representation requires a subtle change in attitude and the acceptance of a wide range of media and technological tools and symbols. Inclusion of visual representations in communication processes has important implications for language arts teaching methods and curriculum planning.

Developing Concepts with Visuals

Consider the concepts addressed in this book and in your class. Select one that interests you and consider how you might represent that topic through visual symbols. Visual symbols could include objects, artifacts, artwork, pictures, computer graphics, and videos. Collect the visual symbols and use them as a springboard for discussion with classmates. After your discussions, consider how construction of knowledge differs when it results from building meaning through visual representations.

Visual Instructional Aids

While observing in a classroom, note the number of visual instructional aids the teacher uses. Does he or she regularly use videos, projected computer images, graphs, pictures, and other visual representations? Observe student responses related to visual representation. Are the students using drawings, computer graphics, cartoons, or other visual representations to complete their assignments? Summarize your findings in a visual representation. Compare what you found with your university peers. Discuss with them any differences in the use of visuals between grades or subject areas. Do you think the use of visual representations has anything to do with the age or comfort level of the teacher?

Classroom Considerations

Visual literacy instruction does not necessarily mean that the language arts curriculum will include a visual literacy unit or multiple visual literacy lessons; it may mean that important concepts related to visual communication are taught during any subject area lesson. Occasionally a discussion or lesson may focus specifically on visual literacy, but it is not usually necessary to design specific lessons; many opportunities to teach about and with visual representation exist throughout the curriculum. Language arts instruction, for example, lends itself to exposing and encouraging students to use a wide range of visual experiences during reading and writing activities. Visual experiences during language arts instruction should include many of the same media students use in their lives outside of school. Television, movies, cartoons, and computer graphics will help communicate ideas and concepts. Classrooms should be "similar to the resource rich, interdisciplinary environment that students currently live in outside the school day" (Kist, 2000). When done in the appropriate way, visual representations and accompanying media support become so common and expected that they are easily integrated with daily practice (Bruce & Hogan, 1998).

A fairly common example of visual literacy instruction in the elementary grades occurs when the teacher reads a picture book to children (see Article II in this chapter). Together the teacher and the children focus on words and text to make meaning from the story. The text and pictures work in tandem to form meaning, allowing students to experience the importance of visual representations. Picture books use expanded visual representations—both texts and pictures—to convey meaning.

Picture books help discussions about visual literacy, including how the arrangement or size of words communicates meaning. Some picture books use word visuals to communicate meaning. In *Ducky* (Bunting, 1997), the author and illustrator creates visuals with words by changing the arrangement and size of the words to convey direction and noise, as in the following:

DOWN
    DOWN
        DOWN it went
We tumbled around inside,
Yellow ducks, green frogs, blue
Turtles, and red beavers.
BUMP
    CRASH! (p. 6)

The way the words are displayed conveys meaning: the falling visual presentation of "down, down, down" visibly illustrates a fall, and the large, bolded print for "bump" "crash" suggests a loud noise.

English Language Learners and Visual Literacy

Displaying knowledge with multiple symbol and media representations recognizes and enhances the differences in the way individuals comprehend. Students who are from different cultural and language backgrounds or who are learning to speak English may be more comfortable communicating when support from a wide range of visual symbols is available. Students who wish to explain something from their native culture may be greatly assisted by pictures, animation, artifacts, or actual examples, as they talk about concepts familiar to them but not their classmates. For example, a recent immigrant from Mexico who wishes to explain the costumes associated with Cinco de Mayo might enrich the verbal description with movie clips from the Internet of Cinco de Mayo events in a Mexican community. Another student explaining the festivities associated with Kwanzaa to her peers might convey information about the holiday by sharing photos of family celebrations.

A picture, video, graphic, or artwork will help any student understand vocabulary and learn important concepts. A picture or movie changes the way students look at ideas or concepts and helps them understand from differing perspectives. ELLs in particular benefit from the support that instructional use of visual representations provides. Visual communication allows the teacher to recognize and "reflect the greater . . . communication needs [of students]" (Tompkins, 1998, p. 23).

Wordless Picture Books

Select a wordless picture book and share it with a child or a small group of children. Audiotape the conversation that takes place as they interpret the pictures. Complete the activity as a language experience activity (LEA) by listening to the tape and writing the story, using their words and expressions to demonstrate how they interpreted the pictures. Repeat the process with another child or second group of children. Compare the stories that the visual representations produced. How do you account for the differences in how the two stories evolved? Can you speculate on the impact of the visual symbols—the pictures—on how the children tell the story?

INSTRUCTIONAL STANDARDS AND GOALS

The rapid growth of technology and the pervasive and unrelenting impact of the media on day-to-day lives have brought about an expanded definition of literacy that includes visual representations. Visual literacy is an essential skill that includes all the communication media of the 21st century, while supporting the traditional areas of reading, writing, listening, and speaking. The National Council of Teachers of English (NCTE) includes the idea of visual literacy in its introduction of language arts standards: "Language as it is used here encompasses visual communication in addition to spoken and written forms of expression" (NCTE/IRA, 1996, p. 2).

Texas is one state that has developed visual literacy standards as a component of language arts instruction. Its state curriculum guide introduces visual literacy as follows: "The English language arts curriculum framework for Texas encompasses a strand entitled viewing and representing. Students in grades 4–12 are expected to interpret visual images, messages, and meanings; analyze and critique visual images; and produce visual images." Texas language arts standards for grades 4 through 8 illustrate how visual representation parallels skills in traditional language arts processes (see Exhibit 6.1).

A complete view of language arts instruction values all symbols that are used to convey meaning. Text, photography, paintings, drawings, computer graphics, videos, and film are all literacy tools that communicate ideas and concepts. It makes sense that language arts would include opportunities for students to interpret and make meaning with all types of symbols.

exhibit 6.1   *Texas Essential Knowledge and Skills for Language Arts related to viewing, representation, and interpretation, grades 4 through 8.*

(23) Viewing/representing/interpretation. The student understands and interprets visual images, messages, and meanings. The student is expected to:

(A) describe how illustrators' choice of style, elements, and media help to represent or extend the texts' meanings (4–8);

(B) interpret important events and ideas gleaned from maps, charts, graphics, video segments, or technology presentations (4–8); and

(C) use media to compare ideas and points of view (4–8).

(24) Viewing/representing/analysis. The student analyzes and critiques the significance of visual images, messages, and meanings. The student is expected to:

(A) interpret and evaluate the various ways visual image makers such as graphic artists, illustrators, and news photographers represent meanings (4–5); and

(B) compare and contrast print, visual, and electronic media such as film with written story (4–8).

(25) Viewing/representing/production. The student produces visual images, messages, and meanings that communicate with others. The student is expected to:

(A) select, organize, or produce visuals to complement and extend meanings (4–8); and

(B) produce communications using technology or appropriate media such as developing a class newspaper, multimedia reports, or video reports (4–8).

VISUAL LITERACY INSTRUCTION

Students' continual exposure to visual representations on the Internet and in movies, advertisements, video games, computer software, cell phones, e-mail, and other media builds certain visual abilities naturally. However, it would be incorrect to assume that students will learn to negotiate meaning through visual literacy simply by everyday experiences and exposure (Yenawine, 1997). Facilitating the development of visual communication skills requires interaction, broad exposure, and an instructional focus on visual representations. No single method teaches all the visual skills that students need to understand complex images. But three approaches to visual literacy instruction—discussions, modification of existing lessons and strategies, and lessons focusing on visual literacy—provide examples of how creative teachers integrate visual representation in their teaching and learning activities.

Classroom texts are usually well illustrated and provide opportunities to build meaning from the visual representations that accompany the text.

Discussions

A simple way to build awareness and knowledge about visual representation is through small and large group discussions. For example, to help students learn to value multiple symbolic representations, you might discuss the role of visual symbols throughout history and in different cultures. The fascinating remains of early communication processes—Sanskrit, cave drawings, the visual symbols of Native American people, and carvings in ancient tombs—illustrate early human written language. The topic of visual literacy incorporates visual representations and provides an historical context for communication.

Modifying Traditional Strategies

In the Window to the Classroom that opens this chapter, Sami, the teacher, uses a well-known strategy to encourage her students to share what they learned from pictures and to frame questions about what they would like to know. The KWL format is usually used with text, but as Sami's lesson illustrates, it adapts easily to any visual form. The KWL format allowed Sami to evaluate what her students had learned and provided some questions to guide future activities. (For more about the KWL format, see Chapter 3, Article IV.)

Like KWL, most traditional language arts activities are easily adapted to include a visual aspect. Presentations such as oral reports often rely on graphs, pictures, overhead notes, and other visual representations. Presentations that use technology tools such as PowerPoint can move easily from film to the Internet to slides. In particular, writing instruction can incorporate visual representation in numerous ways. Students may use visual representations of any type as a way to select topics and find ideas for writing. Sami helped her students take a first step in writing about Native American tribes, a summary statement about what they learned from the pictures. Movies, videos, cartoons, and graphics may provide an impetus for writing texts. Visual representation enhances student-authored texts with illustrations. Drawings, graphs, photographs, and even clip art from the Internet allow students to add meaning to their writing through visual representation.

Modifying an Existing Strategy to Integrate Visual Literacy

1. Review visual literacy standards for your state and identify one that will guide planning for a lesson at your grade level.

2. Select a strategy introduced in text or one that the teacher in your classroom uses regularly. The strategy could be KWL, literature circles, mini-lessons, or any other.

3. Modify the strategy so that it includes a definite link to visual literacy skills (consider the example in this chapter's Window to the Classroom).

4. If possible, try your strategy with a group of students.

5. Evaluate how well the strategy worked. Did the students enjoy the activity? Did they exhibit the behavior described in the standards?

6. Place a copy of your lesson in your portfolio as an example of a visual literacy lesson.

Lessons That Focus on Visual Literacy Skills

Occasionally, a teacher will design specific lessons to provide visual literacy activities. Exhibit 6.2 provides an example of how a teacher could design activities to focus on visual literacy.

FINAL REFLECTIONS

Today's students tend to rely a great deal on visual representation to understand the world around them. New technology and media offer additional ways to communicate, interpret, and produce meaning. It makes sense that literacy instruction should provide opportunities for students to expand their visual literacy capabilities. As Sankey writes, "Focusing on the needs of the student and facilitating the best possible learning experience by utilizing multiple communication tools should lead . . . to greater student satisfaction and possibly even better academic results" (2002).

An upper-grade elementary lesson focusing on specific visual literacy skills.

LESSON: Comparing Elements of a Photograph

OUTCOMES: Students will be able to identify structural elements within a picture's composition.
Students will be able to compare two photographs.

SETUP

Write the following "Glossary" on a transparency, white board, or handout:

1. Foreground: the part of the picture that is nearest to the viewer
2. Background: the scenery behind something (usually whatever is in the foreground)
3. Symmetry: an exact correspondence of form on two sides of a plane, resulting in balance
4. Asymmetry: lack of balance or symmetry
5. Tone: the intensity of light and dark
6. Shape: the basic geometric shapes, such as triangles, squares, and circles, that are apparent in a visual image's composition
7. Motion: the illusion of motion within a visual image

SUGGESTED PROCEDURE

LOOKING FOR STRUCTURAL SIMILARITIES (LARGE GROUP BRAINSTORM, 10–15 MINUTES)

- Ask students to describe what they see in the two images. Concentrate on the content: What do you see? Describe what is in each photo. How are they alike? How are they different?
- After discussing the similarities and differences in terms of the content, ask the students to look at the structure of the visual image. How are the pictures composed? What is similar about their compositions?
- Provide the students with some strategies for reviewing the images for visual similarities. Tell them that they can look from top to bottom or from left to right.

INTRODUCING THE GLOSSARY (LARGE GROUP DISCUSSION, 10 MINUTES)

- Explain that how the picture is arranged is called its composition.
- Introduce the terms from the glossary, explaining that these are some terms that might help the students to discuss the visual image's composition.
- Ask the students to discuss the two pictures using the glossary terms.
- Ask questions, such as: *What do you see in the foreground? What's in the background? Is this a symmetrical or asymmetrical composition? Is motion implied in the image? What is the tone of the image? Can you identify any shapes within the composition?*

Picture Books and Visual Literacy

Visual representations and symbols are important components of students' language and communication processes in and out of school. Pictures, for example, serve to support the description of an important idea in the accompanying text. Conversely, students can help others understand what they know by producing pictorial representations. The pictures they draw as they read and write allow adults to understand how they comprehend information. Connections between communication and visual representation are inevitable. Language arts instruction that ignores the importance of visual representation in the communication process will not be complete.

Embedding creative and visual arts in the language arts curriculum is not a novel idea. One customary approach for including visual literacy in the language arts classroom is to use picture books. Not only are the pictures in children's books beautiful to look at, but they also make important contributions to the meaning of the books and affect readers' responses (Sipe, 1995). When the visual arts' power to make meaning is applied to picture book illustrations, readers' comprehension is extended beyond the interpretation of words (Kiefer, 1996).

Students usually greatly enjoy exploring picture book illustrations independently; however, picture books are also important assets during instructional activities. Instructional activities designed to enhance students' understanding will increase their enjoyment of picture books. Because of their merging of word and image—and because children enjoy them—picture books have been an important tool for language arts instruction in the past and will remain an instructional staple in the future.

PICTURE BOOKS AS VISUAL REPRESENTATION

Picture books, by definition, depend on both pictures and text to build meaning (Sipe, 1995). The close connections between the pictures and the words assure that the meaning goes far beyond either element individually. Not only do students absorb the plot of the story, but the pictures also allow them to add another layer of understanding to their experience with the literature (Kiefer, 1995). Sendak's (1988) text describes the "wild things" that "gnash their terrible teeth and roar their terrible roars" but the pictures of its famous characters add boldness and energy to the meaning of the text. The format, visual elements, and media of picture books all make important contributions to understanding and increase the impact on the reader.

Picture Book Format

A picture book is a visual experience, and the construction of meaning starts with the first glance, even before the book is opened. Everything about a high-quality picture book conveys a message. The format, or how the book is presented, provides the first visual clue about the story. The size, shape, and arrangement of the book introduce the mood of the text. The page layout conveys messages. From discussions of a book's format and why it was selected, children gain insights into the importance of visual representation in constructing meaning.

One example of a book with an unusual format is *Black and White* (Macaulay, 1990). The story is divided in four panels per page, each focusing on a different story line. Eventually the arrangement of pictures, text, and other formatting aspects begins to link the stories together. Another unusual format is that of *Officer Buckle and Gloria* (Rathman, 1995), which is written in a rather cartoonish style that conveys a funny story with an important lesson about safety and jealousy. Other books, such as Zelinsky's *Rumpelstiltskin* (1997), have an elegant, classic format that sets off their beautiful artwork and classic stories.

Visual Elements

Picture books provide a vehicle to introduce the basic elements of visual representations. By becoming aware of these elements (see Exhibit 6.3), readers learn to appreciate the aesthetic dimension of books and extend and enrich their textual and visual experiences (Lynch-Brown & Tomlinson, 2001).

A picture book is a visual experience, and the construction of meaning starts with the first glance and continues during reading and rereading.

Visual elements of picture book illustrations contribute a great deal to the reading experience. In the book *Smoky Night,* the illustrator David Diaz (1994) uses a combination of acrylic paint and collage techniques to illustrate a story that takes place during an urban riot. The pictures, which spread across facing pages, bring together central components of the story to portray important scenes. For example, to illustrate a scene of looters taking cartons of cereal and rice from a market, Diaz uses cereal and bits of broken tile and glass to convey the destruction of the store. The characters are drawn with dark, solid lines, and their distinct features imply strong personalities. Both the lines and colors emphasize the urgency and seriousness of the riot. Softer acrylics or watercolors would not have had the same effect. The overall composition, as well as the combination of techniques, provides teachers and students with a study in effective uses of visual elements. Art critics and children's literature scholars provide helpful, detailed analyses of picture-book illustrations. To read more about the elements in picture books, consult any of the books listed at the end of the chapter under "Books About Children's Picture Books."

exhibit   6.3   *Elements of picture book illustrations.*

Line: The boldness and definition, or lack thereof, of the strokes and lines create and convey meaning and emotion. The lines may be bold, wavy, faint, pastel, etc.

Color: The brightness and hue of colors stimulate additional feelings and meanings. Colors may be intense or faded, pale or opaque. The hues may come from any part of the color spectrum. The colors should complement the text.

Shape: Forms may be rounded or squared off, simple or complex, contributing to qualities such as realism, humor, gentleness, and so forth.

Texture: The texture of the picture suggests a tactile feeling. The textures of illustrations may be smooth, pointed, squared, soft, and so on.

Composition: The arrangement of visual elements within the illustrations (how they are composed) implies relationships among the characters and objects. In composition, color, line, shape, and texture work together to contribute to the meaning of the story. The illustrator arranges the various elements to produce visual impact. *Composition* refers to the total effect.

Media

Picture book artists are often extremely innovative in selecting media and tools for their illustrations. Woodcuts, paints, pencils, crayons, photographs, and collage are commonly used to illustrate high-quality literature (see Exhibit 6.4), and the tools may be brushes, woodcuts, cutouts, and many others, depending on the effect the artist seeks to convey. Artists may focus on one medium or mix media. Comparing books helps learners understand how artists create different moods and emotions by their selection of media. For example, reviewing several versions of fairytales such as Snow White or Cinderella can demonstrate to students how the same story may be presented in different ways. For an example of glorious artwork, see Zelinsky's *Rapunzel* (1997); for a more cartoon-like, comical version of the same story, read Zemach's *Duffy and the Devil* (1973).

The formats, visual elements, and media of picture books can serve as the basis of discussions about different ways of communicating ideas (Sipe, 1995). These conversations can motivate students to consider how artists communicate ideas, and some may even be inspired to try their hand at producing illustrations themselves. Students may work independently or cooperatively with others to experiment with media and see how it affects the visual impression. Watercolor, oil paint, pastels, colored pencils, crayons, woodcuts, and collage are just a few of the many media children can explore to express their moods, emotions, and understandings. Teachers can also provide opportunities for students to create visual representations in response to assignments and class discussions.

	Media used in children's literature.	*exhibit* **6.4**

TYPE OF ILLUSTRATION	MEDIA USED	EXAMPLES IN CHILDREN'S LITERATURE
Drawing	Pen and ink Colored pencils Pastels (colored chalk) Charcoal pencils Computer graphics	*The Mysteries of Harris Burdick,* written and illustrated by Chris van Allsburg *Jambo Means Hello,* written by Muriel Feelings and illustrated by Tom Feelings
Collage	Real objects of assorted textures and designs, such as lace, birch bark, buttons, torn paper, and cotton	*Smoky Night,* written by Eve Bunting and illustrated by David Diaz *Golem,* written and illustrated by David Wisniewski *Alexander and the Wind-Up Mouse,* written and illustrated by Leo Lionni
Printmaking	Woodcuts Linoleum prints Block prints Lithography	*Drummer Hoff,* written by Barbara Emberley and illustrated by Ed Emberley *Shawdow,* translated and illustrated by Marcia Brown
Photography	Black and white Color Digital	*A City Under the Sea: Life in a Coral Reef,* by Norbert Wu *Wild Babies,* by Seymour Simon
Painting	Oils Acrylics Watercolors Gouache Tempera	*My Many Colored Days,* by Dr. Seuss *Pink and Say,* by Patricia Polacco

Adapted from Tomlinson, C., & Lynch-Brown, C. (2001). *Essentials of children's literature* (pp. 35–36). Boston: Allyn & Bacon.

Illustrator Study

Select one book or a series of books by one illustrator. Record your impressions of the format, elements, and media. Point out how the format and media contribute to the overall composition of the book. How do the illustrations influence your understanding of and response to the story? Be prepared to share your impressions with your classmates.

personal reflection

THE TEACHER'S ROLE

Most elementary teachers, especially those who teach language arts, become familiar with many aspects of children's literature and are great fans of picture books. Teachers who know and care about picture books and their illustrators and authors are prepared to use these books to develop students' visual literacy skills. Students eagerly pick up teachers' enthusiasm for children's literature.

Teachers who begin introducing the language of visual representation early, especially during the early elementary years, provide a strong basis for students to develop visual literacy. Young students are capable of using concepts such as media, color, lines, and textures to talk about pictures they enjoy. When a teacher points out that the bright colors in *Where the Wild Things Are* (Sendak, 1988) are appropriate for loud, rambunctious characters or the soft, beautiful colors of *Owl Moon* (Yolen, 1987) help convey the feeling of a quiet snowy night, it will be only a matter of time before she hears her students using the same language.

Learning from Artists

Attend an art exhibit and assess your way of responding to the visual representations. Do the visual representations remind you of events in your life? Are you able to judge the representations based on the visual elements? Do they present a different view or perspective on a topic? If you can, bring artifacts from the exhibit, such as brochures or postcards, in to the classroom. Write about the impact of visual texts on your understandings and share your thoughts with a classmate. Respond in writing to others' ideas on this topic.

INSTRUCTIONAL CONSIDERATIONS

Opportunities to integrate picture books throughout the curriculum are endless. Because picture books cover a wide range of topics, they can enhance the content and activities in any subject area, and they appeal to all ages. Often, interactions are best when they are open ended, without a structured teaching–learning expectation. One of the most rewarding ways to use picture books is simply to read and enjoy them, share them with others, and savor the experience.

Teachers must be mindful of how they use picture books so they do not take away from the joy, beauty, and personal responses that these books evoke. With the recent emphasis on using children's literature in the curriculum, some educators have raised concerns about the overuse of picture books for instruction (Goodman, 1988). Goodman cautions teachers to be sure that literature is enjoyed first and foremost, and that skills and strategies are taught sparingly so that wonderful literature does not become just another way to provide skill and drill for children. These cautions are particularly applicable to picture books that contain rich, evocative illustrations and texts.

Students' responses to literature will be more or less complex depending upon their experiences (Housen, 1992; Yenawine, 1997). Students who encounter visual representations over time begin to understand essential concepts of visual literacy. They become aware of what is involved in visual representations and learn to recognize their own interests and preferences. As students' visual literacy increases, they become capable of classifying, analyzing, and critiquing what they see. They develop advanced visual literacy skills, such as knowing how to use different shapes and colors to convey meaning in visuals they produce. Pictures in the books that children read can help them develop skills in a particular media. Children become good at drawing illustrations or producing collages that express their ideas. Some children are quite adept at interpreting or creating visual representations, and others may make art an enjoyable lifelong interest. No matter what level of sophistication children acquire, their growth in visual literacy "can enhance the development of other meaning-making systems" (Yenawine, 1997, p. 846).

Classroom activities that include visual representations provide opportunities for the teacher to discuss illustrations, encourage open-ended responses to visual representations, and motivate students to create visual expressions of their own. Students should feel free to use a variety of visual representations to interpret what they are learning and feeling (Kist, 2000). This practice allows them to experiment with conveying their ideas and observe the results. By doing so, they begin to see things in new ways. In addition, when students are able to see or express a concept visually, they often discover ways to articulate or represent complex, underlying feelings or responses more completely.

English Language Learners

Illustrations in picture books help students express and convey their ideas when their English language skills are limited. Students who are learning English may not be able to understand all the concepts associated with written or spoken English text, but illustrations convey the story and concepts in a way that helps all students comprehend.

Picture books allow students with a wide range of cultural and language backgrounds to participate in the curriculum. Multicultural literature, in particular, helps students connect to a wide spectrum of experiences and life events, representing people and lifestyles from around the world and across time. These books showcase a variety of lifestyles, perspectives, and cultures through depictions of diverse home and community experiences. The representations of scenes and people may be familiar to some students, but other children may need introductions to cultures that are new to them.

INSTRUCTIONAL STANDARDS AND GOALS

Language arts and reading standards reflect the important role that picture books play in instruction. Connections between picture books and visual literacy are implied in the Texas learning standards (see Exhibit 6.5). The descriptions of expected behaviors in the standards suggest that picture books are an important tool for developing students' visual literacy.

The standards are written specifically for grades 4 through 8; however, students typically encounter picture books much earlier, as one of their first literacy experiences. Teachers of preschool and early elementary grades can use the standards for older students as a guide. Conversely, teachers of students in grades 4 through 8 may overlook an important resource if they believe picture books are only for younger students. Picture books are an important tool in meeting instructional goals at all levels.

INSTRUCTIONAL ACTIVITIES

The ways in which teachers integrate picture books into instruction are almost endless. Not only do picture books provide a great wealth of material for reading, writing, speaking, listening, and visual literacy development, but they also help with teaching the content areas. Picture books are indispensable in social studies, science, mathematics, and other types of instruction for conveying information and concepts and encouraging children to produce images of their own—from simple drawings to highly sophisticated interpretations. Almost every teacher has favorite activities that are supported by picture books. The remainder of this article offers a few examples of the wide range of activities available for picture books in the classroom.

exhibit **6.5**   *Texas Essential Knowledge and Skills for language arts, grades 4–8.*

(23) Viewing/representing/interpretation. The student understands and interprets visual images, messages, and meanings. The student is expected to:
- (A) describe how illustrators' choice of style, elements, and media help to represent or extend the text's meanings (4–8);
- (B) interpret important events and ideas gleaned from maps, charts, graphics, video segments, or technology presentations (4–8); and
- (C) use media to compare ideas and points of view (4–8).

(24) Viewing/representing/analysis. The student analyzes and critiques the significance of visual images, messages, and meanings. The student is expected to:
- (A) interpret and evaluate the various ways visual image makers such as graphic artists, illustrators, and news photographers represent meanings (4–5); and
- (B) compare and contrast print, visual, and electronic media such as film with written story (4–8).

Lesson Development

Plan a mini-lesson that presents a picture book to students and heightens their awareness of the role of the illustrations. Be sure to attend to the interaction between pictures and words and help the students consider how the visual elements contribute to the effectiveness of the storytelling. Encourage the students to respond to the book in the same form as the illustrations. For example, if the artist uses collage, have students create their own collages.

Sketch-to-Sketch

The sketch-to-sketch strategy (Whitin, 1996) encourages readers to draw symbols or signs representing events or ideas in the story. As the students read or listen to a story, they draw simple pictures with a pencil, trying to reproduce aspects of the story that have meaning to them. Sketch-to-sketch is like a visual brainstorming activity; the purpose is not to create elaborate illustrations, but quick sketches note ideas and concepts from the story. The sketches are done during the reading, just as if readers were taking notes to help them remember what they would like to discuss or clarify during post-reading discussions. By creating and sharing their drawings, they deepen their understandings in several ways. The process of creating visual representations helps students realize the power of visual representations, improves their comprehension, and serves as a basis for sharing responses and discussing interpretations.

Artist's Workshop

The methods of reading and writing instruction may also be used as an approach to teaching art (Ernst, 1994). Artist's workshop is time regularly scheduled for learning about artists and their techniques. In language arts classrooms, artist's workshops focus on artwork or illustrators who have been or will be studied in depth during language arts. The artist's workshop typically includes a mini-lesson to introduce and explain techniques and media, but it is mainly a hands-on, creative activity. Students select their own artistic project related to the topic. They may draw, paint, paste, or even write. Materials should be available for student use, and collaboration among students should be encouraged. As the students work, the teacher also has an art project, modeling the artistic and illustration processes just as he models reading and writing activities. After the workshop, students' work may be exhibited, either on classroom bulletin boards or in a schoolwide show.

With the sketch-to-sketch strategy, after reading or listening to a story, readers are encouraged to draw simple pictures with a pencil trying to reproduce aspects of the story that have meaning to them.

Artist's workshops are appropriate in both art classes and language arts classrooms. Art teachers are helpful in planning and implementing artist's workshops. Through collaborative planning, teachers can connect art to reading, writing, speaking, and listening across the curriculum.

Illustrating Stories

Illustrations are very helpful during the writing process. Drawing pictures before writing helps students think about what they want to write, and illustrating finished stories strengthens the link between visual representation and language arts and makes stories stronger and more interesting. Illustrating their own texts provides closure to students' writing process and prepares them for sharing their work with others. Student-authored and -illustrated texts may prove to be some of the most popular books in your classroom's library.

Although illustrations are especially helpful for very young children and ELLs who might have difficulty expressing their ideas in English, producing visual representations of responses to literature is an important process for students of all ages.

Illustrator Study

An interesting way to study the elements and media of picture books is to conduct an illustrator study. The class selects a favorite illustrator and researches his or her life and work on the Internet and in other resources. Students often become experts on a particular illustrator, spending long hours poring over illustrations and deepening their ability to interpret visual symbols in the process.

Any illustrator can be the focus of a study, but some have unique aspects that make a study even more intriguing. Chris Van Allsburg, an illustrator who started as a sculptor, always hides a dog in one of the illustrations in each of his books. Sometimes the dog is easy to find, as in his Caldecott Award–winning book *Jumanji* (1981), where a dog puppet is apparent on the bed headboard in an illustration early in the book. Other times, the dog is more difficult to find, as in the book *Two Bad Ants* (1988), where the dog is barely visible as a piece of garbage swirling down a drain. Not only is Van Allsburg's high-quality artwork worthwhile to study, offering many insights into elements, techniques, and literary quality, but children also enjoy finding the white dog with the spot over one eye. Illustrators such as Van Allsburg tend to have interesting lives that may inspire class discussions.

Numerous websites help children and teachers research authors and illustrators. A few are:

www.acs.ucalgary.ca/~dkbrown/authorsmisc.html
http://falcon.jmu.edu/~ramseyil/childlit.htm
http://falcon.jmu.edu/~ramseyil/biochildhome.htm

Art Centers

Encourage students to try the media or techniques that they are exploring in picture books. After you introduce the books to the class, make them available for inspection, and provide supplies for creating the same type of artwork. You may not always be able to provide the same supplies and media as the artist used, but children are creative and will make do with similar materials.

With an art center in the classroom, students can experiment with various media. Include stamps, sand, beads, construction paper, clay, leaves, buttons, or twine along with traditional art supplies such as paints, crayons, pens, pencils, and computer graphics. Make available "how to" books to motivate children to try various artistic media. Basic art books that show examples of different media and techniques provide inspiration and enjoyment for students.

Materials and resources may be placed on a table in the classroom and changed occasionally to coincide with the illustrations the class is studying and to keep the center fresh and exciting. The art center should include a display area where students may share their work if they wish. Be sure that guidelines for working with materials such as paste and paint are clearly understood, and establish regular times for working in the art center. Setting a few simple rules will make your job easier and assure that children work at the art center without disturbing others who may be doing other work.

Artist Talks

Consider inviting artists or art specialists to the classroom to share their expertise with children. Many children's illustrators have developed presentations to explain how they develop their artwork and match visual symbols with the written words. If an artist is not available in your area, then a librarian or other resource person who understands artwork can be invited to talk to your class. University children's literature experts or art professors are usually willing to visit classrooms. Encourage students to read ahead, prepare questions, take notes, and use good listening skills when a guest speaker visits the classroom. Visitors offer another way to integrate listening, reading, writing, and speaking with visual literacy.

Sharing

Students should be encouraged to share their own artwork just as they would share their writing. Students may develop portfolios of their artwork in order to preserve it and share it with parents and others throughout the year. By sharing their work, students learn to accept a range of responses and to respond to each other's art in a way that is productive and positive. Creating a supportive environment is paramount to encouraging students to continue their creative efforts (Cecil & Lauritzen, 1994).

FINAL REFLECTIONS

Picture books and related art activities invite students to focus on visual communication in many forms and make connections among language arts activities. The more experiences children have with visual representation, the more visually literate they will become. The visual symbols in picture books encourage multiple interpretations, responses, and ways of thinking (Whitin, 1994), enhancing students' intellectual and creative development.

article

Technology

> One of the most significant results of the recent technological change is the increasing importance of images within the process of handling and communicating information. Multi-modal texts abound in our daily lives, in both print and electronic form. (Downes & Fatouros, 1995, p. 5)

Students in today's classrooms have grown up with computers and multimedia. They play with toys that are equipped with computer chips, and they spend hours with electronic games that feature sound and elaborate graphics. The television shows they watch are so filled with the visual aspects of technology that they have come to take complex presentations for granted. Students' cell phones resemble small computers, with tiny screens that bring visual representation into what used to be a purely verbal communication process. New technology-enhanced communication systems encourage the use of different tools, media, and formats and alter visual, oral, and written communication in ways that were not possible with conventional tools of the past (Carroll, 1999).

Students still need to understand verbal and written communication, but the ways they use traditional forms of communication have changed and will continue to do so. Images and sound are taking on an expanded role. Instead of or in addition to responding to literature by writing, students often demonstrate what they have learned by using graphics, animation, photography, and movies, integrating these media throughout their products and presentations. They are capable of learning from fast-moving images and glitzy animation. They respond to lights, action, and visuals.

Technology continues to impact traditional reading and writing and the language arts instructional processes in ways unimaginable a decade ago. It demands new skills of all partners in communication. An effective language user employing technologically enhanced communication media needs well-developed visual literacy skills as well as an understanding of multiple forms of media. Multimedia text—which may include digitized photos, animations, vocal narration, and music—"combines text and graphics and has brought about the interdependence of language arts and the visual arts" (Flood & Lapp, 1998).

TECHNOLOGY AND THE LANGUAGE ARTS CURRICULUM

A language arts curriculum that includes the computer and Internet as instructional tools embraces choice and flexibility. When these tools are available, students have more choices about how they access information and are able to select media tools that best suit their individual learning processes. In this chapter's Window to the Classroom, Sami, the teacher, enhanced student choice by using the Internet during the instructional process. Her students had a great deal of freedom in the activity she designed to introduce them to the Native American study. She set up the guidelines for the activity and selected the museum site, but her students selected the tribes they wanted to explore and the pictures they felt accomplished their purposes. From their computers they could explore a wide range of information, far beyond what would have been available in their classroom textbooks, encyclopedias, and literature selections.

Technology tends to encourage and reward collaborative efforts. In Sami's classroom, all the students pursued the Native American topic, but small groups and pairs discovered different ways to accomplish the assignment. They used computers collaboratively to learn about the topic, complete their research, and engage in electronic conversations.

English Language Learners

The computer and the Internet facilitate learning in classrooms where cultural and language differences exist (Gorski, 2001). Visual and multimedia approaches to presenting information expand opportunities for students who are learning English to learn vocabulary and investigate their interests. Pictures and graphics on the Internet help ELLs understand information. In Sami's Native American unit, the Internet allowed all students, no matter how adept they were at speaking English, to gain some understanding of the topic. As we discussed earlier in this chapter, visual representations contribute to concept development and help learners acquire background so that all students can engage in reading, writing, listening, and speaking activities.

Teachers who need ideas or resources to meet the needs of ELLs can find excellent support on the Web. For example, **www.iLoveLanguages.com,** a commercial website, offers more than 2,000 language links. The links include online language lessons, translating dictionaries, literature in various languages, translation services, and information about many languages. Such a wide range of resources provides students opportunities to learn about multiple perspectives.

Other Internet resources for the classroom are discussion boards and chat rooms for teachers and students, such as those on *Multicultural Forum* (www.edexchange.org/multicultural/payboard/payboard.html) and *McGraw-Hill Multicultural SuperForum* (www.mhhe.com/socscience/education/multi/sites/forums.html) (Gorski, 2001). The Creative Connections Project at www.ccph.com links classrooms from around the world through e-mail and the Internet. This site links more than 750 classrooms in places around the world, including Africa, the Arctic Circle, and China. Internet resources such as these help expand and enhance teachers' ideas and explanations by providing real-life experiences, perspectives, voices, and ideas.

Teacher Resources

Teachers can find a great deal of support on the Internet. A very useful site is Ed Web, at www.edweb.gsn.org, which provides ideas and theories about technology and education, as well as many helpful links for classroom activities. Most textbook publishers maintain websites for teachers and provide direct support for curricular enhancements. Check the reading/language arts textbook series used in your classroom to see if the publisher provides teacher support on the Internet. Houghton Mifflin, for example, provides thematic units, educational guides, and resources for parents at www.eduplace.com/hmco/school.

Teachers often consult the Internet to find answers to specific questions students ask during class discussions. The website Ask the Experts, at www.sciam.com/askexpert_directory.cfm, allows visitors to post questions for experts to answer, such as "What makes Kansas, Oklahoma, and Texas so prone to tornadoes?" "Why can't people tickle themselves?" "Do corked bats allow baseball players to hit the ball farther?" The site also provides a process for developing questions to ask while students study a particular topic.

personal reflection

Internet Resources

Find two websites, one related to content taught in the elementary classroom and one related to teaching strategies for language arts. Familiarize yourself with the sites. Write a description of each site, including a short evaluation, and compile them with other reviews done by your classmates to develop a list of Internet resources.

TECHNOLOGY STANDARDS AND GOALS

Technology innovations affect every aspect of life at home and school, but the most important effects on the way we communicate continue to result from two tools: the computer and the Internet. Instructional goals must go beyond helping students learn the parts and basic operation of the computer—how to turn it on, insert disks and CDs, or navigate from program to program. Most students come to school with basic computer skills or at least the propensity and motivation to learn them quickly. Instead, the overall goal of instruction should be to prepare students to be adaptable and able to learn and use innovations as they come along.

Many states have specific standards that establish instructional goals for technology education; some states, however, have embedded technology and media skills related to language and communication within the language arts curriculum. Examples from the Texas standards in Exhibit 6.6 illustrate how computer and Internet skills are implied in language arts standards.

Some state standards illustrate the impact of technology on the writing process; others are more directly identified as aspects of visual literacy. It would be difficult to meet the goals expressed in standards without preparing students to use the computer keyboard, software, and Internet search engines effectively. Teachers who use technology such as the Internet in their classrooms need to assess and measure their students' existing knowledge and experiences and provide opportunities for them to develop technology skills. Some students have major gaps in their technical abilities, but others are very knowledgeable. Formal measures are available, but your observations as you monitor students' work on computers is also valuable.

Selected items from the Texas Essential Knowledge and Skills related to computer and Internet skills.   *exhibit* **6.6**

(21) Writing/inquiry/research. The student uses writing as a tool for learning and research. The student is expected to: . . .

(C) take notes from relevant and authoritative sources such as guest speakers, periodicals, or online searches (4–8);

(E) present information in various forms using available technology (4–8) . . .

(22) Writing/connections. The student interacts with writers inside and outside the classroom in ways that reflect the practical uses of writing. The student is expected to: . . .

(B) correspond with peers or others via e-mail or conventional mail (4–8).

(23) Viewing/representing/interpretation. The student understands and interprets visual images, messages, and meanings. The student is expected to: . . .

(B) interpret important events and ideas gleaned from maps, charts, graphics, video segments or technology presentations (4–8); and

(C) use media to compare ideas and points of view (4–8). . . .

(25) Viewing/representing/production. The student produces visual images, messages, and meanings that communicate with others. The student is expected to: . . .

(B) produce communications using technology or appropriate media such as developing a class newspaper, multimedia reports, or video reports (4–8).

Checklists, anecdotal notes reflecting students' responses to computers, and conversations with students can provide teachers with a great deal of information about students' capabilities.

COMPUTER TOOLS

Computers have evolved into multimedia workstations, complete with full-color screens and plenty of storage to hold large programs and documents. They offer many options for instructional support, but one task for which they are particularly suited is helping us reason and represent ideas visually (Jonassen, 2000). By allowing students to view and manipulate visual representations, computers can help students clarify and understand texts and concepts. Consider how difficult it may be for a student to conceptualize a process such as photosynthesis. With a computer and the Internet, students can access visual representations of the concept. A student might use a search engine such as Kids Ask Jeeves (**www.ajkids.com**) and type the question, "What is photosynthesis?" Links lead to a short animated movie that explains photosynthesis and illustrates terms like *glucose, stomata, chloroplasts,* and *chlorophyll.* Students replay the clip, stop it when necessary, and print out the graphics to increase their understanding of the concept.

Computer tools for creating visual representations assist students as they respond to topics and explain what they have learned. A student who is able to draw the parts of a plant using computer graphics, label the structures, and color the image appropriately is demonstrating a great deal of knowledge. Just as a student's crayon-and-paper drawings provide important information about what she has learned, the way a student uses a computer and the Internet to describe or illustrate a concept suggests what she knows and understands.

Computer Software

Software available for the classroom changes daily, making it nearly impossible to include an up-to-date list of programs in a textbook. Several categories have been popular for a while, however, and the examples below will probably still be available in one form or another while this edition remains in print. The following three categories—concept organization software, presentation software, and paint and draw software—provide tools for creating visual representations and multimedia productions during teaching and learning activities.

Concept Organization Software

Inspiration and Kidspiration are software programs that promote visual thinking and learning. Inspiration is intended for older students and adults, while Kidspiration is more appropriate for students up to fifth grade. Both programs support visual learning methods such as webbing, idea mapping, and concept mapping. The software helps students express themselves visually and learn through the use of visuals, audio, and other multimedia. They permit teachers and students to create large visual displays about concepts. Additional information about Inspiration and Kidspiration software may be found at **www.inspiration.com**.

Presentation Software

Presentation software allows students to create multimedia presentations—including photographs, animation, clip art, film excerpts, speech, or music along with text—with relative ease. Presentations on the computer offer a new way for students to respond to literature, write directions, demonstrate research findings, and illustrate their own writing. Two of the most commonly used presentation programs are HyperStudio and PowerPoint. HyperStudio (**www.hyperstudio.com/index.html**) helps elementary students combine text and pictures. The program provides figures that children can animate and add to their stories along with sounds, video, photographs, and original graphics. A search on the Web reveals that teachers use HyperStudio in every subject area, including language arts. Hyperstudio's text-to-speech feature makes it a good tool for beginning language learners, as well. PowerPoint is widely used in business and education. It allows a presenter to design visual aids with a variety of typefaces and pictures, graphs, and other media. PowerPoint is more appropriate for older children, but it is simple to use and readily available in many settings.

Many teachers encourage their students to work in groups to plan, design, and create presentations. Students thereby both demonstrate what they have learned about a topic and practice working together and making decisions about organization, design elements, source material, navigational procedures, and media.

Paint and Draw Programs

Software programs such as Kid Pix, SuperPaint, and Painter allow users to create "freehand" drawings and color them. The programs also include pictures that users can modify and include in drawings or documents.

To read more about paint and draw programs, visit **www.inficad.com**.

An example of a slide created by a student using presentation software.

The game by Michael

We went to a bulls basket ball game. They won by 1 basket. The game was at night so I got to stay up very very very late!

Example of a student-authored text illustrated with paint and draw software.

Software Resources

Select a software program that students at your school use to produce visuals. Familiarize yourself with the software and, if possible, observe a student using the program. Write a description of the program, along with a short evaluation, and list suggestions for ways teachers can use the software. Compile it with other reviews done by your classmates to develop a resource file on computer software.

CLARE, VETERAN TEACHER ▶ I was a bit intimidated by the knowledge that some of my fifth graders had about computers and the Internet. In fact, I hesitated to use the Internet in the classroom because I was not confident about my own knowledge and skills. I finally attempted to use the "smart board" in the classroom. (The smart board projects the Internet image on a white board and allows a teacher to highlight visuals, make notes, draw pictures, and transfer them to the computer so they can be printed.) Some of my students had a great deal of experience on the Internet and were able to use the smart board in ways I couldn't. Other students needed a great deal of support to develop important Internet skills. All of my students were very patient as I tried out the new technology. It became a collaborative activity in which all of us learned together. From now on, I won't hesitate to use the computer in the classroom. I know that my students and I will learn a great deal about the Internet by exploring it together.

Contributions of the Internet

The Internet expands the amount and types of information available in the classroom, providing students with access to an almost infinite number of current resources and materials (Gorski, 2001). The Internet also opens up the possibility of contacting people all over the world. Another advantage of the Internet is that it offers up-to-the-minute information. Newly formed countries are recognized, recent scientific discoveries are reported, and new literature is reviewed. Textbooks and other printed resources cannot match the currency of the Internet, so when students need the most recent information, the Internet is the tool to use.

An important benefit of the Internet is that it offers information and ideas in multimedia form. In this chapter's Window to the Classroom, Sami introduced a study of Native Americans by using picture archives from a museum collection. The activity encouraged her students to learn from pictures, write about what they learned, and share with others. Virtual museums are one of many ways the Internet brings visual material into the classroom. Text documents, photographs, videos, animation, and three-dimensional graphics provide current information to students in a variety of forms and levels of sophistication, accommodating students with varying needs and learning styles.

Hypertext

Hypertext is simply text that includes links allowing readers to move from one document or site to another with just a click of the mouse. This simple concept has far-reaching ramifications for learning and problem solving. First, hypertext allows learners to explore concepts in a text freely, when they need or want deeper or broader information. Second, hypertext includes many types of media. If a student reading an Internet text about Thomas Jefferson (Exhibit 6.7) wants to understand more about the text, she clicks a highlighted phrase and immediately a short video clip, complete with narration, animation, and music, explains, for example, the weathervanes at Monticello. The links or hot spots embedded in hypertext or hypermedia texts easily transport the user to another Internet location, where information may be explained more deeply, in different ways, or through different media. The strength of hypertext is that it provides immediate, continuous, and repeated access to content and concepts (Wepner, Valmont, & Thurlow, 2000). The user controls what information is accessed, the speed of presentation, and the number of times it is reviewed. Hypertext supports learning by providing students quick access to information in ways that were not possible in the past. Students may also create hypertext for their own text or Web pages that reflect individual perspectives or understanding. In the process of developing hypertext documents, students construct their own understandings, consider the role of visual representation, and use a wide range of media.

To benefit fully from the Internet, students must be comfortable with using hypertext. In addition, the Internet requires that users extend their reading, writing, and problem-solving skills in unique ways (Valmont, 2000). Some of the special skills students need in order to navigate the Internet have to do with identifying key words, employing search engines, evaluating websites, and using the information they discover in an appropriate way.

Key Words

A key word is a word or phrase that is entered into the search window of an Internet search engine to search the Web for pages or sites that include the key word and information related to it. An understanding of key words is crucial for navigating the Internet. To help students with key words,

Example of a hypertext link. *exhibit* **6.7**

"He also recorded the direction and speed of the wind and the amount of precipitation. From indoors, Jefferson could see a <u>weathervane (weathervane.qt, 840K)</u> positioned over the East Portico of the house; he could also read the wind direction off a compass dial (connected to the weathervane directly above it) on the East Portico's ceiling." (Retrieved Aug. 29, 2004, www.monticello.org/jefferson/dayinlife/sunrise/home.html)

teachers may scaffold appropriate behaviors. For example, a teacher who wishes for students to research a children's illustrator guides the students to use the key words *children's literature* and *children's book illustrators*. A search on these terms returns many sites, and the teacher needs to show students how to select the sites that seem most appropriate and offer the best information. An effective way to show students how to make these choices is to think aloud, demonstrating the process of selecting sites to explore. Students should be encouraged to scan the sites that have been listed and decide which to visit. They should also be aware that it is acceptable to leave a site immediately if it doesn't appear to have the needed information.

Students' Recognition of Internet Graphics

Ask children to show you their favorite graphics on the Web or in a piece of software. Ask them to explain why they like these graphics and what attracts their attention. They may explain to you how visuals motivate them to enter a website and what they learn from the visuals. Try to find out why they enjoy the website. What do the graphics contribute to their learning? Is it colors, well-known icons, or animation that draws them to graphics? Or is it the content? Does what they want to learn motivate them to access a website, learn from a graphic, or work with software? What implications might children's responses to visuals and illustrations have for instruction and the use of software or Internet sites in the classroom?

Search Engines

Search engines provide great support for the research process, but using them effectively requires practice and preparation. Many search engines are available, and each of them searches for concepts in a slightly different way. Students may be directed to use the search engine that is best for their purposes, but often the best search engine is the one with which the child feels familiar and comfortable. Search engines that have been reviewed, filtered, and approved for children include:

> www.AJKids.com
> www.Yahooligans.com
> www.Alfy.com
> www.StudyWeb.com

Internet Safety and Evaluation

With all its possibilities, the Internet does also have drawbacks. It is wonderful to have so much information at students' fingertips, but much Internet content is neither relevant nor appropriate for students. Furthermore, when students are online they are vulnerable to contact by individuals who prey on children. For these reasons, both teachers and parents should be vigilant when students use the Internet. To protect students from accessing inappropriate or dangerous sites, most schools use blocking filters. To learn about how to restrict students' access to the Web, visit **www.cybersitter.com** or **www.surf watch.com.** For more information about using the Internet safely, search on the key words *children* and *Internet.*

Parents should be encouraged to enforce limits on their children's Internet exploration. You might find it interesting to review a contract designed to help parents and children establish guidelines for working on the Web, available at **www.ResponsibleKids.net/ebcontract.htm.**

After choosing an appropriate website to visit and opening the site, students next need to scan the site and decide whether to spend time at that site. Many sites are unreliable, and students must learn how to evaluate them and the information they present. See Exhibit 6.8 for questions and

---

Evaluating websites. *exhibit* **6.8**

When you are evaluating a website, consider the sources of the material, the accuracy and clarity of the content, and the purpose of the site. Ask the following questions:

1. *Can you determine who developed the site?* If not, you may want to take a cautious approach to its contents. *If you can discover the developer, is it a reliable source for the information you are seeking?* A noted authority on the topic or an agency of the government would be considered reliable. If the developer is someone you have not heard of before, *is enough information on the site developer provided so that you can check the person's qualifications?* If not, be cautious and investigate further.

2. *Are sources provided for information on the site, so the user can cross-check information?* If they are included, this is a definite plus.

3. *Does any of the information conflict with reliable sources that you have consulted?* If some of the information is in question, all of it is suspect.

4. *Is the layout of the site busy and confusing, making information difficult to locate and evaluate?* Disorganization is a particularly bad sign. And *is site navigation easy?* Sloppy navigational methods may indicate a lack of attention to detail.

5. *Is the material grammatically correct? Is it free from errors in spelling and mechanics?* These qualities reflect on the material's clarity and accuracy.

6. *Is the site free of advertising?* If not, look for possible bias in the information, based on the advertising.

7. *If currency of information is important, can you tell when the page was developed and last updated?* If not, be careful in accepting the information. If currency is not a factor—for example, for a Civil War site on which the material is not likely to become dated—this will not be a major concern.

Adapted from Roe, B. D. (2000). Using technology for content area literacy. In S. B. Wepner, W. J. Valmont, & R. Thurlow (Eds.), *Linking literacy and technology: A guide for K–8 classrooms* (p. 133). Newark, DE: International Reading Association.

guidance for evaluating websites. Website evaluation is extremely important, and children will need a great deal of guidance and supervision as they learn to select and use dependable websites. Website evaluation forms are available on the Internet. Visit **www.wiu.edu/users/mfbhl/evaluate.htm, http://school.discovery.com/schrockguide/eval.html**, and **www.lesley.edu/ library/guides/research/evaluating_web.html**.

Website Development

By using an HTML editor, students may develop their own classroom websites. These sites provide a space for students to write about their projects, provide information about what they are studying, publish their work and research findings, or establish links to other relevant websites. Instead of developing a printed class newspaper and making hard copies, students may post class news on the Web, or after studying a concept in history, science, or language arts, they may develop a website to demonstrate what they have learned.

Most Web-based publishing is written in HTML, a programming language developed to display multimedia documents. HTML is not difficult to use, and online tutorials are available. An Internet search will turn up many online sources of assistance. HTML software editors, such as Claris, HomePage, PageMill, and Microsoft FrontPage make the process even easier.

Teachers and students should be very cautious about placing personal information on websites. It is best not to include names, addresses, or other personal identification on Web pages, and the use of students' pictures must be considered carefully. Some schools' policies restrict the use of students' names and images.

Website developers must conform to copyright laws when they consider using material that others have created. When and how they may incorporate text, photos, graphics, video, and other materials they have accessed on the Web is an important lesson for all students. Permission is often necessary to use material from other sources, and proper referencing and citations are always necessary when students duplicate or copy material onto their own pages. For links to information about references and citations, visit **http://school.discovery.com/schrockguide/referenc.html#copyright**. Clear, concise instructions for elementary students on how to use citations may be found at **www.tekmom.com/cite/** and **http://tlc.epsb.ca/plagiarism/citations.htm**. Visit **http://oslis.k12.or.us/elementary/howto/cited/** to use a "Citation Maker"—it displays a correct citation when students fill in the online form.

Interactive Internet Options

The Internet dramatically alters notions of reading, writing, and communication (Bolter, 1998). One intriguing contribution is the increased opportunities for immediate interactive communication through written language. Whereas printed language has always been viewed as a relatively permanent communication medium, and letter writing has traditionally been viewed as an artful communication process that requires formal writing skills and interposes a delay of at least several days between mailing and delivery, the situation with electronic mail is quite different. With e-mail the printed word becomes an immediate, informal communication medium. E-mail messages often consist of short phrases and informal written language, and they may be exchanged as quickly as one could talk face to face. As revolutionary as this development may be, it is only the beginning of technological innovations in communication.

Bulletin boards. A bulletin board is an area of a website where users can read messages and post messages for others to read. Each bulletin board usually focuses on a certain subject, and messages appear in "threads" on specific topics that are rather like conversations. Unlike conversations, however, discussions on bulletin boards are "asynchronous"—participants may log in at any time, catch up on the postings made since their last visit, and pick up any strand of conversation.

Public bulletin boards are available for anyone to use and are often associated with websites for news, finance, or other subjects of broad interest. Again, because of the public nature of the Internet, the use of bulletin boards requires caution. Generally it is not a good idea to encourage students to use bulletin boards unless adults are monitoring their safety. To be sure of the nature of the information children read, a teacher or other trusted adult should guide them to bulletin boards that are filtered and controlled. Teachers who set up a bulletin board in the classroom should install monitoring devices to protect children. Some schools require all contacts to come through the teachers' e-mail addresses (Jonassen, Peck, & Wilson, 1999), in effect prohibiting students' use of bulletin boards at school. Be sure you understand your school's policies regarding Internet posting before encouraging children to read and post messages.

Because of the public nature of the Internet, generally it is not a good idea to encourage students to use bulletin boards or chat rooms unless an adult is monitoring their safety.

Chat rooms. A chat room is "a place or page in a website or online service where people can 'chat' with each other by typing messages which are displayed almost instantly on the screens of others who are in the 'chat room'" (retrieved Aug. 29, 2004, www.getnetwise.org/glossary.php). Participants from all over the world may join in these "real time" online conversations. As with bulletin boards, teachers must exercise caution when they allow students to conduct discussions with unknown parties. A safe way to use chat rooms is to connect with other classrooms where the teacher knows the students and the context.

More elaborate chat rooms establish a virtual room in which users may visualize entering a lobby and walking into a room that supports brainstorming, discussion, or presentations. In some cases the virtual rooms provide visual representations of the setting and participants that create an illusion of physical existence. Some "cutting edge" chat rooms merge visualizations, visual representations, and printed conversations in ways that blur their boundaries and change communication processes.

Most chat rooms are devoted to specific subjects. To chat about ESL education and related issues, visit **www.eslcafe.com/chat/chatpro.cgi** (this chat room requires free registration).

FINAL REFLECTIONS

Computers and the Internet have the potential to redefine some of our long-standing assumptions about language arts instruction. They have quickly changed our ideas about visual representation and how print is used, forcing us to amend reading and writing processes that have been in place for years. Indeed, as one educator writes, "Electronic technology is radically changing education and the teaching profession" (Smith, 1999, p. 414). The computer and the Internet are not a panacea for failures of communication or a sure solution for teaching communication skills; however, they will offer creative teachers and learners many new options in language arts instruction.

Media

The popular media inundate us with information and images that shape our thoughts, evoke our emotions, establish our values, and impact our views of the world. Television, radio, movies, newspapers, magazines, books, and Internet sites entertain us, consume our daily conversations, contribute to the way we think about issues, and define politics, economics, and social issues (Downing, Mohammadi, & Sreberny-Mohammadi, 1990). We are immersed in a culture of media, where literate individuals must be able "to understand, interpret, and criticize [its] meaning and messages" (Kellner, 1995, p. iv).

Even the types of media themselves seem endless. Electronic media—television, video (on disks, tapes, and cameras), compact disks, cellular telephones, radio, cable, and digital photography—are available in multiple formats for viewing under almost any circumstances. Print-related media—newspapers, magazines, books, comics, advertising, junk mail, travel brochures, and self-published "fanzines"—continually compete for young peoples' attention and affect their views of their world. The Internet combines multiple media into one experience with the power to overwhelm the user with information. And that's not all: the media continually evolve and alter our work, leisure, and communication processes with formats and texts that become increasingly sophisticated.

The most pervasive popular medium in modern life is the television. Americans spend over half their leisure time watching television. Some estimates indicate that by the time a person reaches the age of 21, she has seen more than 350,000 commercials (Hammer, 1995). No other medium interprets our lives so convincingly. Much of what we know and understand and believe about our world is filtered through the visual representations of television (Postman, 1995). The impact of television on young people is especially dramatic, as the statistics in Exhibit 6.9 indicate.

Watching Television

personal reflection

Spend some time watching television and focusing on the messages of the visual images. Organize the class to watch different types of programming—commercials, news, children's shows, prime-time shows. Pay particular attention to children's programming and the commercials that children watch. Turn off the sound and watch a commercial, news program, drama, or sitcom. What messages are communicated through visual images? Do you agree with the messages? Are you affected by those messages? Each group should share its findings with the entire class and develop ideas about the contribution of television to our views of the world.

Indications of the impact of popular media on students.   *exhibit* **6.9**

According to Angelfire.com,

- By age 18, an average teen will have seen 350,000 commercials.
- 50 percent of seventh to twelfth graders have a television in their room; 18 percent have a television and VCR in their room.
- Children between ages 9 and 13 watch more television than any other segment of the population except the elderly.
- 25 percent of all prime-time and weekend daytime commercials advertise food, 50 percent of which is "junk" food.

Retrieved August 16, 2003, from www.angelfire.com/ms/MediaLiteracy/Demo.html.

Television is only one way the media inundate us with images and messages. We scan the newspaper in the morning and listen to early-morning news radio or TV news programs while we get ready for the day. On the way to work or school, we pass dozens of huge billboards while listening to the radio play the latest hit from the current pop icon. Class assignments and work responsibilities require us to log in on the computer, communicate with e-mail, and review information on the Internet. At lunchtime, we talk with our friends about the movie we have just seen or what occurred on "reality TV" last night. Before we start home, we check in on our cell phone to see if friends or family members need us to bring something home for the evening meal. Meanwhile, our VCR is taping soap operas or talk shows so we can watch them later in the day. Our daily routines involve interactions with popular media in such rapid succession that we seldom notice the impact.

Similar to adults, elementary students spend a great deal of time engaged with popular media. They often have their own computers, e-mail accounts, cell phones (with text messaging ability), and personal stereos. As a result, they are highly conscious of commercial logos such as Coke, Nike, and McDonald's. They recognize and can name famous sports figures, rappers, and pop divas. The words of popular music are as familiar to them as nursery rhymes. They are greatly affected by current events, which are as vivid to them on television—wars in faraway places, a blackout in New York, the arrests of professional athletes, the success of an American competing in the Tour de France, and any event that is played over and over on the news.

MEDIA LITERACY

Both children and adults require a certain level of media literacy to navigate the complex messages in our high-tech world, and students learn a great deal about how to interpret popular media messages outside of school. Because of the predominance of the media in American culture, elementary students arrive at school capable of recognizing and interpreting a wide range of media presentations. It is astonishing to realize that for the most part, "literacy in the social media is unconscious, inarticulated, and unrecognized" (Hammer, 1995).

Traditional literacy is generally associated with printed materials—literature and writing are the core of the K–12 curriculum (Leland & Harste, 1999; Hobbs, 1997). Little attention is given to the importance of media literacy in the language arts curriculum, how students use media skills to interpret their daily lives, and how teachers should approach media literacy in the broader instruction of communicative skills. This neglect continues despite the fact that "we live in an era that is no longer dominated by the primacy of print . . . most Americans get most of their information about themselves and their world from television, not textbooks—pictures, not print" (Considine & Haley, 1999, p. xvii). A broader view of literacy implies that literacy skills must be applied to "messages in a variety of forms" (Hobbs, 1997, p. 8), including the primarily audiovisual messages of popular media. Recognizing the influence of popular media on literacy and communication will deeply affect the way teachers plan and implement language arts instruction.

Observing Media Influence

Visit **www.visualsummit.com/Media/MLLessons.html** and take the test on how much you know about the impact of media on students. How does this quiz rate your media literacy skills?

For one week, record evidence of popular media in the classroom. Note references in children's language, including their oral, written, and visual productions. Observe evidence such as pictures and words on clothing, school supplies, lunchboxes, and so forth. Compile a list of popular media representations, and identify the most common influences in children's lives. Plan a lesson in which students bring examples of popular culture to write about or discuss in class.

STANDARDS AND GOALS RELATED TO MEDIA

In the past, the United States has not viewed media education as an important component of schooling, but other countries such as Canada, Australia, and England believe that the study of media is an important part of becoming a well educated, literate person. The Ministry of Education in Ontario has described media literacy as the process of

> understanding and using mass media. It is also concerned with helping students and children develop an informed understanding of the nature of mass media, the techniques used by them and the impact of these techniques. More specifically, it is education that aims to increase students' understanding and enjoyment of how media work, how they produce meaning, how they are organized, and how they construct reality. (http://interact. uoregon.edu/MediaLit/HomePage)

Attitudes about media education in the United States may be changing. The American Academy of Pediatrics recognized the importance of media in children's growth and development and formally recommended that parents, teachers, and pediatricians work to promote "critical television-viewing skills among children" (http://interact.uoregon.edu/ MediaLit/FA/MLArticleFolder/kubey.html). The term "critical media literacy" (Alvermann, Moon, & Hagood, 1999) has been associated with reading and language arts instruction. Media literacy is defined as "providing individuals access to understanding how the print and nonprint texts that are part of everyday life help to construct their knowledge of the world" (Alvermann, Moon, & Hagood, 1999, p. 3). This definition implies that readers and writers must learn to understand and use popular media communication processes.

A review of three states' curriculum standards, California's, New York's, and Ohio's, revealed that state standards do mention media in language arts and reading standards; however, media literacy skills are not represented as extensively as are more traditional language arts skills. The examples in Exhibit 6.10 illustrate how state standards typically present media literacy instructional goals.

exhibit **6.10**   *Three examples of state language arts standards referencing popular media.*

CALIFORNIA LEARNING STANDARDS

English–Language Arts

Listening and Speaking

–2.0 Speaking Applications (Genres and Their Characteristics)   Grade 4

■ Make informational presentations: Incorporate more than one source of information (e.g., speakers, books, newspapers, television, or radio reports).

1.0 Listening and Speaking Strategies   Grade 6

■ Identify persuasive and propaganda techniques used in television and identify false and misleading information.

NEW YORK STATE ELEMENTARY STANDARDS

■ Gather and interpret information from children's reference books, magazines, textbooks, electronic bulletin boards, audio and media presentations, oral interviews, and from such forms as charts, graphs, maps, and diagrams.

■ Read and form opinions about a variety of literary and informational texts and presentations, as well as persuasive texts, such as advertisements, commercials, and letters to the editor.

OHIO STANDARDS FOR ELEMENTARY LEVEL

In the benchmark statement for K–12 language arts, the State of Ohio identifies the importance of applying . . . the reading process to various texts including . . . multimedia and electronic sources. More specifically the elementary standards include the following:

■ Communicate visually and in writing through multimedia.

■ Give presentations using a variety of delivery methods, visual materials and technology.

Integrate Media with Language Arts

field note

6.8

Review the language arts standards for your state or your elementary schools' local curriculum. Does it include standards that deal with media, either explicit or implied? Review standards in other subject areas and search for references to media. If your state or local standards include technology education, you will most likely find references to media there. Survey textbooks used at your grade level and note any references to media. Collect lessons or suggested activities associated with media and be prepared to share them with your university class. Sharing with your classmates can be the first step to creating a collection of instructional ideas and activities that will help you integrate media with language arts.

The media's influence on elementary and middle school students far outweighs the focus given to it in instructional settings (Alvermann, Moon, & Hagood, 1999). However, a teacher may reduce the imbalance by incorporating popular media into language arts curriculum. Topics related to media that are of interest to students serve as an excellent basis for listening, speaking, reading, and writing activities while meeting standards in language arts and other subject matter areas. Media education is probably best when it is connected to the traditional skills of language arts instruction. Moreover, the use of popular media in instructional tasks is highly motivational for elementary students. Teachers who use television, movies, computer games, popular music, and teen magazines as instructional materials capture students' attention and engage them in relevant and meaningful learning processes.

Teacher Viewpoint

CARLA, BEGINNING TEACHER ▶ I am always trying to keep up with what my fourth grade students are doing in their spare time. They are always impressed when I know about movie and recording celebrities they discuss or when I can talk about the video games they play. During the past couple of years, I've been using media as a way to introduce the chapter books they are reading. Sometimes I use the video version just to motivate them to read the book, but I also use it as a tool for teaching them about the role of visual presentations. A standard technique I use is to have students compare books and movies with the same title. I have a set of Newbery Award stories and videos that make it easy to develop instructional activities.

Last year I wanted to study the impact of media on students' lives in a different way, so I designed a unit so that students could see how they are influenced by video games. I divided my class into different groups who answered questions such as how video games were used, where they were developed, and how much time and money students their age spend engaged in video games. Much of the research was completed on the Internet. As we studied the topic, I observed an enormous involvement in the reading, writing, and speaking activities that supported their research. I worried that parents might think I was taking time away from language arts instruction, but I had good evidence in the students' reading, writing, and speaking behaviors that they were taking this opportunity to improve their communication skills while also realizing how popular media impacts their lives.

MEDIA EDUCATION

Media literacy comprises many of the same skills needed to interact with books and literature, but in somewhat different forms. The major differences may result from the formats of the "texts," the presence of audio and visual illustrations, and the context or site where the presentation is found. Literate consumers of media must access and understand texts by listening to, viewing, and reading. Students also must be able to evaluate and respond to the messages they hear and see in popular media. Three processes—accessing and understanding, evaluating and analyzing, and responding—provide a framework for media education (Hobbs, 1997) in language arts instruction (see Exhibit 6.11).

Accessing and Understanding

Students who are media literate know where and how to find media texts, and they recognize and understand these texts. Most students come to school already adept at accessing media. They watch television, search the Web, play video games, listen to music, and have viewed or heard thousands of ads on television and in newspapers and magazines. They understand many of the messages conveyed by media representations, especially the commercial messages directed at them, but they benefit from learning more about the role of media in their lives. Teachers can increase students' ability to access and understand popular media by using and referring to media during instruction. Television, videos, and the Internet may serve as engaging ways to introduce topics and explain concepts. Classroom media experiences are especially beneficial in that they allow students to build on common experiences. For example, students who see the movie *Whale Rider* before studying a unit on New Zealand will have a common reference and examples that are familiar to everyone.

Discussion is a simple strategy teachers often use to help students learn to access media texts. Many teachers start the day talking about current events and ask children to talk about what they saw on television or read in the newspaper. This sort of discussion is particularly relevant during times of national celebrations or crises. Students are aware of and concerned about faraway wars, national energy shortages, and celebrities running for state or national offices. They hear about these topics throughout their day and are often very interested in focused discussions, continued research, and opportunities to read and write about these subjects. Media-related activities are important classroom contributions to children's understanding of day-to-day happenings, and they are relatively easy and enjoyable to implement. Students enjoy discussing subjects that affect their daily lives.

Media logos and icons permeate students' lives. Musicians, television stars, and commercial signage appear everywhere students go. Even very young children are familiar with visual signs and logos associated with television and other media. To start a discussion, teachers might ask students to talk about what these signs and logos mean. As students recognize the presence of logos and signage in their lives, they develop an awareness and understanding of the messages they convey. Additional discussions might explore the economic impact of logos on students' lives (familiarity with certain brands might encourage them to spend their money) or aspects of design (see Article II in this chapter). Students could speculate whether a particular logo would mean the same thing if it were pink instead of red and begin to understand the impact of color and other design elements on the messages of visual representations.

Reading skills and activities applied to popular media texts help students improve their comprehension and analytical skills. In the same way that effective teachers help students through the reading process, they guide students before, during, and after they interact with popular media. For example, a teacher who is using the movie *Whale Rider* as an introduction to the study of New Zealand, might ask the class to predict what they think the movie is about. Students would probably guess that the movie is about a whale and imagine that someone would ride a whale. They would undoubtedly make some predictions unrelated to the movie. The teacher could then ask students to watch the movie and consider which of the predictions were confirmed. About halfway through the movie, the teacher could stop the movie and talk about which original predictions were con-

Framework for integrating media education in language arts curriculum.	*exhibit*	**6.11**

SPECIFIC GOAL	DESCRIPTION	EXAMPLE ACTIVITIES

Access and Understanding	Develop technological skills for manipulating media
	Recognize messages
	Comprehend messages
	Apply messages
	Use information
		Share experience—view and listen as a class
		Discuss logos and icons
		Apply traditional language arts strategies:
		   DRTA
		   KWL
		   Retelling

Evaluating and Analyzing	Make judgments Examine Compare Decide	Discuss "Did you like . . . ," "Why or why not?" Compare media presentations Apply literature elements Critique commercial messages
Responding	React Create new ideas Develop opinions	Write and discuss Create visuals Produce media

firmed or not, and have students make new predictions. When the movie is over, the class would discuss the film, reviewing their predictions and retelling their favorite parts. As with books, prediction activities help students improve their comprehension of movies and other media and provide a flexible framework for discussions, writing, and listening.

Analyzing and Evaluating

A media-literate person makes judgments, examines, compares what he sees and hears, and comes to informed decisions about relevance and accuracy. Activities that involve analysis and evaluation may be simple and spontaneous, naturally arising during discussions, or planned in detail to meet specific instructional goals. For example, after watching a movie or video or interacting with an Internet presentation, the class might discuss questions that require analysis and evaluation skills. Questions such as "Did you like the movie? Why or why not?" are the first steps to analyzing and evaluating what students have seen.

Comparing film and literature versions of the same story is an excellent way to analyze and critique a movie. Film and literature comparisons, where students assess the differences between film versions and original texts and their effect on themes, characterization, and enjoyment, increase students' analytical abilities and help them learn strategies for identifying good movies. One way to guide a comparative discussion is to use a Venn diagram, noting things that are different and similar (see Exhibit 6.12).

The ability to analyze and respond appropriately to advertisements is a critical aspect of media literacy. Students might review a series of advertisements to identify what is being sold and what messages are being sent. They could point out values that advertisers promote along with their products—athletic prowess, good looks, popularity—and consider why advertisers would exploit these values. The class might develop advertisements of their own, using techniques they have observed in actual ads.

Students may analyze and critique popular media "texts" just as they do print literature. For example, a teacher who uses *Whale Rider* in the classroom might ask the class to complete Internet research and decide if the representation of the Maori children in the movie is realistic. They might evaluate elements as in a literature study, such as genre, character development, and conflict and resolution, as a familiar framework. By applying the criteria that they would use to evaluate good literature and their knowledge of visual representations, students may evaluate the overall quality of the movie. Reading reviews from professional critics will give them a sense of how movies are evaluated, and these reviews themselves may serve as texts for evaluation.

By providing students with a format for evaluating what they see, teachers can guide them to be more analytical. Teachers can encourage students to follow up their own media experiences by evaluating and analyzing in written form and to read professional reviews and discussions related to television and movies. All of these activities will contribute to students' traditional literacy skills as well as their media literacy.

Venn diagram comparing movies and books.   **exhibit** **6.12**

BOOKS

Characters are imagined

Authors talk about characters' thoughts

Descriptions, details, events are written, and reader imagines

Readers make connections between the words and their own imagination

Pictures are created in the readers' minds, or they use illustrations to form mental pictures

BOOK AND MOVIE

Common title

Common characters

Events are similar (some events may be made for movies)

Similar plots, although the plot is often modified for movies

Settings are similar (some changes may be made for movies)

Time period is the same

MOVIES

Character is personified by an actor

We see what characters do instead of know their thoughts

Settings are built or in actual locations

Special effects may be used to enhance the storytelling

Some events differ so they are appropriate for movies or TV

Endings are often different

Music helps the plot development (e.g., it foreshadows events)

Movie makers interpret the events for the viewer

Responding

Media-literate people are capable of communicating their responses to media texts—their emotional responses, intellectual insights, and opinions. They can describe their responses to others and explain how their media experiences affected them. They can articulate their responses to both fantasy events (the story in a movie) and real-life media events (an awards show), and they may do so by writing, by speaking, or by creating their own visuals. Teachers can learn a great deal about students' lives and their views of the world by observing their reactions to and opinions about media texts.

Advertisements, movies, and websites that feature eye-catching special effects can spark discussions about media production. By studying how advertisers and directors enhance their messages with graphics, pictures, and simulations, students grow to appreciate the effects of visual representations.

Educating students in the methods of media production is an effective way to explore the role and influence of the media (Griffin & Schwartz, 1996). Creating media productions is a particularly rewarding way for students to respond and an excellent way for them to demonstrate what they have learned. Creating a script, advertisement, newspaper article, or website provides opportunities for students to interpret, critique, collaborate, and enjoy while they engage in hands-on activities. Photography, cinematography, and other video productions require students to conduct research, write scripts, and practice other traditional literacy skills. They may use media tools to enhance their responses to books and other media experiences, or to help explain what they have learned during research projects.

The Internet is a rich source of media lessons and suggestions for including media in the curriculum. The list of activities shown in Exhibit 6.13, retrieved from the Public Broadcasting Service's website, illustrates the support teachers can find on the Internet and suggests ways to teach media literacy skills.

exhibit **6.13**   *Language arts and media activities suggested by the Public Broadcasting Service.*

Ask students to count the ads they see or hear for a whole day. This might include billboards, flyers left on car windshields, and logos on clothes. As students share results, ask them to define what's advertising and what's not: a label on a sweater? A name on a mailbox at a private residence? Together, create a definition for "advertisement."

Evaluate Web sites—a great training ground for media literacy. Who sponsors the site? How long has the site been around and do you know how often it is updated? Do links work? Are sources provided for quotations, research results, etc.? How does it compare with similar sites? Write site reviews and develop evaluation rubrics. Are the questions the same for other sources of information? Check out the K.I.D.S. Scout Report for some great sample reviews.

Ask students to evaluate the credibility of sources. Is the author's name given? What do you know about the author? Does the author seem to have anything to gain one way or another from the situation?

Ask students to look for patterns of representation in certain types of media. What do you "always" see in sitcoms? Comic books? Magazine ads? Movies? Stage a debate or discussion to evaluate which medium does the best job with accurate representation.

If advertising is used in your school (Channel One, posters, etc.) engage students in an analysis of the ads. What do they sell and why? How do the advertisers use colors, music, editing, etc. to appeal to you? Students might write editorials about advertising in schools, or focus on advertising production techniques and script advertisements pitching a product to an unlikely audience.

Exhibit 6.13 is excerpted with permission from www.pbs.org/TeacherSource and is used with permission of the Public Broadcasting Service.

FINAL REFLECTIONS

The importance and relevance of media literacy has never been greater, and it is clear that the impact of popular media will only increase with time. Unfortunately, specific references to media education and popular culture are not prevalent in traditional language arts curriculum. However, many teachers recognize the importance of popular media and use it as a "text" when they teach reading, writing, listening, and speaking. Students have a natural interest and motivation to attend to issues related to popular culture and are easily encouraged to study how media impacts their own learning, understanding, and communication processes. It is a very important aspect of their personal literacy skills. Griffin and Schwartz write,

> McDonald's, Coke, Nike, shopping malls, the 5000-channel universe and computers are not going to go away. Students need communication strategies to understand and interpret popular media. It is naive to believe that traditional language arts skills consisting of literature, grammar, spelling, and writing will equip today's students for the audiovisual media environment they live in. (1996, p. 41)

Integrating Multimedia in Instruction

As you observe or deliver instruction in your classroom, note the media used to support lessons. Develop a lesson that integrates one or more types of media. Experiment with how different media motivate and interest students and influence their responses. For example, present a lesson based on print from a newspaper, then present the same content with videos, or include Internet presentations. What are some positive effects of media on language arts instructional processes?

PROFESSIONAL REFLECTIONS

Review the field notes from this chapter and develop one or more into a component of your portfolio. To continue to reflect on your field note responses, consider the following suggestions:

- Use the material you developed for Field Note 6.1 and create a visual representation of the media that affect children in your classroom. Consider using a concept map, web, or collage.
- Review the popular media lesson you developed for Field Note 6.9, making any changes you feel are necessary based on your reflections and assessment. Include your evaluation and samples of children's responses in your portfolio.

Professional Readings

To expand your understanding of the content of this chapter, you may wish to read some of the following books:

Alvermann, D. E., Moon, J. S., & Hagood, M. C. (1999). *Popular culture in the classroom: Teaching and researching critical media literacy.* Newark, DE: International Reading Association.

Alvermann and her colleagues make a case for the importance of developing an awareness of popular culture during language arts instruction. This book not only argues for teaching about popular culture, but it also provides motivating and interesting teaching strategies. This book will help you consider why and how to teach about popular culture.

Bang, M. (2000). *Picture this.* Boston: Bulfinch/Little, Brown.

The author uses the story of Little Red Riding Hood to describe how pictures tell stories. She changes the illustrations that accompany the story to demonstrate the impact of color, lines, shapes, and other visual elements.

Dresang, E. T. (1999). *Radical change.* Bronx, NY: H. W. Wilson.

Dresang discusses more than 200 excellent, provocative books that children's librarians and teachers should know about. They range from picture books to YA fiction, from informational nonfiction to poetry and beyond, pushing the boundaries to include formats that are nonlinear or offer unconventional points of view.

Gorski, P. C. (2000). *Multicultural education and the internet.* Boston: McGraw-Hill.

Gorski makes a case for using the Internet to increase the representation of multiple perspectives and views of the world. This short text lists many valuable websites that can help teachers integrate the Internet into their instructional procedures.

Books About Children's Picture Books

Doonan, J. (1993). *Looking at pictures in picturebooks.* Gloucestershire, UK: Stroud: Thimble Press.

Kiefer, B. (1995). *The potential of picture books: From visual literacy to aesthetic understanding.* Englewood Cliffs, NJ: Merrill.

Marantz, S. (1992). *Picture books for looking and learning.* Phoenix, AZ: Oryx Press.

Nodelman, P. (1988). *Words about pictures.* Athens, GA: University of Georgia Press.

Stewig, J. (1995). *Looking at picture books.* Fort Atkinson, WI: Highsmith Press.

Some children's books provide insights about the impact of visual presentation on readers' responses. Review a few of the books listed here and talk with your classmates about how the illustrations and graphics help you understand visual literacy.

Children's Books

Jonas, A. (1990). *Round trip.* Clarksville, IN: Mulberry House.

This inventive format tells two stories. You read the book through and then turn it over for another story. The pictures take on a different meaning depending on which way the book is held. Children can learn that images can mean more than one thing depending on how you look at them.

Macaulay, D. (1990). *Black and white.* Boston: Houghton Mifflin.

The visual presentation of this book is part of the story. Macaulay intermingles several stories, and the illustrations help us understand how the stories are connected. The visual presentations in this remarkable picture book provide new perspectives with each rereading.

Martin, B., & Archambault, J. (1989). *Chicka, chicka, boom, boom.* Illustrated by L. Ehlert. New York: Simon & Schuster.

This classic book uses visuals to represent the rhythm and motion of language. It is an alphabet book in which colors help young readers remember letters and the alphabet.

Other children's books mentioned in this chapter are:

Brown, M. (1982). *Shadow.* New York: Charles Scribner's Sons.

Bunting, E. (1997). *Ducky.* Illustrated by D. Wisniewski. New York: Clarion.

Bunting, E. (1994). *Smoky night.* Illustrated by D. Diaz. San Diego: Harcourt Brace & Co.

Ehlert, L. (1995). *Snowballs.* San Diego: Harcourt Brace & Co.

Emberley, B. (1967). *Drummer Hoff.* Illustrated by E. R. Emberley and B. Emberley. Englewood Cliffs, NJ: Prentice Hall.

Feelings, M. (1974). *Jambo means hello.* Illustrated by T. Feelings. New York: Dial.

Hendershot, J. (1987). *In coal country.* Illustrated by T. B. Allen. New York: Alfred A. Knopf.

Jarrell, R. (1972). *Snow White and the seven dwarfs.* Illustrated by N. E. Burkert. New York: Farrar, Straus, and Giroux.

Lionni, L. (1969). *Alexander and the wind-up mouse.* New York: Alfred A. Knopf.

McDermott, G. (1972). *Anansi the spider: A tale from the Ashanti.* New York: Scholastic.

Polacco, P. (1994). *Pink and say.* New York: Scholastic.

Rathman, P. (1995). *Officer Buckle and Gloria.* New York: Putman and Sons.

Sendak, M. (1988). *Where the wild things are.* New York: HarperCollins.

Seuss, Dr. (1996). *My many colored days.* New York: Alfred A. Knopf.

Simon, S. (1997). *Wild babies.* New York: HarperCollins.

Van Allsburg, C. (1981). *Jumanji.* Boston: Houghton Mifflin.

Van Allsburg, C. (1984). *The mysteries of Harris Burdick.* Boston: Houghton Mifflin.

Van Allsburg, C. (1988). *Two bad ants.* Boston: Houghton Mifflin.

Wisniewski, D. (1996). *Golem.* New York: Clarion.

Wu, N. (1996). *A city under the sea: Life in a coral reef.* New York: Atheneum Books for Young Readers.

Yolen, J. (1987). *Owl Moon.* Illustrated by J. Schoenherr. New York: Philomel.

Zelinsky, P. O. (1997). *Rapunzel.* New York: Dutton.

Zemach, H. (1973). *Duffy and the Devil.* Illustrated by M. Zemach. New York: Farrar.

REFERENCES

Albers, P. (1997). Art as literacy. *Language Arts, 74,* 338–350.

Alvermann, D. E., Moon, J. S., & Hagood, M. C. (1999). *Popular culture in the classroom: Teaching and researching critical media literacy.* Newark, DE: International Reading Association and Chicago, IL: National Reading Council.

Anderson, C. (1995). The role of picturebook illustration in visual literacy. *The New Advocate, 8,* 305–312.

Baskin, B. H. (1996). The role of computer graphics in literacy attainment. In J. Flood, S. B. Heath, & D. Lapp (Eds.), *Handbook of research on teaching literacy through the communicative and visual arts* (pp. 872–874). Newark, DE: International Reading Association.

Bolter, J. D. (1998). Hypertext and the question of visual literacy. In D. Reinking, M. C. McKenna, L. D. Labbo, & R. D. Kieffer (Eds.), *Handbook of literacy and technology: Transformations in a post-typographic world* (pp. 3–14). Mahwah, NJ: Lawrence Erlbaum Associates.

Bruce, B. C., & Hogan, M. P. (1998). The disappearance of technology: Toward an ecological model of literacy. In D. Reinking, M. C. McKenna, L. D. Labbo, & R. D. Kieffer (Eds.), *Handbook of literacy and technology: Transformations in a post-typographic world* (pp. 269–281). Hillsdale, NJ: Erlbaum.

Carroll, J. M. (1999). *Five reasons for scenario based design.* Proceedings of the Hawaii Conference on System Science. Maui, HI: IEEE Computer Society. Retrieved June 10, 2004, www.computer.org/proceedings/hiccs/0001/00013/00013051.PDF.

Cecil, N. L., & Lauritzen, P. (1994). *Literacy and the arts for the integrated classroom: Alternative ways of knowing.* New York: Longman.

Considine, D. (1994). Strategies for media literacy. *Telemedium: The Journal of Media Literacy, 41*(2).

Considine, D., & Haley, G. E. (1999). *Media literacy: The purposes, principles, and curriculum connections.* Englewood, CO: Teachers Idea Press.

Daiute, C. (1992). Multimedia composing: Extending the resources of kindergarten to writers across the grades. *Language Arts, 69,* 250–260.

Davis, R. W. (1996). *Art and children: Using literature to expand creativity.* Lanham, MD: Scarecrow Press.

Desmond, R. (1996). TV viewing, reading, and media literacy. In J. Flood, S. B. Heath, & D. Lapp (Eds.), *Handbook of research on teaching literacy through the visual and communicative arts* (pp. 23–30). New York: Simon & Schuster/Macmillan.

Downes, T., & Fatouros, C. (1995). *Learning in an electronic world.* Sydney, Australia: Primary English Teaching Association (PETA).

Downing, J., Mohammadi, A., & Sreberny-Mohammadi, A. (1990). *Questioning the media: A critical introduction.* Newbury Park, CA: Sage.

Eisner, E. W. (1991). Rethinking literacy. *Educational Horizons, 69,* 120–128.

Ernst, K. (1994). Writing pictures, painting words: Writing in an artists' workshop. *Language Arts, 71,* 44–52.

Fisherkeller, J. (2000). "The writers are kind of desperate": Young adolescents, television, and literacy. *Journal of Adolescent & Adult Literacy, 43,* 596–606.

Flood, J., & Lapp, D. (1998). Broadening conceptualizations of literacy: The visual and communicative arts. *The Reading Teacher, 51,* 342–344.

Frei, R. (1990). Making meaning with art: Children's stories. *Language Arts, 76,* 386–392.

Galda, L., & Cullinan, B. (1997). Introduction. In J. Flood, S. B. Heath, & D. Lapp (Eds.), *Handbook of research on teaching and literacy through the visual and communicative arts* (pp. 789–792). New York: Macmillan.

Garner, R., & Gillingham, M. G. (1998). The Internet in the classroom: Is it the end of transmission-oriented pedagogy? In D. Reinking, M. C. McKenna, L. D. Labbo, & R. D. Kieffer (Eds.), *Handbook of literacy technology: Transformations in a post-typographic world* (pp. 221–231). Mahwah, NJ: Lawrence Erlbaum Associates.

Goodman, K. (1988). Look what they've done to Judy Blume!: The "basalization" of children's literature, *The New Advocate, 1,* 24–29.

Gorski, P. C. (2001). *Multicultural education and the Internet: Intersections and integrations.* New York: McGraw-Hill.

Greeno, J. G., & Hall, R. P. (1997). Practicing representation: Learning with and about representational forms. *Phi Delta Kappan, 78,* 361.

Griffin, M., & Schwartz, D. (1996). Visual communication skills and media literacy. In J. Flood, S. B. Heath, & D. Lapp (Eds.), *Handbook of research on teaching literacy through the visual and communicative arts* (pp. 40–47). New York: Simon & Schuster/Macmillan.

Hammer, R. (1995). Rethinking the dialectic: A critical semiotic meta-theoretical approach for the pedagogy of media literacy. In P. McLaren, R. Hammer, D. Scholle, & S. Reilly (Eds.), *Rethinking media literacy: A critical pedagogy of representation* (pp. 34–85). New York: Peter Lang.

Hobbs, R. (1997). Literacy for the information age. In J. Flood, S. B. Heath, & D. Lapp (Eds.), *Handbook of research on teaching literacy through the communicative and visual arts* (pp. 7–14). New York: Simon & Schuster/Macmillan.

Hortin, J. A. (1994). Theoretical foundations of visual learning. In D. M. Moore & F. M. Dwyer (Eds.), *Visual literacy: A spectrum of visual learning* (pp. 5–29). Englewood Cliffs, NJ: Educational Technology Publications.

Housen, A. (1987). Three methods for understanding museum audiences. *Museum Studies Journal, 2*(4), 41–49.

Housen, A. (1992). Validating a measure of aesthetic development for museums and schools. *ILVS Review, A Journal of Visual Behavior, 2,* 213–237.

Jonassen, D. H. (2000). *Computers as mindtools for schools.* Upper Saddle River, NJ: Merrill.

Jonassen, D. H., Peck, K. L., & Wilson, B. G. (1999). *Learning with technology: A constructivist perspective.* Upper Saddle River, NJ: Merrill.

Kellner, D. (1995). Preface. In P. McLaren, R. Hammer, D. Sholle, & S. Reilly (Eds.), *Rethinking media literacy: A critical pedagogy of representation* (pp. xv–xvii). New York: Peter Lang.

Kiefer, B. (1995). *The potential of picturebooks: From visual literacy to aesthetic understanding.* Englewood Cliffs, NJ: Merrill.

Kiefer, B. (1996). The visual arts made accessible through picture books. In J. Flood, S. B. Heath, & D. Lapp (Eds.), *Handbook of research on teaching literacy through the visual and communicative arts* (pp. 820–821). New York: Simon & Schuster/Macmillan.

Kist, W. (2000). Beginning to create the new literacy classroom: What does the new literacy look like? *Journal of Adolescent & Adult Literacy, 43,* 710–718.

Kubey, R. (2001). *The case for media literacy* [Electronic version]. Retrieved June 16, 2004, http://interact. uoregon.edu/MediaLit/mlr/readings/articles/kubey.

Kubey, R., & Baker, F. (1999, October 27). Has media literacy found a curricular foothold? *Education Week, XIX*(9), 56, 38.

Leland, C. & Harste, J. (1999). Is this appropriate for children? Books that bring realistic social issues into the classroom. *Practically Primary, 4*(3), 6–10.

Lynch-Brown, C. & Tomlinson, C. (2001). *Essentials of children's literature.* Boston: Allyn & Bacon.

McGee, L. M., & Richgels, D. J. (2000). *Literacy's beginnings: Supporting young readers and writers* (3rd ed.). Boston: Allyn & Bacon.

Messaris, P. (1997). Introduction. In J. Flood, S. B. Heath, & D. Lapp (Eds.), *Handbook of research on teaching through the visual and communicative arts* (pp. 3–5). New York: Simon & Schuster/Macmillan.

Ministry of Education (1989). *Resource guide: Media literacy.* Ontario, Canada: Ministry of Education.

Moore, D. M., & Dwyer, M. (Eds.). (1994). *Visual literacy: A spectrum of visual learning.* Englewood Cliffs, NJ: Educational Technology.

National Council of Teachers of English & International Reading Association (1996). *Standards for the English language arts.* Urbana, IL: NCTE and Newark, DE: IRA.

Norton, D., & Norton, S. (1994). *Language arts activities for children.* Upper Saddle River, NJ: Merrill.

Nueman, S. (1996). Television as a learning environment: A theory of synergy. In J. Flood, S. B. Heath, & D. Lapp (Eds.), *Handbook of research on teaching literacy through the visual and communicative arts* (pp. 15–21). New York: Simon & Schuster/Macmillan.

Postman, N. (1995). *The end of education: Redefining the value of school.* New York: Knopf.

Reinking, D. (1997). The 1994 technology and cognition group at Vanderbilt University reported in "Me and my hypertext: A multiple digression analysis of technology and literacy." *The Reading Teacher, 50,* 626–643.

Remer, J. (1996). *Beyond enrichment.* New York: American Council for the Arts.

Sankey, M. D.(2002). Considering visual literacy when designing instruction. *The e-Journal of Instructional Science and Technology, 5*(2).

Schirato, T., & Yell, S. (1996). *Communication and cultural literacy: An introduction.* St. Leonard: Allen & Unwin Pty. Ltd.

Sipe, L. (1995). Connecting visual and verbal literacy: Second graders learn about art techniques in picture books. *Teacher Research: The Journal of Classroom Inquiry, 2,* 61–73.

Sipe, L. (1998). Learning the language of picturebooks. *Journal of Children's Literature, 24*(2), 66–75.

Smith, F. (1999). When irresistible technology meets irreplaceable teachers. *Language Arts, 76,* 414–421.

Tomlinson, C., & Lynch-Brown, C. (2001). *Essentials of children's literature.* Boston: Allyn & Bacon.

Tompkins, G. (1998). *Language arts: Content and teaching strategies.* Upper Saddle River, NJ: Merrill/Prentice Hall.

Valmont, W. J. (2000). What do teachers do in technology-rich classrooms? In S. B. Wepner, W. J. Valmont, & R. Thurlow (Eds.), *Linking literacy and technology: A guide for K–8 classrooms* (pp. 160–217). Newark, DE: International Reading Association.

Valmont, W. J., & Wepner, S. B. (2000). Using technology to support literacy learning. In S. B. Wepner, W. J. Valmont, & R. Thurlow (Eds.), *Linking literacy and technology: A guide for K–8 classrooms* (pp. 2–18). Newark, DE: International Reading Association.

Wepner, S. B., Valmont, W. J., & Thurlow, R. (2000). *Linking literacy and technology: A guide for K–8 classrooms.* Newark, DE: International Reading Association.

Whitin, P. (1994). Opening potential: Visual response to literature. *Language Arts, 71,* 101–107.

Whitin, P. (1996). *Sketching stories, stretching minds: Responding visually to literature.* Portsmouth, NH: Heinemann.

Yenawine, P. (1997). Thoughts on visual literacy. In J. Flood, S. B. Heath, & D. Lapp (Eds.), *Handbook of research on teaching literacy through the visual and communicative arts* (pp. 845–846). New York: Simon & Schuster/Macmillan.

One of the greatest challenges that Delray has in his new career as a teacher is deciding how to make instructional decisions in his classroom. He meets this challenge by basing instructional choices on assessment of his students. For example, based on his own teaching philosophy and state learning standards, he has set an instructional goal to help children read a wide variety of materials. He teaches in Florida, and one of the standards he is responsible for addressing in his third-grade classroom is, "The student constructs meaning from a wide range of texts." To address this standard, he implemented instructional strategies such as reading aloud to the class, introducing new books, leading book discussions, setting up literature circles in his classroom, providing a classroom library with a wide variety of texts, and giving students daily time to read.

He also planned how to assess his students' reading performance. Delray consistently measures this by using anecdotal records, checklists, and summaries of his students' book reviews. The information that he collects lets him know whether he is meeting his instructional goals and indicates what instructional experiences he should continue to provide for his students. For

Chapter 7

USING ASSESSMENT TO MAKE INSTRUCTIONAL DECISIONS

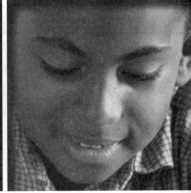

example, at the end of a grading period, Delray found that most of his students were reading a wide range of children's literature. Most of the young readers in his classroom were beginning to read a range of books, including short novels, informational texts, and picture books. However, he identified three students who were reading only humorous picture books. Based on his assessments, Delray decided to plan experiences for these three students that would encourage them to read a wider range of materials.

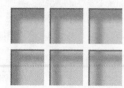

Delray views assessment as a collaborative process. For example, to assess the range of material being read in his classroom, Delray has students fill out checklists about the types of books they read and liked. He then discusses some of his observations about the books they are reading. He even has his students write down observations of their own reading behaviors. After reviewing all this information together, he and his students discuss and evaluate their reading behaviors and identify goals for the semester. Periodically the students evaluate their own progress and determine what they would do to read a wider range of texts. In addition, Delray holds conferences with students individually and goes over what they are reading in a systematic way. Together he and his students make decisions about their reading goals and what they should work on to expand their reading.

Delray is also concerned about the statewide assessment that is given at his grade level. Although he believes literacy is best measured by a series of assessment tools, he prepares his students for the spring test by familiarizing them with the language and nature of the testing processes. The statewide standardized test becomes one more way for him to assess the students in his classroom. He is familiar with the state standards for language arts, and he knows how well his district's curriculum guide fulfills them. He uses the curriculum guide to plan his weekly instruction, making sure he is addressing the required standards in his teaching, while also considering the needs of his students and his goals for their learning.

Beyond his classroom, school, district, and state, Delray knows that there are expectations for his students' learning. Through faculty meetings and reading information from the Florida Board of Education, Delray has learned about the No Child Left Behind Act (NCLB), a wide-sweeping federal law that requires schools to show that students are making adequate yearly progress (AYP) in key academic areas, including the language arts. By engaging in ongoing assessment in his classroom, Delray is able to keep track of what his students know and can do and what he still needs to teach. He recognizes that assessment is a powerful link to improved learning for all of his students.

INTRODUCTION

Delray works hard to collect information from his students that helps him make decisions in his classroom. He knows that assessment should be closely linked to instruction and that effective assessment and evaluation are keys to instructional planning. But making the link between assessment and instruction is not always straightforward. Simply put, assessment and evaluation provide information that supports teachers' instructional decisions (Winograd & Arrington, 1999).

GUIDING QUESTIONS

Consider these questions as you read this chapter. Jot down your initial responses to each question. After reading the articles, revisit your responses. Would you make any changes to them? If so, what would those changes be? Discuss your responses with one or more of your classmates, your professor, or your mentor teacher.

1. What are the purposes of assessment and evaluation?
2. How can teachers involve their students in the evaluation and decision-making processes?
3. How can instruction and assessment be linked?
4. What is the No Child Left Behind Act, and how will it affect your teaching?
5. What is the role of standardized testing in language arts instruction?
6. How are standards and testing connected?

The Nature of Assessment and Evaluation

Delray recognizes that his students' language abilities change and grow daily and that measuring their growth and development is an important aspect of language arts teaching. Assessment is necessary for good teaching, and it depends on teachers knowing as much as they can about individual students. Assessment takes place naturally in the classroom, reflecting what students are learning and how they are feeling about language arts.

Assessment refers to the ongoing process of collecting information about students' performance through a variety of techniques, including observations, conferences, work samples, checklists, and self-evaluations (Routman, 2000). Evaluation occurs when someone summarizes, analyzes, and interprets this information (Routman, 2000). Assessment and evaluation are both extremely complex processes whose purpose is to inform children, parents, teachers, and the community at large about children's skills. By connecting assessment and instruction, teachers can make appropriate decisions and take effective action to improve teaching and learning. Certain types of assessment and evaluation stir controversy and debates, but no matter how they are accomplished, assessment and evaluation should inform and support language arts instruction and learning.

Your Experiences with Assessment and Evaluation

What are your personal experiences with assessment and evaluation as a student? What types of assessments do you tend to perform best on? Why? What types of assessments tend to be difficult for you? Share your experiences with several peers. Are your experiences the same or different? How can you explain this? What insights can you draw about the benefits and limitations of various types of assessment in teaching and learning?

THE SCOPE OF ASSESSMENT AND EVALUATION

Most educators have a similar understanding of assessment and evaluation, but individuals use the words to mean slightly different things. Although the terms "evaluation" and "assessment" are often used interchangeably, they actually have different yet related meanings. Traditionally in language arts, *assessment* means collecting information from students in order to make instructional decisions. *Evaluation* involves making judgments about the progress children are making, on the basis of assessment information. Evaluation, defined in this manner, requires some type of judgment about the appropriateness of children's language productions and performance.

Teachers compare children of the same age with regard to their development and language behaviors. Evaluation also refers to program evaluation and how effective the language arts curriculum is in meeting goals established in state standards. Students' test results, for example, can serve as a yardstick to evaluate the language arts curriculum or specific programs. Regardless of how the terms are defined, there is no doubt that assessment and evaluation are closely linked, occur in many forms, are used for many purposes, and can result in multiple interpretations.

The emphasis of assessment and evaluation varies for different audiences and different contexts. For example, during the past decade, many people outside the schools have demanded to know about the literacy skills of school children. Legislation such as the No Child Left Behind Act (NCLB, 2002) requires that states show, through the use of standardized testing, that their students are making adequate yearly progress.

PURPOSES FOR ASSESSMENT AND EVALUATION

Many people are interested in students' language arts learning and performance, including teachers, parents, administrators, community members, and students themselves. Each of these groups has different purposes for wanting to know about students' performance. Providing various audiences with appropriate information requires differing methods of evaluation and reporting (Farr, 1992). (See Exhibit 7.1.)

Multiple purposes of language arts assessment.   exhibit   **7.1**

AUDIENCE	PURPOSE
Public (the community, legislators, etc.)	Measure the effectiveness of schools in the community, state, and nation.
Administrators	Summarize the performance of children in their schools and districts.
Parents	Understand the growth of their own children.
Teachers	Facilitate and monitor classroom instruction and learn about their own teaching processes.
Students	Find out how they can improve and gain motivation for continued growth.

Adapted from Farr, R. (1992). Putting it all together: Solving the reading assessment puzzle. *The Reading Teacher, 46,* 26–37.

personal reflection

What Can Teachers Do to Help the Community Understand Testing?

Consider the final statement in the Teacher Viewpoint below: "I wonder if there might be a better way." If you were Marilyn, what additional information would you want to share with the community? What methods could you use to share that information to help educate the community about the range of outcomes that occur in language arts instruction? Discuss your ideas with your mentor teacher to gain additional insight into the ways school districts support or limit teachers' efforts to explain testing outcomes. Share your insights and findings with your classmates.

Community Members

Since tax money supports schools and pays teachers' salaries, the public has a legal right to know about the effectiveness of schools. Community members and legislators hold schools and teachers accountable for what children are learning about language arts. Statewide testing has evolved out of the need to understand if schools in communities and states are effective in promoting high achievement. Usually, reporting to the public requires a standardized evaluation tool that compares schools across communities and possibly even across states. These reports give more attention to the academic achievement of specific grade levels across a school district, city, or state and much less to reporting performance of individual children. Unfortunately, when test scores are made public, contextual information about the curriculum, progress across the year, class sizes, socioeconomic issues, and other factors are not provided to help community members understand and interpret the test results fully.

TEACHER Viewpoint

MARILYN, VETERAN TEACHER ▶ I cringe each spring when the results of our state tests are printed in the newspaper. They break down the scores by school and grade level. Since I teach in a small school with only two teachers at each grade level, it's pretty easy to guess which scores belong to which teacher. Unfortunately the scores don't mention how far the children have come over the year and the amazing amount they have learned since September. I know the public has a right to know how our schools are doing, but I wonder if there might be a better way.

Administrators

School administrators, superintendents, and principals are interested in how their school, grade levels, and classrooms are doing. Although their concern about the performance of the entire school should not imply that they are not interested in individual students, their main interest is in monitoring and being able to describe the growth and development of large numbers of students. Tests and other evaluative tools show superintendents and principals how much progress each teacher's students are making. They use this information to guide their decisions about program selection, curriculum development, and professional development for teachers. Assessments also provide administrators with information about students' strengths and needs for instructional attention. They can find out which subgroups are successful (or not) and use this information in planning.

School administrators talk about student growth in terms of test scores, percentages, and comparisons to standards or benchmarks. They are interested in

- the percentage of their students who passed tests.
- comparisons with previous years and other schools in similar contexts.
- indications that the curriculum is helping students meet state and local standards.

The No Child Left Behind legislation holds administrators responsible for adequate yearly progress (AYP) of all students. School administrators are required to review standardized tests scores and ensure that students are making adequate yearly progress based on a statewide definition. Not only does the school as a whole (*all* students) need to make AYP targets, but eight subgroups of students (African American, American Indian, Asian/Pacific Islander, Hispanic, White, English language learners, economically disadvantaged, and special education students) also need to make the same AYP target.

To read more about adequate yearly progress, visit the U.S. Department of Education's website at **www.ed.gov/admins/lead/account/ayp/edlite-index.jhtml.** Check with your state education department to learn how schools in your state define AYP.

Parents

Parents may also have concerns about the test scores of an entire school, but their primary purpose is to understand how their own children are doing. Test scores are not always the most meaningful way to report to parents, and as a teacher you may need to help them interpret the results. More commonly, the basic reports to parents are in the form of report cards and parent–teacher conferences. In addition, collections of artifacts such as writing samples, reading lists, projects, video and audiotapes, and other classroom assignments can help parents understand their children's language arts abilities. Parents tend to be most concerned that their children are learning to read and write, achieving in the school setting, and can transfer what they have learned to life outside the classroom.

Teachers

Teachers depend on assessment and evaluation information that indicates whether and how students are learning. For teachers, the purposes of evaluation are

- to gain information that guides planning and implementation of instruction.

- to monitor children's learning.
- to guide reflection about the teaching process.

Evaluation and assessment are critical for effective instruction. The more teachers know about their students, the more effectively they are able to plan instruction and interactions that support language development. Teachers have a responsibility to use assessment and evaluation practices that give them accurate and sufficient information about students' learning and development.

Students

Students need feedback regarding their language growth. An important purpose of assessment is to develop students' own awareness of their progress and encourage them to continue language development. Feedback and evaluation are critical to motivating them to become effective language users.

The feedback students receive during language arts instruction affects their opinion of themselves as effective language users. Most of us believe we are good, mediocre, or poor writers or readers based on our school experiences and the feedback we received. If teachers felt we were good readers and writers, we usually carry that perception with us throughout life. The reverse is also true: some adults who feel they are poor writers and readers developed that belief as a result of feedback they received during their elementary language arts instruction.

Because different groups of individuals have different purposes for assessing students, various ways of measuring have evolved. Options range from the traditional approaches that teachers have used in schools for decades to a broader, more subjective approach that has recently emerged—authentic assessment.

personal reflection

Views of Assessment and Evaluation

Review newspapers and other current periodicals and identify articles, commentaries, and information items about educational assessment, evaluation, and testing. Bring examples to class and use them as a basis for discussing the impact of public perceptions on assessment. Consider the viewpoints presented and discuss the impact that public opinion has on classroom assessment and evaluation.

TWO APPROACHES TO ASSESSMENT

Educators often talk about the distinctions between traditional and authentic assessment. Wiggins (1990) explains the difference as follows:

Assessment is authentic when we directly examine student performance on worthwhile intellectual tasks. Traditional assessment, by contrast, relies on indirect or proxy "items"—efficient, simplistic substitutes from which we think valid inferences can be made about the student's performance at those valued challenges. (p. 1)

Traditional Approach to Assessment

What usually comes to mind when language arts teachers refer to traditional evaluation and assessment is standardized tests. Standardized tests have been one of the most prevalent and influential methods of determining children's reading and writing achievements, and they have had a great impact on language arts instruction. Teachers and schools have depended on standardized measures to describe complex language behaviors and to report students' academic achievement to parents, the community, and others.

There are several standardized test formats, but all of them focus on gathering objective information about a student's performance compared to a standard or norm. In the most common format used to measure reading abilities, a passage of one or more paragraphs is followed by multiple-choice questions. Standardized writing tests are usually more open ended, consisting of a prompt or a picture and space for students to respond. All standardized tests by nature are normed and administered, scored, and interpreted in a standard, prescribed manner. (Article III of this chapter discusses the standards and processes associated with standardized tests in more detail.)

Standardized Test Use

Interview your mentor teacher or another teacher to find out what standardized tests are given in her or his school. If possible, review information about the tests to learn what they measure and what types of information they provide. Ask the teacher to share how the standardized test results are used in the school district, school building, and classroom. Share your findings with your peers.

Standardized testing is an important influence on language arts instruction. It is mandated at the school, district, and state levels and used to compare students across various groups. The general consensus is that standardized tests can produce information that is valuable for some purposes: they tell us how well students have acquired basic facts (Herman, Aschbacher, & Winters, 1992) and how they compare to others who are the same age or grade level. They do not, however, provide a total picture of the language user. They cannot reflect all the goals of instruction or all the language processes that need to be measured. By themselves, they provide only part of the picture of a student's language arts abilities. Standardized tests are sometimes described as capturing a snapshot of a student's abilities at a specific time and place and on a specific task.

NCLB and Standardized Testing

Visit the No Child Left Behind website at **www.ed.gov/nclb/landing.html** to learn more about this important education legislation. Investigate the role of standardized testing in the NCLB Act. Discuss your findings with your classmates.

Authentic Approach to Assessment

Authentic assessment, also called alternative assessment and performance assessment, suggests a broad perspective on assessing students. Authentic assessment measures literacy behaviors as they would be used in real-life settings (Ryan, 1994). It takes into account students' interest and developmental levels. It occurs during the teaching and learning process and provides information that helps teachers make instructional decisions. The purposes of authentic assessment are closely linked to instructional goals.

Authentic assessment has several components. First, assessment that is authentic allows teachers to determine if they have met their instructional goals. Second, the teacher evaluates a student's achievement by reviewing his previous work in comparison to his current work instead of comparing it with other students. Third, instead of using one test or score to describe students' language growth, teachers collect multiple work samples over a long period of time. Examples of authentic assessment tools include portfolios, rubrics, and performance assessment tools. Observation tools such as checklists and anecdotal records may also be used to document progress. (See Article II in this chapter.)

A challenging aspect of teaching is to develop assessment practices that measure learning. Some forms of assessment, such as standardized tests, may narrowly define what a teacher wishes to measure. They may measure skills such as vocabulary knowledge or punctuation, but they do not present an entire picture of the language user. Consider, for example, a student who reads enthusiastically during silent reading time each day and then is required to take a vocabulary test based on words extracted from one of the books she has read. She gets only half of the words right and receives a failing grade, which is recorded in the grade book as a score for reading comprehension. Does this form of assessment truly reflect her reading comprehension? To determine what students really know, teachers must use assessment practices that are student centered, collaborative, extensive, and continuous (Brualdi, 1998; Wiggins, 1990). When an assessment has these qualities, it is defined as authentic. If you can answer "yes" to each question listed in Exhibit 7.2, you are implementing authentic assessment.

	Framework for identifying authentic assessment.	*exhibit* **7.2**
Student Centered	Does assessment focus on individual students?	
Collaborative	Does assessment involve the learner and capitalize on different perspectives?	
Extensive	Does assessment make use of a variety of different methods and sources?	
Continuous	Is the assessment process long term and ongoing?	

Student Centered

Authentic assessment focuses on student learning. More specifically, it focuses on what students do as they use language in their day-to-day activities, in contrast to some of the more traditional assessments, which compare children's work. Lucy Calkins (1994) explains that "In the end, a classroom is student-centered if and only if our teaching happens in response to individual students" (p. 314). Authentic assessment occurs when teachers use student interviews, focus on student responses, and allow time for themselves as well as students to reflect on what they have accomplished during the school day.

The judgments made about students during authentic assessment processes result from comparing students' work over a period of time. Most important, "Information gathered about students' literacy during daily instructional events can be used to plan instruction that addresses students' needs, expands their interests, and challenges them" (Rhodes & Dudley-Marling, 1996, p. 33).

Collaborative

Collaboration between students and teachers is mutually beneficial and has a positive impact on classroom learning (Graves, 1994; Tierney, Crumpler, Bertelsen, & Bond, 2003). From an early age, children are able to communicate their own interest, strengths, and weaknesses in their learning processes. Authentic assessment captures their ideas. Jane Hansen (2001), a language arts researcher, found that children as early as first grade could articulate their interests and desired learning outcomes. Hansen noted that "As the teachers included more and more opportunities for their students to reflect and plan, their initial surprise at their students' ability to evaluate themselves changed to an assumption that their students could evaluate their growth" (p. 80).

Choice is an important aspect of collaborative assessment. Students should have the opportunity to take an active role in assessment processes.

Effective assessment does not occur on one day but rather results from a teacher continuously collecting documentation over a period of time.

"What did you learn during this activity?" "What did you do well on in this assignment and what do you still need to work on?" and "Where do you see growth in your own language arts behavior?" are examples of questions teachers can ask to gain student feedback during the assessment process.

Delray, the teacher in this chapter's Window to the Classroom, worked with his students to identify the goals they wanted to accomplish related to reading a wider range of materials. Then his students provided their ideas about how the class was meeting the goals. The students helped him collect information and provided feedback about how his strategies were affecting their behavior and learning. Students were aware of the instructional goal and knew how he was assessing their progress. They helped their teacher decide if they were meeting their goals. Encouraging students to assess their own learning has many benefits, including helping them learn to understand and articulate their own strengths and weaknesses—an ability that is important to lifelong learning.

Collaborative assessment processes can also include parents. Parents may be asked to help interpret the information that has been collected. They can help teachers determine why students are not performing well or give teachers ideas about how to motivate their children. A parent may describe what a student is reading at home or relate reactions to homework or class assignments. Their insights offer another perspective, one that includes cultural and family-related interpretations of how students respond to language arts instruction.

Extensive

Assessment is extensive when it uses a variety of methods and sources. If assessment is to help us understand a child, then we should consider how the child functions within different situations, contexts, and assignments. The more sources and methods she incorporates, the better a teacher will be able to understand a student's learning. For example, a writing sample from a journal may provide information about informal writing, whereas a writing sample that has gone through the entire writing process will let the teacher know how much the writer understands about writing conventions, organizational, and presentation. Similarly, before teachers can understand students' recreational reading behaviors, they must know what students actually read at school and at home. By using many methods and types of activities, teachers can best identify the strengths of a learner and also where the learner may need additional support, practice, and experiences (Valencia, Hiebert, & Afflerbach, 1994).

Continuous

Effective assessment does not occur on one day but rather results from a teacher continuously collecting documentation over a period of time. No one test or assessment can effectively measure children's language growth and development. Continuous assessment means measuring performance during day-to-day activities; it also means that teachers are constantly assessing and evaluating in the course of instructional processes. Teachers do not wait until the end of a lesson or unit to evaluate whether and how children are learning concepts and skills. They make constant decisions based on what is happening as the instructional plan unfolds. For example, Delray continuously assessed the variety of materials students read in his classroom, and he worked on increasing the variety as soon as he realized that it was a problem.

CONNECTING ASSESSMENT AND INSTRUCTION

Instruction and assessment are reciprocal processes. In other words, assessment and instruction occur simultaneously. As teachers learn more about their students' performance and abilities, they are able to plan appropriate instruction, which is then assessed, and so on (Cooper & Kiger, 2001). Through several specific strategies, teachers can assure that assessment and instruction are connected.

Establish Common Goals

The goals that are established for instruction should also guide assessment (Ryan, 1994). For example, if an instructional goal is for students to be able to determine their own writing topics, then instructional planning should provide opportunities to learn how to choose topics. A parallel assessment goal would be to evaluate students' ability to select their own topics when involved in writers' workshop. The teacher might base assessment on a review of journals in which students wrote about topic selection, a review of their lists of possible topics, teacher–student conferences, and final written products in which students successfully choose their own topics. A multiple-choice test would not effectively measure the student's understanding related to this goal. Rubrics, self-evaluations, and records of student–teacher conferences would, however, document the extent to which students are meeting this instructional goal.

Use Assessment Findings to Make Instructional Decisions

When assessment procedures are closely related to the goals of instruction, the information gained about students can inform instructional planning. Assessment results indicate what instruction is appropriate for individual students (Johns, Lenski, & Elish-Piper, 2002). For example, if, after reading the students' journals and reviewing the lists of topics they have provided, the teacher finds that several students are still struggling with topic selection, then she can work with them to demonstrate strategies. On the other hand, when assessment procedures indicate that some students are already capable of selecting their own topics, they can spend their time on other aspects of writing.

Assessment Strategies

Observe and record the methods of assessment used by your mentor teacher during one school day. Interview your mentor teacher to determine his or her purpose, methods, and uses for assessment. Create a chart that illustrates the connections between assessment and instruction.

FINAL REFLECTIONS

Assessment and evaluation will be critical to your success as a teacher. With increasing scrutiny and demands on teachers to document student achievement and mandates by legislation such as the NCLB Act, it is imperative that you develop skills and strategies to assess and evaluate your students' performance in language arts. By linking findings from ongoing assessments of students to your instructional planning, you will be able to support the learning of all your students—just as Delray sought to do in this chapter's Window to the Classroom.

Using Authentic Literacy Assessment

Literacy development has many dimensions, and it can be described and assessed in many ways. Teachers must know enough about assessment to develop methods and procedures that capture the complexity of children's literacy development (Popham, 1999). Assessment is not limited to defining what needs improvement. Not only does a teacher need to know which children's literacy behaviors need development, they should also understand children's strengths. Assessment reveals what to teach and how well students are learning what is taught.

Authentic assessment is more than giving good grades to those who do well and poor grades to those who do not. It provides much more information than a test score or grade can convey. Teachers make many decisions as they teach language arts—during instructional planning, when instruction is being implemented, and when reviewing students' products (Rhodes & Shanklin, 1993). Authentic assessment supports that continuous process, emerging out of day-to-day classroom observations, interactions between teachers and students, and literacy products.

THE ROLE OF OBSERVATION

Teachers can gather a great deal of information about literacy development by watching children during daily instructional activities. Observation is one of the major components of authentic assessment. Throughout classroom instruction, teachers observe and compare what they see to what they hope to accomplish during instruction.

Observation can be informal, but at times teachers need to use more organized observational formats that utilize structured methods of collecting, organizing, managing, and interpreting information. Experienced teachers frequently use checklists and anecdotal records to collect observational data systematically.

KENDRA, BEGINNING TEACHER ▶ I use observation constantly in my teaching. I look at the children's faces when I'm explaining something. I watch them closely and listen to their conversations when they work in small groups. I am definitely a "kid-watcher"! Observation is the best tool I have to figure out if they "get it" or if I need to re-teach something.

Checklists

Checklists are flexible assessment instruments that teachers can adapt for almost any literacy activity. Some teachers design their own checklists tailored to classroom literacy activities and their objectives. They are simple to create: add a grid to a class roster, and fill in dates when behaviors are observed, check marks to record literacy behaviors, or more detailed notes. Checklists can be correlated to specific state goals and school district learning objectives to help teachers focus their observations in these areas. Sample teacher-made checklists are shown in Exhibits 7.3, 7.4, and 7.5, along with the specific state goals they address.

Many checklists are available for teachers to help them capture observations about almost anything that occurs in the classroom. Some textbooks and teacher guides include checklists. While commercially prepared checklists may be helpful, teachers will want to compare them to their state goals, district curriculum, and classroom instructional plans and make modifications where necessary.

exhibit 7.3 *Teacher-made pre-reading strategies checklist.*

Florida Sunshine State Standards for Grades 3–5, Reading Standard 1:

The student uses the reading process effectively

1.1 Uses a table of contents, index, headings, captions, illustrations, and major words to anticipate or predict content and purpose of a reading selection.

NAME _____

BEFORE READING:	DATE	TEXT	COMMENT
Uses the following text features to anticipate or predict the content and purpose of a reading selection.			
Table of contents			
Index			
Headings			
Captions			
Illustrations			
Major words (boldfaced type)			

exhibit 7.4 *Teacher-made observational checklist.*

Georgia Quality Core Curriculum Standard for Grade 1, Language Arts, Area: Literature

Demonstrates an interest in various types of self-selected literature through daily reading.

NAME _____ **DATE** _____

In the two-week period, has the child:	Yes	No	Notes
1. Seemed happy when engaged in reading activities?	☐	☐	_____
2. Volunteered to read aloud in class?	☐	☐	_____
3. Read a book during free time?	☐	☐	_____
4. Mentioned reading a book at home?	☐	☐	_____
5. Chosen reading over other activities (playing games, coloring, talking, etc.)?	☐	☐	_____
6. Made requests to go to the library?	☐	☐	_____
7. Checked out books at the library?	☐	☐	_____
8. Talked about books she or he has read?	☐	☐	_____
9. Finished most of the books she or he has started?	☐	☐	_____
10. Mentioned books she or he has at home?	☐	☐	_____

Adapted from Rhodes, L. K., & Shanklin, N. L. (1993). *Windows into literacy: Assessing learners K–8.* Portsmouth, NH: Heinemann.

| Teacher-made checklist for class oral presentations at the end of a unit of study. | exhibit | 7.5 |

Illinois State Learning Goal, Grades 1–2:

Speak effectively using language appropriate to the situation and audience.

+ = demonstrated consistently   O = demonstrated occasionally
✓ = demonstrated some of the time   N = not demonstrated at this time

Student Name	Speaks at appropriate rate	Uses language appropriate for presentation to class	Speaks clearly so others can hear	Looks at others while speaking	Stays on topic while speaking	Sequences information logically while speaking	Uses visuals or props to illustrate oral presentation
Alex							
Amy							
Bradford							
Devon							
Dontrell							
Elena							
Jackie							
Joo-Hee							
Jorge							
Kamal							
Maria							
Michael							
Nadia							
Quiana							
Rasem							
Sean							
Shanita							
Shelby							
Steven							
Tyler							
Ukyong							

Checklists can also be completed by students. Completing checklists helps students take responsibility for their learning and encourages them to reflect on their strengths and needs. Exhibit 7.6 gives an example of a checklist to be completed by students.

Anecdotal Records

Anecdotal records are observations in which the teacher describes how students respond to classroom activities. The teacher describes a specific event, behavior, or outcome in a clear and objective way that avoids opinions. Teachers may make anecdotal records during instruction or any classroom literacy event, then review their notes as they make instructional decisions. The record should describe the event or behavior in enough detail so that when the teacher reviews it, she can mentally reconstruct the actual event to facilitate planning for instruction (Rhodes & Nathenson-Mejia, 1992). Teachers might want to keep anecdotal notes, for example, when they want to remember students' responses to a particular classroom activity or to note a specific literacy behavior. In essence, the teacher looks for important literacy events, takes notes as the event is happening or immediately afterward, and reviews them to gain insights that might be helpful during instructional planning.

Teachers may compile anecdotal records for each child (their behavior during writers' workshop, for example) or for the entire class. If one student is having a particularly difficult time during reading or writing activities, the teacher might focus on that student to look for patterns of behavior that contribute to his or her difficulties. A good time for teachers to write anecdotal records is when the entire class, including the teacher, is writing. Some teachers keep a journal narrating classroom events and use this record to plan instruction or guide their work with individual children.

exhibit **7.6**   *Student checklist.*

NAME _____   DATE _____

Mark an X next to each activity you have completed successfully.

☐ 1. I have completed retelling the story I read.

☐ 2. I have retold the story to one of my classmates.

☐ 3. When retelling the story, I told it in sequence (correct order).

☐ 4. I used eye contact and expression in my voice to keep my listener interested.

☐ 5. I have retold the story to someone at home.

☐ 6. I wrote about this activity in my journal.

☐ 7. I am prepared to tell the story in front of the whole class.

Anecdotal Records

During your field experience, focus on observing an individual student during language arts instruction. Write an anecdotal record to document that student's engagement and performance during the instruction. Focus your anecdotal record on observable behaviors or outcomes rather than your opinion. Repeat this process with several students. Share and discuss your anecdotal records with your cooperating teacher.

Interest Inventories

Interest inventories, such as the one shown in Exhibit 7.7, and incomplete sentence surveys give teachers important information regarding children's attitudes toward literacy. Students can complete the forms themselves by writing, audio recording, or discussing their answers. Young children can complete questionnaires orally with a parent or teacher noting their responses.

Reading interest inventory.   *exhibit* **7.7**

NAME _____   DATE _____

1. I am very good at _____ .

2. I would like to learn more about _____ .

3. The best book I ever read is _____ .

4. My favorite author is _____ .

5. My favorite CD or song is _____ .

6. In my spare time I like to _____ .

7. Reading is _____ .

8. My favorite television show is _____ .

9. My favorite movie is _____ .

10. If I spend time on the Internet I search for _____ .

11. If I could meet anyone in the world, it would be _____ .

12. I usually read _____ .

13. Good stories are about _____ .

14. I like it when people read aloud stories about _____ .

INTERACTIVE ASSESSMENT PROCESSES

A teacher can gain a great deal of information about students' feelings and attitudes toward language learning by discussing literacy behaviors with them. Among the many interactive formats that will help a teacher collect valuable information are interviews, conferences, and interactive anecdotal records.

Interviews

Through interviews, teachers can gain insight into students' perceptions about their learning. Teachers may conduct interviews during one-on-one conferences or with the entire class at once, inviting the students to respond in writing. Interviews conducted at the beginning of the year and again at intervals throughout the year provide information about children's changing literacy behaviors. Exhibit 7.8 provides a sample interview about writing.

Conferences

Teachers may conduct conferences with students either one-on-one or in small groups. During conferences, students can discuss such topics as books they are reading, movies they have watched, Internet research they are doing, or writing projects they are completing. In addition to obtaining information about how students respond to classroom instruction, teachers can use conferences to provide feedback, focus children's attention, and support literacy development.

Teachers typically hold conferences to talk about reading and writing, but almost any aspect of language arts can be covered. For example, technology and other visual communication processes may be the focus. A

exhibit 7.8 *Example of a writing interview.*

1. Is there something that gives you trouble during the writing process?

2. What do you find are the easiest (hardest) parts of the writing process?

3. What do you feel best about when you read your own writing?

4. What makes you feel less confident when you read your own writing?

5. In the past you had difficulty with _____ during the writing process. Do you still have problems with _____? Why do you think that is so?

6. What can I do to help you with your writing?

Adapted from Rhodes, L. K., & Shanklin, N. L. (1993). *Windows into literacy: Assessing learners K–8.* Portsmouth, NH: Heinemann.

exhibit	7.9

Guiding questions for student conferences.

1. What are you reading or writing now? Tell me about it.

2. What literacy activities do you enjoy the most? What products make you most proud?

3. What do you want to accomplish next?

conference is an excellent time for students and teachers to discuss literacy behaviors, attitudes, and concerns as well as establish goals for learning.

The teacher's main role in a conference is to listen to what students are saying about their literacy development. To prompt students' comments, beginning teachers may find guiding questions useful. Exhibit 7.9 provides sample guiding questions for conferences.

Literacy Conference

field note

7.4

Meet with a student to discuss a book she or he is reading, a writing product, an oral report, or another type of literacy activity. Ask questions that encourage the student to talk about his or her process. Use a checklist or anecdotal notes to record the student's responses. In your record, summarize the conference along with any instructional suggestions that might be appropriate, and discuss your observations with your mentor teacher.

HILDA, PRESERVICE TEACHER ▶ My mentor teacher conducts really short conferences with her students every week. She moves around the classroom with a clipboard to take notes, and she asks four or five kids questions each day so she gets to all of the kids each week. The questions are usually open-ended ones like, "What can you tell me about your reading this week?" or "What problems have you been having in reading or writing?" She spends no more than a few minutes with each student, but she gets such good information. It is amazing how well she knows her students. When I asked her how she can know all 25 of her students so well, she told me it is her conferences. I have started to try using these conferences on the days I'm in the classroom, and I am excited to use them next semester when I'm student teaching.

An *interactive anecdotal record* allows children to respond to their teachers' observations. The result is collaborative, ongoing assessment between teachers and children. The teacher writes his observations to be read by his students, who in turn read and respond, providing input from their perspectives. Students may add their own observations, explain their behaviors, or question what the teacher observed. Alternatively, children could be encouraged to write the initial observations and teachers could add their perspectives.

Interactive anecdotal records are particularly helpful when a new instructional activity is introduced in the classroom and the teacher would like feedback from the students' perspectives. For example, the teacher who wrote the 11/18 note in Exhibit 7.10 shared the observation with her students and let them respond, providing additional reactions and ideas. Checklists and anecdotal records are flexible methods for capturing classroom responses to literacy instruction. They are useful in numerous settings and adaptable to a wide range of language arts activities.

ASSESSING LITERACY PRODUCTS

Teachers can use many of the literacy products that evolve from daily instruction to measure literacy growth and development. Almost any response to classroom activities can become part of the assessment process. Assignments students complete offer a great deal of information that will help teachers plan for instruction. Some of the most useful activities are written and oral retelling, journals, and portfolios. After collecting these materials, teachers must analyze them—often by using a rubric.

Written and Oral Retellings

Teachers can assess a student's understanding and comprehension of something that has been read (Johns, Lenski, & Elish-Piper, 2002) by asking for a written or oral retelling. After reading a text, the student is asked to write or tell everything she remembers about it. The teacher may choose to ask probing questions to gain a more complete idea of what the student understood.

Teachers use a variety of methods to record what the child retells. Some create an outline of the story or list major events so they can record what the child remembers of each part. Others take notes as the child retells the story. Teachers may audiotape the interaction for further analysis. The information collected during the retelling allows the teacher to analyze the student's level of comprehension. Retellings are flexible and can provide information about more than reading comprehension. They can serve as an authentic assessment method to show that children are developing their abilities to understand and comprehend what they see, hear, and read. Exhibit 7.11 outlines a procedure for retellings.

Some teachers use a retelling checklist to evaluate children's retellings and compare them. By using the same

Retellings are flexible and can serve as an authentic assessment method to show that children are developing their abilities to understand and comprehend what they see, hear, and read.

Examples of anecdotal records.	exhibit	7.10

TEACHER ANECDOTAL RECORD   **Individual Student: Juanita, First Grade**

10/24—Points to individual words when reading aloud. Is more fluent than at the beginning of the year—made improvements in confidence of sounding out words, too! Enjoys rereading In the Small, Small Pond by Denise Fleming.

10/30—Phone call from parents—we are all proud of her reading!

11/15—Is feeling inhibited about inventive spelling. Note: Continue to talk about sounding out strategies. Work with small group to develop individualized strategies. Encourage her to collaborate with peers to feel more comfortable.

INTERACTIVE ANECDOTAL RECORDS   **Individual Student: Georgio, Fourth Grade**

11/16—Mini-lesson: Using dialogue in stories—Today, when we learned about using dialogue in stories, Georgio pulled out a book from his backpack and shared an example from his SSR book, The Indian in the Cupboard. Later, he wrote a story in his journal where he used quotation marks. At times, he was confused about what punctuation went where, but he is working on it! We will continue talking about punctuation marks. Mrs. W

I am using quotation marks in my stories. It is cool. Sometimes I don't know where to put my commas—inside or outside the marks? Georgio

I am proud of how Georgio is writing. He showed me his story at home and we worked a little more on it. He read it to his little sister and to his dad. Georgio's Mom

---

INTERACTIVE ANECDOTAL RECORDS   **Entire Class**

11/18—Field Trip—Today we went to the science museum. The kids conducted an experiment where they made volcanoes. They really liked it! I haven't done a lot of experiments in the classroom yet, but the kids seem really interested in them. They used lots of great talking and vocabulary to describe the volcano activity. Mrs. W.

The trip to the museum was really fun! I learned about the scientific method and I made a volcano! I want to do more experiments, Mrs. W! Ronzell

I liked the trip, too! I did an experiment in my after-school class that I could teach the class. We made telephones out of cups and string. Can I show the class soon? Juanita

exhibit 7.11 *Setting up a retelling and analyzing the results.*

TO SET UP THE RETELLING:

1. Choose a text to read. Select a text the student can read independently.

2. Tell the student that she is to read the story and will retell it after she has finished.

3. After the student reads the text, ask her to retell everything she remembers about the story, either aloud (oral retelling) or in writing (written retelling). Then an adult listens to or reads the child's retelling.

4. The teacher can use prompts to draw out more information. For example, he may say:

    Tell me more about ____.

    Why do you think _____ happened?

    What was the problem in this story?

    Describe ____ at the beginning of the story.

    How did ___change by the end of the story?

    What was the moral of the story?

TO ANALYZE RETELLINGS, ANSWER THE FOLLOWING QUESTIONS:

1. How close to the original text material was the retelling?

2. Did the retelling include explicit and inferred information? If it included inferred information, were the inferences logical?

3. Did the retelling reflect the structure of the text?

4. How is the student's knowledge and experience reflected within the retelling?

5. Did the retelling demonstrate sequential structure, and were the details related to each other?

6. Did the retelling reflect understanding of what the student read?

retelling checklist with multiple texts over time, the teacher can pinpoint each student's strengths and areas for improvement in relation to reading comprehension and retelling. Exhibit 7.12 provides a sample retelling checklist for a fiction book.

Journals

Teachers analyze students' journal writing to observe and understand their growth as writers and learners. Regular journal entries reflect students' acquisition of spelling conventions, writing rules, written expression, and the ability to develop ideas. Students can be guided to reflect on their own writing growth by reviewing their journal entries over time.

| Retelling checklist for fiction. | *exhibit* | **7.12** |

NAME _____   **DATE** _____

BOOK TITLE _____

Indicate the degree to which the student's retelling:	HIGH	MODERATE	LOW	NONE
1. includes information directly stated in the text.				
2. includes information inferred from the text.				
3. includes the main idea.				
4. includes main characters.				
5. includes the setting.				
6. includes key events.				
7. includes the problem.				
8. includes the solution.				
9. sequences the retelling logically.				

Adapted from Opitz, M. (1998). *Flexible grouping in reading.* New York: Scholastic Professional Books.

Journals can serve as the basis of student and teacher conferences and as a springboard for reflection about important aspects of the writing process. By looking at journal entries, the teacher can gain insight into students' process for topic selection, their responses to literature, and even how their understanding of subject matter evolves. Teachers evaluate journal entries in numerous ways. Whatever method you choose, remember that the journal should be a nonthreatening space for students to reflect and write without concerns about being graded. Assigning grades or making corrective comments discourages expression. A more appropriate assessment method might be a checklist or anecdotal records.

Portfolios

Most teachers develop a system to organize and keep track of students' literacy products. Many rely on portfolios—collections of students' work, sometimes including classroom work samples and pieces that students have completed in other contexts, that demonstrate their growth and development. Some of the portfolio components should be repeated or duplicated during the school year so that changes in literacy behaviors can be measured (Koch & Schwartz-Pettersen, 2000). For example, structured self-evaluations that are completed three or four times a year can clearly indicate changes in students' attitudes and behaviors. Samples of work that might be included in a language arts portfolio include the following:

Questionnaires that measure attitudes toward reading, writing, and visual literacy

Responses to literature

Writing samples

Visual representations of knowledge

Reading and writing journal entries

Reading and writing logs

Teacher's observations

Self-evaluations

Writing, both completed and in progress

Classroom tests

Observational checklists

List of texts read during silent reading

Story maps

Other language arts projects

Portfolios are more effective when teachers and children plan and develop them collaboratively (Rhodes & Shanklin, 1993). Together they can decide what should go into the portfolio and the purposes for collecting information; they may even work together to interpret and evaluate the material in the portfolio. At the outset, students and teachers should establish specific guidelines for what information should be placed in the portfolio and who will be responsible for contributing that information. Students should be expected to help as much as possible with the record keeping and logistics of building the portfolio. For example, they could help develop the list of items that will be included in the collection. (See Exhibit 7.13.)

Not everything a child completes should go into the portfolio; instead, teachers and children should be selective, choosing material that illustrates students' growth throughout the year. One teacher established a portfolio system that consisted of two collections of work. Students each had a "work" folder to which they added all the literacy products they liked. At the end of each two-week period, the teacher asked them to decide which of the samples represented their best work. Each student moved that work into a "collection" portfolio that was continuously updated throughout the year. Several times during the year, the teacher asked the students to review the work in their collection folder and write reflections about their own growth. These writings became an important component of the portfolio.

Teachers and students should set up and maintain their portfolios in ways that reflect their instructional purposes and needs. Teachers may need to experiment a bit before they find the best format for their classroom.

Portfolios come in many shapes and sizes. Manila folders are the least expensive and most readily available storage spaces for children's work. File folders are easily accessible. Expandable files allow children to categorize their artifacts and add reflections and written feedback. Large binders can

Portfolio contents checklist.   *exhibit* **7.13**

This Portfolio is the property of _____

It contains samples of my work in these areas:

Writing   _____
                   _____
                   _____

Reading   _____
                   _____
                   _____

Listening   _____
                   _____

Speaking   _____
                   _____

Visual Representations _____
                   _____
                   _____

Adapted from Ryan, C. (1994). *Middle school assessment.* Westminster, CA: Teacher Created Resources.

hold accumulated projects, and two pieces of poster board, taped or stapled together, make a large portfolio suitable for visual artwork.

Teachers evaluate portfolios in many ways, depending on the purposes of the portfolio. They may choose a descriptive evaluation technique or a numerical evaluation (checking off the number of items included in the portfolio). Students may perform a self-evaluation by checking off the artifacts they have added to the portfolios, without judging the quality of the work.

Portfolios provide a system for collecting documentation of progress and events in a language arts classroom. They are one of the most frequently used authentic assessment tools and are particularly effective because they focus on the literacy behaviors of individual children. Like all true authentic assessment methods, they are child centered, collaborative, extensive, and continuous (see Exhibit 7.14). Portfolios should be an integral component of authentic assessment in all language arts classrooms (Tierney, Crumpler, Bertelsen, & Bond, 2003).

exhibit 7.14 *Assessment tools that demonstrate characteristics of authenticity.*

	CHILD CENTERED	COLLABORATIVE	EXTENSIVE	CONTINUOUS
Written/Oral Retelling	■ Focuses on one child's responses	■ Can include collaborative activities in which students reconstruct, discuss, and retell the story	■ Relies on listening, oral expression, and writing ■ Can be used in different content areas	■ Allows students to participate many times throughout the year
Journals	■ Focuses on child's ideas, observations, and writings	■ Can be interactive among children, teachers, parents, and others	■ Includes ideas, observations, and writing from a variety of subject areas, contexts, and experiences	■ Occurs regularly throughout the year
Interactive Anecdotal Records	■ Focuses on child behavior and actions	■ Can involve parents, students, and teachers	■ Includes notes from a variety of contexts and activities ■ Can be used in a variety of settings	■ Should be based on observations throughout the school year and build on prior observations
Portfolios	■ Represents student-selected work ■ Involves students in assessment of writing progress ■ Makes students part of goal setting	■ Used as a tool for conferencing ■ May involve peers, parents, and teachers ■ Can represent collaborative work	■ Includes a variety of writing, including letters, lists, stories, reports ■ Collects multiple representations of growth	■ Collects products created over the entire school year
Rubrics	■ Focuses on individual child's responses ■ Establishes method to compare child's work ■ Communicates growth and progress to child ■ Can be designed and modified based on child's development	■ Can be jointly constructed by teachers and children ■ Can be used as a component of collaborative goal setting	■ Can identify various practices and learning experiences ■ Can be used over a period of time or modified based on developmental growth or changes in learning goals	■ Measures overall writing goals throughout the year ■ Can be continuously modified

GWEN, VETERAN TEACHER ▶ I have used portfolios with my students for about five years. I started small, with only writing portfolios the first year. Students chose one writing sample to include each week. I conferenced with students about every six weeks to review their portfolios and set new goals for their writing. By starting out small, I learned a lot of things "to do" and "not to do" with portfolios. That made it easy to add to the portfolio process each year.

AMI, BEGINNING TEACHER ▶ During my student teaching, I learned how to use portfolios for language arts from my mentor teacher. We had students keep their work in a folder each week, and every Friday we spent about 20 to 30 minutes in the afternoon having the students choose two items to add to their portfolio. One was a "student choice" item, usually something they were really proud of; the other was a "teacher choice" item that connected to the curriculum and specific learning goals. We talked to each student to find out why they selected the "student choice item," and we also discussed the "teacher choice item." When students finished the process, we let them read silently, go to the listening center, or write in their journals. We used expandable folders for the portfolio, and we kept them in a file cabinet in the classroom. This system worked really well during my student teaching, and now I'm using it in my own second-grade class.

Portfolio Assessment

Collect literacy products from a single student over several weeks. (If children are developing portfolios, use their collections.) Meet with the student to talk about his or her work. Let the student describe his or her strengths and needs for improvement. Use the products along with your review of the products to summarize in writing what you have learned about the child's literacy development. Develop at least three instructional recommendations to address the child's needs and build on his or her strengths as a language user. Implement at least one of your instructional recommendations.

Analysis and Interpretation

With an organized set of literacy products from each child, the teacher can proceed to the heart of evaluation: analysis and interpretation. This step varies depending on the teacher's and students' needs.

Describing a child's work, identifying patterns, recognizing inconsistent behavior, establishing benchmarks, and comparing data with other children or earlier representations of the same child's work all can provide important insights about student learning and information for planning instruction.

Consulting with other teachers may help confirm patterns and recognize inconsistencies in classroom experiences. They can review assessment information and provide additional insights. Students should also have opportunities to help analyze their products and portfolios. They may uncover patterns or offer insights that the teacher would never have considered. Children are capable of explaining certain behaviors, talking about what influenced their responses, and describing their processes in ways that may complement the teacher's views.

Rubrics

Rubrics are tools that help teachers and students analyze the information they have collected in portfolios, daily work, projects, or other learning activities (Rickards & Cheek, 1998). A rubric explicitly identifies the literacy behaviors that a teacher expects to see as a result of literacy teaching and learning (Valencia, Hiebert, & Afflerbach, 1994) and places these behaviors along a continuum reflecting various levels of achievement. To use the rubric, the student or teacher identifies the student's position on the continuum, sometimes awarding points for each level. Usually a teacher designs a three-point rubric, with descriptors for above-level performance, at-level performance, and below-level performance. In the process of creating the rubric they may review samples of work that students have already completed in order to define an appropriate set of descriptors. A rubric may be holistic or analytic, generic or task specific (Lewin & Shoemaker, 1998). Rubrics may also be based on specific state goals or school district objectives. The rubric in Exhibit 7.15 represents a holistic measure of student writing samples. The rubric in Exhibit 7.16 is an analytic rubric correlated to a specific state writing goal.

 7.15   *Holistic rubric for student writing.*

Score of 3
Writing samples demonstrate mature and original use of language.
Writing samples demonstrate well-developed ideas.
Writing samples demonstrate good skill in organization and mechanics.

Score of 2
Writing samples demonstrate competent use of language.
Writing samples show fairly well-developed ideas.
Writing samples demonstrate some skill in organization and mechanics.

Score of 1
Writing samples partially suggest competent use of language.
Writing samples show little or no sign of original ideas.
Writing samples show little skill in organization and mechanics.

Adapted from Ryan, C. D. (1994). *Authentic assessment.* Westminster, CA: Teacher Created Resources.

| Analytical rubric for student writing. | *exhibit* | **7.16** |

State Goal, Texas Essential Knowledge and Skills, Grade 5:

The student selects and uses writing processes for self-initiated and assigned writing.

NAME _____   DATE _____

WRITING SAMPLE(S) _____

E = Exceeds   M = Meets   N = Does not meet

PREWRITING	E	M	N
Brainstorming	☐	☐	☐
Graphic organizers	☐	☐	☐
Notes	☐	☐	☐

DEVELOPING DRAFTS	E	M	N
Categorizing ideas	☐	☐	☐
Organizing ideas into paragraphs	☐	☐	☐
Blending paragraphs into longer texts	☐	☐	☐

REVISING DRAFTS FOR COHERENCE, PROGRESSION, AND LOGICAL SUPPORT OF IDEAS	E	M	N
Adding or elaborating on ideas	☐	☐	☐
Deleting ideas	☐	☐	☐
Combining ideas	☐	☐	☐
Rearranging text	☐	☐	☐

EDITING DRAFTS FOR	E	M	N
Standard usage	☐	☐	☐
Varied sentence structure	☐	☐	☐
Appropriate word choice	☐	☐	☐

Rubrics

Meet with your mentor teacher and together identify a project or an assignment that the students will soon be completing. Develop a rubric to assess student performance on that task. Use it to help your teacher evaluate student products.

field note

7.6

FINAL REFLECTIONS

Teachers use numerous methods of observing student performance and collecting samples of students' work, as well as many techniques to interpret the results. The goal should be to use authentic assessment to support literacy instruction. Classroom instruction that reflects authentic reading, writing, listening, and speaking processes is best measured and assessed with authentic measures. Exhibit 7.14, shown earlier, summarizes how each of the assessment tools discussed in this article meets the criteria for authentic assessment.

As you work toward becoming a teacher, it is important that you consider the types of assessment and evaluation that will allow you to understand the strengths and needs of each of your students. By carefully considering your state goals, district objectives, curriculum, and personal teaching philosophy, you will be able to select the tools and techniques that best match your classroom. Although you may choose from a variety of approaches to assessment and evaluation, the bottom line must always be to improve teaching and learning for all students.

article

Standards and Testing

Ideally, teaching and learning decisions are the responsibility of teachers and other educators who know and understand the students, the classroom, and the community. But the forces that determine instruction and assessment go far beyond the classroom and community settings (Sizer & Rogers, 1993), and some of the factors that influence language arts instruction are external to both classrooms and children's lives. National and state initiatives influence assessment and instruction processes, in some cases taking these processes out of the hands of teachers, educators, and the community. By becoming well informed about state and national mandates, you will be better prepared to understand these expectations and how they affect you and your students.

National and state standards and testing programs, aimed at improving educational and instructional processes and measuring teacher effectiveness (Popham, 1999), have become an important aspect of literacy education. The results of state tests are widely reported to the public and used for school-to-school, state-to-state, and even international comparisons. With standards and tests being used to measure school and educational effectiveness, teachers are under a great deal of pressure to improve student achievement as measured on standardized tests.

The passage of the No Child Left Behind Act on January 8, 2002, has resulted in closer scrutiny of student performance, teacher quality, and school performance. Complete information on this Act is available on the NCLB website located at **www.ed.gov/nclb/landing.html.** Some key components of the NCLB Act are summarized in Exhibit 7.17.

The NCLB Act has far-reaching consequences for education. State boards of education decide which specific tests to use to measure student progress, how to define highly qualified teachers, and what options they will provide to parents whose children are enrolled in low-performing schools.

NCLB in Your State

Visit the "More Local Freedom" section of the No Child Left Behind website (**www.ed.gov/nclb/landing.jhtml**) to learn how your state is responding to the NCLB Act. Ask your mentor teacher how the Act has affected his or her school and classroom. Share your findings with your peers.

field note

7.7

Key components of the No Child Left Behind (NCLB) Act.   *exhibit* **7.17**

Accountability for Results: Each state must measure every public school student's progress in reading and math in each of grades 3–8 and at least once during grades 10–12. These assessments must be aligned with state academic content and standards. The results of these assessments are designed to be used by teachers to develop high-quality instruction. In addition, the results are used by administrators to assess how much progress each teacher's students make and to guide decision making in their schools.

Practices Based on Scientific Research: Federal funding is targeted to support educational programs and practices that are proven to be effective through scientific research studies. By focusing on programs and practices that work, the quality of education and student achievement is expected to rise.

Parental Information and Options: States and school districts must give parents easy-to-read report cards on schools and districts that show which schools are performing well and those that are not. Achievement data is publicized and broken down by race, ethnicity, gender, language background, migrant status, disability status, and low-income status. Information about the professional qualifications of teachers must be made known. In the event of a school's ongoing poor performance, parents may request a transfer to a higher-performing school in their area or receive supplemental educational services such as tutoring, after-school programs, or remedial classes.

Source: www.ed.gov/nclb/landing.html

STANDARDIZED TESTING

As a key component of the NCLB Act, standardized tests are a reality for all teachers. In addition, most states and many districts have specific requirements for standardized tests at certain grade levels. Standardized tests include achievement/readiness tests, diagnostic tests, and intelligence tests. They usually require students to respond with multiple-choice or short-answer responses. They are timed, and the test taking environment is strictly controlled. Strict procedures determine scoring and interpretation.

Standardized tests are developed by private companies. Before companies publish a new test, they administer it to large numbers of children representing the types of children who will take the test after it is released. From these results and statistics about the test group, the company determines the test average, grade and age equivalencies, and percentiles. This procedure, known as *norming,* allows comparisons between groups of students.

After a teacher administers a standardized test, she submits the results for scoring. The scores are presented in tables and graphs that allow teachers to compare their students' achievement with that of the norming population. One score is a number with a decimal that indicates the grade equivalency of the student's performance. For example, a score of 3.2 suggests that the student's performance on that test compares to the performance on the same test of an average third-grade student in the second month of school. Norming also establishes percentiles. A student who scores in the 82nd percentile performed as well as or better than 82 percent of students in the testing group at that grade level. Standardized tests often report stanine scores, as well; these rank student performance on a scale of 1 through 9. The lowest stanine score is 1, and the highest is 9. Stanines 1, 2, and 3 indicate below average performance, stanines 4, 5, and 6 imply average performance, and stanines 7, 8, and 9 indicate above average performance. Stanines are based on the statistical normal curve, meaning that most students will score in the middle, and only a small number will score at the high and low ends.

Standardized Tests

Ask your mentor teacher to share the results of a recent standardized test, if possible. Examine the scores and discuss the standardized testing process with your mentor teacher. What types of scores are reported? What do the scores mean? How does the teacher use the results of the tests? What does she view as the benefits and drawbacks associated with standardized test results? How do the students in your school respond to standardized tests?

Legislators see standardized tests as a way to demonstrate what children are learning at school. Most states use some form of testing to measure students' literacy achievement, and the NCLB Act also requires testing in math and reading in grades 3 through 8 and once during grades 10 through 12. To find out whether your state requires specific testing, visit your state department of education's website.

Interpreting and Explaining Standardized Test Scores

Assume that a third-grade student achieved the following scores on a standardized test during the fourth month of school. How would you explain each score to a parent? Role-play with a partner. Share your ideas with your mentor teacher and ask for his or her suggestions for presenting standardized test scores to parents. Share your findings with your classmates.

Reading Comprehension: 42nd percentile   Vocabulary: Stanine 3

Writing Mechanics: 2.8 grade equivalent

The Role of Standardized Tests

Historically, teachers, parents, and others (such as college admissions officers) have used standardized test scores to compare students. Because they measure student achievement, they are also considered to be a measure of school effectiveness (Popham, 1999). More and more these tests are also used to measure the effectiveness of individual teachers.

Although standardized tests have been around for many years, in the last decade their role in educational settings has expanded. The "testing movement" has exerted pressure on all aspects of the curriculum, but it has been focused most intensely on language arts performance, as parents' and communities' concern about children's levels of literacy has grown. Statewide standardized tests have come to exert a large influence on reading and writing instruction.

Standardized Tests

Review a standardized test manual (you may be able to obtain one from your mentor teacher or methods course instructor). What are the procedures for administering the test? What directions are provided to teachers? Examine the types of scores the test provides, and, if available, review a sample of the test. What are the uses and limitations of the test? Share your findings with your peers.

Concerns About Standardized Tests

Several concerns are associated with statewide testing. One is that teachers often "teach to the test." With so much pressure for students to perform well, teachers may allow the test content to guide their curricular and instructional decisions. Even more troublesome is that test preparation may take time away from authentic language arts activities that would be of more benefit. Another negative aspect is that children's standardized tests reduce complex literacy processes and successes to a single score, failing to recognize the uniqueness of each language learner. In addition, some children may experience test anxiety, which causes them to perform poorly in comparison to their daily work and reduces the accuracy of the test results.

An important concern about standardized testing is that it may disadvantage diverse learners (Eisner, 1995). Since the tests do not reflect learners' differing experiences and backgrounds, the results show bias against students who are members of various cultural, racial, language, and socioeconomic groups. A large gap persists between the scores of students who are members of particular minority groups and students from the majority or mainstream culture. The various levels of achievement on the tests may be the result of any number of factors, but most observers suspect they are related to cultural differences—students who have different cultural backgrounds may have different learning styles. An even more obvious impediment to testing culturally different children is the mismatch between the test material and the background experiences of the test takers. If the test's reading passages feature events, activities, or ideas different from a child's experiences and background, the child is likely to achieve lower scores. If illustrations and examples on the test are from cultures other than one they have experienced, children may interpret them differently than a "mainstream" child would.

Language differences may also impact test results. Obviously, students who do not speak English well (or at all) are likely to achieve lower test scores. It is extremely difficult for children to succeed on standardized tests when they are unfamiliar with English. In fact, it may not be possible to evaluate a child's literacy in English fairly until he or she has a strong command of the English language. Teachers should use a variety of measures to evaluate and monitor *all* students' literacy development, but this is particularly crucial with English language learners (ELLs). Authentic assessment is highly recommended for ELLs, as it provides a more inclusive view of their development and achievements. Teachers will be able to understand ELLs' language arts skills and abilities best when they use a variety of assessments rather than just standardized tests. In addition, allowing students to express their understanding through various modes—drawing, dramatizing, graphic organizers, discussions, and so forth (Chamot & O'Malley, 1994)—will yield more accurate information about what ELLs know and understand.

Overreliance on standardized tests frequently leads educators to label children. This has important implications for students who come from different backgrounds and experiences. White middle-class children traditionally outperform children of other groups. This does not reflect a difference in intelligence or abilities as much as a cultural incongruity in the tests. Although test developers have tried to eliminate racial, cultural, and socioeconomic biases from test items, gaps still exist between the performance of some groups of students and students from the mainstream group.

Poor test performance has profound and long-term effects on a student's literacy. Self-concept, motivation, and self-perceptions often suffer, and children who do not perform well may be placed in special education classes, labeled as deficient, and subjected to stifling, low expectations.

Some extremely detrimental practices have developed out of standardized testing. One of the most potentially damaging is high-stakes testing—testing that has a long-term impact on a student's future, based on performance on a single test. As the result of a single score, older students may be prevented from graduating from high school and younger children may not be promoted to the next grade. High-stakes testing also refers to testing situations where students' poor performance could affect a teacher's salary or evaluations. These practices increase the pressure on teachers to raise student scores on achievement tests, sometimes at the expense of genuine teaching and learning.

Standardized tests are not in themselves a detriment to literacy development, if teachers use them appropriately. Teachers who know their students should be able to contextualize their students' performance on standardized tests. If children perform very differently than expected, the teacher should look for the causes. Teachers should interpret test results carefully and use them in combination with authentic measures. By combining the results of standardized and authentic assessments, teachers can develop a complete picture of their students' language processes and abilities.

ELAINE, VETERAN TEACHER ▶ One year, I was teaching fifth graders, but many of them had not mastered the fourth-grade curriculum. Because of my belief in a child-centered approach to teaching, I focused on helping my students develop the skills, strategies, and knowledge they needed from the fourth-grade curriculum before we moved on to the fifth-grade curriculum. It's just common sense. Why would I teach things they weren't ready for yet? Unfortunately, my principal found out and insisted that I abandon the fourth-grade curriculum and teach what was in the fifth-grade curriculum so the students would do well on our state proficiency test. I know why he told me to do this, but I felt like I abandoned my philosophy and beliefs of teaching.

Advocating for Your Students

Imagine that you had the experience Elaine describes in the Teacher Viewpoint. How would you explain your decision to focus on the fourth-grade curriculum to your principal? If your principal was not supportive of your approach, what would you do to advocate for your students so they would receive educational experiences that match their needs and strengths? Discuss your ideas with your classmates.

JESSICA, BEGINNING TEACHER ▶ I was so nervous about the standardized test I had to give my students this year. The directions were clear, and I knew what I was supposed to do to give the test, but I was worried about preparing my students for it. I know in my teacher education program they told us not to "teach to the test" because it is a waste of classroom time, but I wasn't sure what I should do now that I'm responsible for my own classroom and students. I talked with some experienced teachers in my building and my principal, too. They assured me that if I taught the curriculum and provided lots of meaningful educational experiences my students would do well. They also suggested that I spend a little time teaching my students a few basic test-taking skills so they would be ready. I spent a little time doing mini-lessons on choosing the best answer on multiple-choice tests, budgeting time during a timed test, and other basic test-taking strategies. I am glad I did these mini-lessons, because my students seemed more confident to take the test. I'm also proud that I didn't abandon the district curriculum to "teach to the test." It's a tough situation; I'm just glad my teaching colleagues and principal were there to guide me through it.

BALANCING AUTHENTIC AND TRADITIONAL ASSESSMENT

Standardized testing may seem to stand in stark contrast to the authentic assessment strategies that support effective language arts instruction. Although the two types of assessment seem dramatically different, teachers can strike a balance between authentic and traditional assessment (Calkins, 1998).

Students in classrooms that focus on authentic language activities need exposure to testing experiences and strategies. Teachers can provide this exposure by introducing test formats and working aspects of test preparation into the curriculum. To familiarize children with what they will see on tests, teachers may review test formats and invite the children to practice with sample tests or test materials that are no longer being used (Popham, 1999). Students also benefit from help with general test-taking strategies, such as how to "bubble in" test responses, make calculated guesses, or budget scheduled time. Mini-lessons and teacher think-alouds work well. Some test-taking strategies can help children on more authentic assessments as well. Exhibit 7.18 lists some test-taking strategies that will help students feel more comfortable with and improve their performance on standardized tests.

CATHY, VETERAN TEACHER ▶ One of my students knew that she did not do well on multiple-choice comprehension questions. "I always forget the answers by the time I get to the end of the reading. I know to go back and find the answer in the passage, but I get too confused to find out where it is," she told me. I told her that maybe she should try another strategy, such as reading the questions before she reads the passage. We practiced that strategy until she felt confident in using it. This conversation with my student reminded me how important it is to talk with students about how to take tests.

| *Strategies for taking standardized tests.* | *exhibit* **7.18** |

- Underline important parts of the question or reading passage.

- Use scratch paper to work out problems.

- Eliminate answers that you know are incorrect.

- Check answers after you finish the test.

- Read the directions carefully.

- Use a bookmark or place holder.

- Practice bubbling in responses completely so your answers are counted.

- Become familiar with the wording and language used in test directions.

Teachers who feel that testing is not the optimal method of assessment may not have a choice about administering tests to their students. State- and federally mandated tests are the law. Teachers should be prepared to guide their students through the test-taking process and help them to perform as well as they are capable. If teachers keep a positive attitude, talk about the uses of the tests, and help students learn test-taking skills, their students will be more likely to approach testing with an attitude that helps them perform well.

Children need opportunities to talk about the tests. Discussions of how the tests will be used and who will see the results help put children at ease. Teachers can explain to students that their yearly performance will be reviewed to measure how much they have learned in the last year. Standardized tests should be viewed as another fact of life that is important, but not overwhelming.

THE LINK BETWEEN STANDARDS AND TESTING

A great deal of the pressure on teachers to achieve high standardized test scores has resulted in a link with educational standards. Standards are intended to assure consistency in learning in schools across a state. They were developed only as guidelines, but too often they come across as mandates (Murray, 1997), and at their worst they are viewed as an impediment to authentic instruction. In truth, standards should not exclude local content or discourage divergent thinking. However, their link with statewide testing may become an overriding concern of teachers and other educators.

Standards and testing that are determined by outside-of-school constituencies can become obstacles to delivering authentic language arts instruction. It is important to acknowledge that education does not exist in a vacuum; it is shaped by cultural, community, and social factors, and testing is part of the existing culture. Even though testing and standards may impede teaching and learning and impose a great deal of stress on both teachers and students, they appear to be here to stay.

Teachers should recognize that good language arts instruction is the best way to prepare students to do well on tests. Authentic teaching and learning strategies remain the best approach to helping students meet state learning standards and consequently do well on standardized tests. Good teaching, with a healthy balance of attending to and recognizing the role of standards and testing in language arts, will result in positive achievement in most classrooms.

Some teachers and parents are voicing concerns about the amount of standardized testing taking place in schools (Sacks, 2001). As you enter the teaching profession, consider how you can be an advocate for good instruction and appropriate assessment policies. Sacks (2001) suggests that teachers advocate for developing alternative test formats that more closely match classroom instruction, implementing portfolios, and lowering the stakes associated with test scores.

While you may feel that as an individual teacher you have little control over policies that govern education, you can help work toward sound educational and testing policies. First, you can write letters to the local newspaper editor, communicate with your legislators, and share your views with your school and district administration. If you join with groups of professional colleagues, you can speak with a stronger voice. For example, by joining professional organizations such as the National Council of Teachers of English (NCTE), International Reading Association (IRA), or your state chapters of NCTE and IRA, you can vote on position papers, get involved with their legislative affairs committees, and contribute to lobbying efforts to share the organizations' views with policy makers. The FairTest website (**www.fairtest.org**) provides resources, fact sheets, and suggestions for advocating for appropriate assessment policies at the state and federal levels.

personal reflection

How Can a Teacher Advocate Against Inappropriate Use of High-Stakes Testing?

Consult one of the following resources for information about high-stakes testing. Identify at least one way you could advocate against the inappropriate use of standardized testing. Share your ideas with your classmates. In small groups or as a class, identify at least one advocacy idea that you can carry out yourself or with your classmates.

International Reading Association: **www.reading.org**

National Council of Teachers of English: **www.ncte.org**

FairTest: **www.fairtest.org**

Alfie Kohn: **www.alfiekohn.org**

Students Against Testing: **www.nomoretests.com**

GRADING

Most teachers are required to submit traditional grades (letter or numeric) for language arts on a regular basis throughout the school year. If handled appropriately, the grading process can provide helpful feedback to students and parents. Grade reports help students and parents understand the student's successes and challenges with language arts, and they can motivate a student to continue progress (Rhodes & Shanklin, 1993). Grade reports or report cards can take many forms, including traditional A through F grades, checklists, or narrative summaries. Many school districts have redesigned their report cards to correspond to state standards.

Reviewing a Report Card

Find out what kind of report card is used in the school where you are doing your field experience. Ask your mentor teacher to share a copy of it. Discuss the strengths and limitations of the report card with your mentor teacher. Share your findings with your peers.

field note

7.11

Students and parents often place a great deal of importance on grades. Students may fear earning failing grades, or they may compete with siblings or classmates for good grades. Later, in secondary school, grades are a factor in college admissions and work-related training options. To be productive, grades should serve as feedback and a way to enhance the communication among teachers, parents, and students. It is imperative that teachers carefully consider whether their grading actually reflects what they intend to measure. Teachers may choose to grade every assignment or grade only selected assignments. One of the most successful ways to grade student work is to help them understand their own progress when measured against past performance (Rhodes & Shanklin, 1993).

Making judgments about complex literacy development may be challenging, but it is possible to be fair when the criteria for grading are clear and explicit. Teachers should base their judgments on multiple assessments that document students' progress and accomplishments (Calfee, 1996). The starting point for such judgments is a set of defined expectations for each assignment. If children are aware of expected criteria, most of them will try their best to meet those expectations.

Establishing clear criteria is a necessary first step, but grading remains a complex process. It is easy to recognize a good student-authored poem, for example, but it is more difficult to assign a grade to that poem. Teachers may define criteria to help students understand the assignment and to guide the grading process. In some cases, teachers and students may work together to establish grading criteria. Teachers may find it helpful to complete the assignment themselves before establishing the criteria for evaluation. (See the discussion about collaboration in Article I of this chapter.)

Another way to establish criteria is to sort the students' work into three groups: above average, average, and below average, then use the work in each of the groups to create a list of criteria. Although this method is popular, it has one important disadvantage: students cannot be given clear criteria before they do the work.

Some teachers arrive at grades by recording points. Each day that a student follows the teacher's guidelines, the student receives points. Teachers use a variety of point scales; in the most common one, the scores add up to 100 points. Teachers assign points for such items as homework completion or classroom participation. Before starting the point system, the teacher must be sure to identify the factors that will affect points and decide how much the factors will count (Popham, 1999). Some homework assignments, for example, might be worth more points, reflecting their level of challenge or difficulty.

The example shown in Exhibit 7.19 is one way a teacher might grade a research paper. Notice that the grade is based on many different aspects of the process. The aspects are weighted (receive more or fewer points) depending on the teacher's emphasis. Ideally, the teacher would share this form with students when she gives the assignment so that they could understand the association between the requirements and the final grade.

The teacher will need to be involved in most grading, but occasionally it may be appropriate for children to be involved. Students can actually learn by grading their own work. They may use teacher-established criteria, or they may assign their work a grade based on their own judgment. They can be asked to provide a rationale for assigning the grade to their work (Rhodes & Shanklin, 1993). The teacher will make the final decisions, but students can contribute to the process. For example, students could com-

exhibit 7.19 *Grade evaluation for a research paper.*

Component	Points Possible	Your Score
Journal entries demonstrating topic selection	15	_____
Notes about research	15	_____
First drafts	15	_____
Final draft		_____
Punctuation	5	_____
Vocabulary	5	_____
Neatness	5	_____
Content	40	_____
Total points	100	_____
Grade		_____

plete the grade evaluation for their research paper (see Exhibit 7.19) and turn it in with the paper. The teacher could consider the student's own evaluation as part of her grading process.

Assigning Grades

Ask your mentor teacher how he or she determines grades for student work. Ask to see the grade book. How does your mentor teacher use it to record and average grades? Share your findings with your peers.

field note
7.12

FINAL REFLECTIONS

Although evaluation, assessment measures, and standards are often maligned and dreaded because of misuse, these are all tools that help teachers make instructional decisions. Standards provide general guidelines, and assessments and evaluations help teachers understand the impact of language arts instruction on their students. The most important thing to remember about standards, assessment, and evaluation is that when linked to instruction, they can help all students learn. As you enter the teaching profession, you will need to reflect on the strengths and limitations of various literacy assessment tools and strive for a balance of authentic and standardized measures that provides a complete picture of your students and their language arts abilities.

PROFESSIONAL REFLECTIONS

Review the field notes from this chapter and develop one or more into a component of your portfolio. To continue to reflect on your field note responses, consider the following suggestions:

- Compile newspaper and magazine clippings about testing, and describe the perceptions of testing portrayed in the media. Write or illustrate a reflective response that conveys your philosophy about the role of testing and assessment in your future classroom.
- Review the samples of work collected from one child and develop a literacy profile. Illustrate and describe the student's literacy behaviors, and give instructional recommendations to support his or her continued growth in literacy.
- Review the lesson plans you have developed throughout the semester. Focus on the assessment component of your lessons, and use the framework in Exhibit 7.14 to determine whether you have produced authentic assessment procedures to accompany your instruction.

Professional Readings

To expand your understanding of the content of this chapter, consider reading the following books:

Lewin, L., & Shoemaker, B. J. (1998). *Great performances: Creating classroom-based assessment tasks.* Alexandria, VA: Association for Supervision and Curriculum Development.

This is an excellent source for developing classroom assessment processes. It includes examples of assessment tools that can be easily adapted for any classroom and for many subjects. This a very practical book that will help teachers measure students' learning.

Ohanian, S. (1999). *One size fits few: The folly of educational standards.* Portsmouth, NH: Heinemann.

This book explains how the standards movement impacts classroom learning. Ohanian focuses on the impact of standards on diverse learners. Her perspective provides a critical view of standards.

Rhodes, L. K., & Shanklin, N. L. (1993). *Windows into literacy: Assessing learners K–8.* Portsmouth, NH: Heinemann.

Rhodes and Shanklin provide a thorough and comprehensive view of the assessment process. They present assessment as a collaborative endeavor among students, parents, teachers, and others and suggest how assessment can be a motivating factor in students' lives. They give specific examples of assessment techniques and provide step-by-step directions for assembling a portfolio.

 Form a small group with three or four peers. Select one of the children's books listed below and read it. Individually, write down one or more issues that the book poses about assessment, evaluation, or testing. Discuss the issues in your group.

Children's Books

The following children's books relate to the topics in this chapter.

Finchler, J. (2000). *Testing Miss Malarkey.* Illustrated by K. O'Malley. New York: Walker and Co.

Miss Malarkey's school is getting ready for standardized testing, and everyone is worried. This picture book examines standardized testing with humor.

Gilson, J. (1980). *Do bananas chew gum?* New York: Lothop, Lee & Shepard.

In this chapter book, Sam is in sixth grade, but he only reads and writes at a second-grade level. He acts like a smart-aleck to avoid looking dumb. His family just moved to a new town, and Sam worries how long he will be able to keep his secret.

Hoban, L. (1983). *First grade takes a test.* Illustrated by M. Cohen. New York: Dell Books for Young Readers.

This picture book describes a group of first graders who take a standardized test. They struggle with the structure of the test, which does not always let them show what they really know.

Kraus, R. (1971). *Leo the late bloomer.* Illustrated by J. Aruego. New York: Simon & Schuster.

This picture book tells the story of Leo, who didn't talk even though everyone was watching him and waiting for him to develop. They waited and waited, until finally Leo bloomed and talked.

REFERENCES

Brualdi, A. (1998). Implementing performance assessment in the classroom. *ERIC/AE Digest.* College Park, MD: ERIC Clearinghouse on Assessment and Evaluation. ED 423312.

Calfee, R. (1996). Assessing development and learning over time. In J. Flood, S. B. Heath, & D. Lapp (Eds.), *Research on teaching literacy through the communicative and visual arts* (pp. 144–166). International Reading Association. New York: Macmillan.

Calkins, L. M. (1994). *The art of teaching writing.* Portsmouth, NH: Heinemann.

Calkins, L. M. (1998). *Raising lifelong learners: A parents' guide.* Boulder, CO: Perseus.

Chamot, A. U., & O'Malley, J. M. (1994). *The CALLA handbook: Implementing the cognitive academic language approach.* Reading, MA: Addison-Wesley.

Cooper, J. D., & Kiger, N. D. (2001). *Literacy assessment: Helping teachers plan instruction.* Boston: Houghton Mifflin.

Eisner, E. (1995). Standards for American schools: Help or hindrance? *Phi Delta Kappan,* 385–390.

Farr, R. (1992). Putting it all together: Solving the reading assessment puzzle. *The Reading Teacher, 46,* 26–37.

Graves, D. H. (1994). *A fresh look at writing.* Portsmouth, NH: Heinemann.

Hansen, J. (2001). *When writers read.* Portsmouth, NH: Heinemann.

Herman, J. L., Aschbacher, P. R., & Winters, L. (1992). *A practical guide to alternative assessment.* Alexandria, VA: Association for Supervision and Curriculum Development.

Johns, J. L., Lenski, S. D., & Elish-Piper, L. (2002). *Teaching beginning readers: Linking assessment and instruction.* Dubuque, IA: Kendall/Hunt.

Koch, R., & Schwartz-Petterson, J. (2000). *The portfolio guidebook: Implementing quality in an age of standards.* Norwood, MA: Christopher Gordon.

Levin, H. M. (1998). Educational performance standards and the economy. *Educational Researcher, 27*(4), 4–10.

Lewin, L., & Shoemaker, B. J. (1998). *Great performances: Creating classroom based assessment tasks.* Alexandria, VA: Association for Curriculum and Supervision.

Murray, D. M. (1997). The seeing line. *Voices from the Middle, 4*(3), 3–5.

Opitz, M. (1998). *Flexible grouping in reading.* New York: Scholastic.

Popham, W. J. (1999). *Classroom assessment: What teachers need to know.* Boston: Allyn & Bacon.

Rhodes, L. K., & Dudley-Marling, C. (1996). *Readers and writers with a difference: A holistic approach to teaching struggling readers and writers.* Portsmouth, NH: Heinemann.

Rhodes, L. K., & Nathenson-Mejia, S. (1992). Anecdotal records: A powerful tool for ongoing literacy assessment. *The Reading Teacher, 45,* 502–509.

Rhodes, L. K., & Shanklin, N. L. (1993). *Windows into literacy: Assessing learners K–8.* Portsmouth, NH: Heinemann.

Rickards, D., & Cheek, E. H. (1998). *Designing rubrics for K–6 classrooms.* Norwood, MA: Christopher Gordon.

Routman, R. (2000). *Conversations: Strategies for teaching, learning, and evaluating.* Portsmouth, NH: Heinemann.

Ryan, C. D. (1994). *Authentic assessment.* Westminster, CA: Teacher Created Materials.

Sacks, P. (2001). *Standardized minds: The high price of America's testing culture and what we can do to change it.* Boulder, CO: Perseus.

Sizer, T., & Rogers, B. (1993). Designing standards: Achieving. *Educational Leadership,* 381–383.

Tierney, R. J., Crumpler, T. P., Bertelsen, C. D., & Bond, E. L. (2003). *Interactive assessment: Teachers, parents, and students as partners.* Norwood, MA: Christopher Gordon.

Valencia, S. W., Hiebert, E. H., & Afflerbach, P. P. (1994). *Authentic reading assessment: Practices and possibilities.* Newark, DE: International Reading Association.

Wiggins, G. (1990). (ERIC Document Reproduction Service No. ED328611.) *The case for authentic assessment.* Washington, DC: Eric Digest.

Winograd, P., & Arrington, H. J. (1999). Best practices in literacy assessment. In L. B. Gambrell, L. M. Morrow, S. B. Neuman, & M. Pressley (Eds.), *Best practices in literacy instruction* (pp. 210–241). New York: Guilford.

Debra is implementing new language arts grouping procedures and activities she learned during a school-sponsored workshop. The workshop introduced her to new strategies that the whole district is attempting to implement. Now she and the other fourth-grade teachers at her school are collaborating to adopt the new ideas into their language arts routines. Their main focus is to use flexible grouping procedures, organizing children into small groups according to instructional needs. In Debra's classroom, she has grouped children together who are still having difficulty writing on their own to focus on developing fluency of ideas. Another group of children is focusing on improving the vocabulary they use during writing. Several other groups are formed based on other needs. In addition, Debra and the other fourth-grade teachers have decided to implement writers' workshop in their classrooms. They have already been using readers' workshop during language arts instructional time, and the district's focus on writing instruction has motivated them to try some new strategies. Debra's principal is aware of her grade level's team efforts and is eager to see how the instructional and grouping procedures will work.

Chapter 8

THE LANGUAGE ARTS PROFESSIONAL

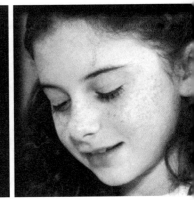

Debra is satisfied as she works with the new writers' workshop procedures and small group instruction. Her informal observations indicate that most children in her classroom are responding well to the group work. However, occasionally, she is frustrated with the students' behavior during small group work. She feels her fourth graders demonstrate too much off-task talking and behaviors when they are supposed to be working. She is also concerned about four children who never seem to listen and who dominate the

conversations, as well as two other children who never talk in the small groups. Debra decides to collect data about her students' listening skills so she can understand better what is happening during small group interactions. She wants to answer the question, "What listening patterns do my fourth graders exhibit during small group work?"

She begins writing anecdotal records about her entire class's listening during small group work, but she focuses specifically on the students whom she thinks talk too much or too little. She designs a checklist to help her focus on the students' behaviors. After two weeks of collecting information about her students' listening habits, she finds that the four talkative students are actually very engaged in the small group work and are not allowing others to participate. The quiet students are not joining in because they cannot compete with the students who dominate the conversation. One child is uncharacteristically quiet during small group work, and Debra notes that she should talk to the parents to see if they can provide information that might encourage his participation.

Debra begins to build on what she learned in the school-sponsored workshop and sets about adding to her knowledge about listening during small group work. She reviews the materials from the district workshop and reads additional material available in professional books. She finds several articles in the journal *Language Arts* about improving listening skills. Most important, she shares her findings with her colleagues at the next grade-level meeting, and they all work together to find ways to improve her students' listening behaviors. One of the ideas that her colleagues help her implement is a student self-evaluation of listening skills. A second idea the teachers suggest is to design a mini-lesson about listening skills in small group sessions. Since some of the other teachers are having the same difficulty, they also benefit from the collaborative planning session. Debra refers to professional books, articles, and Internet resources as she begins to implement their suggestions. She is excited to continue to learn about improving listening in her classroom, and she feels that she has developed as a professional through specific training offered in her district, reading professional materials, and collaborating with her colleagues.

INTRODUCTION

There is always more to learn about teaching. The workshops, professional readings, and collaborative learning that Debra experienced illustrate some of the ways teachers continue their professional growth after they graduate from their teacher education programs. Continuous learning helps teachers keep up with the trends and issues in language arts instruction, and it familiarizes teachers with new strategies and innovative instructional processes. Professional organizations help teachers keep up to date with developments in the field. Effective teachers are continually learning, both independently and together.

Debra's experience shows how collaboration can be an important component of a teacher's professional life. Often collaboration goes beyond the classroom and even the school in which the teacher works. Teachers are constantly communicating and working with family and community members to learn more about the children in their classrooms. For example, Debra intended to talk to one student's parents to discover why he was not participating in small group settings. Teachers also collaborate and communicate with other teachers at professional conferences, in graduate classes, and in online discussions about education.

GUIDING QUESTIONS

Consider these questions as you read this chapter. Jot down your initial responses to each question. After reading the articles, revisit your responses. Would you make any changes to them? If so, what would those changes be? Discuss your responses with one or more of your classmates, your professor, or your mentor teacher.

1. What are some of the ways teachers continue their learning after they start their teaching careers?

2. How do teachers collaborate with family and community members to improve classroom instruction?

3. What are some of the issues and trends in language arts instruction that may impact your first years of teaching?

article
1

Continuing Professional Development

You may think that when you finish your teacher-training program you will understand everything you need to know about teaching and learning. You may believe that some of the elusive answers and problem-solving techniques associated with teaching will come to you naturally as you complete your student teaching experience. This is not the case. Debra felt very prepared when she graduated from her teacher preparation program, but she recognized that she still had a lot to learn, as did her veteran colleagues. Experienced teachers know that their growth is a never-ending, lifelong process. Teachers will always need to learn new techniques, plan for innovative instruction, read professional journals, and listen to other teachers and professionals who can provide new information about teaching and learning.

PROFESSIONAL DEVELOPMENT

Learning new instructional strategies and new ideas about teaching and learning is the key to staying current and up to date. *Professional development* is the term often used to refer to the continuous professional growth of a teacher. *Staff development* is the term used to describe the education and training required by a district. A teacher's professional development, whether the district plans it for her or she initiates it independently, helps her remain vibrant and involved, and it contributes to student achievement as well.

Professional development of teachers is a crucial component of the teaching profession. Your university program is the first step, but it is certainly not the end of your professional development. The district that hires you, the profession in general, and your own needs will motivate you to continue your growth and development as a language arts teacher after you complete your university courses. Professional development activities will be an important factor throughout your career, and as early as your first week as a teacher you may find that your district requires attendance at planned activities and training. A "new teacher workshop" or orientation session will help you learn about your job. Usually your first professional development activities in a new school introduce you to the district-wide curriculum and how it aligns with state standards, acquaint you with the benefits and policies related to your teaching position, and provide you with valuable hints for success in your first days on the job.

Professional development continues far beyond assisting a new teacher to learn about the district. The implementation of new instructional programs or schoolwide purchases of new tools, such as textbooks, computers, software, or other media tools, means that teachers need to learn new ways of doing things. Evolving assessment and evaluation systems also require teachers to learn new strategies and methods. Many schools train teachers to implement specific, required strategies to prepare students for state proficiency tests and district-wide assessments. Most school districts have a planned sequence of professional development activities for teachers. Never before have educators enjoyed so many staff development opportunities designed to help them extend, build, and enrich their knowledge and skills for effective teaching and learning. Furthermore, many states require teachers to engage in continuing education to maintain their teaching certificates. Regardless of the specific requirements in a school district or state, teachers who wish to meet the needs of their students will be constantly reading about recent research on learning, and reading further to understand how that research impacts their daily practice (Magestro & Standford-Blair, 2000).

LIFELONG LEARNING ACTIVITIES

Professional development is a personal and professional commitment never to quit learning. Effective teachers feel a need to improve their teaching, and each year they learn new ways to improve their classroom processes. Teachers may depend on a familiar teaching routine, but each year they will find themselves adding something new, trying a different approach, or abandoning a practice that is no longer effective. This constant learning process keeps teaching fresh and alive, and it provides a model for students who see that their teachers are always learning.

Many professional development activities are designed to improve teachers' skills in reading and language arts instruction. In the past, the language arts were viewed as a set of skills to be mastered. Over the past few years, however, that has changed, and the language arts are now viewed as a multidimensional communication process. The evolving views of literacy require new ways of teaching and suggest new instructional strategies, such as readers' workshop and literature circles. The goal of many new approaches is to build positive student attitudes toward language learning and use. Practices that worked 10 years ago may no longer work due to changes in student demographics, increased emphasis on state standards, and the availability of technology. For all these reasons, teachers must continue to grow and evolve in their teaching.

The lifelong learning of a teacher goes beyond classroom strategies. Good language arts teachers are constantly developing their personal communication skills. They possess a curiosity and drive to understand their own literacy processes so that they can help their students become the best language users possible.

Your current university program is part of your lifelong learning process, but it is only the first step. No matter how long you work in a classroom, "teaching should be a continuing expedition of self-discovery, from growing toward the profession as a student to growing in the profession as a practitioner" (Duck, 2000, p. 42).

CAMI, PRESERVICE TEACHER ▶ I am really busy with my education classes, my field experience, and my job, but I make time to read and talk to teachers. I subscribe to *Language Arts* and *Teaching K–8,* and I visit teaching websites on the Internet. I have an aunt who is a teacher, and I talk to her about teaching every time I see her. I also study with some of my friends who are in the teacher education program. I even went to our state language arts conference in the spring. It was amazing how much I learned! I am so excited to be a teacher, and I'm always trying to learn as much as I can.

JAVON, BEGINNING TEACHER ▶ I just finished my first year of teaching, and I learned so much during that year. I have lots of plans for the summer to get myself prepared for the coming year. I have several professional books that my colleagues recommended, and I just started getting *The Reading Teacher* because I joined the International Reading Association. I signed up for two workshops this summer: one is offered by the local university, and the other is sponsored by a publishing company. One of my colleagues will be going with me so we can plan how to use the new ideas in our classrooms.

MAYRA, VETERAN TEACHER ▶ I read journals and books, and I go to at least one language arts conference each year. I also read lots of children's literature so I know what to recommend to my students. After teaching for 18 years, I realized that I wanted not only to do professional development for myself, but to help other teachers as well. For the past year I have been the mentor for a new teacher in my building. We learned so much together. I have also volunteered to do a workshop on teaching writing across the curriculum for my school next year. I'm challenging myself to keep learning, and my teaching continues to get better each year.

ENGAGING IN REFLECTIVE PRACTICE

The best way to improve your teaching is to learn what good teaching is by constantly analyzing, comparing, and contrasting classroom practices. Teachers engaged in reflective practice experiment with new instructional strategies, ask questions about their teaching and how their students are learning, gather evidence about their teaching, and revisit and modify their instruction based on their reflections (Costa & Kallick, 2000). The ultimate purpose of reflection is to promote student learning by understanding better ways of teaching.

Reflection is second nature to effective, experienced teachers who have been asking questions and considering ways to improve classroom instruction throughout their careers. Sometimes a teacher engages in reflection while planning for instruction or making classroom decisions. It may begin with a casual observation and lead to instructional decision making. For example, a teacher may recognize that children are having difficulty writing descriptive prose. A reflective teacher will gather information and look for the reasons why students struggle with descriptive writing and then provide experiences and activities that will improve their writing skills. If teachers do not reflect on what is happening in the classroom, they may continue to follow weekly plans or district-wide curriculum without considering the students' needs. A reflective teacher attempts to adjust instruction to meet those needs.

Reflective practice means taking the time to reflect and learn. Teachers need time to think, analyze, and reflect on what they are doing. It also takes time for them to write and record their observations, insights, and reflections. It is not always easy to find the time to continue the learning process, but it is well worth the effort.

COLLECTING DATA ABOUT YOUR OWN TEACHING

A teacher may plan a systematic approach to reflecting on his teaching practices. He might write down the reactions to classroom events or record the steps that lead up to an event. These structured observations or notes can be indispensable when the teacher is trying to identify how to improve instruction.

Reflection can also be collaborative. Informal sharing can take place over lunch, or teachers may organize a more structured way to share, such as in small groups during grade-level meetings or after school. Sharing ideas about classroom teaching and learning helps teachers recognize and understand their own beliefs and ideas. Some ways teachers can reflect on their teaching, individually or collaboratively, are described below.

Reflective Journal Writing

For many teachers, the key to their professional development and reflective practice is journaling (Routman, 2000). A journal helps teachers keep track of their classroom successes, their instructional problems, and the ways they address enduring classroom concerns. Journal entries document a teacher's growth within the profession and help her develop a professional development plan. (A professional development plan, often required by the district or state, establishes professional goals and activities for a period of time and encourages teachers to engage in workshops, graduate classes, professional reading, and other learning situations.)

Teachers often begin their journals by writing down their reactions to classroom activities. To reflect on instructional processes, a teacher might answer questions such as, "How did my students respond to the activity?" "Was I happy with the instructional procedure?" "What can I improve?" A teacher might then focus on students' reactions and answer questions such as, "Which students seemed to respond well to the activity?" "Which students did not participate in the activity?"

Action Research

Action research is a systematic process that helps teachers clarify the impact of their teaching on student learning and see how to make changes based on evidence they collect in the classroom. The purpose of action research is to improve the quality and effectiveness of teaching. Teachers design and implement action research projects in order to analyze information to improve their own practice. Action research can be done by individuals or by teams of colleagues; the team approach is called *collaborative inquiry.*

Action research has the potential to generate genuine and sustained improvements in classroom instruction. It gives teachers opportunities to reflect on and assess their language arts teaching; to explore and test new ideas, methods, and materials; to assess the effectiveness of new approaches; to share feedback with team members; and to make decisions about which new approaches to include in the team's curriculum, instruction, and assessment plans.

Following are the steps to develop an action research project (Calhoun, 1994) (also see the summary in Exhibit 8.1).

The best way to improve our teaching is to learn what good teaching is by constantly analyzing, comparing, and contrasting classroom practices.

1. *Identify an area of focus in the classroom.* Recurring questions about a topic or a desire to improve instruction in a particular area might spur the focus. For example, a teacher of language arts might be concerned with students' ability to listen carefully during whole-class discussions. The teacher would focus on students' listening behaviors and how they respond to current lessons. He would also think about how his students have listened in the past and how their listening behaviors have changed over time.

2. *Collect information or evidence related to the focus of the inquiry.* Collect information about the topic from as many sources as possible. One place to start would be information that is already available, such as the contents of writing folders, reading records, or other collections of children's work. The teacher who is focusing on listening behavior might collect audiotapes of whole-class discussions, conduct a survey by asking children about their own listening skills, or talk to colleagues who teach the same group of students and find out how their listening behavior is described in other settings. She could also collect anecdotal data during whole-class discussions to learn more about the class's listening behaviors.

3. *Organize the information in some way that makes it easy to begin to search for answers to the problem or issue.* For example, count instances of behaviors, summarize anecdotal records, organize artifacts, or provide examples of communication processes. Checklists are useful for organizing certain types of information.

4. *Analyze and interpret the data.* Through this analysis teachers begin to see how to deal with the issue. For example, a review of a checklist or table that notes listening behaviors in one classroom may reveal that only one group of students is causing disruptions during instruction or that most interruptions are related to the topic of discussion which implies that students are hearing what is being said. From analysis of the information, the teacher can decide what to do about the listening behaviors during the next steps of action research.

5. *Study what others have found out about the topic.* Professional literature is an excellent source of information about many topics, offering examples of what others have done in similar situations and suggestions for action that might be most promising in your classroom.

6. *Take action based on the inquiry.* Select a course of action that makes sense based on what you learned by analyzing the information and what you read in the professional literature. For example, the teacher who is monitoring listening behavior would use the data from the classroom and information from journal articles to design classroom strategies that might help her address the problem. She can modify existing instructional strategies or plan different instruction strategies based on what she found through her action research.

7. *Evaluate the effectiveness of the action.* An action research project is not complete without a review of the process. Think about whether the right question was asked. For example, the teacher who collected data about her students' listening behaviors may find that it was not entirely a listening problem but instead had to do with her students' background on a topic. Determine whether the information was collected, organized, and analyzed in a way that was productive and useful. If the teacher in the example

Steps for action research. *exhibit* **8.1**

1. Identify a problem or ask a question about instruction.
2. Collect information or evidence related to the problem or question.
3. Organize the information.
4. Analyze and interpret the information.
5. Study what others have learned.
6. Take action based on the analysis and interpretation of information:
   - Learn more.
   - Develop a plan.
   - Read and reflect.
   - Modify instruction.
7. Evaluate the effectiveness of the action.

exhibit   8.2   *Sample action research topics.*

What can I do to encourage English language learners to participate in small group and large group discussions?

How can I maximize language arts instructional time by minimizing time needed for transitions between activities?

What strategies and materials will motivate reluctant readers to engage in reading during sustained silent reading (SSR) time?

Based on projects completed by Harlem Interns in the Harlem–NIU Partnership.

reviews the process and finds that she missed an entire week of collecting information about her students' listening process, she may want to repeat the data collection procedures to assure that her data will yield helpful conclusions. The most important aspect to consider, however, is the effectiveness of the classroom strategy identified to address the problem. Use the data you collected to see if the strategy or activity you initiated was effective. Often teachers work together to review the effectiveness of their action research activities, including the new instructional strategies. Collaborative effort in action research development, implementation, and review is a most rewarding form of professional development.

Action Research

Identify a question, challenge, or problem that you have in your field experience classroom. Plan an action research project based on your question. Plan how you will collect data, make observations, review student work, or keep anecdotal records to learn more about the problem. Consider how you will organize and analyze the data. Will you keep it in chronological order, search for patterns in the anecdotal records you keep, or tally behaviors you have observed? With your mentor teacher's support, implement your plan. Collect information and meet with a small group of your classmates to share what you find. Read textbooks or professional journals to help you address the issue. Continue to share with your classmates as you learn about your problem or question.

Portfolios

You will likely develop a professional portfolio as you go through your teacher education program—a collection of artifacts, visuals, writings, children's work, and other materials that document your growth as a teacher

(Farris, 1999). Your portfolio might include a statement of philosophy about your choice of teaching style, classroom management techniques, sample activities, lessons, projects, photographs of classroom interactions, and videotapes of instruction. The process of documenting your competencies and experiences as a teacher will continue as you begin your career. You should consider it an important activity related to being a professional educator (Rieman, 2000). Portfolio material may be collected in a three-ring notebook, kept in a file folder, collected on a computer disk, or compiled online, in an electronic form.

A portfolio can provide the basis for professional development and help ensure ongoing self-renewal. Some states and districts require teachers to develop portfolios for use in assessment and evaluation of their teaching effectiveness. In this case, a committee of teachers will review the portfolio to make sure that the teacher is providing students with effective instruction. A portfolio can also assist teachers as they search for jobs.

An important part of the portfolio is the evaluation and summary written by the teacher herself. Reflecting on your own practice will help you monitor and adjust your instruction to meet student needs. When teachers regularly reflect upon their teaching, communication skills, and knowledge, they increase the effectiveness of the teaching and learning processes in the classroom, and students benefit (Rieman, 2000). A professional portfolio charts your growth within the profession and contain your plans for self-renewal (Duck, 2000).

Portfolio Summary

Review all the products you have produced during field-based activities and professional reflections this semester or quarter. Gather your classroom observations, the lessons you have taught, the community activities you completed, and other products or responses that represent what you have learned during this course. Organize them in a way that makes sense. Review with your classmates what you have learned. Write a summary of your activities.

PARTICIPATING IN DISTRICT AND PROFESSIONAL ORGANIZATION ACTIVITIES

Teachers participate in an array of professional development activities. Some are arranged by school districts, others by professional organizations. Teachers can also participate in professional networks that help them learn, reflect, and try new strategies. Effective teachers take advantage of professional development activities and resources throughout their careers.

School-Sponsored Activities

Professional development activities are a key component of a school's improvement goals and plans. Ongoing professional development activities help teachers improve their personal teaching performance and learn new skills. When a school district adopts a new reform effort, introduces a new instructional strategy, or requires that teachers implement new instructional programs, then it usually provides opportunities for teachers to learn about the innovation. School districts that adopt an instructional theme, such as problem solving or cooperative learning, also require their teachers to take part in staff development activities. They may call on consultants from outside the district or teachers from within the district to provide professional development activities. For example, if a school district decides to implement process-writing activities, it might hire an experienced teacher from another district who is familiar with the concept to explain and help the district implement these strategies. Or, when reading across the curriculum is the focus of staff development, the school may rely on the expertise of the building's reading specialist.

Professional Organizations

The National Council for Teachers of English (NCTE) and International Reading Association (IRA) are the major language arts professional organizations. When teachers join these organizations, they can receive journals such as *Language Arts, Voices from the Middle, English Teacher, The Journal of Adolescent and Adult Literacy,* and *The Reading Teacher,* which offer articles about recent research findings in language arts, new instructional strategies, and descriptions of teachers' experiences. These organizations hold national meetings each year, as well as regional, state, and local meetings. The professional meetings consist of sessions presented mostly by teachers and university professors who share some of the latest research and instructional strategies. These organizations and their journals offer teachers a way to keep up to date with the most recent trends in language arts instruction.

   To learn more about IRA and NCTE, visit their websites: **www.reading.org/main.html** and **http://ncte.org.**

personal reflection

Professional Meeting

Attend a local, regional, or national professional meeting related to language arts instruction. Attend at least several sessions. If there are exhibits of educational materials, look through them and gather samples, if possible. Keep notes on new ideas you gained from the meeting and share them with your classmates.

Professional Networks

Teachers often work in isolation, so many enjoy becoming a part of a network that explores issues of teaching and learning collaboratively. Connecting with others is an important aspect of teachers' professional development. By sharing ideas, asking questions, and challenging one another's beliefs, teachers can reflect on their practice and make improvements for the future. As Debra and her colleagues demonstrated in this chapter's Window to the Classroom, by sharing their ideas, experiences, and observations, all teachers, regardless of level of experience, can improve their practice.

Networks may be established at the school where you teach, at the district level, in graduate programs, or even through the Internet. Joining a group of individuals or colleagues provides opportunities to discuss concepts and problems that arise during staff development activities or in the classroom, helps teachers find ways to integrate new concepts with other aspects of instruction, and contributes to a shared professional culture in which teachers develop common understandings of instructional methods. Simply being part of the network may encourage teachers to try new strategies.

Mentoring

Many states and school districts offer mentoring programs, in which an experienced teacher assists a new teacher who is entering the profession. If such a support mechanism is not available for you when you start teaching, then you should seek a mentor yourself. Try sharing a success or challenge with experienced teachers; if they seem genuinely interested in your efforts and questions, then any of them could be a good mentor (Duck, 2000). You will have many questions during your first year of teaching, and a strong mentor can be a great help.

Graduate Work

Most teachers will return to the university setting at some point to take a course, upgrade their skills in a particular area, or obtain an advanced degree. Teachers who do this often find that university course work becomes extremely relevant after a year or two of teaching. Taking a course in reading or children's literature after gaining experience in the classroom helps teachers learn new strategies and reflect on their work. Graduate programs in particular require teachers to do a great deal of reflecting and thinking about their own practice. Most school districts offer incentives for taking graduate courses, increasing teachers' pay once they have completed a specific number of credit hours. Graduate courses are an excellent way to fulfill state professional development certification requirements. Some school districts offer tuition assistance or arrange for classes to be taught in schools. A university may have a satellite campus close to your own school that would make it convenient to attend after the workday.

National Board for Professional Teaching Standards

Some teachers choose to improve their practice by becoming certified through the National Board for Professional Teaching Standards (NBPTS). This organization's rigorous certification process is closely linked to professional development activity. To earn NBPTS certification, teachers must critically assess their own teaching through a portfolio that contains videotapes of classroom teaching, samples of student work, and written commentary. They also must demonstrate knowledge, skills, and abilities in their teaching field. The entire process focuses on practice and teaching performance. Generally, teachers must have a great deal of experience in order to pursue National Board certification. You may wish to keep it in mind as a goal for the future.

FINAL REFLECTIONS

A teacher is a learner. Professional development activities will help you pursue the lifelong learning you will need for an effective career. Informal and formal learning opportunities keep your teaching fresh, provide new ideas, and rejuvenate you. As you enter the teaching profession, you will continue to be involved in learning activities that promote better teaching and learning in your classroom.

article

Professional Collaboration and Communication

An important part of your job as a teacher will be to communicate and collaborate with a wide range of family and community members from cultures and socioeconomic settings that may be different from your own (Daiute, 1996; Payne, 1998). Communication is crucial for gaining the collaborative involvement of parents, care givers, and community members in children's education. By working with parents and others in the community, teachers can support the literacy development of all students. As Debra plans for the school year, she considers ways to involve students' families and community members to enhance the quality of the language arts instruction she provides. She takes into account the support and resources that other teachers can provide. In short, Debra is aware that collaboration and communication are important aspects of teaching.

FAMILY CONNECTIONS

Literacy development begins at home, where parents influence children's attitudes toward school and literacy. It is important to note that some children do not live with their own parents, but the adults who serve as their primary care givers are just as important as parents to those children's literacy development and school success. In this discussion we use the terms "parents" and "family members" to describe children's primary care givers; however, it is important to realize that some children may live with grandparents, aunts or uncles, older siblings, or foster families, in group home settings, or in other arrangements.

Family members' attitudes toward literacy are crucial in children's acquisition of reading, writing, listening, and speaking skills. The way significant people in children's lives view and value literacy will greatly affect children's language arts learning. When parents and family members support and understand literacy activities, teachers and students are more likely to succeed.

When parents and family members support and understand literacy activities, teachers and students are more likely to succeed.

The most important role of family members in literacy development is their initiation and demonstration of language and communication processes at home and in daily life. Interactions between children and their parents, the ways reading and writing are used in the home, how stories are told among friends and families, and even the role of television at home are important factors that impact personal literacy development (Binstock, 1996).

The influence of family members on early literacy development is well documented, but evidence also suggests that parental and family involvement in and understanding of school activities have positive results in students' school experiences (Christenson & Sheridan, 2001). When family members and teachers connect and communicate, everyone learns more about the child.

Parents and family members can be a great help to teachers who want to understand their students' language learning. They provide another perspective on a student's behavior, and they can support what is happening in the classroom. Contacts with the family may help teachers understand issues at home, such as a new sibling, excitement about a holiday, or neighborhood events affecting the child's school behavior patterns. Similarly, parents may learn that the child is talented in writing or storytelling, or that he is currently engrossed in reading a particular book. When adults share what is happening in children's lives, they can be more supportive of literacy development. Each time a teacher talks to a family member and each time a family member participates in school activities, both parties develop more understanding and acceptance.

Children benefit in subtle ways when parents and teachers work together. Family and parental interest in school activities signals to the child that literacy and learning are important. Observing that adults in their lives value and support literacy learning further strengthens students' sense of the importance of language learning. When family members are interested and involved in school, children are likely to reflect that interest in their own activities.

CHALLENGES TO FAMILY INVOLVEMENT

Even if a teacher understands and embraces the role of families in children's educational processes, certain attitudes and situations can inhibit communication and collaboration. For example, if parents or family members speak a different language, then they may feel uncomfortable and ill at ease at school. If the student's parents were not successful in school or never learned to read or write in English, it may be very difficult for them to understand how much they can influence their children's literacy development. Parent and family members who tend to feel uncomfortable at school will be more motivated to take part in school events when the environment makes them feel comfortable and welcome (Smith & Elish-Piper, 2002).

Teachers can help parents and family members who speak a different language to feel more comfortable in the school or when interacting with the teacher. They can make sure that an interpreter is available for conversations. The interpreter may be a family member who is bilingual—these individuals can provide important support to teachers. They can serve as interpreters for children who are developing English skills or for family members who do not speak English. They can also make presentations in class to help the entire class learn about their language. Teachers should remember that even when language is an obstacle, involving all parents in classroom activities will help build strong and collaborative home school links.

Parents and family with language, cultural, educational, or socioeconomic backgrounds that differ from the teacher's may hesitate to visit the school because they are not sure how to act or what to say. Often teachers misread this reluctance to take part in school activities as a lack of caring about the child's school activities (Smith & Elish-Piper, 2002). Almost all parents and family members are concerned about their children and are eager to do what they can to help their children be successful at school. Teachers may need to make special efforts to help some parents and family members feel comfortable at school—by honoring their perspective, asking their advice, or enlisting their assistance in finding ways to improve the child's classroom learning experiences. All parents have something to offer if they have the right encouragement. They can help pass out lunch tickets, read to an individual or small group, translate for children who do not speak English, or share their hobbies. Their presence in the classroom acknowledges that there are unique opportunities for them to collaborate in their children's education (Elish-Piper, 2002; Moll, Amanti, Neff, & Gonzalez, 1992).

Often parents' work schedules make it difficult for them to communicate and collaborate with teachers. Many schools recognize this barrier and schedule meetings and conferences in the evenings or early mornings, when parents are off work. Personal or family problems, too, can affect how and when parents interact with teachers. If a family is experiencing a divorce, a family member's illness, or transportation problems, it may be difficult for parents to work with teachers. In each of these situations, the more teachers know and understand about the family, the better they are able to understand the parents' and the child's situation and find ways to meet the needs of the entire family. For example, a single mother will appreciate meeting with a teacher after work, and a Spanish-speaking parent will be more comfortable with a translator (Smith & Elish-Piper, 2002).

If new teachers have not personally observed the benefits of working and collaborating with parents and families, they may view it as a hindrance to the day-to-day classroom schedule. With so many things to do in establishing a language arts classroom, it is not easy for a new teacher to think about collaborating with parents. However, the payoff for collaboration with parents is great, and efforts to communicate and collaborate with families will make a great impact on students' literacy development.

ENCOURAGING FAMILY INVOLVEMENT

Teachers inform parents about daily school activities through informal chats, telephone calls, personal letters, e-mail messages, and parent–teacher meetings. Parents' nights, open houses, and parent–teacher meetings are usually regularly scheduled so that parents can meet the teachers and learn about school routines, policies, and schedules. Teachers can further support communication between home and schools and invite parents and other important family members to collaborate and support literacy development with strategies such as regular reports, conferences, and home visits.

Regular Reports

Informing parents about school-related activities will require many methods for communicating. One of the most common ways to convey what is happening at school is end-of-term reports. These reports may take the form of grades or summaries that describe the child's growth. Systematic grade reports have served as a reporting system to parents for a long time, but if the truth be known, a letter grade does not tell a parent a great deal about what is happening at school.

To inform parents more fully about what is happening in school, teachers may give them written reports. For example, the teacher might describe the writing skills a child has consistently displayed during the reporting period. The teacher might attach examples of the child's work to provide concrete illustrations.

Child-authored material communicates to parents what is happening at school and demonstrates children's communication abilities. The entire class might publish a newsletter that is sent home or posted on the Internet, or children can write letters to their parents, telling them what they have been doing during language arts instructional activities.

When written messages are sent home from the classroom, teachers should consider the languages spoken in homes. Parents may not be able to read the messages unless they are translated. Many schools routinely publish information in Spanish or other languages that are dominant in the community where the children live. If the school has no formal process for translating messages, perhaps bilingual children will be able to translate homebound messages for their parents. If children cannot translate the messages, community members from service organizations, houses of worship, and agencies might assist with translation. Parents will be grateful and more ready to support language arts instruction if teachers make the effort to ensure they can read and understand the messages sent home from the classroom.

Translation programs are also available free on the Internet, but teachers should use these with great caution since they tend to rely on word-by-word translation, not accurately translating idioms or slang. Two popular translation programs are Babel Fish (**http://babelfish.altavista.com**) and PROMPT's Online Translator (**www.translate.ru/eng/other.asp**).

Interview Parents

Interview at least two parents of school-age children to learn about the role, questions, and concerns of parents related to education. To identify parents to invite for interviews, you might wish to work with your mentor teacher or with others in your community. Try to interview at least one parent whose racial, ethnic, socioeconomic, or language background differs from your own. Consider asking:

- What is the most important thing you want your child's teacher to know about him or her?
- What goal(s) do you have for your child in language arts this year?
- What is the best experience you have had with your child's school or teacher?
- What is the worst experience you have had with your child's school or teacher?
- What advice do you have for a new teacher about working with parents?

You may wish to add other questions to the list. After completing your interviews, share your findings with your peers. Discuss the general conclusions you can draw about working with parents in your future teaching.

In addition to considering the language of materials they send home to families, teachers should be aware of the difficulty of the materials. Before sending home a newsletter or parent letter, use the "Tools" feature in Microsoft Word or WordPerfect to measure the readability or difficulty of the text. These tools calculate both the grade-level difficulty and vocabulary complexity (reading ease) of the texts. If you find that the materials are too difficult, revise them to make them more accessible to parents and family members (Smith & Elish-Piper, 2002).

Communicating with Parents

Work with your cooperating teacher to collect the messages and packets that are sent home with children during an entire grading period. Analyze the messages. What overall feeling do they convey? What information do parents learn about their child? How accessible are the messages to all parents? What changes might make the information more accessible and useful to parents? Share your findings with your peers.

field note
8.4

Conferences

Conferences are an important means of communicating with parents. Traditionally, schools require parent and teacher conferences and schedule them around certain grading periods. They typically last about 15 to 20 minutes, and the discussion revolves around report cards and other progress reports for the grading period.

To plan a conference with parents, start by establishing the purpose of the meeting (Burke, Fogarty, & Belgrad, 1994). The goal might be to discuss long-term language development or talk about a recent classroom event. Next, decide who should take part in the conference and when the conference will take place. Finally, plan the conference itself. Select strategies for introducing topics or eliciting discussion among all in attendance. Encourage parents to come with questions, and ask them to select a work sample they would like you to explain or discuss (Canter & Associates, 1998). Exhibit 8.3 outlines these steps.

Planning a conference.   *exhibit* **8.3**

Set goals for the conference.

Identify participants, time, and place.

Plan discussions and questions.

Select examples of children's work.

Work collaboratively to set goals for student learning.

Conferences should be relaxed and comfortable; give special attention to making the family members feel at ease. They will enjoy reviewing their children's work with the teacher. Describe school behaviors by sharing samples of work and anecdotes from classroom life. Use pictures, videos, writings, drawings, and other print and nonprint representations to clarify the child's roles and behaviors in the classroom. Portfolios, folders, work samples, and other records will also enhance discussions and encourage conversations. Ask parents to tell you about the child's literacy development at home and encourage them to express their pride and enjoyment in the child's progress. An important aspect of parent–teacher conferences is to work collaboratively with parents, providing opportunities for them to help make plans and participate in their child's classroom experience. By giving thought to the conference arrangements, the teacher can provide a comfortable situation for everyone to communicate.

Most conferences focus on the teachers and parents, but in some cases students can take part in conferences (Burke, Fogarty, & Belgrad, 1994). A conference that involves the student reflects a different relationship among the teacher, student, and parents, because it invites the student to take part in analyzing his own work and discussing it with his parents and teachers. The student may even take the lead in conducting the conference, selecting the materials that will be available during the conference and practicing how she will talk about her learning. Even if students do not attend the conference, they can help the teacher review and summarize their work.

Teachers need to prepare students for participation in a conference (Ryan, 1994). Together the class can discuss how the conferences will progress and what students can talk about with their parents. The teacher and students may discuss and identify the literacy products they will bring. After they have decided what they will show their parents, they can script a discussion and questions they will ask their parents (see Exhibit 8.4). Before students lead a conference, the teacher can model the process and role-play conferences with the students. Teachers may also need to prepare the parents, by explaining the process in advance, perhaps in a letter or during an after-school meeting.

exhibit 8.4   *Script of student's questions and comments during a conference.*

What questions do you have about my work?

Is there any activity you would like me to talk about?

This represents work that I am very proud of. The reason why I am so proud is _____.

Here is some work that I think I can improve. The way I would improve this work is _____.

If I were to summarize my work in language arts, I would say _____.

Although teachers are present to expand and clarify what children present to parents (Rhodes & Shanklin, 1993), the children have the main responsibility for conducting the conference. At the end, the student can be asked to leave if there are things that would be better discussed between parents and teachers. When conferences are viewed as a collaborative process, with teachers, parents, and children each making important contributions, they help to establish a comfortable team approach to literacy learning.

MATEO, BEGINNING TEACHER ▶ Today I tried student–parent conferences for the first time! I worked with the students to help them develop their presentations. We selected materials, students wrote their assessments of themselves, and then organized their portfolios so that when parents came in, the students would be ready to talk about their progress this quarter. I had two different shifts of conferences so that there would be enough room for each family to confer. I think they went really well! Some parents were concerned that I was not a major part of the conference, even though I told them how much I worked with the students to help organize their discussion tonight. For those parents, we made separate arrangements to either meet another time or discuss their children's progress on the phone. Most parents were really impressed at how much their children had learned and could do. I think they were amazed that the conferences were so productive and interesting. The children were also really proud of their involvement in the conferences. Things went so well, I plan to do this again!

Conference Planning

Help one child plan a conference with his or her parents. Along with your mentor teacher, the child, and the parents, take part in the conference. Afterward, review the meeting and write a summary of its positive aspects and the challenges or problems that arose. Include your insights about how to improve the process in future situations.

Home Visits

Another form of the parent–teacher conference is home visits. If families are willing and your school district permits home visits, they can help a teacher understand more about students' home cultures (McIntyre, Kyle, Moore, Sweazy, & Greer, 2001). To conduct a home conference, the teacher should think of questions that will encourage the family to tell about their home language and learning. For example, a teacher may ask a younger student, "Will you show me what you read at home?" Teachers of older students may want to see where they do their homework and have them explain their hobbies. Visiting parents in surroundings where they are comfortable may make it easier for them to share about their children.

Teachers can plan and prepare for home visits so that parents will know what to expect. For example, before the conference, the teacher might make up a packet that includes the questions she may ask, the role of the child during the conference, and some of the things she'd like the family to share. She might encourage the family to be ready to talk about hobbies, pets, favorite television shows, and favorite books. Some families may prefer not to have the teacher visit the home, and it is important to honor this response. Furthermore, some children may be homeless, may live in a shelter, or may move from one home to another as they stay with family members and friends. In these situations, meeting at school, in another community location such as the public library or community center, or at a fast-food restaurant are other options.

Teachers use many creative strategies to encourage parents to explore their own literacies (Taylor, 1997) during home visits. They might ask parents to share something personal, such as a photograph, an item of clothing, a letter, or a song, and write about its special meaning. If parents don't feel comfortable writing about the item, they can tell the story aloud. One teacher visited homes where he was invited to share read-aloud stories with the families. Parents who became interested in reading stories to others after his visit volunteered to read in schools or in the community. As these ideas show, home visits can encourage a wide range of interactions and responses among everyone involved.

TEACHER Viewpoint

DENA, VETERAN TEACHER ▶ I always begin home conferences by asking, "Will you show me where you read at home?" I want to see where my students do their homework and understand whether they have space to work at home. Often students tell me things they wouldn't tell me at school, or they may share things that are important to them. I often meet family pets and hear about a day in the life of these students. I sit down with the families, have tea, and meet siblings, grandparents, and neighbors. I see the gardens, hear about pictures on the walls, and find out about parents' concerns related to their child. Maybe it's the informal setting of the home that makes them more comfortable. When I learn about their home and meet their parents, my students seem to understand that a link between school and home has been made, and after my visit, parents seem more comfortable contacting me and coming into the classroom.

FAMILY CLASSROOM INVOLVEMENT

Parents can be involved with their children's literacy learning by visiting the classroom or engaging in activities at home. By providing various opportunities for family involvement, teachers encourage links between school and home (Elish-Piper, 2002).

Classroom Visits

Involving parents in classroom activities improves collaboration and communication. Family members should feel welcome to visit the classroom, and when they do visit, they should feel comfortable and encouraged to contribute to the instructional activities.

To encourage family classroom visits, teachers might specify a certain time when visitors are welcome. Visitors may be invited to watch literacy activities and listen as children communicate during regular classroom activities. Children can serve as hosts for classroom visitors. They may sit with the family members, explaining what is happening and what to expect. By visiting the classroom, family members become familiar with routines and schedules and begin to feel comfortable in the classroom environment.

After family members become familiar with classroom activities, they can begin taking part in the activities. They might read their favorite books aloud, read silently as the class engages in SSR, work with children who are researching topics on the Internet, or help edit a class book. Family members' presence during literacy activities provides powerful reinforcement for the importance of literacy sharing. Family members might also volunteer to help with special jobs or activities: helping younger children write stories, reading aloud to small and large groups of children, setting out materials for painting and drawing, overseeing computer-related activities, or helping the class clean up after major projects.

Programs designed to educate and support parents can be a part of the parental involvement program (Christenson & Sheridan, 2001). For example, the schools might provide a space and time for parents to gather and meet with a teacher, nurse, or counselor to discuss issues that they would like to learn about. Inviting parents to help choose the topics and organize the discussions is a good way to demonstrate that you value the ideas and contributions of parents and family members.

Classroom Visits

Observe a parent or family classroom visit, or help your mentor teacher plan an open house. What do family members do when they come to the classroom? Do they appear to be comfortable? Are they observers, or do they actively take part in classroom activities? How do children respond when their own family members come to the classroom? Did you learn anything about the child whose parents or family members visited the classroom? Share your findings with your peers.

Home Activities

Working parents may not be able to visit the classroom regularly, but they can still collaborate and participate in their children's literacy development. Single parents, parents with young children or elderly family members to care for, and parents who lack transportation to the school may find it difficult to visit the classroom on a regular basis. There are still many roles that parents can play after school or at home to support the child and feel involved in the classroom.

Of course, the most beneficial at-home activity is parents' participation with their children in reading experiences. Parents can read to their children and talk to them about books and stories. Speaking a different language should not be an impediment; these parents can still support the importance of literacy activities by reading and discussing books in their own language. Parents can look at books with their children and encourage their children to read aloud and tell them about their reading and literacy experiences. Family members who listen to children reading and become involved in their literacy activities are a great support to the language arts activities in the classroom. Teachers can encourage parental involvement in school activities by suggesting reading materials or planning classroom activities that require meaningful home collaboration.

The three-way notebook is an instructional activity that involves parents in their child's literacy development. Rhodes and Shanklin (1993) describe this strategy, in which students and teachers keep a notebook about what they are learning at school. Students select an assignment each month and examine their communication processes as well as their feelings and ideas about the assignment. Students may write about what they learned during mini-lessons, reading assignments, or Internet research, or from visual representations. They can reflect on their communication processes and how they have improved their writing, reading, or understanding as a result of the activity. Children can also evaluate the activity and their work, describing what they liked best or what they want to do differently the next time.

At least once a month, the teacher responds to the child's reflections by writing in the notebook. Then the notebooks are shared with the parents, who are asked to respond in writing to their child's and teacher's journal entries. The notebooks are a way to encourage collaboration and develop parents' understanding of classroom activities and events. Rhodes and Shanklin (1993) report that the three-way notebooks can foster a sense of community among the parents, students, and teachers.

It can be a challenge for teachers to involve parents who work all day, who may speak a language other than English, or who might not yet feel comfortable with teachers and the school. But there are many ways to make the classroom welcoming and to encourage parents to become involved in their child's literacy development. Teachers' efforts to do so will benefit all involved. Involving parents and other family members in the educational process is an important component of teaching the language arts (Flood, Lapp, Tinajero, & Nagel, 1995).

CONNECTING WITH OTHER TEACHERS

Teachers have many opportunities to work together. It is common for teachers at the same grade level or in the same subject area to meet regularly to plan together and share ideas. All the fourth-grade teachers in an elementary school or all the language arts teachers in a middle school may meet regularly, for example. Your meetings with other teachers will be both informal and formal.

Teachers interact formally in teacher meetings, grade-level planning meetings, and professional development activities. They work, learn, and plan together, sharing ideas and ways to teach language and literacy skills. Some teachers become close colleagues—working together to teach, research, and even team-teach selected units or lessons. During informal conversations in school hallways or the teacher's lounge, they pass along ideas, favorite books, and instructional strategies.

Teachers also frequently meet with cross–grade level groups, special education teachers, bilingual teachers, and teachers who have different roles than their own, for example when they gather to plan for children with special needs. Often these collaborative meetings take the form of *staffings* or evaluation meetings that involve students (especially when they are in upper grades), parents, classroom and special education teachers, and possibly school psychologists and administrators (Rhodes & Shanklin, 1993). The group discusses the child's progress based on information collected from various perspectives. For a child who needs special services, teachers and others collaborate to develop an individual educational plan (IEP). Staffings allow educators and families to work together to find the best way to provide educational contexts and learning support for the child.

Professional colleagues are important collaborators. When teachers work with their peers, they experience some of the most important professional connections they will make. It is almost impossible to work in a school building without communicating and collaborating with other teachers. Cooperation, collaboration, and communication can make a teacher's job easier and provide support for trying innovative strategies and improving students' literacy learning.

COMMUNICATING WITH ADMINISTRATORS

Teachers benefit from communication and collaboration with the administrators in their school. The principal is usually the most important administrator in teachers' daily interactions. They inform the principal of student behavior and classroom events, especially when there is a serious discipline problem or the need arises to contact parents or other professionals about a child's behavior or learning. But when things are going well in the classroom, the principal should hear about that, too!

Teachers can communicate with the principal about literacy classroom activities by inviting the principal to be involved—to read aloud, watch a dramatic presentation, or view visual representations produced by the students. Principals who are able to observe literacy learning may offer their own suggestions.

Principals are an important part of the school environment, and they can make significant contributions to literacy instruction when invited to collaborate and participate in classroom activities. They often help set the tenor of language arts teaching in a building. They will usually support teachers' efforts to innovate and improve instruction, when teachers are able to explain how what they are doing fits into the larger picture. If teachers offer plenty of evidence and clarify their ideas, principals usually encourage their innovations. For example, a group of teachers may decide to integrate language arts, social studies, and science instruction. The implementation of an interdisciplinary unit means that their daily schedule would be different from the established school schedule. Their principal would likely be willing to support their plan if they come to her and explain why they want to reorganize the day, explain their ideas, and describe the benefits. The principal should be seen as an important partner in literacy instruction.

CONNECTING WITH COMMUNITIES

The first step to connecting with the larger community is to recognize and acknowledge its importance. Teachers can signal their respect for the community in many ways. They might design activities that recognize holidays and cultural events important to the community, and include referents and representations of various cultures in instruction. Literature, books, and newspapers representing differing cultures should be present in the classroom. Community members may serve as resources and bring the life of the community into the classroom. An effective language arts teacher will accept the various languages and cultures of the community while at the same time encouraging students to expand their personal views of language and culture so they will feel comfortable in the mainstream culture of our society.

Community members are usually very concerned about school children's literacy skills and ability to communicate with others. Religious leaders, business people, and other community members often take a great deal of interest in test results and other measures of success at school. Teachers should find ways to communicate what is happening in the classroom to the community. Developing a good relationship with the local newspaper is one effective way to get information into the community. You might invite a newspaper reporter to visit your classroom if you are putting on a play or doing a special literacy project. The class could work together and submit letters or reports of their classroom experiences to the local newspaper, informing them of books they are reading, surveys they have done, or writing experiences that focus on community interests.

Community members can be asked to participate in learning activities. They may serve as speakers when they know about topics that are related to units of study, such as biology or art. Other visitors might share special hobbies or travel experiences or read their favorite books. Few people can resist an invitation to visit a classroom to talk to children about something they know. Health professionals, police officers, tradespeople, business owners, and firefighters can also be invited to participate in classroom activities. Involving community members in classroom activities enhances the students' experience while also creating a relevant link between school and community and building support for teachers and schools.

FINAL REFLECTIONS

Students are greatly influenced by their families and the community in which they live. To build strong connections among the school, family, and community, teachers collaborate and communicate with a wide range of people, including family and community members, other teachers, and administrators. New teachers may find that learning to work collaboratively with families and communities takes time, but it is well worth the effort.

Trends in Language Arts

article

III

Our society's communication infrastructure is becoming more and more complex. The number of languages spoken in the United States, the technological innovations that impact our communication patterns, the information revolution that adds new knowledge daily, and the strong influence of media are changing traditional ways of communicating and conducting our everyday affairs (Luke, 1998). Educational processes in general, and therefore language arts processes in particular, are affected by technological, legislative, demographic, and scientific developments. Teaching professionals must continually review and consider how these shifts transform classroom instruction.

Some trends come and go; others leave a mark and will continue to influence how teachers teach and students learn language arts. Many of the issues are complex and interrelated, and a listing of only a few may appear too simplistic, but a review of several themes that have been woven throughout this text will clarify their importance. It will not be possible to discuss all the issues nor approach trends from differing perspectives; the goal in this article is to focus on a few important trends that will impact the teaching profession as you begin your career. These trends are:

- Changing definitions of language arts
- Increasing language and cultural diversity
- Inclusion of media and technology
- Impact of state and federal policy
- Importance of testing and accountability

Tracking Trends

Ask three to five teachers in the school where you are doing your field experience about trends that have affected them during their teaching careers. Which trends impacted language arts instruction most directly? Which trends brought about the most change? Have any trends reappeared during veteran teachers' careers? Bring the results of your survey to class and compare your list with your classmates'. Arrange your findings in categories, and label each group of trends. Does your list resemble the list in this article? How do the lists differ?

CHANGING DEFINITION OF LANGUAGE ARTS

(Reference further information and examples related to this trend in this textbook: Chapter 1, Articles I & II; Chapter 4, Article IV; Chapter 6, Articles I–IV.)

Conventional views of literacy suggest that language arts instruction should focus on reading and writing; in the past, literacy was considered the ability to read and produce printed materials effectively. Language arts teachers have long operated under the assumption that once their students could read and write effectively, the literate abilities they had acquired would serve them well in work, family, and leisure activities. However, this view of language arts is rapidly changing and expanding. In today's culture, reading/writing-based communication is no longer adequate, and an expanded notion of literacy is emerging as the foundation for language arts instruction. The definitions that have guided language arts instruction in the past seem rudimentary in the context of the new systems of language and symbol representation that are currently being used by literate people (Smagorinsky, 2000).

The social and cultural changes related to media require an expanded definition of literacy education. Much modern literacy is based on new, continually emerging technology. Film, television, and other mass media directly impact our students' lives and our own. The influence on young people is particularly strong. Students communicate about topics that seem to become part of the mainstream culture overnight. They use new words and expressions associated with popular music and video games. Their communication processes regularly include animation, electronic sound, voice activation, and image making. Issues related to media literacy are beginning to be referenced in language arts curriculum, but the impact will be felt even more in the future. Innovations in communication require new skills and behaviors, but these are also grounded in the reading, writing, listening, and speaking skills that have always been present in language arts curriculum.

Literacy requirements are rapidly changing and will continue to change. Language arts curriculum in turn should reflect instructional approaches that are responsive to modern communication trends. It is not enough to stay abreast of innovations; teachers must also develop new approaches, determine how students learn effectively, and reflect on what constitutes literacy (Luke, 1998). Literacy educators are coming to recognize that literacy is not simply a matter of learning to read and write, but that literate individuals possess "the ability to access, analyze, evaluate, and communicate messages in a variety of forms" (Hobbs, 1997, p. 7).

These technological changes and recent research in education and development have contributed to the current debate about how to teach reading. No other discussion in language arts has impacted the field so greatly. It encompasses questions about the amount of phonics presented to young children, the way in which literature is used in classroom instruction, and how reading skills are presented. During the past decade, language arts education experts have swung from the view that phonics is best taught in an integrated way throughout reading and writing instruction to a commitment to teaching phonics directly with drills and routines. What makes sense to most educators is that reading and writing instruction should rely on multiple strategies and instructional approaches. Dorothy Strickland, a former president of International Reading Association, provides the guidelines shown in Exhibit 8.5 as a way to maintain balance during language arts instruction.

The waves of reform led by trends in how we define language arts will continue throughout your career. They may or may not require new training, but they will certainly require openness to change and a commitment to preparing all students to meet the demands of a complex communication process.

Literacy requirements are rapidly changing and will continue to change.

Five rules of thumb for maintaining balance.	*exhibit* **8.5**

1. **Teach skills as a way to gain meaning.** Skills are not ends in themselves.

2. **Each day, include time for both guided instruction and independent work.** Otherwise, students will never internalize skills and make them their own.

3. **Avoid teaching children as if they were empty receptacles for knowledge.** Instead, allow them to build knowledge in a process-oriented way.

4. **Integrate print and electronic materials effectively.** That way, your classroom will reflect the multimedia world in which students live.

5. **Always consider standardized test scores in light of informal assessment data.** Encourage parents to do the same.

Adapted from Strickland, D. (n.d.). Balanced literacy, *Instructor.*

INCREASING LANGUAGE AND CULTURAL DIVERSITY

(Reference further information and examples related to this trend in this textbook: Chapter 1, Articles I & II; Chapter 3, Articles I–IV.)

Today's classrooms reflect many different cultures and languages. The number of children whose culture differs from the mainstream and whose language is not English is larger and more dominant than ever before (Olsen, 2000). A small Texas school recently reported that 26 languages were represented in its student population, and the metroplex of Houston reported that 106 languages were spoken among its students. The most common language other than English spoken by students is Spanish, but students also speak Vietnamese, Mandarin Chinese, and languages of the Southern Pacific Islands—just to mention a few.

Teachers may find it challenging to understand, instruct, and assess the literacy practices of students who speak a different language. ELLs are not all the same: some children come to school speaking their own language poorly, and very little English, while others may be completely literate in two or more languages. Children may know how to read well in their first language, or they may not have acquired reading skills in any language. Providing language arts education for children who speak English as their second language will continue to be an important challenge for the teaching profession.

Because the basic literacy processes are rooted in culture, the way students experience their everyday lives impacts the way they use language and how they learn in school. Children from different cultures communicate in a variety of ways (Daiute, 1998). In the past, language arts instruction has not always recognized the importance of culture in students' language learning processes, and it has focused on a primarily white, middle-class view of communication. This is no longer appropriate in today's multicultural and multilingual classrooms. From 2000 to 2015, the total minority school-age population is projected to increase in all but two states. By 2015, minority students will make up more than 50 percent of the school-age population in at least five states (Olsen, 2000). This majority-minority population has already changed dramatically in some areas of the country, such as the Bronx, Houston, Washington, D.C., and Chicago. Cultural changes are apparent among the school-age population, but teachers continue to come from mostly white, middle-class backgrounds. Language arts teachers, whose backgrounds and language experiences usually differ from those of the children they teach, must recognize the need to make connections between the school and the learner's culture. It is very important in today's multicultural classrooms to understand students' home life, social and cultural structures, and language development and how each of those factors impacts their language learning. Teachers who develop awareness about cultural and language differences and honor those differences in their classrooms will facilitate the learning of all children, no matter what their background.

INCLUSION OF MEDIA AND TECHNOLOGY

(Reference further information and examples about this trend in this textbook: Chapter 5, Article IV; Chapter 6, Articles I–IV.)

Technology and media have generated new communication forms, content, social structures, communication styles, and symbolic systems (Luke, 1997). Consider the print and literacy symbolic systems that a person must use when browsing the Internet. He must read words of different sizes, interpret animated symbols, ignore or attend to flashing messages, and interpret voice animation. A successful user of the Internet must understand how to select hyperlinks that lead to the intended destination. Many elementary students are literate enough to traverse the Internet with ease. Already, we often take the literacy behaviors and skills associated with media and technology for granted. As technology continues to become more and more common in schools and homes, it is important to note that some children do not have access to technology at home or in their community. This is typically a concern in low-income areas, where computers are uncommon in homes and public libraries may be poorly equipped in the area of technology. For this reason, it is important that all children have the opportunity to learn to use technology in meaningful ways in their school settings.

Language arts teachers do not have a choice about integrating technology and other media into classroom instruction. If students are to succeed in tomorrow's society, they must understand and be able to use technology tools. Language arts teachers are already accustomed to integrating computers, the Internet, and educational software in their classrooms. The presence of technology tools itself changes the way language arts instruction is viewed. Remember, it was not long ago that people were concerned about the impact of word processors and spellcheckers on children's writing processes. The use of word processors in the classroom is no longer a concern but an accepted and expected skill that children need to learn.

New technologies continue to provide tools and processes that dramatically change the way we communicate and interact. The explosion of e-mail as a communication tool seems almost too common to mention. It was only a short while ago that very few people were communicating with e-mail, but now it is a common, everyday experience. In recent memory, no other medium has impacted our communication processes so dramatically—and it will continue to do so.

Our increasing ability to engage in group discussions through Internet chat rooms and electronic bulletin boards reveals the new flexibility and accessibility of worldwide communication. The Internet provides immediate access to people and knowledge: we can access information and opinion about a newsworthy event, or we can hold a conversation with an individual who has made an important scientific discovery. Adults are amazed by how rapidly technology has changed our world, but consider this: The children you teach have grown up *expecting* to communicate through e-mail and the Internet.

We are just beginning to understand the impact of new technology on language and literacy. No doubt technological innovations will continue to impact society's concepts of language and communication. The influence of the new technology may be as impressive as that of the printing press, which made reading possible for all people. It will greatly impact communication processes and ultimately how you teach language arts.

IMPACT OF STATE AND FEDERAL POLICY

(Reference further information and examples about this trend in this textbook: Chapter 7.)

Public concern about the quality of education has engendered greater state and local policy influence in all aspects of education. California Proposition 227, requiring changes in how English language learners are taught in that state, is one example. Many other states have passed laws or mandates for particular curriculum requirements or policies related to teaching English language learners. The No Child Left Behind (NCLB) Act illustrates the impact of federal policy on language arts instruction. NCLB addresses a wide range of educational requirements and mandates, affecting everything from teacher training to safety in the school. A portion of the NCLB bill, "Reading First," includes specific guidelines for teaching reading. The ramifications of NCLB are just beginning to be felt and will continue at least until 2012. (To learn more about NCLB, visit **www.ed.gov/nclb/landing.html.**)

Because reading and writing are widely considered the basic skills of an educated person, language arts is a frequent subject of legislation. State and federal policies set language arts curricular and testing requirements that teachers are expected to implement.

It is no secret that many state and federal policies are highly political and often controversial. Providing the resources to pay for state and federal mandates is a crucial issue facing public education, and debates over the role of state and federal policies in language arts instruction will continue. Because of the importance of language arts learning and the large sums of tax money supporting public education, state and federal involvement in teaching and learning is likely to persist.

IMPORTANCE OF TESTING AND ACCOUNTABILITY

(Reference further information about this trend in this textbook: Chapter 7.)

One outcome of increased federal and state involvement in public education is the growing role of testing and accountability in language arts instruction. State and district testing have been implemented in virtually every public school in the nation, arousing questions and criticism both within and outside the education profession about its impact on teaching and learning (Barksdale-Ladd & Thomas, 2000). In most cases, teachers do not have a great deal of input on the development and use of tests, but they are the ones responsible for administering them, and they are affected by the results.

Standardized testing contrasts starkly to other trends impacting language arts instruction. On the one hand, teachers are encouraged to accept a changing definition of literacy, recognize various languages and cultures, and incorporate complex technological tools in communicative processes. At the same time, the testing movement often requires teachers to view communication more narrowly, as something that can be measured with simplistic tools. Testing children is not new or controversial, but the over-reliance on tests as a measure of communication effectiveness that characterizes the trend does merit debate.

Testing processes contribute a great deal of stress to teachers' lives. Teachers and principals are under pressure to raise and improve test scores each year. Administrators and the community see the test results as a measure of teachers' and schools' performance. Teachers often recognize the problems of overreliance on tests, but they are nevertheless required to administer the tests to their students. The fact that teachers often feel so much pressure for children to perform well on the tests that they "teach to the test" is one of the negative consequences of the testing movement.

Many educators and parents are concerned about the way we assess children's communication skills, and they remain hopeful that standardized tests' role can be decreased (Barksdale-Ladd & Thomas, 2000). The testing issue has impacted language arts instruction for the past two decades, and it will continue to influence language arts teaching in the years to come. There is no doubt that this trend must be critically assessed and questioned. This issue is certain to impact your teaching career for years to come.

Trends and Issues

personal reflection

On any trends or issues, people hold opposing views that may be extreme. For example, proponents of the "back to basics" movement argue that language arts instruction should focus on reading and writing skills, while more liberal proponents advocate an expanded definition of language arts. Some view the mainstream American culture and language as the only approach to communication, while others believe we should teach ELLs with strong bilingual approaches. With a small group, select one of the trends from this article. Develop at least two views on the issue. Formulate strong arguments for each perspective. Research the issue and views in outside resources such as the Internet, interviews of professors and teachers, and newspaper editorials. Be prepared to present a group debate to your whole class.

FINAL REFLECTIONS

This article identifies five trends that will continue to impact language arts instruction as you begin your career: changing views of language arts, language and culture, media and technology, state and federal policy, and testing. Some of these trends will continue for many years; others may come and go. You may experience them in different ways during your career, and other trends may emerge to affect language arts. New information, ideas, and trends will impact language arts teaching. You may find it frustrating that trends seem to dominate instructional processes, but the changes caused by trends are an exciting part of teaching. Trends can freshen perspectives, increase dialogue among professionals, and offer instructional innovations that improve teaching and learning. Teachers who stay abreast of the changes will continually learn and improve their skills.

personal reflection

Reviewing Field Notes

Review your field notes from this course and find evidence of the trends discussed in this article in your own experiences. Specifically, look for the following:

- Evidence of an expanded view of language arts that includes visual and other literacies.
- Classroom examples of the diversity of languages used by children and the effects.
- Evidence that technology is changing practices in language arts instruction.
- Examples of how state and federal policy are influencing language arts curriculum and instruction.
- Evidence of the impact of standards and testing on language arts instruction.

Share the examples with a small group of your classmates.

PROFESSIONAL REFLECTIONS

Review your field notes from this chapter and develop one or more into a component for your portfolio. To continue to reflect on your field notes, consider the following suggestions:

- Review your portfolio and select some of the most meaningful examples of your work. Choose items that are representative of your overall learning. Write a reflective evaluation of your learning—a self-evaluation of your experiences in your university and field-experience classroom settings.
- Write your philosophy of language arts teaching and learning. Use examples from your field notes to illustrate your ideas. In a conference

with one or two of your classmates, your mentor teacher, or your university professor, explain your areas of growth.

■ Write a letter to parents that describes what will happen in your language arts classroom when you begin to teach. Focus on the important ideas and practices that will guide your language arts teaching and learning as you envision it after your experiences this semester. (You might wish to update this document throughout your university coursework and teaching experiences to reflect your current ideas.)

Professional Readings

Some books that will expand your understanding of the content of this chapter include:

Birchak, B., Connor, C., Crawford, K. M., Kahn, L., Kaser, S., & Turner, S. (1998). *Teacher study groups: Building community through dialogue and reflection.* Urbana, IL: National Council of Teachers of English.

This book outlines how and why teacher study groups promote professional development and enhance instruction. This is an excellent resource for implementing a teacher study group in your school.

Commeyras, M., Bisplinghoff, B. S., & Olson, J. (Eds.). (2003). *Teachers as readers: Perspectives on the importance of reading in teachers' classrooms and lives.* Newark, DE: International Reading Association.

This collection of essays examines how literacy teachers use reading in their daily lives, professional lives, and classrooms. This book is an excellent tool to help you reflect on the role of reading in your personal and professional life.

Garan, E. M. (2004). *In defense of our children: When politics, profit, and education collide.* Portsmouth, NH: Heinemann.

This provocative book critiques recent educational policies, including mandated educational programs, scripted teaching, and high-stakes testing.

Graves, D. H. (1991). *Build a literate classroom.* Portsmouth, NH: Heinemann.

Graves, D. H. (1991). *Discover your own literacy.* Portsmouth, NH: Heinemann.

These two books are part of a series designed to help beginning teachers reflect on the language arts classroom. The books provide activities that help you reflect on your own personal literacy behaviors and experiments that you can do to help you develop a literate classroom.

Rieman, P. L. (2000). *Teaching portfolios: Presenting your professional best.* Boston: McGraw-Hill.

This is a concise, easy-to-read guide to developing a professional portfolio. It assumes that the portfolio will encourage reflection and provides suggestions for how you can collect, choose, and organize portfolio materials.

REFERENCES

Barksdale-Ladd, M. A., & Thomas, K. F. (2000). What's at stake in high-stakes testing. *Journal of Teacher Education, 51*(5), 384–397.

Binstock, E. (1996). Student conversations: Provocative echoes. In J. Flood, S. B. Heath, & D. Lapp (Eds.), *Research on teaching literacy through the communicative and visual arts* (pp. 346–354). International Reading Association. New York: Macmillan.

Burke, K., Fogarty, R., & Belgrad, S. (1994). *The portfolio connection.* Arlington Heights, IL: IRI/ Skylight Training and Publishing.

Calhoun, E. F. (1994). *How to use action research in the self-renewing school.* Alexandria, VA: ASCD.

Canter & Associates. (1998). *First-class teacher: Success strategies for new teachers.* Santa Monica, CA: Canter & Associates.

Christenson, S. L., & Sheridan, S. M. (2001). *Schools and families: Creating essential connections for learning.* New York: Guilford.

Costa, A. L., & Kallick, B. (2000). Getting into the habit of reflection. *Educational Leadership, 57*(7), 60–65.

Daiute, C. (1998). Points of view in children's writing. *Language Arts, 75*(2), 138–149.

Daiute, C. (1996). Youth genre in the classroom: Can children's and teachers' cultures meet? In J. Flood, S. B. Heath, & D. Lapp (Eds.), *Research on teaching literacy through the communicative and visual arts* (pp. 323–334). International Reading Association. New York: Macmillan.

Duck, L. (2000). The ongoing professional journey. *Educational Leadership, 57*(8), 42–45.

Elish-Piper, L. (1996). Dialogue journals in family literacy programs: Considering the possibilities. *Illinois Reading Council Journal, 24*(3), 27–39.

Elish-Piper, L. (2002). Icing on the cake: Parent involvement in literacy in the primary grades. *Illinois Reading Council Journal, 30*(3), 12–22.

Farris, P. J. (1999). *Teaching, bearing the torch* (2nd ed.). Boston: McGraw-Hill.

Flood, J., Lapp, D., Tinajero, J. V., & Nagel, G. (1995). "I never knew I was needed until you called!" Promoting parent involvement in schools. *The Reading Teacher, 48,* 614–617.

Hobbs, R. (1997). Literacy for the information age. In J. Flood, S. B. Heath, & D. Lapp (Eds.), *Handbook of research on teaching literacy through the communicative and visual arts* (pp. 7–14). New York: Simon & Schuster Macmillan.

Luke, A. (1998). Getting over method: Literacy teaching as work in "new times." *Language Arts, 75,* 305–313.

Magestro, P. V., & Standford-Blair, N. (2000). A tool for meaningful staff development. *Educational Leadership, 57*(8), 34–35.

McIntyre, E., Kyle, D., Moore, G., Sweazy, R. A., & Greer, S. (2001). Linking home and school through family visits. *Language Arts, 78,* 264–272.

Moll, L. C., Amanti, C., Neff, D., & Gonzalez, N. (1992). Funds of knowledge for teaching: Using a qualitative approach to connect homes and classrooms. *Theory into Practice, 31,* 132–141.

Olsen, L. (2000, September 27). Minority groups to emerge as a majority in U.S. Schools. *Education Week, XX,* 4, 34.

Payne, R. K. (1998). *A framework for understanding poverty.* Highlands, TX: RFT.

Rhodes, L. K., & Shanklin, N. (1993). *Windows into literacy: Assessing learners K–8.* Portsmouth, NH: Heinemann.

Rieman, P. L. (2000). *Teaching portfolios: Presenting your professional best.* Boston: McGraw-Hill.

Routman, R. (2000). *Conversations: Strategies for teaching, learning, and evaluating.* Portsmouth, NH: Heinemann.

Ryan, C. D. (1994). *Authentic assessment.* Westminster, CA: Teacher Created Resources.

Smagorinsky, P. (2000). Snippets: What will be the influences on literacy in the next millennium? *Reading Research Quarterly, 35*(2), 277–278.

Smith, M. C., & Elish-Piper, L. (2002). Primary-grade educators and adult literacy: Some strategies for assisting low-literate parents. *The Reading Teacher, 56,* 156–165.

Taylor, D. (1997). Supporting family literacy: Many families, many literacies. *Preconference Institute, IRA Convention.* Atlanta, GA.

Author/Title Index

Subject Index